Linda White Room 304
Mrs. Anderson

GREGG

Shorthand Simplified

FOR COLLEGES

VOLUME TWO

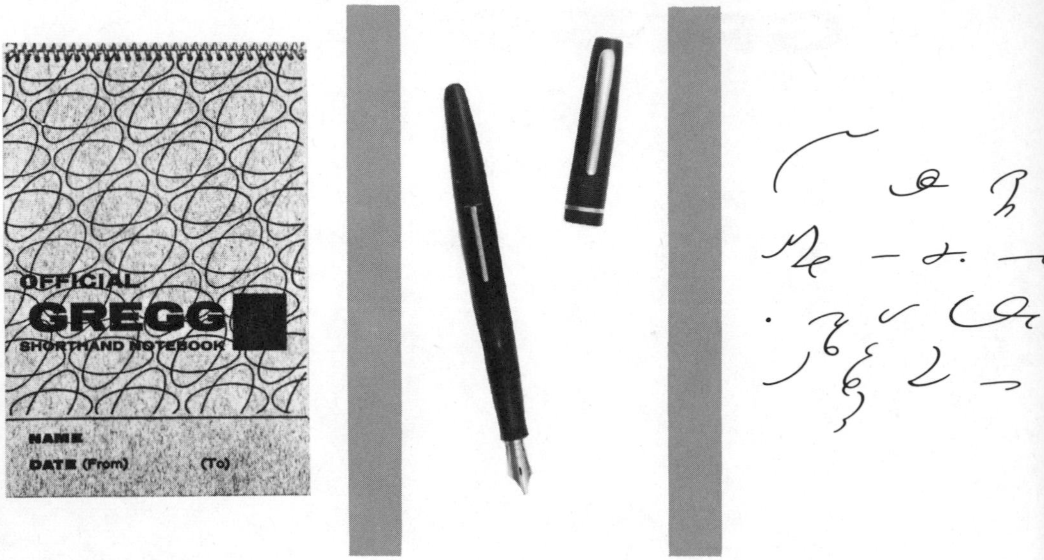

GREGG PUBLISHING DIVISION

McGraw-Hill Book Company, Inc.

New York Chicago Dallas San Francisco Toronto London

GREGG

Shorthand Simplified

FOR COLLEGES

VOLUME TWO
SECOND EDITION

LOUIS A. LESLIE
Coauthor Simplified Revision of Gregg Shorthand

CHARLES E. ZOUBEK
Coauthor Simplified Revision of Gregg Shorthand

RUSSELL J. HOSLER
Professor of Education, University of Wisconsin

Shorthand written by CHARLES RADER

GREGG SHORTHAND SIMPLIFIED FOR COLLEGES • VOLUME TWO • SECOND EDITION

37292

11 12 13 14 15 16 17 18 19 20 RRD-58 2 1 0 9 8 7 6 5

Library of Congress Catalog No. 57-6402

Published by GREGG PUBLISHING DIVISION
McGraw-Hill Book Company, Inc.
Printed in the United States of America

Acknowledgments

The authors wish to acknowledge the valuable help that they received from shorthand teachers in various parts of the country. Special acknowledgment is due Mr. Charles Rader for writing the beautiful shorthand in this book. The authors are also indebted to Miss Tere LoPrete for the attractive design of the book.

PREFACE

Gregg Shorthand Simplified for Colleges, Volume Two, Second Edition, as its title indicates, is intended for use after the completion of *Gregg Shorthand Simplified for Colleges*, Volume One, Second Edition. It serves as a link between shorthand theory and advanced dictation and transcription. It is specifically designed to help the student achieve the following objectives:

1. To review and strengthen his knowledge of the theory of Gregg Shorthand

2. To develop his ability to construct new outlines under the stress of dictation

3. To extend his knowledge and skill in the basic elements of typewritten transcription

4. To lay a foundation for further development of dictation and transcription skill.

The basic pattern of the First Edition has been substantially retained; but many new and useful features have been added, based on constructive suggestions the authors have received from teachers who have used the First Edition.

Theory Review Cycle

Gregg Shorthand Simplified for Colleges, Volume Two, Second Edition, contains 16 chapters and each chapter is divided into 5 lessons. Each chapter contains a 5-drill theory review cycle as follows:

First Lesson: A Chart of Brief Forms and Derivatives

Second Lesson: Useful Business-Letter Phrases and Common First and Last Names

Third Lesson: Word Families

Fourth Lesson: Word Beginnings and Endings and Geographical Expressions

Fifth Lesson: Word Building Practice and, in each even-numbered chapter, an Accuracy Practice.

This cycle not only provides a thorough review of Gregg Shorthand but it also helps to develop the student's power to construct new outlines under the stress of dictation.

Connected Practice Material

In building shorthand speed and accuracy it is highly desirable that the student read and copy a great deal of well-written shorthand. In this volume the student is provided with a wealth of well-written shorthand in each lesson.

1. *Gregg Shorthand Simplified for Colleges,* Volume Two, Second Edition, contains 70,456 words of practice material in shorthand – 56,333 in the form of actual business letters; 14,123 in the form of inspirational, entertaining, or informative articles.

2. The material in each chapter is devoted to a specific line of business or industry. For example, Chapter 1 is built around the wearing apparel industry; Chapter 2, around household furnishings; etc. This arrangement of material gives the student an opportunity to become fairly familiar with the vocabulary of each field. It also makes the student's practice more meaningful and interesting.

3. The opening letter in the first lesson of each chapter is a brief form and phrase letter. It is ideal for warmup purposes on each of the days that the class is working on the chapter in which the letter appears. So that the student may concentrate on the brief forms and phrases, no marginal reminders are given in that letter.

Transcription Helps

One of the significant new features of this Second Edition – a feature strongly recommended by the teachers who used the First Edition – is the greater emphasis placed on transcription. This emphasis is carried out through the following devices:

1. Marginal Reminders. The marginal reminders presented in Volume One are reviewed in Chapter 1 of Volume Two. The explanations of those marginal reminders are repeated at the beginning of Chapter 1, and the marginal reminders are intensively used in the shorthand practice material of Lessons 1 through 5.

In succeeding lessons, the new marginal reminders are introduced one or two at a time and intensively woven into the shorthand practice material of the lesson in which they are introduced. The last marginal reminder is introduced in Lesson 14.

Beginning with Lesson 15, all the marginal reminders are regularly reviewed so that the student has the best possible opportunity to learn to use them correctly.

The punctuation marks and the marginal reminders appear in red. This use of color highlights these marginal reminders so that they will be impressed more firmly on the student's mind.

2. Transcription Word Study. To help overcome one of the most serious deterrents to rapid and accurate transcription – a limited vocabulary – a Transcription Word Study is presented at the head of each Reading and Writing Practice. The Transcription Word Study consists of definitions of a number of words or expressions with which the student may be unfamiliar. These words and expressions are selected from the Reading and Writing Practice.

3. Transcription Quiz. The Transcription Quiz, with which the student is already familiar through his work with Volume One, is designed to do two things – to help the student determine for himself how well he can apply the rules of punctuation he has studied and to develop his ability to supply, with the help of context, words that are missing from the shorthand.

The Transcription Quiz in Volume Two follows this same pattern, but the problems to be solved are more advanced.

Review Charts and Lists. In addition to the brief form charts that appear in the first lesson of each chapter, there is a complete alphabetical list of brief forms of Gregg Shorthand on the back, inside covers of this volume.

The appendix contains lists that review all the word beginnings and endings as well as the major phrasing principles of Gregg Shorthand.

Student Helps. Another new feature of this Second Edition that will appeal to teachers and students alike is the series of student helps throughout the book. These helps give practical suggestions to the student on how to practice, how to take new-matter dictation, what to do about the size of his notes, and the like.

The authors wish to express their gratitude to the many teachers who have used the First Edition and who have shared with the authors their experiences in teaching it. Wherever possible, their suggestions have been incorporated in this volume; as a result, the authors are confident that this Second Edition will enable teachers to do an even more effective job of preparing students for dictation and transcription.

Louis A. Leslie
Charles E. Zoubek
Russel J. Hosler

CONTENTS

PART ONE

wearing apparel
household furnishings
general retailing
aviation

YOUR TASK AHEAD

Before proceeding with the work in Volume Two, let us take inventory of the things you have accomplished thus far.

1. You have learned the alphabet of Gregg Shorthand; consequently, you have the tools with which to construct an outline for any word in the English language.

2. You have learned many helpful abbreviating devices – brief forms, word beginnings, word endings, phrasing – that will enable you to write at high speeds with greater ease and facility.

3. You have given some attention to such nonshorthand factors as spelling, punctuation, and vocabulary, factors that will play an important part in your development as a rapid and accurate transcriber.

Your work with *Gregg Shorthand Simplified for Colleges*, Volume One, has helped you lay a firm foundation for the task ahead of you – developing your ability to write shorthand easily and rapidly and to transcribe your notes accurately on the typewriter.

You are now at one of the most interesting stages of your shorthand course; you will experience the thrill of watching your stenographic skills grow almost from day to day. This growth will be rapid if you practice efficiently at home and in class.

At home. At home you will read and copy a great many letters and articles from shorthand. From this reading and copying, you will derive many benefits. You will review all the principles and abbreviating devices of Gregg Shorthand many, many times. You will stock your mind with correct joinings of shorthand strokes so that you can use them in the construction of outlines under the stress of dictation.

As a by-product of your shorthand reading and copying, you will develop your vocabularly and improve your ability to spell and to punctuate.

Your work at this stage should be easy and pleasant, for you have no new principles or abbreviating devices to learn.

Your home-practice program. To get the most out of your home practice and also to insure that you complete it in the minimum of time, it is important that you practice efficiently. Let us review briefly the procedures you should follow:

1. Always *read* all shorthand before you copy it. Read aloud if possible.

2. When you come to an outline that you cannot read, spell it. If the spelling does not *immediately* give you the meaning, refer to your student's transcript if you have been provided with one. If not, write the outline on a slip of paper and find out its meaning in class the next day. Do not spend more than a few seconds trying to decipher an outline. At this stage, there will not be very many outlines that you cannot immediately read.

Also, be sure to pay particular attention to the marginal reminders.

3. After having read the material, make a shorthand copy of it, reading aloud as you write. Write as rapidly as you can, but be sure that you write readable shorthand.

Don't forget to insert in your own notes the punctuation that is encircled in the shorthand in the text.

In class. In class most of your time will be devoted to taking dictation at constantly increasing speeds. Your teacher will see to it that you get the proper kind of dictation at the proper speeds so that your skill will increase steadily and rapidly.

1

WEARING APPAREL

Marginal Reminders, 1

As part of your preparation for transcription – the production of letters that the employer would have no hesitation in signing – you began giving attention in *Gregg Shorthand Simplified for Colleges, Volume One*, to the factors of punctuation and spelling as you learned new principles and developed your shorthand skill. In Volume One you took up eight of the simpler uses of the comma as they occurred in the Reading and Writing Practice exercises. You also studied the "spelling demons" in those exercises.

In this volume you will take up a number of new and more advanced points of punctuation; you will study good typing style; and you will continue your efforts to become a good speller.

As in Volume One, each punctuation mark in Volume Two appears in the Reading and Writing Practice encircled in red; and a brief explanation for the use of the punctuation mark is given in the left margin. Also in the margin are the words that should be given special spelling attention.

In Chapter 1 you will review the points of punctuation that you studied in Volume One. New elements of punctuation and typing style will be gradually introduced beginning with Lesson 6.

Practice Procedure:

To be sure that you derive the greatest benefit from these marginal reminders, follow these practice suggestions:

1. Read carefully the explanations and the illustrative examples of the marginal reminders that follow these explanations.
2. Each time you meet an encircled punctuation mark as you read the Reading and Writing Practice, glance in the left margin of the page to be sure that you know why that punctuation mark was used.
3. As you copy the Reading and Writing Practice, insert each punctuation mark in your shorthand notes and encircle it.
4. Spell all words in the marginal reminders once, preferably aloud.

In Chapter 1 you will review:

, parenthetical

In order to make his meaning clearer, a writer sometimes inserts a comment or an explanation that could be omitted without changing the meaning of the sentence. These added comments and explanations are called "parenthetical" and are usually separated from the rest of the sentence by commas.

If the parenthetical word or expression occurs at the end of a sentence, only one comma is needed.

> I suggest, therefore, that you see him.
> John was pleased with the result, needless to say.

, apposition

Sometimes a writer mentions a person or thing and then, in order to make his meaning perfectly clear to the reader, says the same thing in different words.

> Our manager, Mr. E. H. Brown, will welcome you.
> I think Monday, June 6, is a good day for the meeting.

An expression in apposition is set off by two commas, except at the end of a sentence, when only one comma is necessary.

> You will be met by our manager, Mr. E. H. Brown.

, series

When the last member of a series of three or more items is preceded by *and*, *or*, or *nor*, place a comma before the conjunction as well as between the other items.

> Please check the headlights, the brakes, and the tires.
> John met his aunt at the station, picked up her luggage, and took her to his home.

As in *Gregg Shorthand Simplified for Colleges*, Volume One, introductory commas will be treated under the following four headings:

, *when* clause
, *as* clause
, *if* clause
, introductory

All dependent clauses beginning with words other than *when*, *as*, and *if* will be classified as ", introductory."

> When the time comes, I will be ready.
> As I wrote you previously, I cannot attend the meeting.
> If you are going, please let me know.
> Although he stayed at the hotel, he did not eat there.

When a sentence begins with the main clause, however, no comma is used between the main clause and the dependent clause.

> I will be ready when the time comes.
> Please let me know if you are going.

A comma is also required after introductory words and explanatory expressions such as *frankly, consequently, on the contrary, for instance*.

> Frankly, I am worried about his condition.
> On the contrary, he was the one who made the mistake.

, conjunction

A comma is used to separate two independent clauses that are joined by one of the conjunctions *and, but, or, for, neither, nor*.

> We have developed the film, but we find that the proofs lack clarity.

The first independent or principal or main clause is

> We have developed the film.

and the second,

> We find that the proofs lack clarity.

Both clauses could stand as separate sentences, with a period after each. Because the thought of the two sentences is closely related, however, they were joined to form one sentence. Because the two independent clauses are connected by the co-ordinating conjunction *but*, a comma is used between them before the conjunction.

Hyphenated before noun
No noun, no hyphen

The presence or absence of the hyphen in expressions like *well known* and *up to date* is a transcription problem that causes many errors. The answer is extremely simple. If a noun follows the expression, hyphens are necessary; if no noun follows, no hyphens are used.

The lecturer was well known. (No noun after the expression.)
He is a well-known lecturer. (Noun follows the expression.)

LESSON 1

1. Brief Forms and Derivatives. The following chart contains 36 brief forms and derivatives. Can you read the entire chart in half a minute?

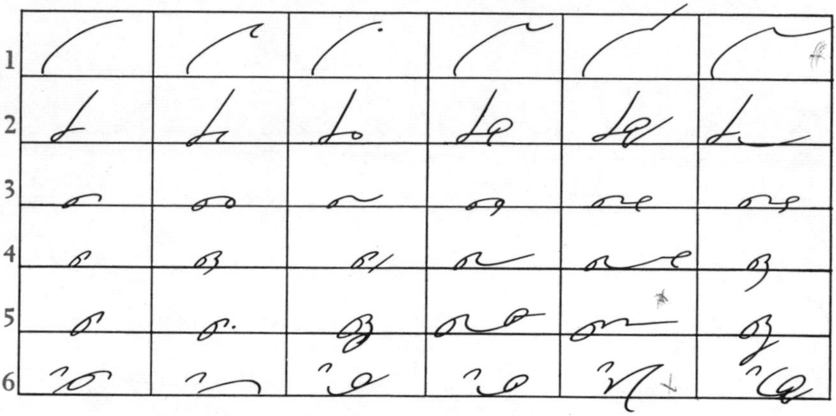

1. Time, times, timing, timer, timed, timeless.
2. General, generals, generally, generalize, generalized, generality.
3. Weak, weakly, weaker, weakest, weakness, weaknesses.
4. Use, uses, used, useless, uselessness, useful.
5. Out, outing, outside, outline, outcome, outfit.
6. Undertake, undergo, underrate, underwrite, understandable, underpriced.

2. Brief Form and Phrase Letter. This letter consists largely of brief forms and phrases. You can profitably read and copy it many times.

Reading and Writing Practice

3. Transcription Word Study. The greater command you have of words, the more efficient stenographer or secretary you will be. In the Transcription Word Study that precedes each Reading and Writing Practice, you will continue to build your knowledge and understanding of useful business words and expressions.

Be sure to read each Transcription Word Study before you begin your work on the Reading and Writing Practice.

literally Not exaggerated.

bonded Insured.

precision Exactness, extreme accuracy.

4.

Brown's colors

day-to-day hyphenated before noun

, introductory

, introductory

regardless

, introductory

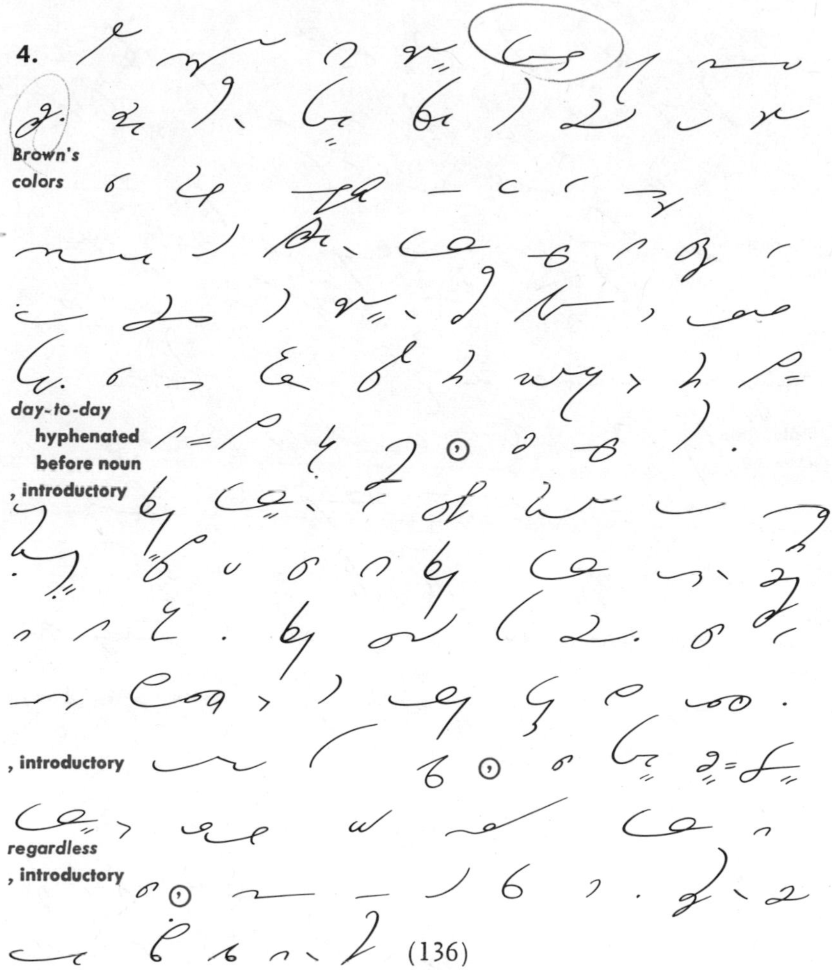

(136)

5.

, introductory

dominated

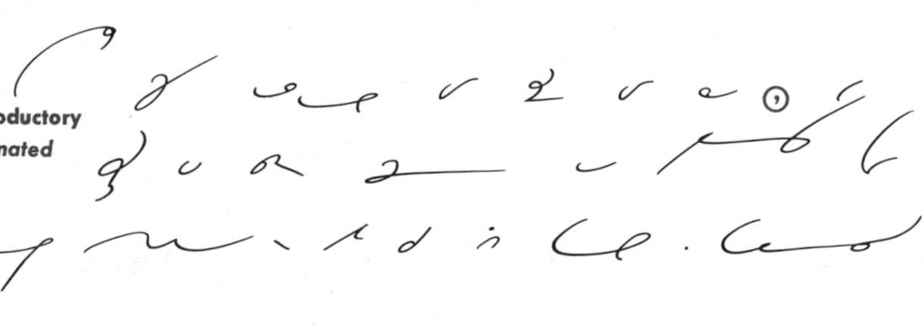

, introductory
announcing
, conjunction
succeeded
formal
, apposition
(139)

6.

well known
no noun,
no hyphen
, introductory
descended
dangerous

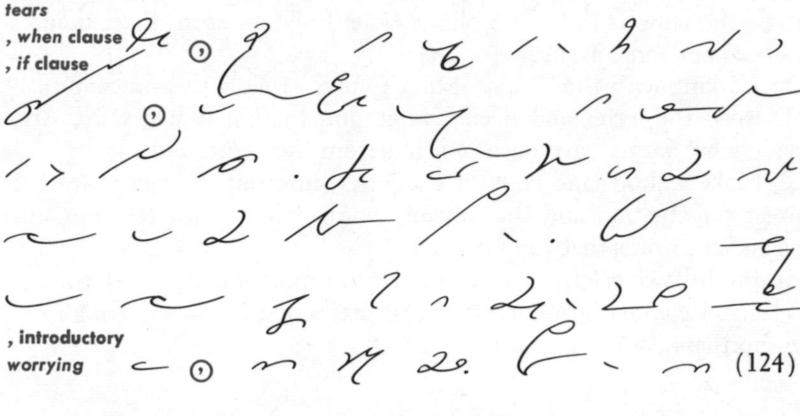

7. 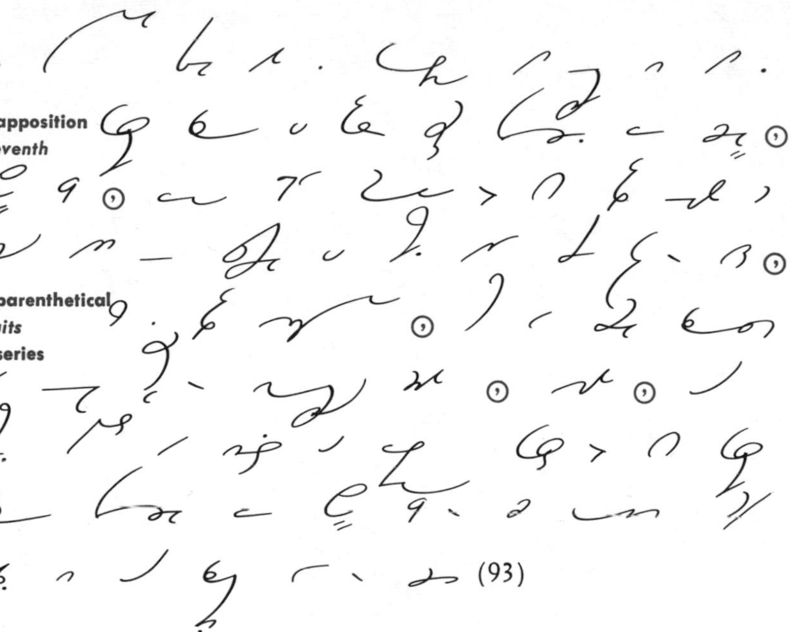

Transcription Quiz. In *Gregg Shorthand Simplified for Colleges,* Volume One, you were introduced to the Transcription Quiz that tested your ability to punctuate and your ability to supply from context words missing from the shorthand.

In Part I of this volume, the problems in the Transcription Quizzes will be the same as those in Volume One. In later lessons these quizzes will become more advanced.

In working with the Transcription Quizzes follow this procedure:

1. Read the letter and decide what punctuation is necessary. Also decide what words have been omitted from the shorthand.

2. Make a shorthand copy of the letter, inserting in your notes the correct punctuation and the missing words. Circle both the punctuation and the words that you supplied.

In the following letter you will have to supply 4 commas—1 comma as clause, 1 comma introductory, 2 commas series; 2 words missing from the shorthand.

8.

(115)

LESSON 2

9. Useful Business-Letter Phrases. There are 37 phrases in this paragraph. Can you read the entire list in a minute or less?

I

1 

He

2 

Who

3 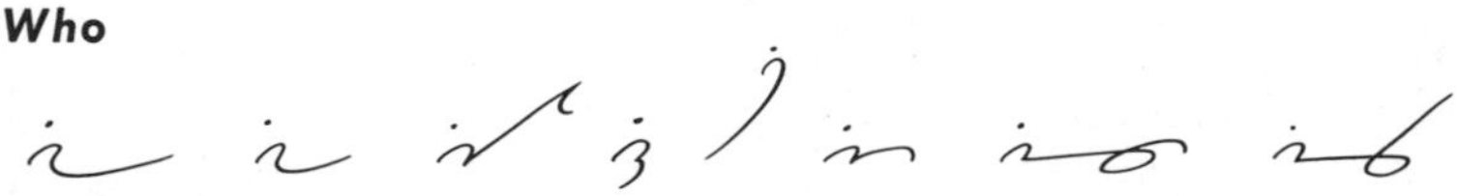

You

4 

1. **I can, I could, I am, I am sure, I do not, I do not think, I did, I have, I have not.**
2. **He is, he can, he may, he will, he will be, he could, he would, he did, he said, he was.**
3. **Who will, who are, who desire, who is, who have, who can, who make, who made.**
4. **You are, you are not, you can, you cannot, you could, you could not, you would, you did, you have, you have not.**

10. Frequent Names. The second lesson of each chapter contains (1) a number of frequently used last names; (2) a number of frequently used men's first names or women's first names.

Read through the list, referring to the key whenever you cannot read a name.

1
2
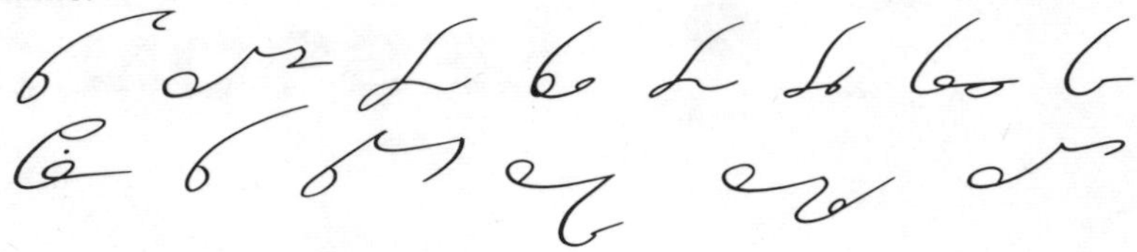

1. **Adams, Anderson, Baker, Barry, Becker, Bennett, Brennan, Brown.**
2. **Abraham, Adam, Adolph, Albert, Alfred, Andrew.**

Reading and Writing Practice

11. Transcription Word Study

minor Small. (Do not confuse with *miner*, which means "a person who works in a mine.")

browsing Reading here and there in a library.

emporium A store, a market.

12.

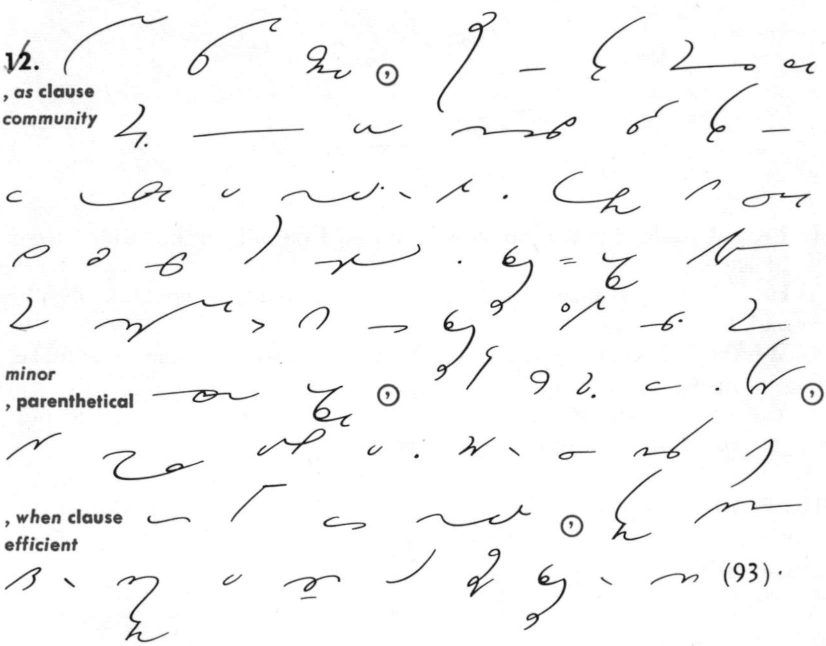

, as clause
community

minor
, parenthetical

, when clause
efficient

(93)

13.

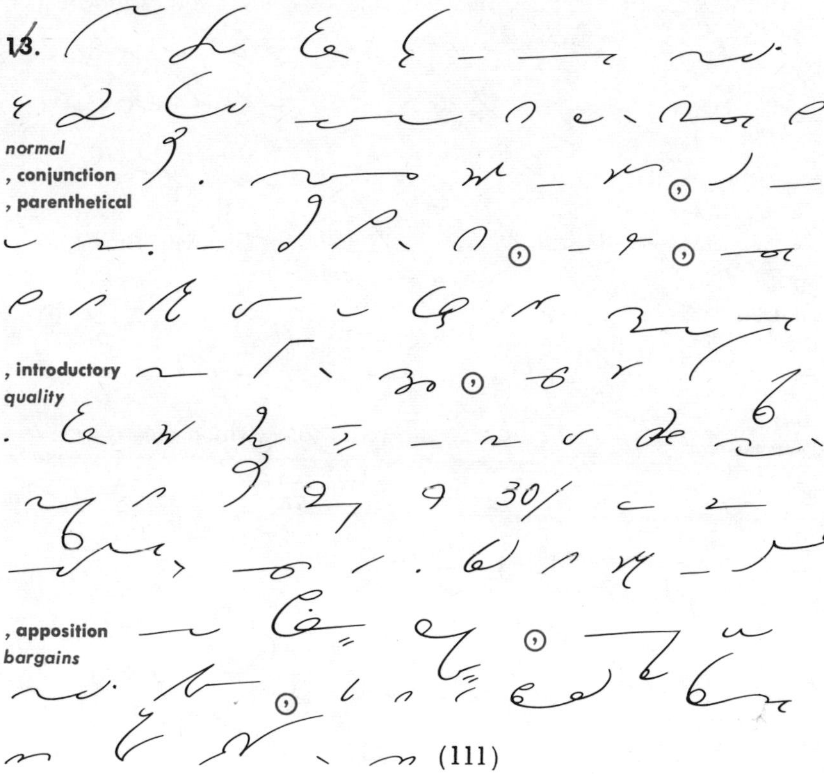

normal
, conjunction
, parenthetical
, introductory
quality
, apposition
bargains

(111)

14.

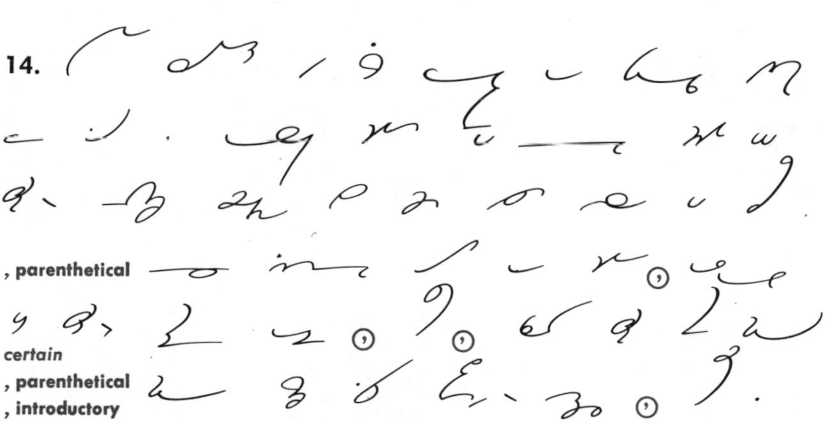

, parenthetical
certain
, parenthetical
, introductory

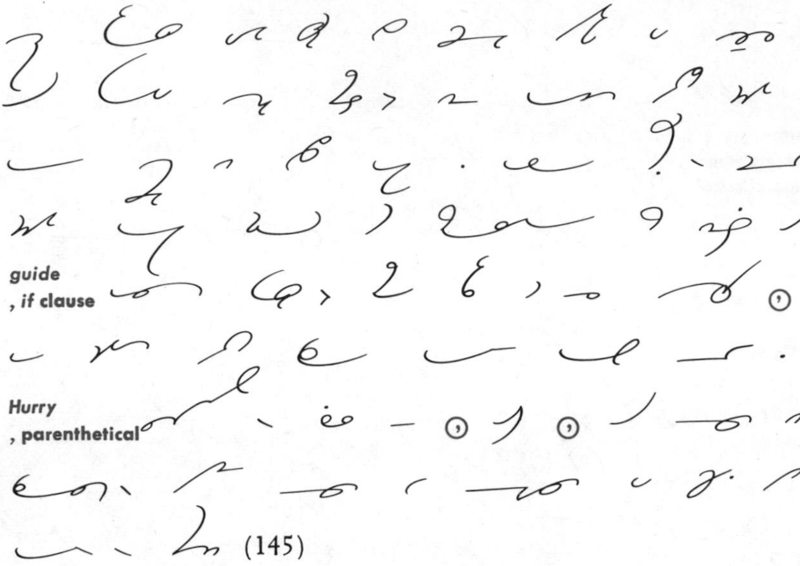

guide
, if clause

Hurry
, parenthetical

(145)

15.

well-read
hyphenated
before noun

well dressed
no noun,
no hyphen

, series
, conjunction
likely

Emporium

, when clause

, series

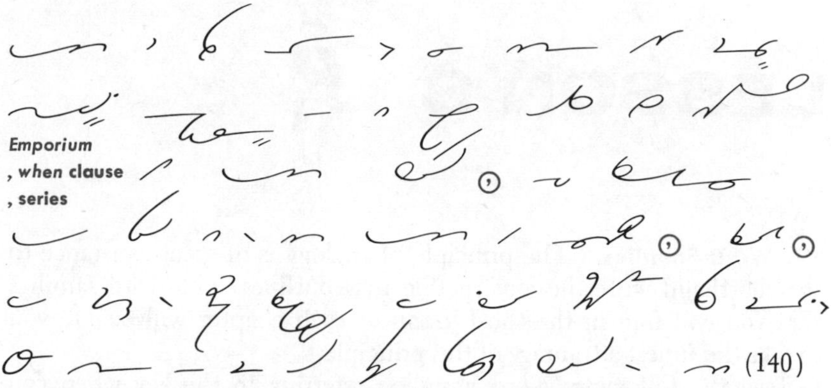

(140)

Transcription Quiz. For you to supply: 5 commas–1 comma *as* clause, 1 comma introductory, 2 commas parenthetical, 1 comma *if* clause; 2 missing words.

16.

(112)

LESSON 3

17. Word Families. The principle of analogy is of great assistance to the shorthand writer in constructing new outlines. The word families that you will find in the third lesson of each chapter will enable you to take the fullest advantage of this principle.

Read the following Word Families, referring to the key when you cannot read an outline.

-ic

1 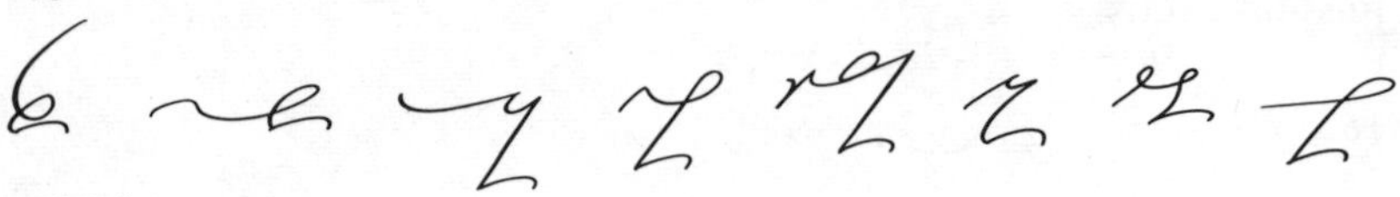

-come

2 

-thing

3 

-some

4 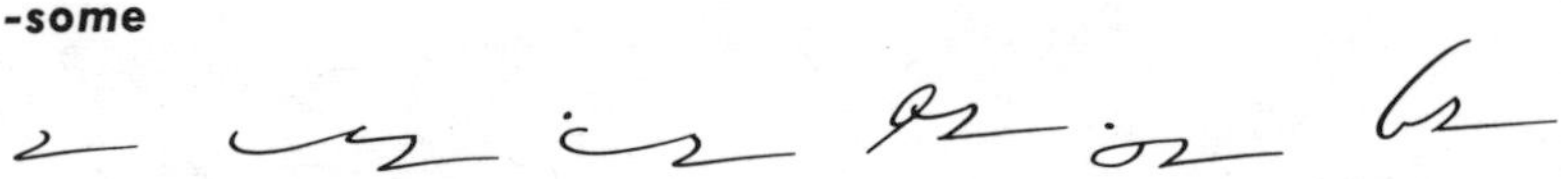

-take

5 

1. Basic, classic, logic, tragic, strategic, topic, terrific, magic.
2. Come, become, outcome, welcome, overcome, income.
3. Thing, anything, everything, something, nothing, plaything, things.
4. Some, lonesome, wholesome, tiresome, handsome, bothersome.
5. Take, overtake, partake, retake, mistake, undertake.

Reading and Writing Practice

18. Transcription Word Study

replenish To stock, to fill.

logic Sound reasoning.

skeptics Persons who approach a situation or problem with doubt.

19.

, apposition
, conjunction
occasion
men's
apparel
, introductory
replenish

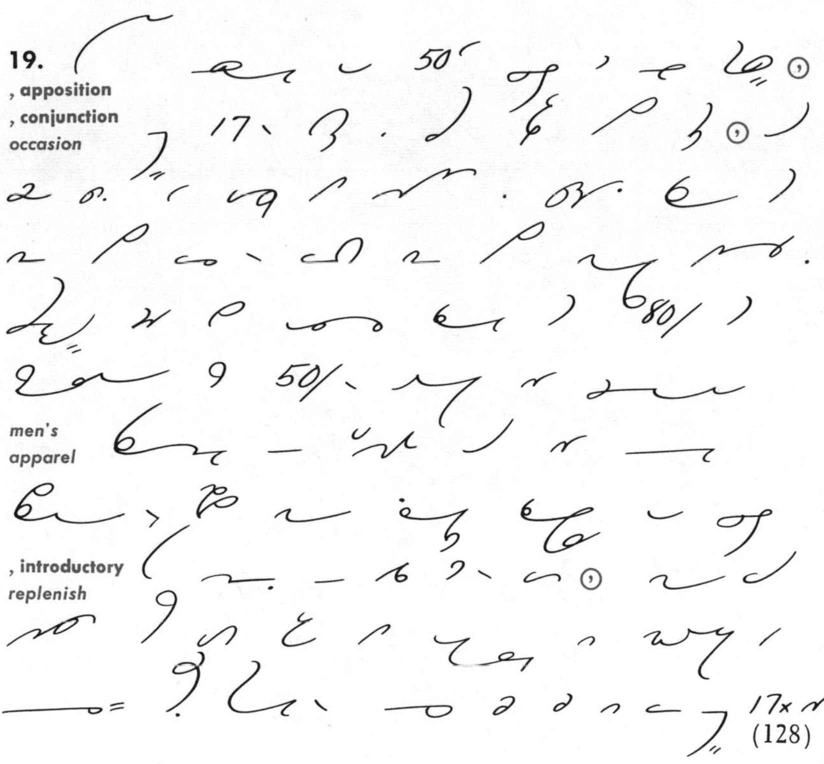

(128)

20.

stronger
, conjunction

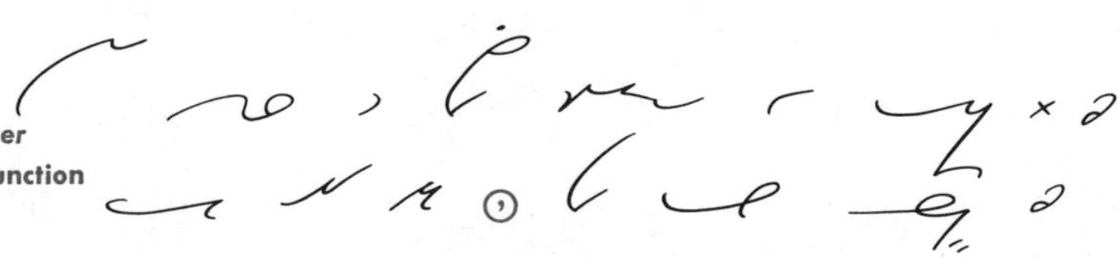

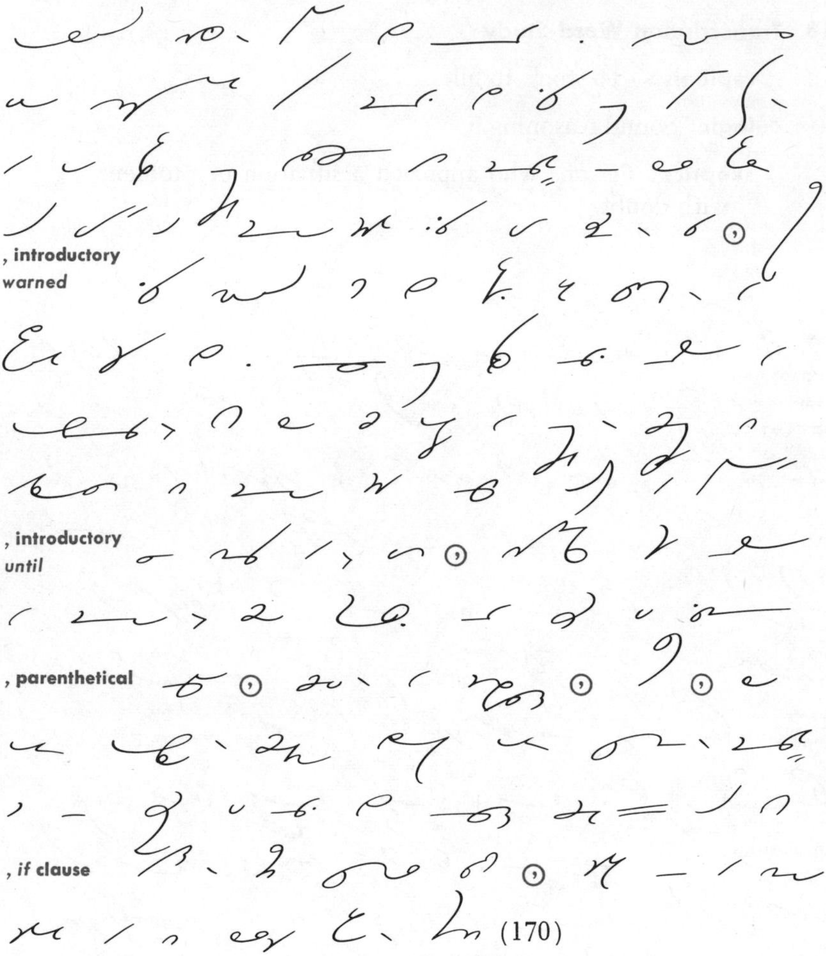

, introductory
warned

, introductory
until

, parenthetical

, *if* clause

(170)

21.

, *if* clause
, apposition
Clothing

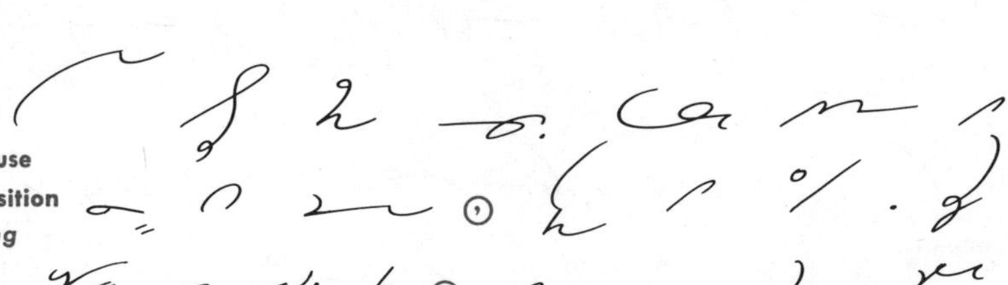

well known
no noun, no hyphen
, conjunction
well-dressed
hyphenated before noun
(93)

22.

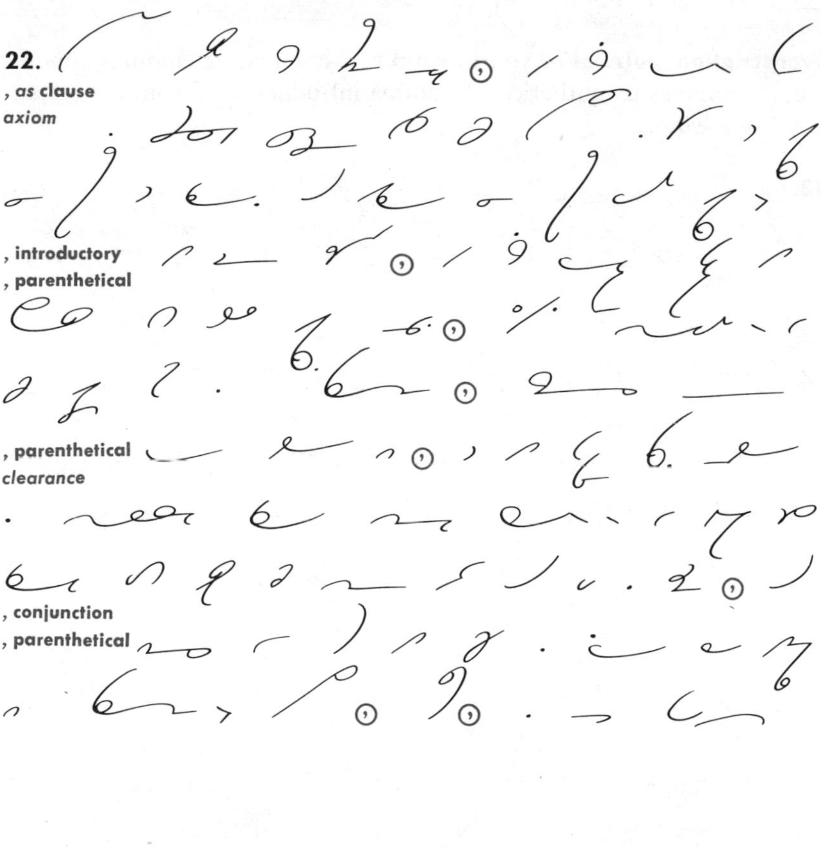

, as clause
axiom
, introductory
, parenthetical
, parenthetical
clearance
, conjunction
, parenthetical

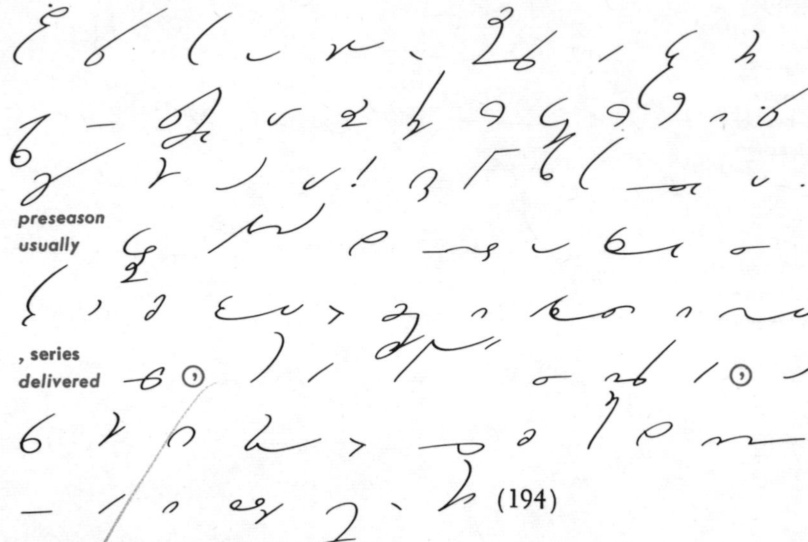

preseason
usually

, series
delivered

(194)

Transcription Quiz. For you to supply: 7 commas–2 commas apposition, 2 commas parenthetical, 1 comma introductory, 2 commas series; 2 missing words.

23.

(101)

LESSON 4

24. Word Beginnings. Can you read this entire list in 30 seconds or less?

After-

1 

Al-

2 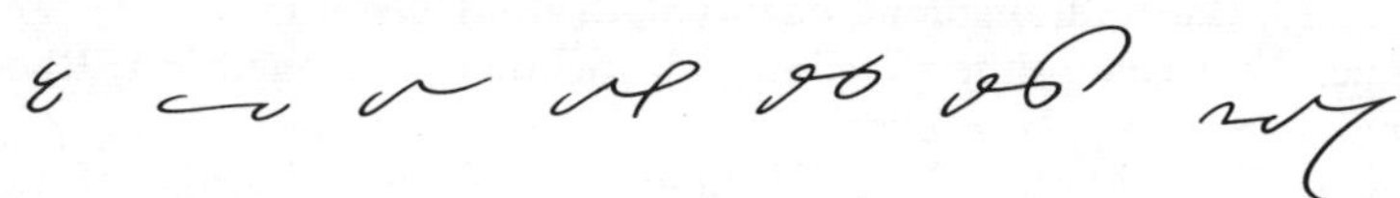

Be-

3 

Circum-

4 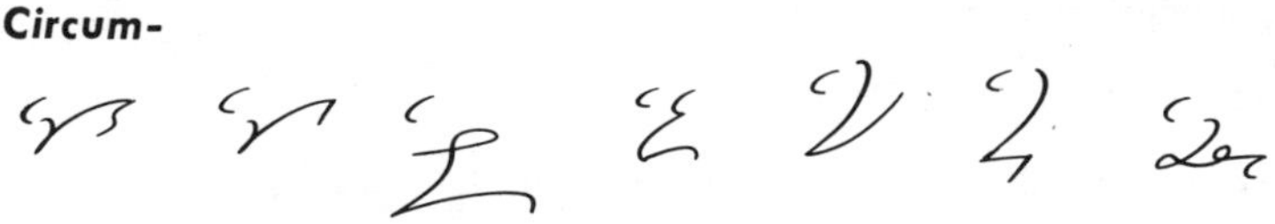

Con-

5 

Com-

6 

1. **Afternoon, aftermath, afterthought, afterglow, aftertaste, afterward.**
2. **Also, almost, alter, alteration, alternate, alternative, unalterable.**
3. **Because, became, becomingly, begin, belittle, beside, beware.**

4. Circumstances, circumstantial, circumnavigate, circumspect, circumvent, circumvention, circumference.
5. Concur, confine, convince, congress, consult, consistent, contribute.
6. Competition, compliment, compete, complaint, compose, comprehend, compound.

25. Geographical Expressions. Read through this list a number of times, referring to the key whenever you cannot read a geographical expression.

1 2 3

1. Stamford, Hartford, Bradford, Cranford, Bedford, Oxford.
2. Maine, New Hampshire, Virginia, Massachusetts, Connecticut, Rhode Island, New Jersey, New York.
3. United States, United States of America, England, Canada, Mexico, Guam, Hawaii.

Reading and Writing Practice

26. Transcription Word Study

torrid Hot, dried by heat.

soliciting Approaching with a request, asking for.

furriers Those dealing in the buying and selling of furs.

27.

, series
altering
offering
, introductory
(124)

28.

, parenthetical
appreciate
tempting
, introductory

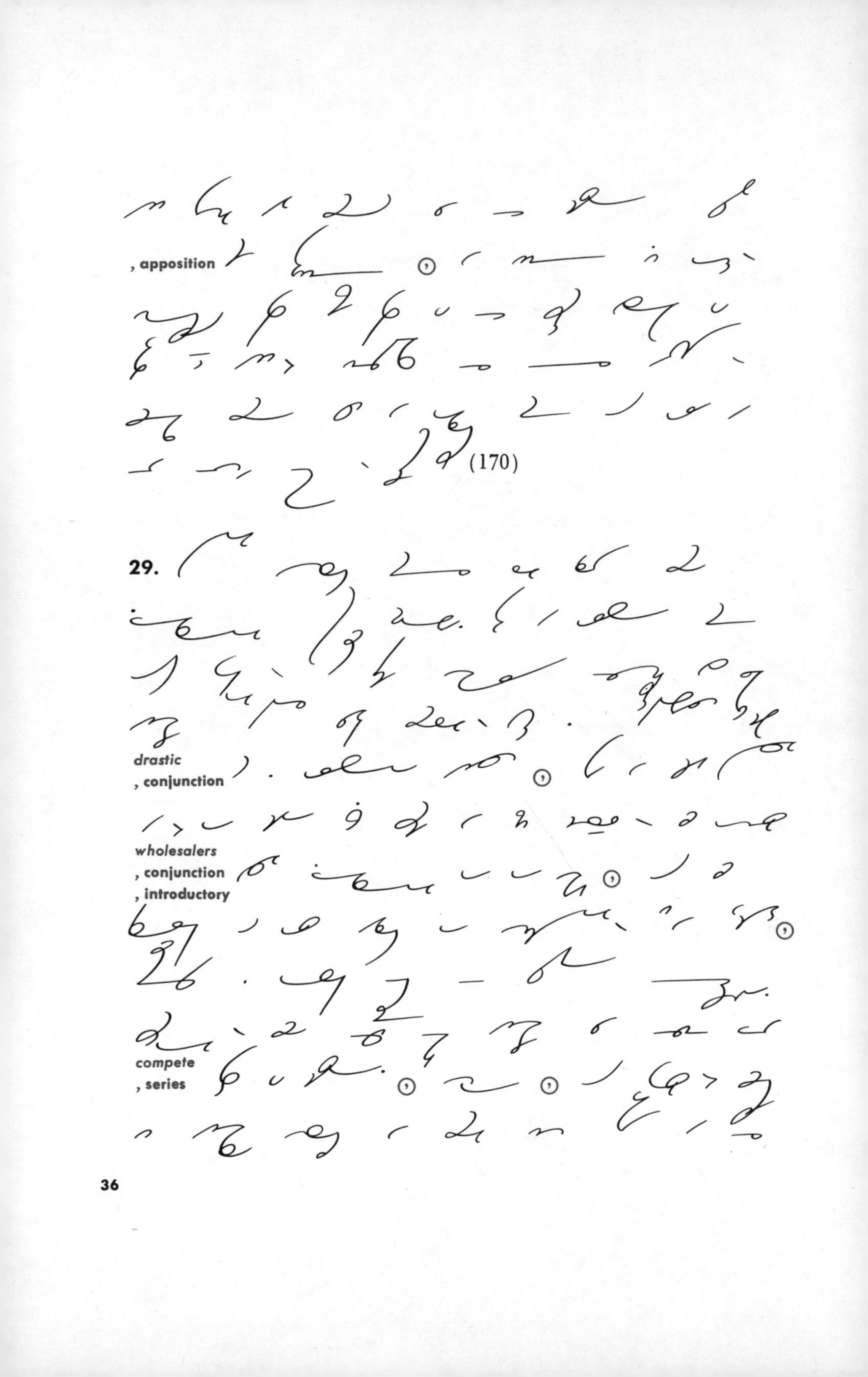

, apposition

(170)

29.

drastic
, conjunction

wholesalers
, conjunction
, introductory

compete
, series

(168)

Transcription Quiz. For you to supply: 5 commas—2 commas series, 2 commas parenthetical, 1 comma introductory; 2 missing words.

30.

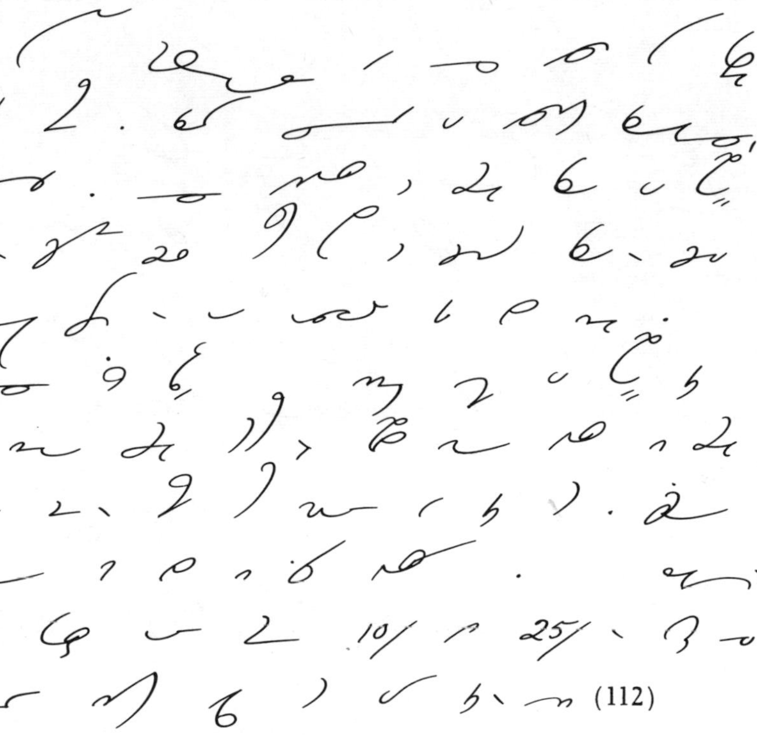

(112)

LESSON 5

31. Word-Building Practice—Diphthongs. These word-building practice drills provide a review of the major theory principles of Gregg Shorthand. Can you read the following list of words in less than a minute?

I

1 

Oi

2 

Ow

3 

U

4 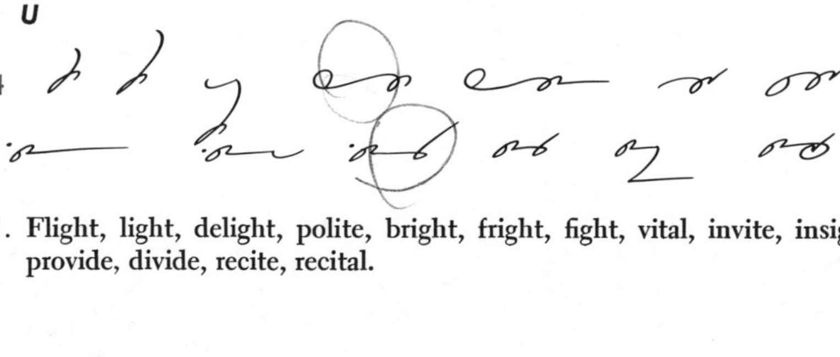

1. **Flight, light, delight, polite, bright, fright, fight, vital, invite, insight, provide, divide, recite, recital.**

2. Joy, enjoy, annoy, boy, toy, destroy, convoy, toil, soil, boil, foil, coil, loyal.
3. Now, cow, plow, brow, mouth, blouse, scout, doubt, doubtless, proud, cloud, powder.
4. Few, view, review, argue, argument, cute, acute, human, humor, humid, unit, uniform, unite.

Reading and Writing Practice

32. Transcription Word Study

chores Odd jobs.

imperative Commanding, not to be avoided.

incredible Difficult to believe.

33. Science and the Traveler

, parenthetical
clothes
, introductory
, introductory
launched
career
, parenthetical

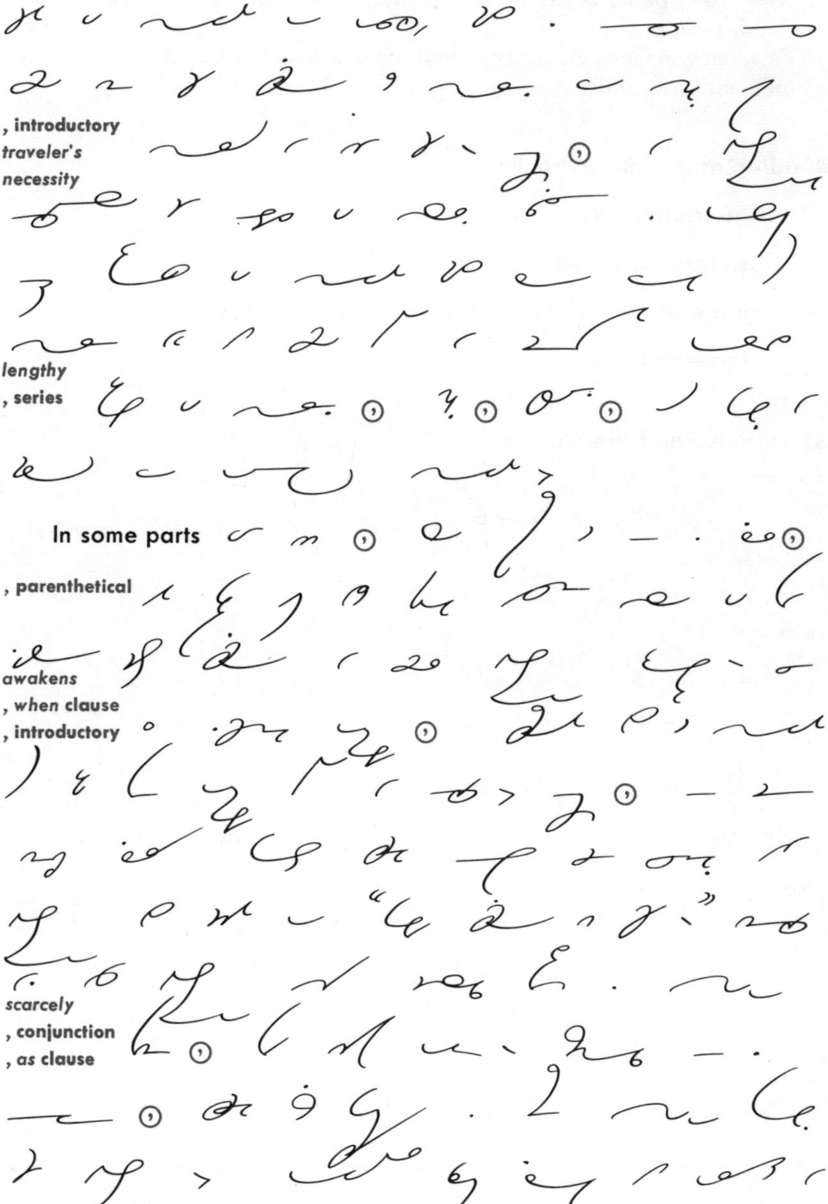
, introductory
traveler's
necessity
lengthy
, series
In some parts
, parenthetical
awakens
, when clause
, introductory
scarcely
, conjunction
, as clause

, introductory

, if clause

leisurely

, parenthetical

arithmetic

two-week

hyphenated before noun

Laundry arithmetic

, parenthetical

week-long

hyphenated before noun

, parenthetical

, introductory
imperative

, parenthetical

Our first traveler

, introductory
, parenthetical

science
, introductory

overnight

, introductory

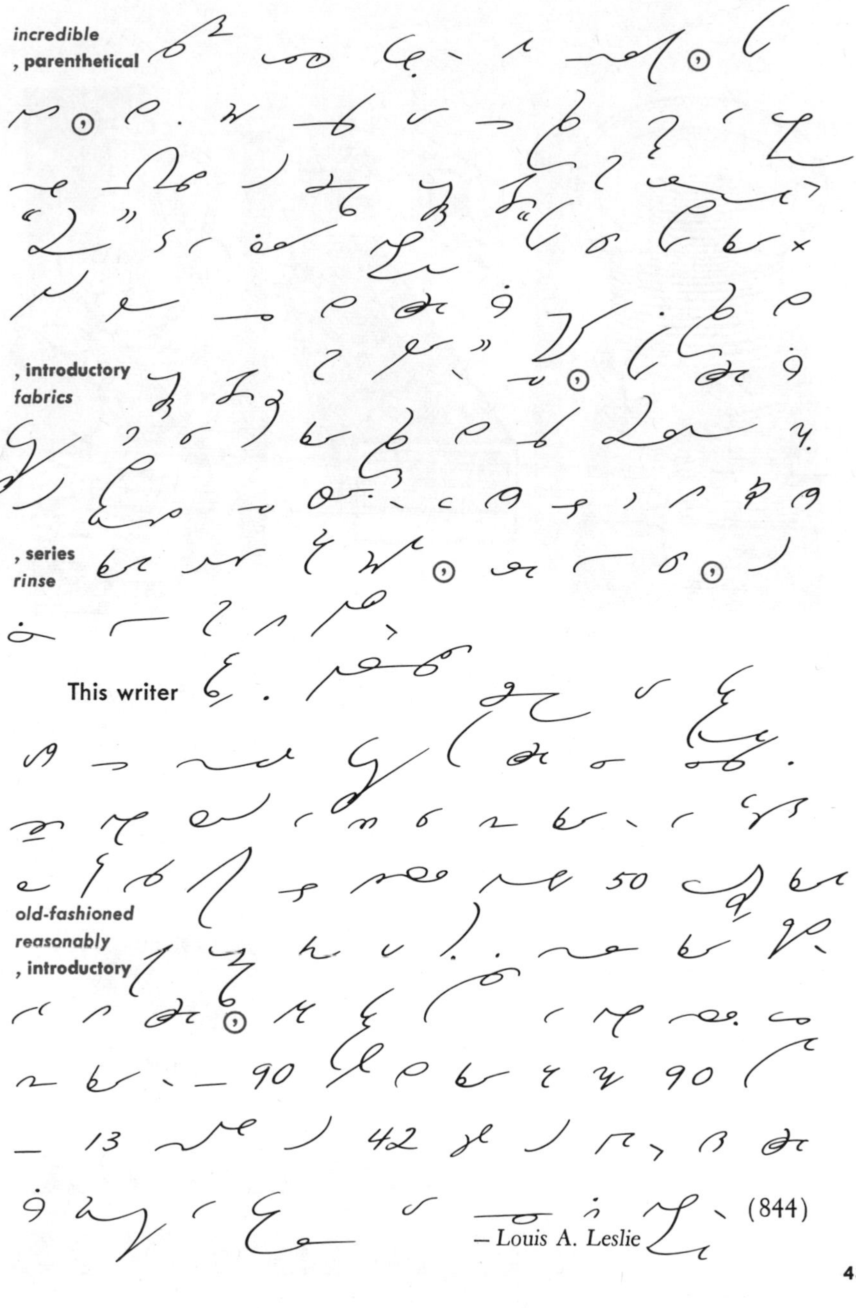
incredible
, parenthetical
, introductory
fabrics
, series
rinse
This writer
50
old-fashioned
reasonably
, introductory
90
90
13
42
(844)
– Louis A. Leslie

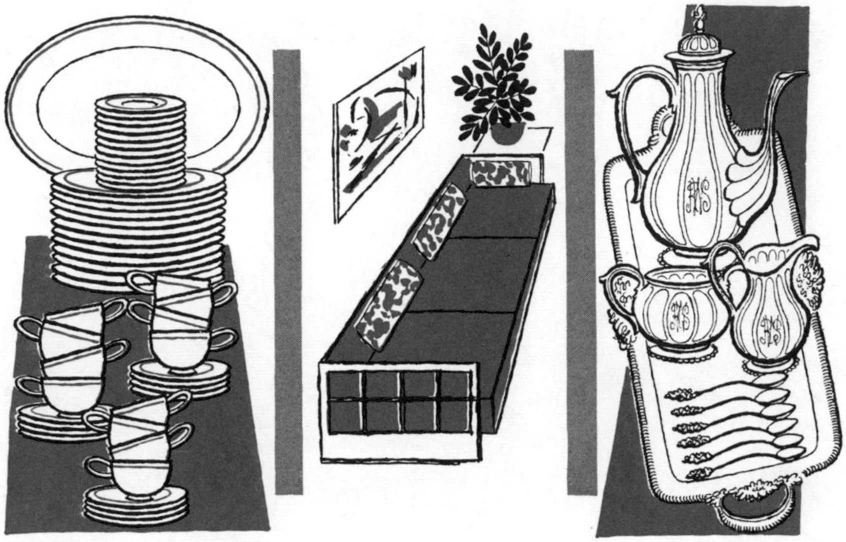

2

HOUSEHOLD FURNISHINGS

LESSON 6

Marginal Reminders, 2

; no conjunction

A semicolon is used to separate two independent, but closely related, clauses when no conjunction is used to connect the clauses.

I will go to the meeting; he will remain in the office.

The above sentence could be written as two sentences, with a period after *meeting*. However, because the two thoughts are closely related, the use of the semicolon seems more appropriate.

34. Brief Forms and Derivatives. Can you read these brief forms and derivatives in 30 seconds or less?

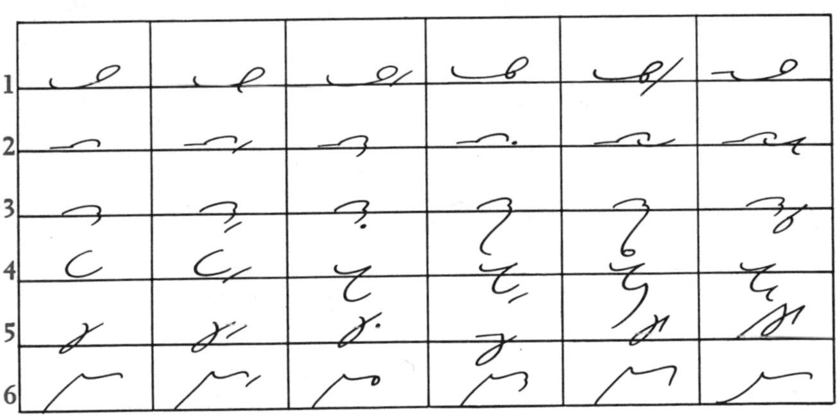

1. Like, likes, liked, likely, likelihood, unlike.
2. Enclose, enclosed, encloses, enclosing, enclosure, enclosures.
3. Consider, considered, considering, considerable, considerably, considerate.
4. Present, presented, represent, represented, representative, represents.
5. Satisfy-satisfactory, satisfied, satisfying, unsatisfactory, satisfaction, dissatisfaction.
6. Direct, directed, directly, directs, direction, indirect.

35. Brief Form and Phrase Letter

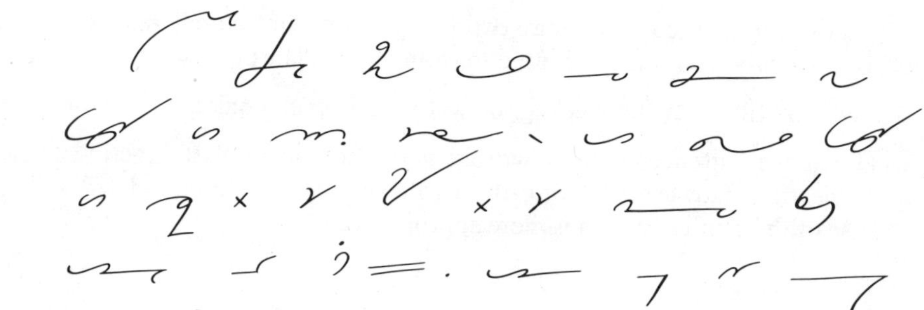

(124)

Reading and Writing Practice

36. Transcription Word Study

reputable Held in esteem.

contemplating Thinking about, considering.

lessen To decrease. (Do not confuse with *lesson,* which means "something that is learned or taught.")

37.

; no conjunction
happiness
, introductory
buy
decide
, apposition
; no conjunction

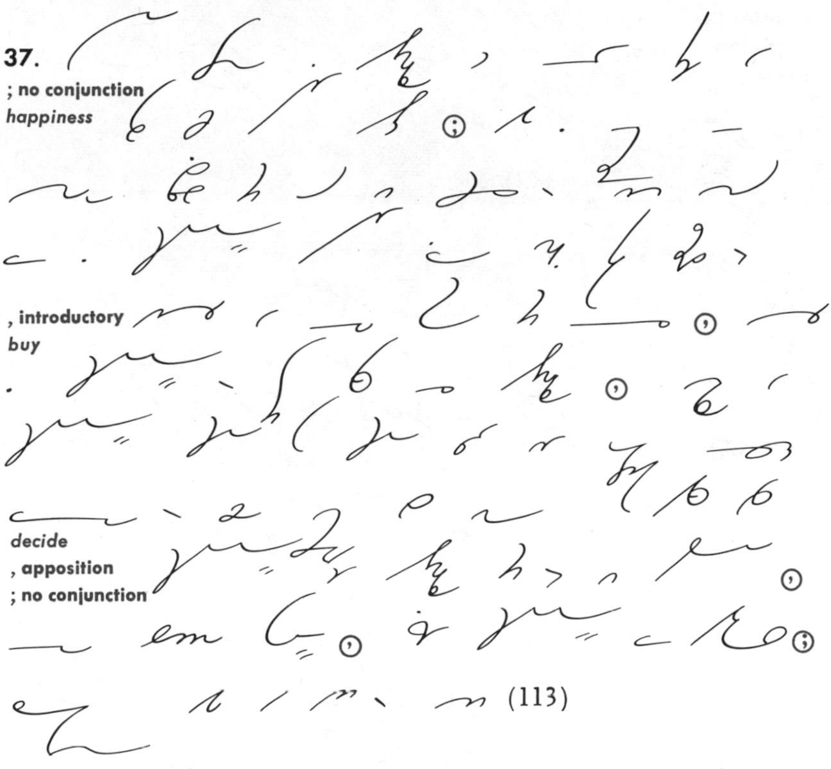

(113)

38.

, introductory
received

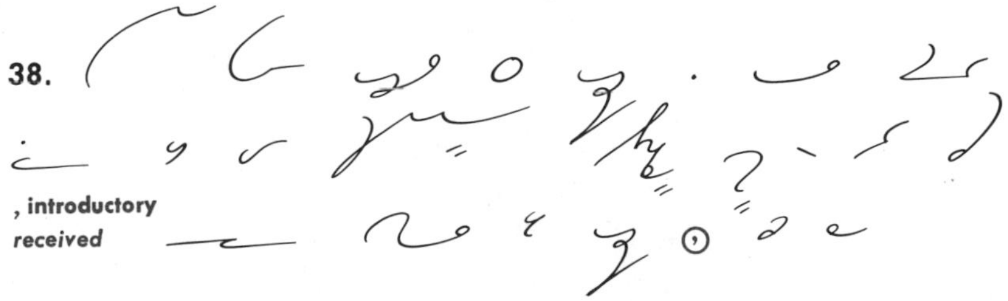

available

, introductory

; no conjunction

, introductory

appliance

(112)

39.

concerning

, parenthetical

indeed

12-month

hyphenated before noun

***, if clause* enclosed**

, apposition

; no conjunction
schedule

familiar
, when clause
, parenthetical

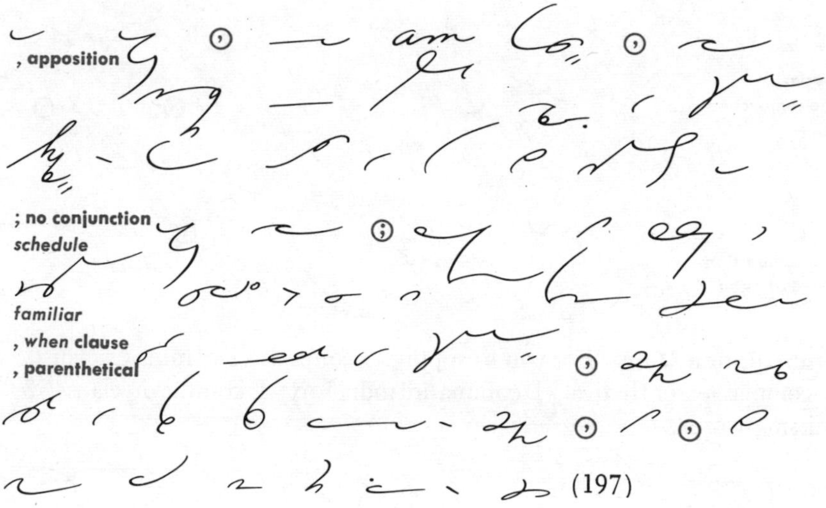

(197)

40.

representative
, apposition

, introductory
appreciation

(73)

41.

operate
, conjunction

carefully

, series
; no conjunction
itself
; no conjunction
demonstration

(69)

Transcription Quiz. For you to supply: 5 commas—1 comma as clause, 2 commas parenthetical, 1 comma introductory, 1 comma *if* clause; 2 missing words.

42.

(131)

LESSON 7

Marginal Reminders, 3

; because of comma

As you have already learned, a comma is used to separate two independent clauses that are joined by a conjunction. When a comma occurs within one or within both independent clauses, a semicolon is used to separate the two clauses.

> So far, I have not heard from you; and I should not be human if I were not worried.
>
> I have not heard from you; and I should not be human, Mr. Smith, if I were not a little worried.

The reason is simple enough. If there are other commas in the sentence, something stronger than a comma is necessary to separate the two parts of the sentence.

No hyphen after *ly*

As you have also learned, a hyphen is used in such expressions as *well known* and *good looking* when they are compound modifiers preceding a noun—*well-known pianist; good-looking dress.*

No hyphen is used, however, when the first word of the compound modifier ends in *ly*. For example, no hyphen would be used in the following sentence:

> It is a widely read magazine.

To be sure that you are not tempted to put a hyphen in such expressions, they are occasionally called to your attention in the Reading and Writing Practice exercises by the marginal reminder "no hyphen after *ly*."

43. Useful Business-Letter Phrases. Can you read the 29 phrases in this paragraph in less than half a minute?

They

1 

We

2 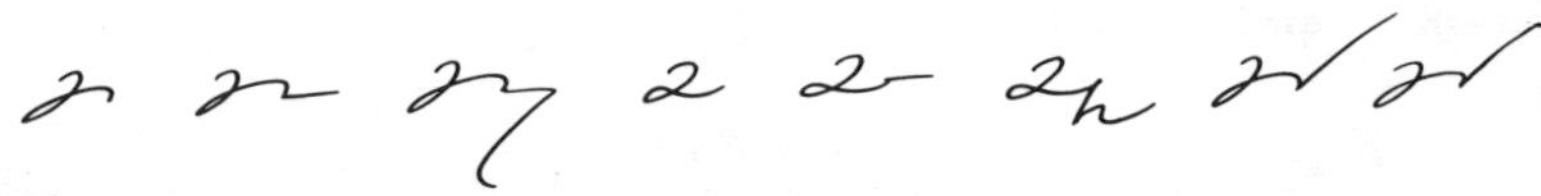

That

3 

This

4 

1. They would, they did, they have, they may, they are, they will, they could.
2. We can, we cannot, we cannot be, we are, we are not, we are sure, we could, we could not.
3. That is, that is not, that is the, that are, that are not, that it is, that it was, that it will.
4. This is, this is the, this is not, this letter, this matter, this might.

44. Frequent Names

1 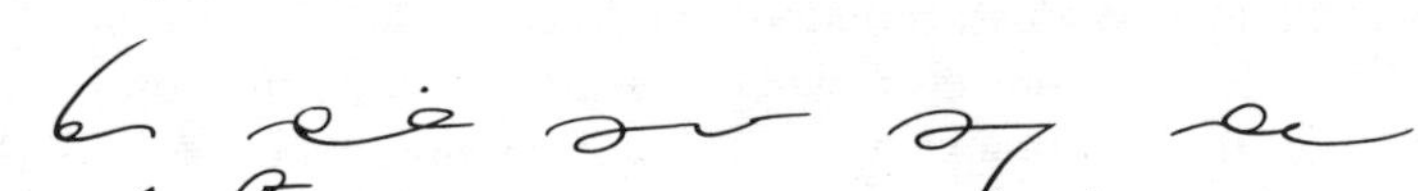

2 

1. Burke, Callahan, Cameron, Campbell, Carroll.
2. Adeline, Agnes, Amelia, Annabell, Augusta, Barbara.

Reading and Writing Practice

45. Transcription Word Study

mart Market, store.

utility Usefulness.

46.

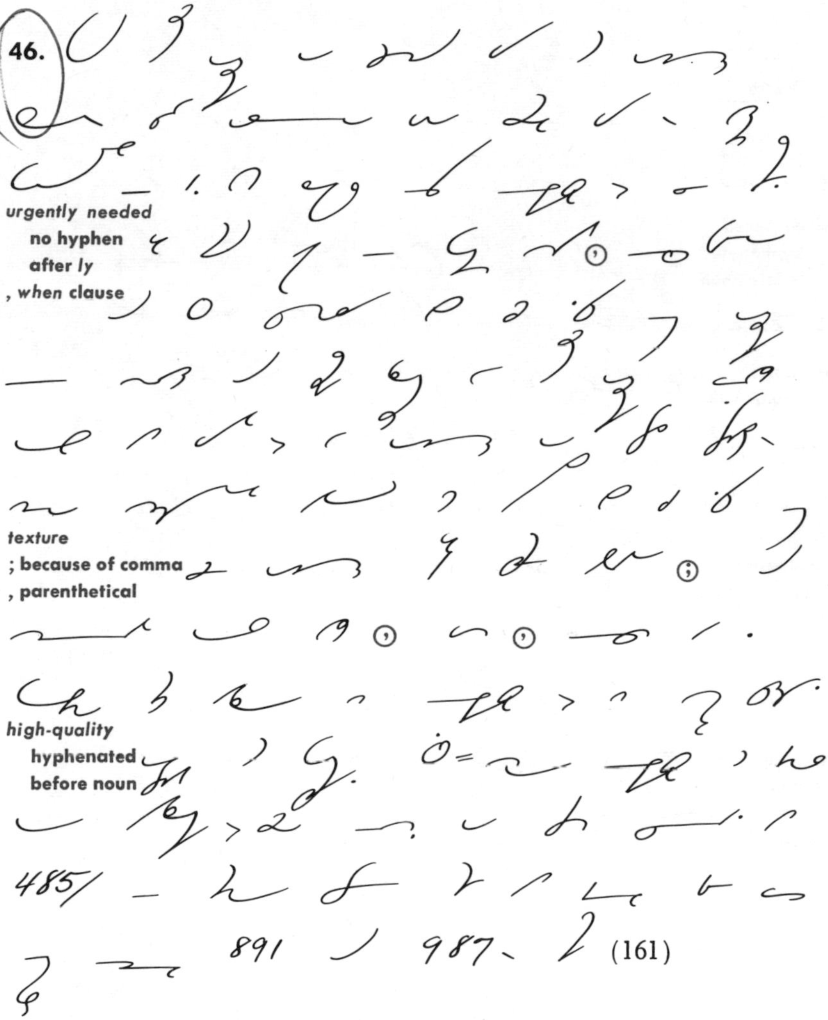

47.

reflected

, series

age-ripened hyphenated before noun

museums

; no conjunction

definitely

, *if clause*

; because of comma

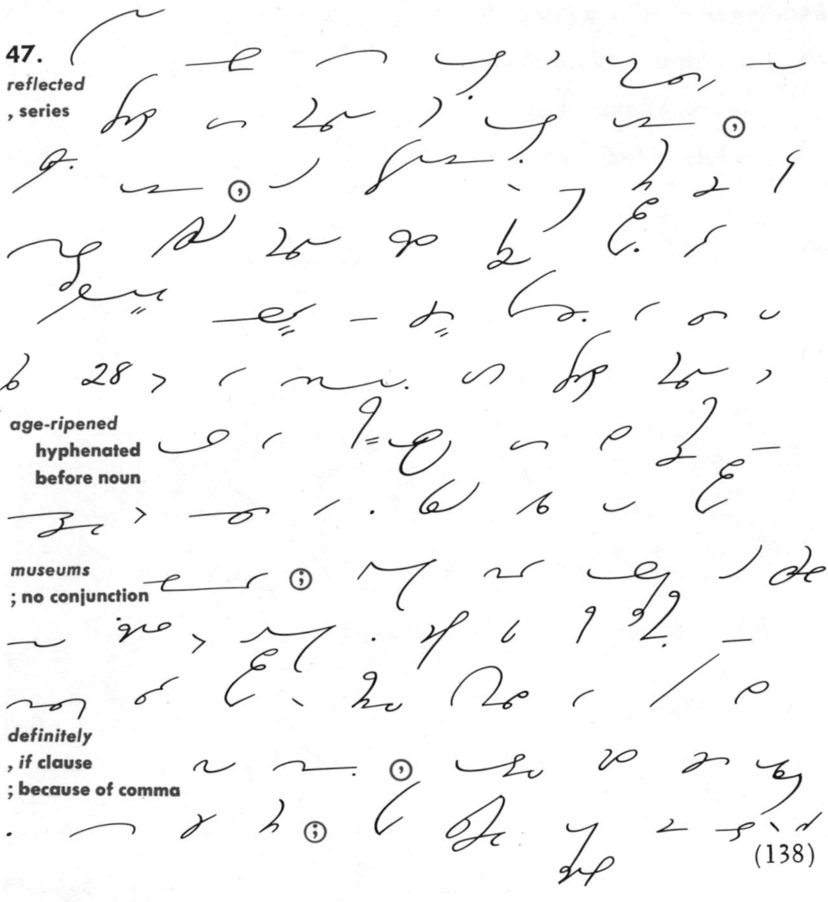

(138)

48.

, apposition

; because of comma

disappointed

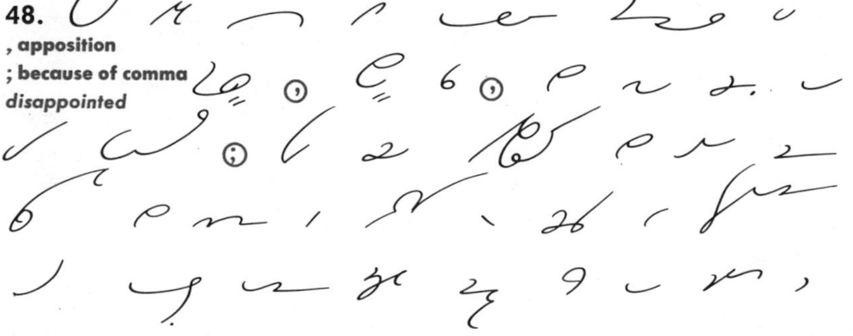

moderately priced no hyphen after *ly*

, parenthetical

catalogue

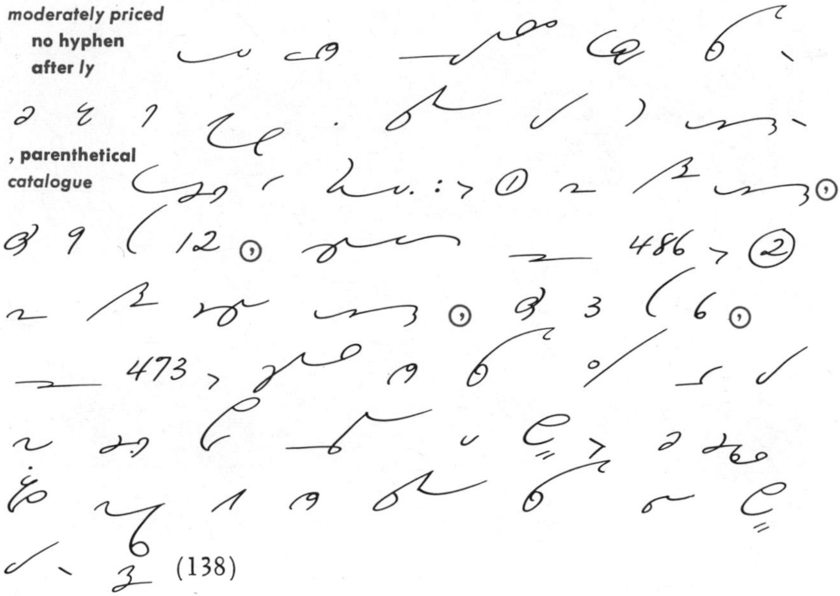

(138)

49.

breakfast

; no conjunction

(47)

Transcription Quiz. For you to supply: 8 commas–2 commas apposition, 2 commas series, 1 comma *if* clause, 1 comma introductory, 2 commas parenthetical; 2 missing words.

50.

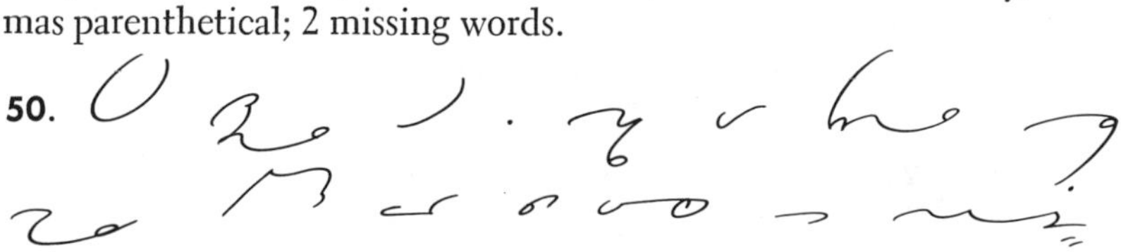

(211)

LESSON 8

Marginal Reminders, 4

Dates

The correct form for transcribing dates is *January 15*, with no *th* after the figure when the month precedes the day. The reminder in the margin reads:

Transcribe:
January 15

Amounts

The correct form for transcribing even amounts of dollars is *$120*, with no decimal point and no ciphers. The reminder in the margin reads:

Transcribe:
$120

Street Address

In transcribing a street address, the form recommended is *115 West 82 Street*—without a *d* after the street number.

More and more authorities are recommending the omission of *th*, *st*, and *d* from numbered street addresses because the omission adds to the readability of the address.

The marginal reminder for the foregoing address would be:

Transcribe:
82 Street

51. Word Families

-long

1 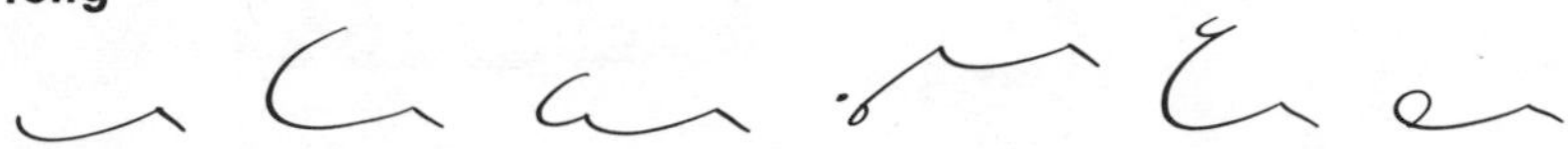

-sign

2 

-let

3 

-count

4 

-serve

5 

-sure

6 

1. Long, belong, prolong, headlong, oblong, along.
2. Sign, assign, design, resign, countersign, assignment, designer.
3. Outlet, pamphlet, bracelet, booklet, inlet, violet.
4. Count, account, recount, discount, miscount, accountant, accountancy.
5. Serve, deserve, conserve, observe, preserve, reserve, deservedly.
6. Insure, assure, treasure, measure, pleasure, reassure.

Reading and Writing Practice

52. Transcription Word Study

compound fracture A fracture in which the bone breaks through the skin.

tibia The larger of the two bones in the part of the leg between the knee and the ankle.

patronize Deal with, trade with.

53.

overdue

Transcribe: *$48*

, as clause

; because of comma

, introductory

Transcribe: *6 per cent*

, if clause

promptly

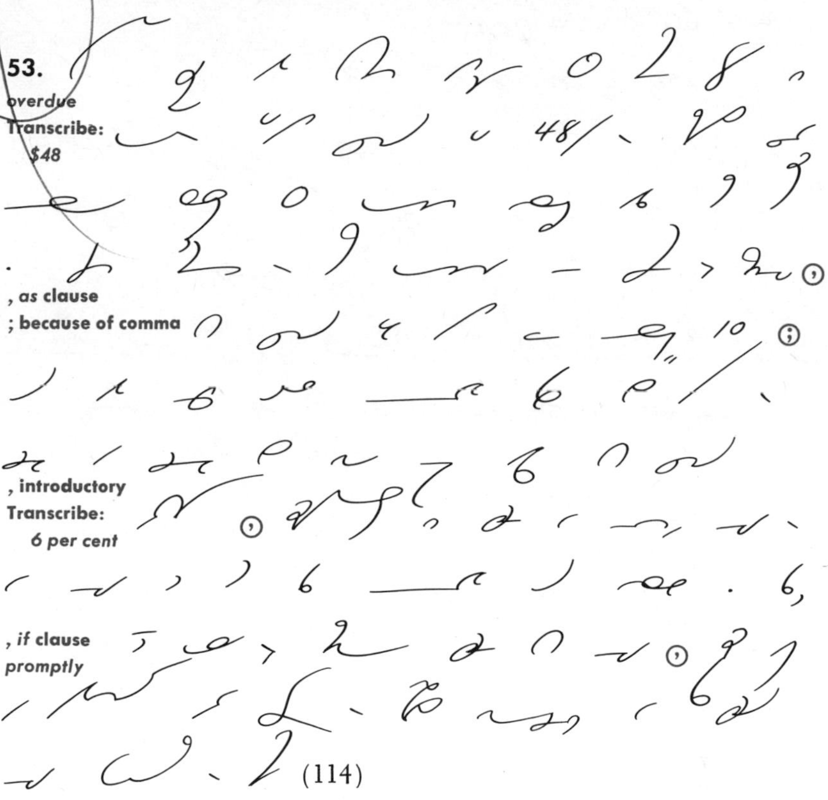

(114)

54.

Transcribe: *$150*

, apposition

, conjunction

, as clause

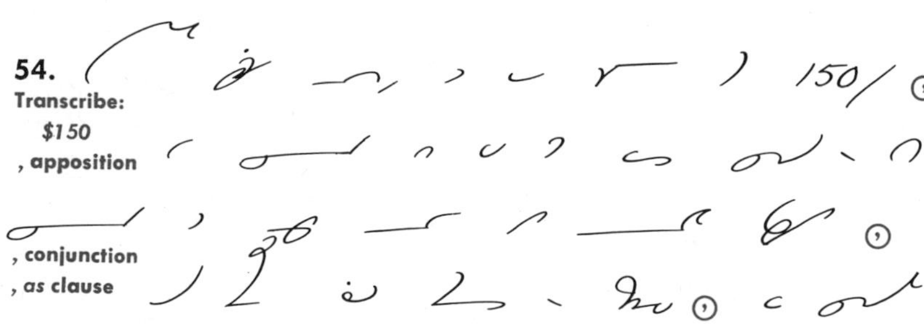

Transcribe:
22 Street
$150
, when clause

10 22 150

; because of comma
, parenthetical

unexpected
, if clause

1940

liberal
, parenthetical
, introductory

(188)

55. Transcribe:
March 1
$150

150 50

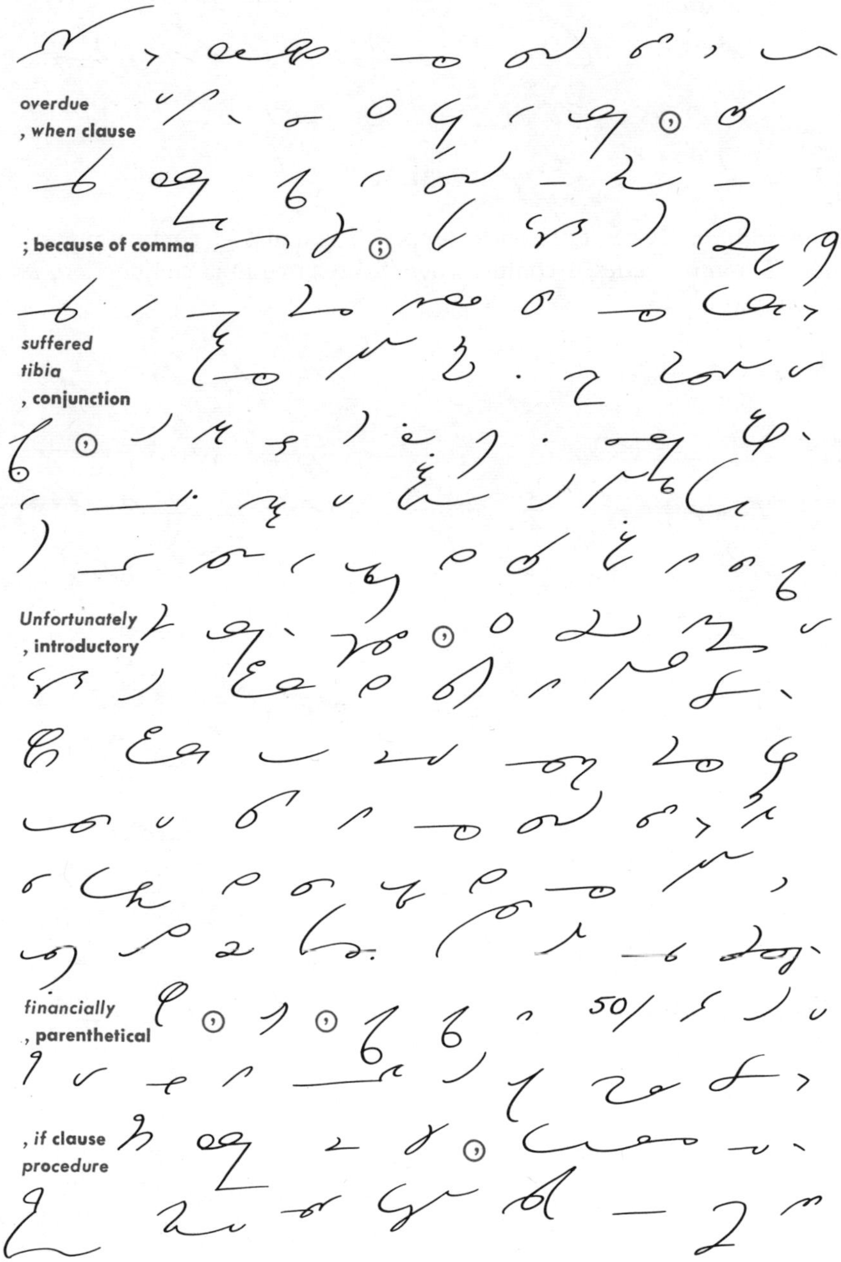

overdue
, when clause
; because of comma
suffered
tibia
, conjunction
Unfortunately
, introductory
financially
, parenthetical
, if clause
procedure

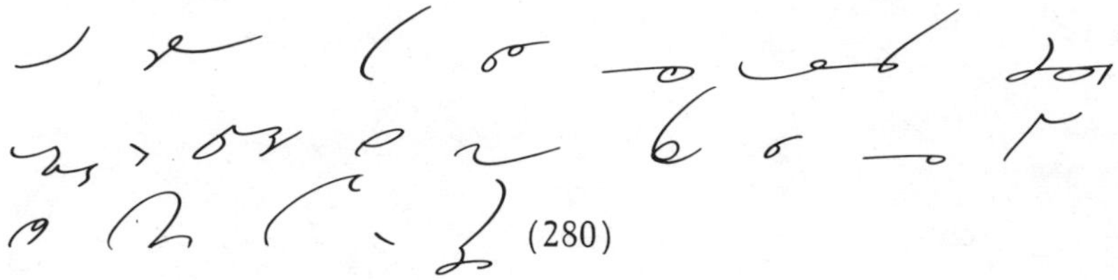

(280)

Transcription Quiz. For you to supply: 5 commas—1 comma apposition, 2 commas series, 1 comma *when* clause, 1 comma conjunction; 2 missing words.

56.

(157)

LESSON 9

Marginal Reminders, 5

. courteous request

Very often one businessman may wish to persuade another to take some definite action. He could make his request for action with a direct statement, such as:

I wish to hear from you by return mail.

A direct statement of this type, however, might antagonize the reader. Many businessmen, therefore, prefer to make such a request in the form of a question.

May I hear from you by return mail.

Where a request for definite action is put in the form of a question, a period is used at the end of the sentence.

This is the way you can decide whether to use a question mark or a period:

1. If the question calls for an answer in the form of action, use a period.
2. If the question calls for an answer in words, use a question mark.

57. Word Endings

-ly

1 

-ally, -ily

2 

-cial, -tial

3 

-ful

4 

-self, -selves

5 

-ble

6 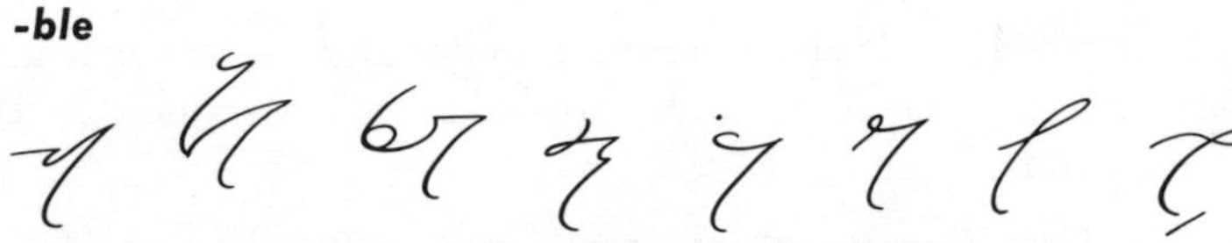

1. Neatly, only, firmly, calmly, badly, simply, namely.
2. Finally, vitally, totally, formally, steadily, readily, family.
3. Special, commercial, substantial, circumstantial, beneficial, essential, initial, initials.
4. Careful, harmful, grateful, helpful, helpfully, helpfulness.
5. Himself, herself, myself, yourself, itself, ourselves, themselves, yourselves.
6. Notable, obtainable, pardonable, sensible, horrible, terrible, table, cabled.

58. Geographical Expressions

1 

2 

3 

1. Bloomfield, Greenfield, Westfield, Winfield, Deerfield, Plainfield.
2. Pennsylvania, Maryland, Virginia, West Virginia, North Carolina, South Carolina, Georgia, Florida.
3. Argentina, Australia, Belgium, Bolivia, Brazil.

Reading and Writing Practice

59. Transcription Word Study

consternation Dismay.

quandary A state of doubt.

embark To engage in, to set out on.

60.

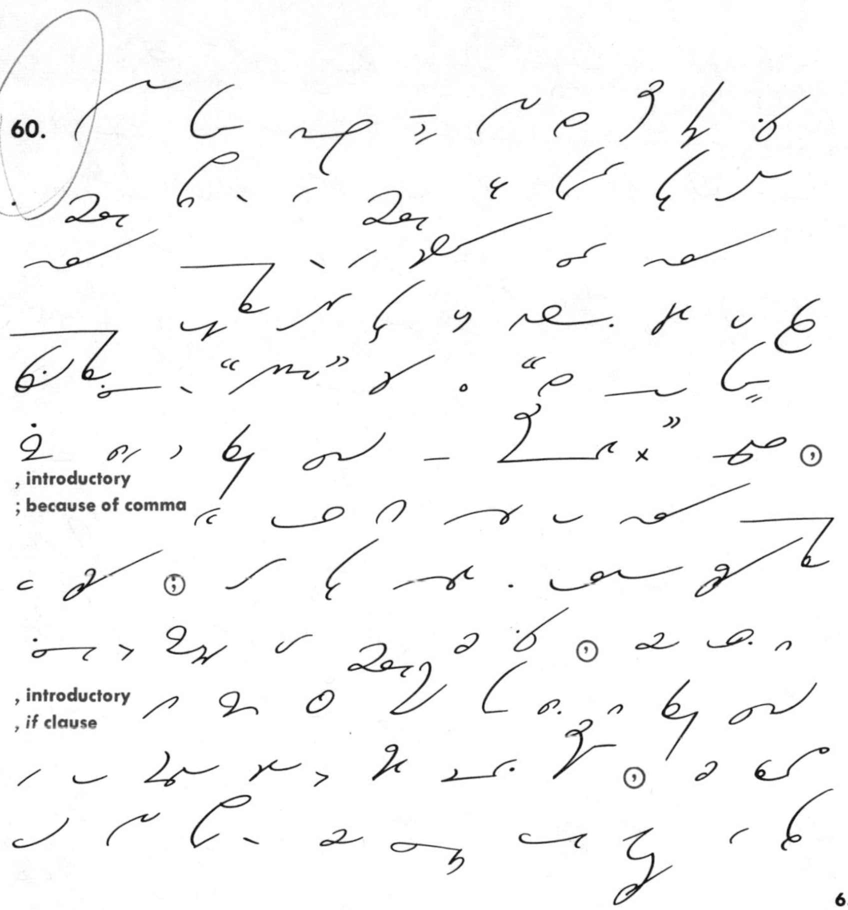

, introductory
; because of comma

, introductory
, if clause

, *if* clause
eager

won't
. courteous
request

(182)

61.

furniture
quite

1956

; no conjunction
buying

household
, introductory

, introductory
exploring

wall-to-wall
first-floor
hyphenated
before noun

estimate
. courteous
request

(208)

62.

, introductory
, parenthetical

30

, as clause
Easy-Payment
hyphenated
before noun

20/

, introductory
. courteous
request

(121)

Transcription Quiz. For you to supply: 6 commas–2 commas parenthetical, 2 commas introductory, 2 commas series; 2 missing words.

63.

(189)

LESSON 10

64. Word-Building Practice — Consonants

Ng

1 

Ngk

2 

Over Th

3 

Under Th

4 

1. **Ring, king, bring, spring, string, sing, hang, sang.**
2. **Blank, frank, tank, sank, ink, bank.**
3. **These, thick, thickness, thief, thieves, thin, thousand, thus, teeth.**
4. **Though, thought, thoughtless, although, threat, thorough, health, wealth.**

65. Accuracy Practice — Straight Lines. The speed with which you can read your notes will depend in part on the accuracy of your penmanship. The Accuracy Practice exercises in this lesson are intended to improve your ability to write straight lines. With this and the other Accuracy Practice exercises in this volume, follow this procedure:

1. Read the entire drill.

2. Practice each group separately, writing it once or twice and making a special effort to keep the straight lines absolutely straight.

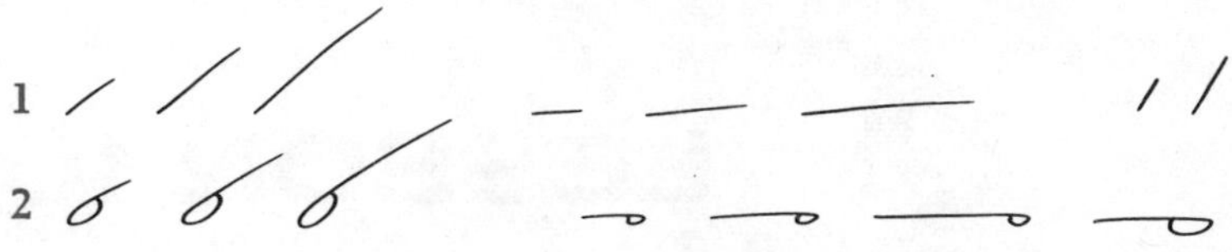

1. It-at, would, did-date; in-not, am-more, men; shall-ship, which.
2. Ate, add, added; any, me, many, may.

Reading and Writing Practice

66. Transcription Word Study

arbitrated Decided, determined.

incurable Incapable of being helped.

storm window A second window placed outside the regular one as protection against cold weather.

67. Father Rests

favorable
lovely

, series
children's
quarrels

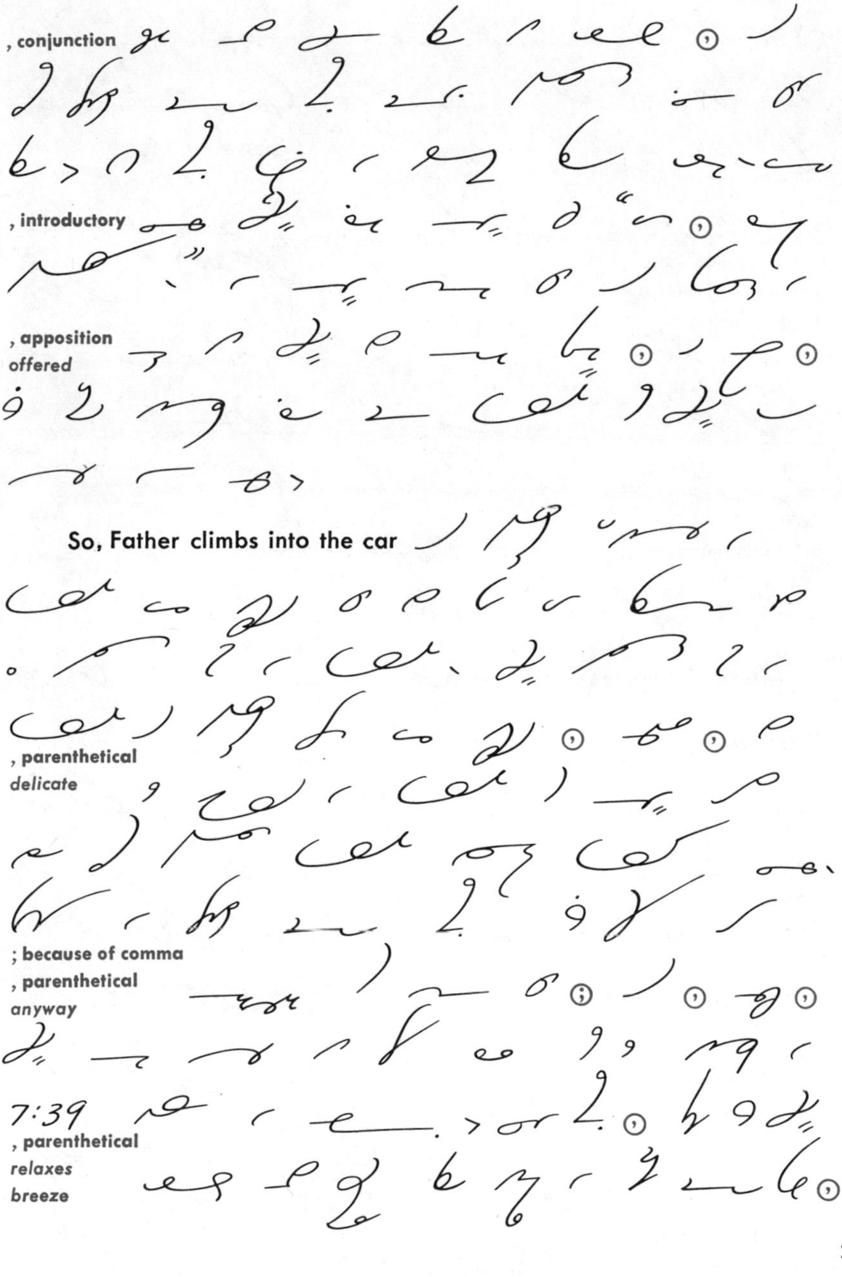

, conjunction

, introductory

, apposition
offered

So, Father climbs into the car

, parenthetical
delicate

; because of comma
, parenthetical
anyway

7:39
, parenthetical
relaxes
breeze

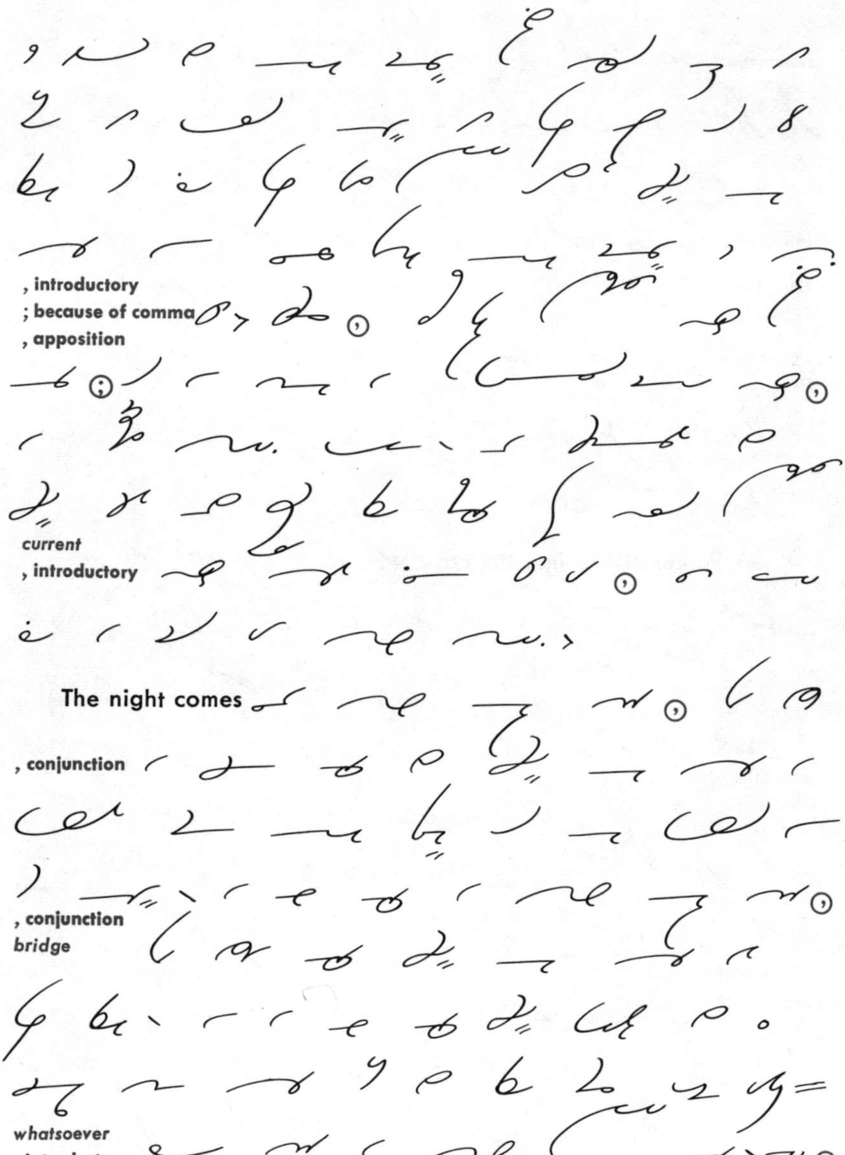

, introductory
; because of comma
, apposition

current
, introductory

The night comes

, conjunction

, conjunction
bridge

whatsoever
, introductory

; no conjunction
, introductory

, introductory

Does Father rest

, as clause
season

, *when* clause
, parenthetical
leaves

, conjunction
screens

, *when* clause

Worst
, introductory

strictly
, series
faucets

Then there are

, *if* clause

adjustment
; no conjunction

apparently

; no conjunction

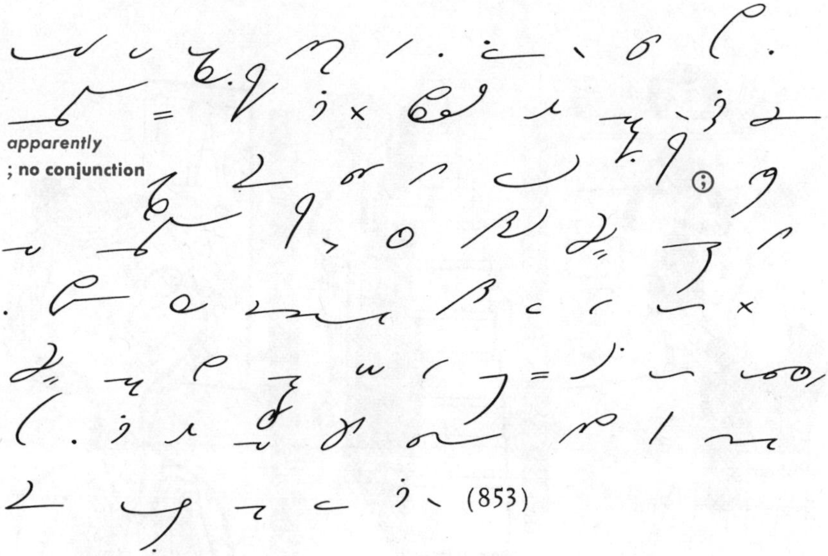

Spelling and Punctuation Self-Check

In your shorthand class you are improving your ability to spell and punctuate as well as building up your shorthand skill. Are you careful, however, to spell and punctuate correctly when you

1. Write compositions, reports, and assignments in your other subjects?

2. Correspond with friends to whom you must write in longhand or on the typewriter?

Make correct spelling and punctuation a habit!

3

GENERAL RETAILING

LESSON 11

Marginal Reminders, 6

, nonrestrictive

Nonrestrictive clauses and phrases are set off by commas. A nonrestrictive clause or phrase is one that may be omitted without changing the meaning of the sentence. The nonrestrictive clause or phrase might be classified as parenthetical. It is important that you follow the meaning of the dictation in order to be able to identify the restrictive and the nonrestrictive clauses and phrases and to punctuate them correctly.

> Restrictive – no commas: The automobile that was speeding was completely destroyed.
> Nonrestrictive – commas: The automobile, which was speeding, was completely destroyed.

In the first sentence above, *that was speeding* is a restrictive clause and must not be set off by commas. The expression *that was speeding* identifies the particular automobile that was destroyed. In the second sentence, *which was speeding* is a nonrestrictive or descriptive or parenthetical clause that must be set off with commas. It does not identify the particular automobile that was destroyed; it could be omitted without changing the meaning of the sentence.

The use of these commas is determined by the meaning of the sentence. You can always tell the dictator's meaning by the inflection of the voice during dictation. It is almost always possible to decide from the meaning of the dictation whether an expression was intended to be nonrestrictive or restrictive–whether it should be transcribed with or without commas.

68. Brief Forms and Derivatives

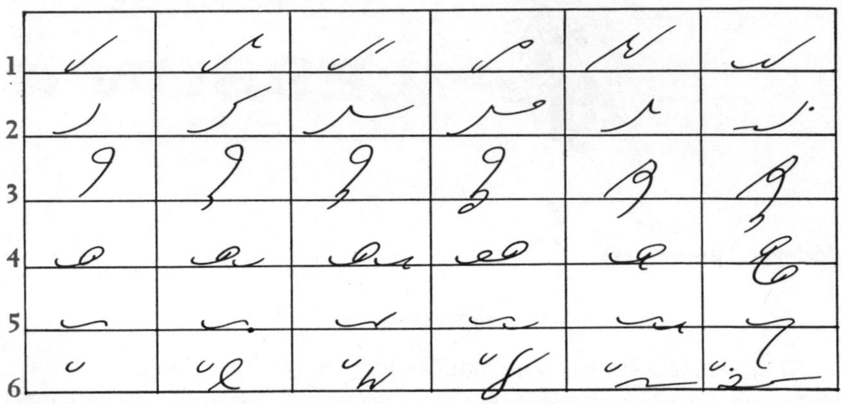

1. Order, orders, ordered, orderly, disorder, reorder.
2. And-end, ended, endless, endlessly, ends, unending.
3. Advantage, advantages, advantageous, advantageously, disadvantage, disadvantageous.
4. Write-right, writer, writers, rewrite, writes-rights, typewrite.
5. Work, working, worked, worker, workers, workable.
6. Over, overtax, overshoot, overpaid, overcome, overwhelm.

69. Brief Form and Phrase Letter

(135)

Reading and Writing Practice

70. Transcription Word Study

Blacktop Black substance, often tar, used for paving roads and streets.

authorization Permission.

converted Changed over.

71.

driveway

, nonrestrictive

, introductory

expensive

. courteous request

advantages

, introductory
dangerous
sun's
, parenthetical
, when clause
; no conjunction
.convenience

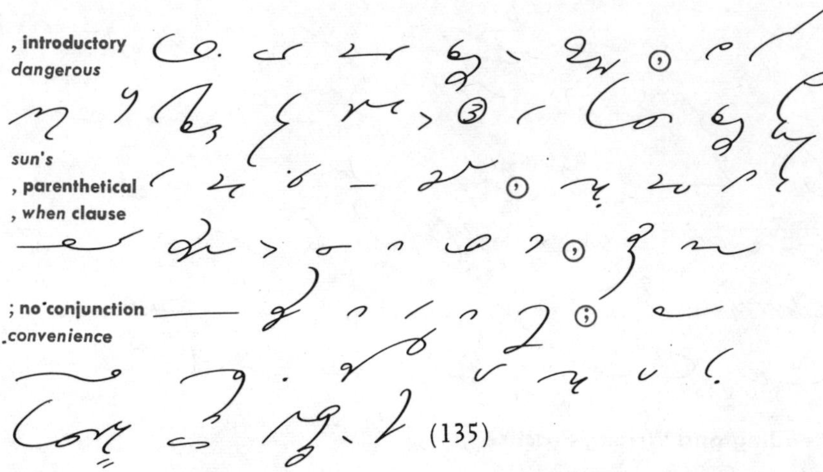

(135)

72.

blacktopping
, nonrestrictive
, conjunction
entrance
estimate
. courteous request
, conjunction

(110)

73.
requested
, as clause
, introductory
Transcribe:
$100
, series
, nonrestrictive
payable
proceed
, if clause

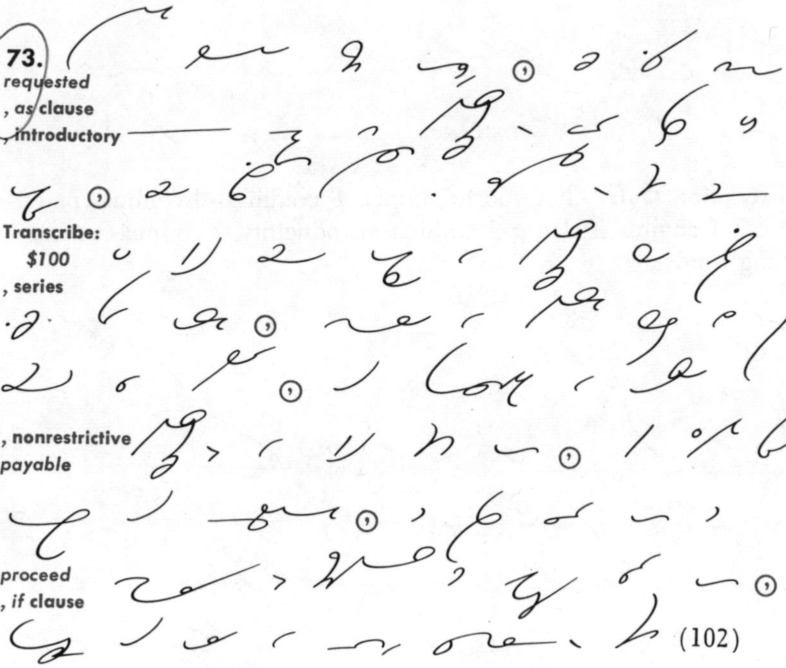

(102)

74.
authorization
accordance
, introductory
satisfied
, if clause

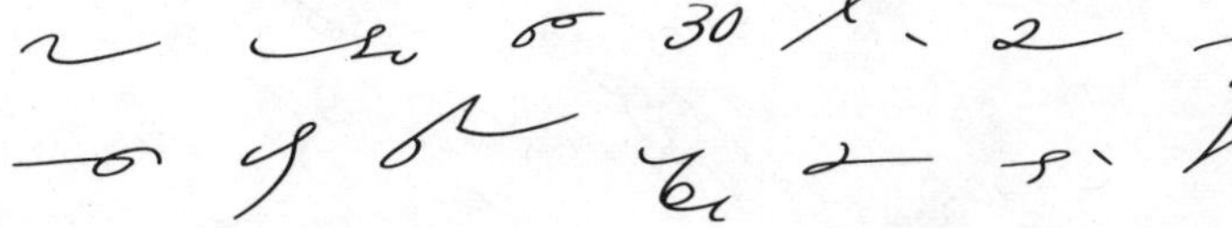

(114)

Transcription Quiz. For you to supply: 8 commas–4 commas parenthetical, 1 comma *if* clause, 1 comma introductory, 2 commas series; 2 missing words.

75.

(166)

LESSON 12

Marginal Reminders, 7

, *and* omitted

Usually, two adjectives preceding a noun are separated by a comma.

It is a clear, bright day.

The comma is not used if the first adjective modifies the combined idea of the second adjective plus the noun.

She wore a beautiful green dress.

, introducing short quote

Short quotations are introduced by a comma.

The boy said, "I must be in class by nine o'clock."

, inside quote

. inside quote

The comma and the period are *always* typed inside the final quotation mark.

She said, "I cannot take the job."
The booklet, "10 Ways to Reduce," is out of stock.

Question marks are placed inside or outside the final quotation mark according to the sense of the sentence.

She asked, "Why did he go?"
Why did she say, "The job is too hard for me"?

Semicolons and colons are *always* placed outside the final quotation mark.

> Be sure to mark that letter "Confidential"; then place the carbon copy in my personal file.
>
> Shipments of the following goods should be marked "Fragile": china, glassware, ceramics.

76. Useful Business-Letter Phrases

Which

1 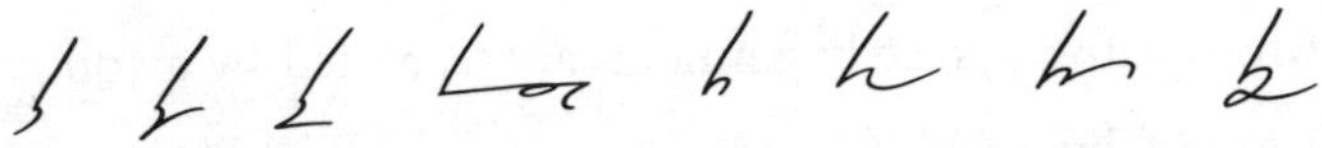

We

2 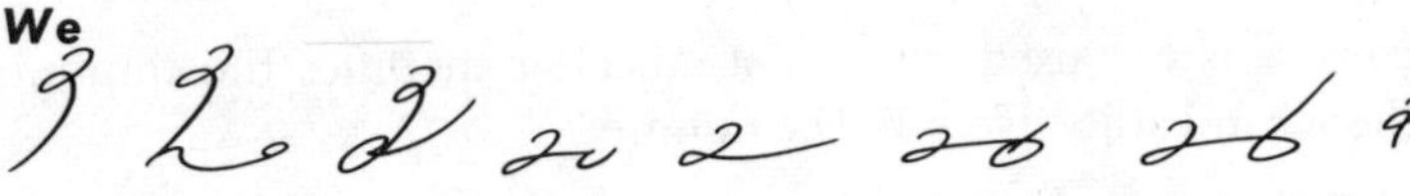

You

3 

It

4 

1. **Which is, which is the, which is not, which means, which you, which you are, which you can, which we are.**
2. **We have, we have your letter, we find, we know, we will, we might, we made, we shall.**
3. **You might, you must, you may, you may be, you may be sure, you may have, you should.**
4. **It is, it is not, it isn't, it is the, it will, it will not, it will not be, it was not.**

77. Frequent Names

1 

2 

1. Clark, Cohen, Cohn, Collins, Connell, Cooper.
2. Beatrice, Belle, Bertha, Bridget, Caroline, Catherine, Celia.

Reading and Writing Practice

78. Transcription Word Study

tyro A beginner, a novice.

indestructible Incapable of being destroyed.

deterioration Worsening.

79.

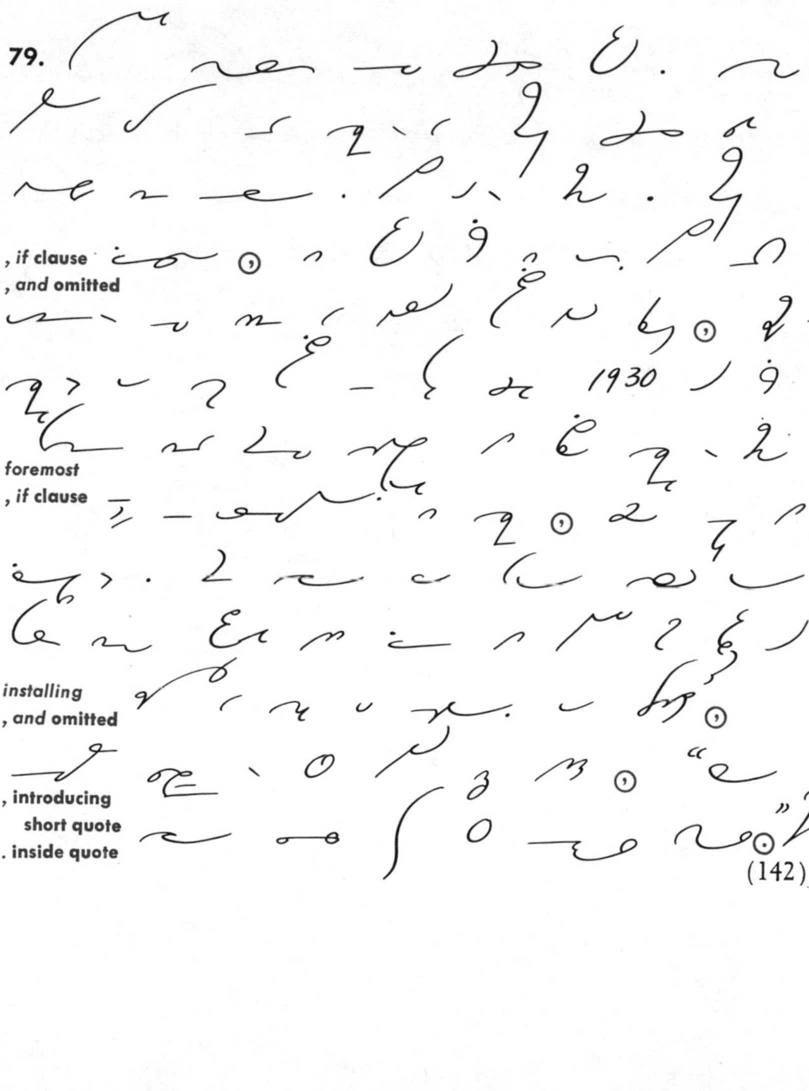

, *if clause*
, *and omitted*

foremost
, *if clause*

installing
, *and omitted*

, *introducing short quote*
. *inside quote*

(142)

80.

, *and* omitted
practical
, introductory
, introductory
wealthy
, parenthetical
, series
Transcribe:
12 feet
, introducing
short quote
amazingly
. inside quote
, parenthetical
, introductory
, *if* clause
opportunity

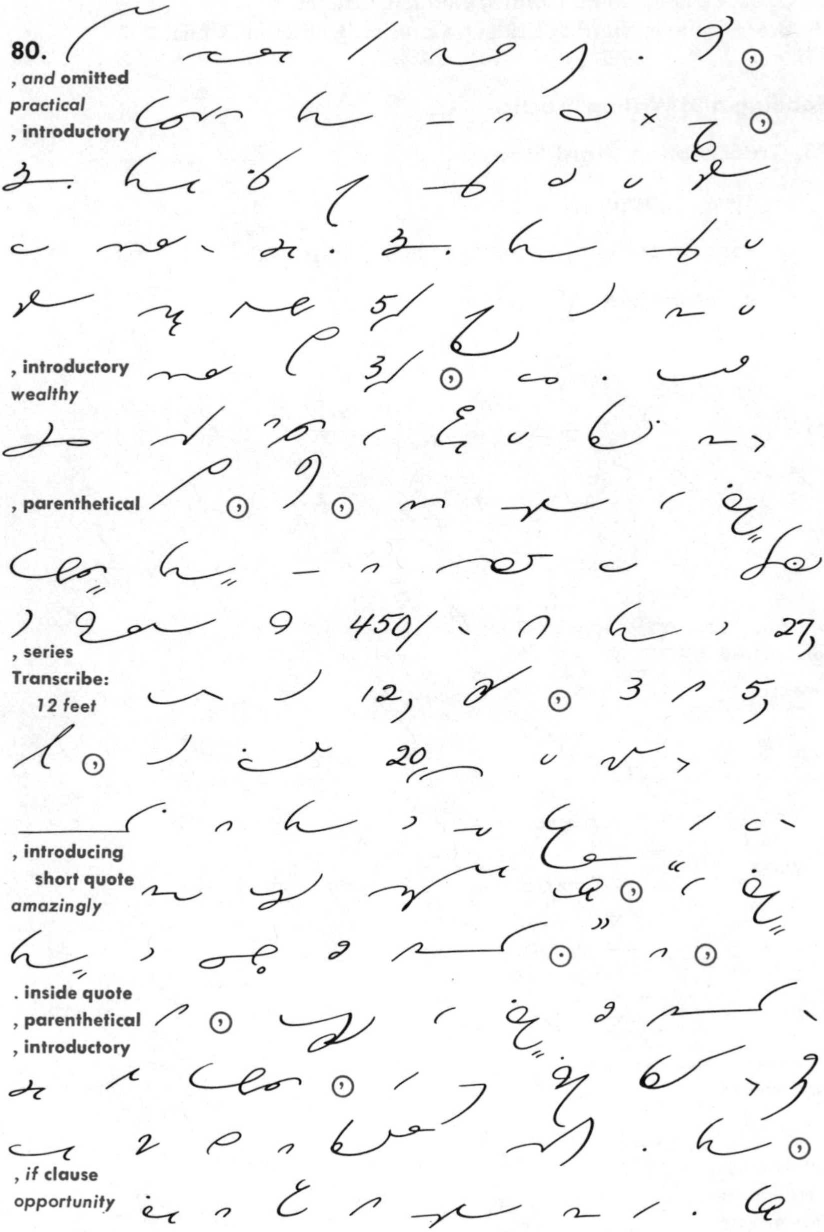

postal
, apposition
. courteous
request

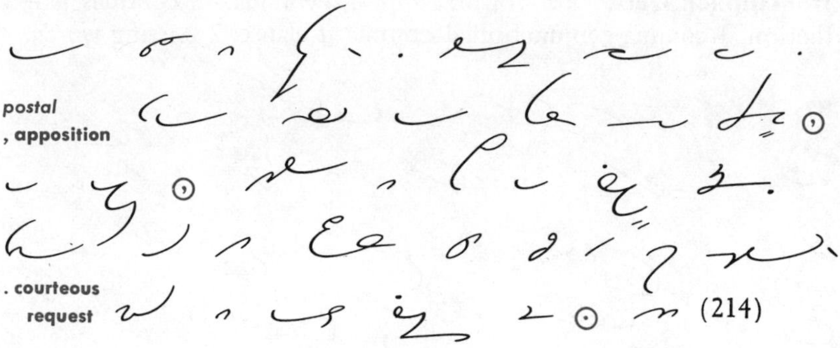

(214)

81.

wife's
, and omitted
carefully planned
no hyphen
after *ly*
tyro
well-designed
hyphenated
before noun
self-addressed
, conjunction

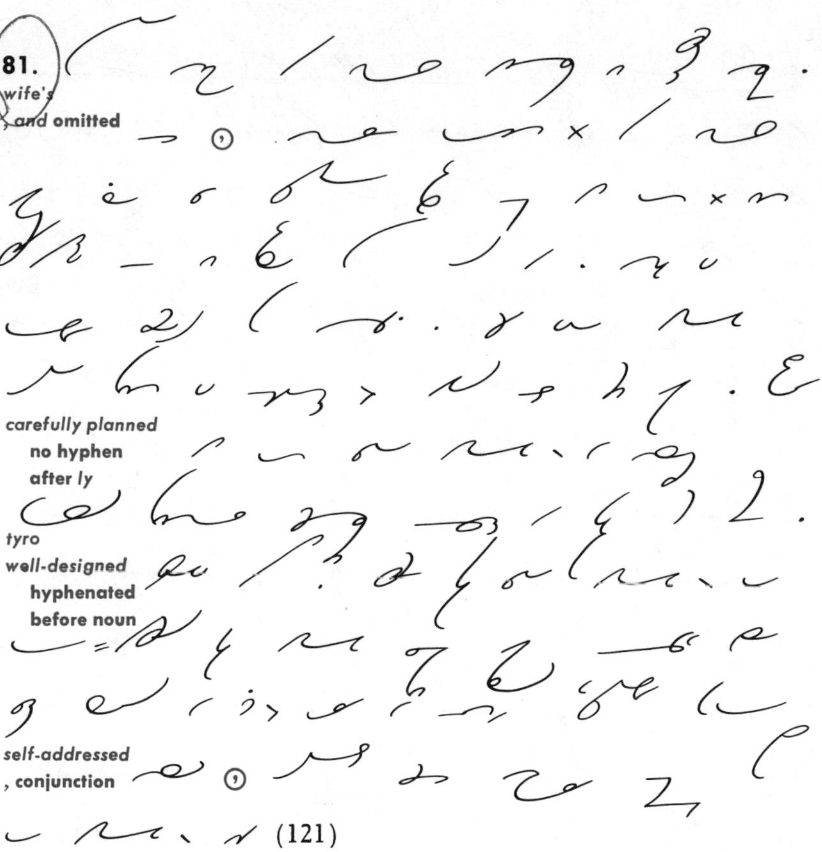

(121)

Transcription Quiz. For you to supply: 6 commas—4 commas parenthetical, 1 comma conjunction, 1 comma *if* clause; 2 missing words.

82.

(184)

LESSON 13

Marginal Reminders, 8

: introducing long quote

Long quotations are introduced by a colon.

> The boy said: "I have studied for many years to prepare for this work, and I hope that you are willing to help me find a place either here or in some neighboring city."

: enumeration

A colon is used after an expression that introduces some following material, such as an explanation of a general statement, a list, or an enumeration.

> There are three requirements: speed, accuracy, and artistry.
>
> The new washing machine has this advantage over other washing machines: it uses very little soap.

83. Word Families

-son

1 

-time

2 

-most

3 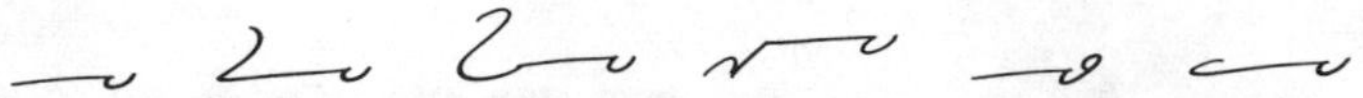

-vent

4 

-rate

5 

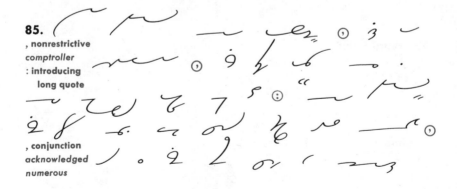

1. Son, reason, unison, person, garrison, comparison, crimson.
2. Time, noontime, sometime, pastime, daytime, nighttime, lifetime.
3. Most, foremost, uppermost, utmost, mostly, almost.
4. Vent, invent, event, convent, prevent, circumvent, advent.
5. Rate, operate, separate, generate, commemorate, enumerate.

Reading and Writing Practice

84. Transcription Word Study

comptroller (pronounced *con*-troller) An officer whose job it is to check expenditures.

reluctant Unwilling.

striking Remarkable.

85.

, nonrestrictive
comptroller
: introducing
long quote

, conjunction
acknowledged
numerous

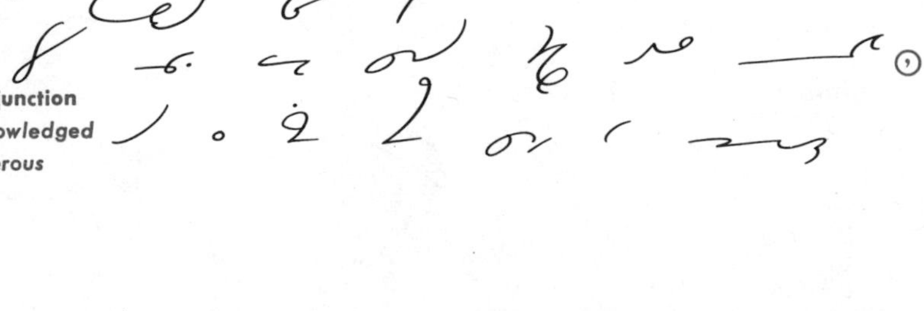

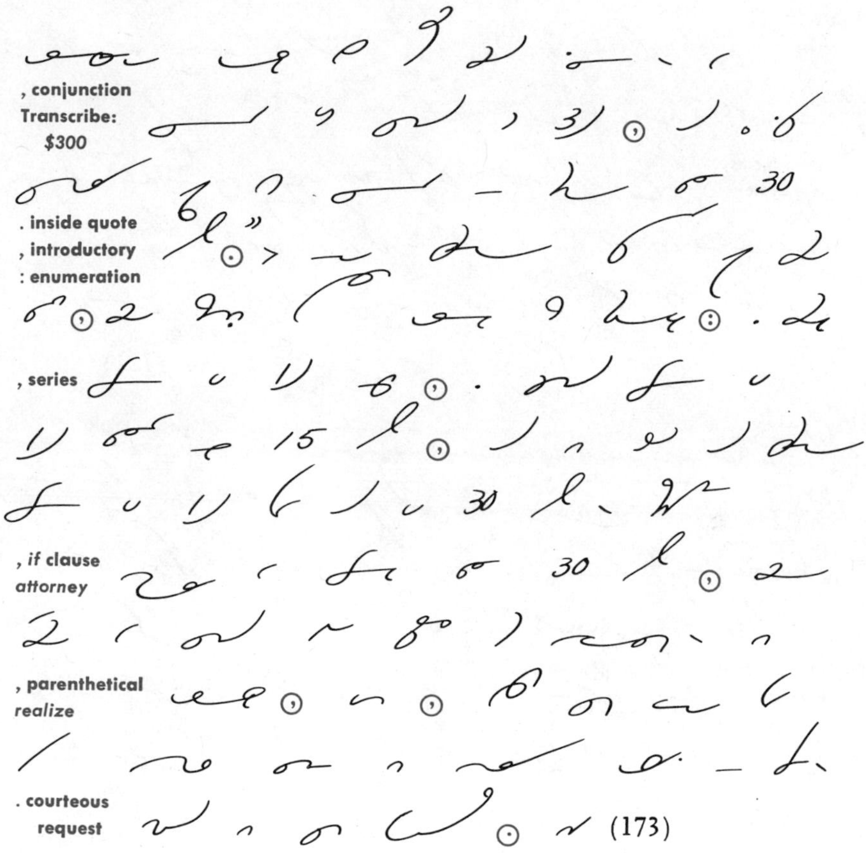

, conjunction
Transcribe:
$300
. inside quote
, introductory
: enumeration
, series
, *if* clause
attorney
, parenthetical
realize
. courteous
request

(173)

86.

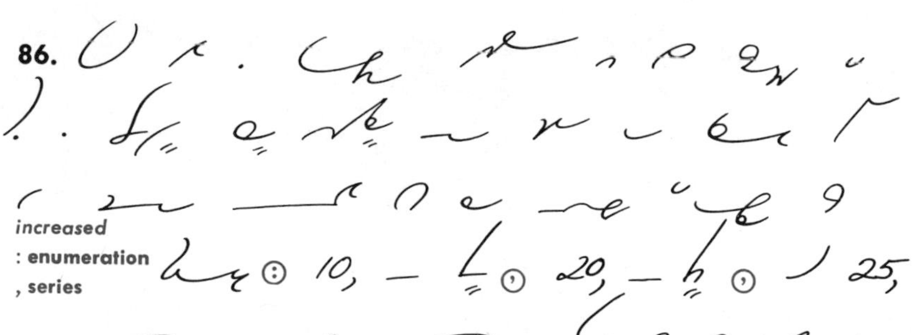

increased
: enumeration
, series

, introductory
, apposition
advice

(124)

87.

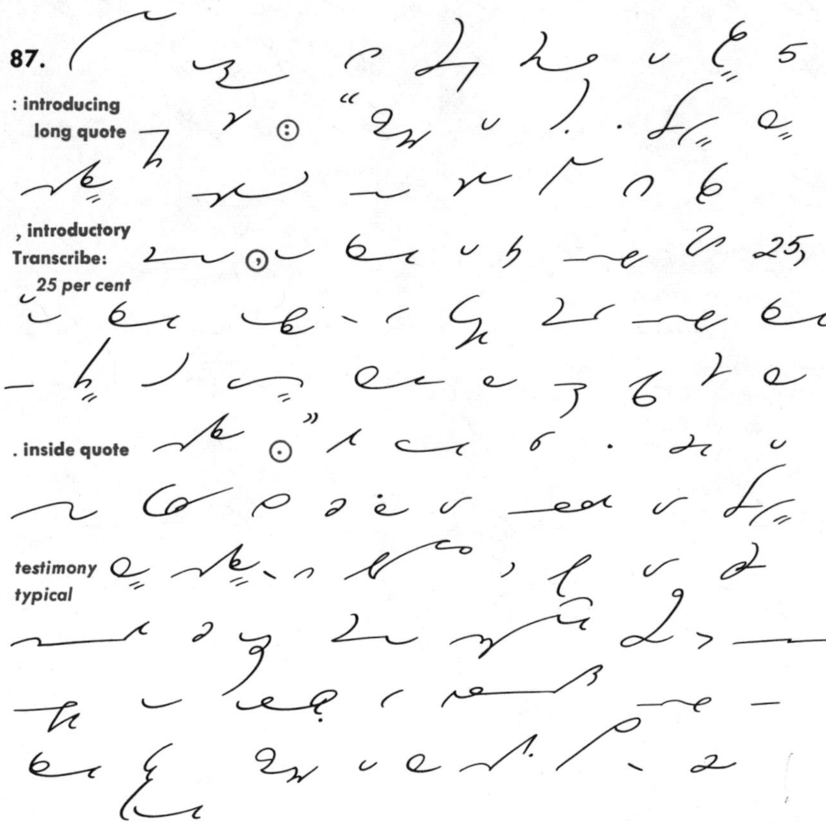

: introducing long quote

, introductory
Transcribe:
25 per cent

. inside quote

testimony
typical

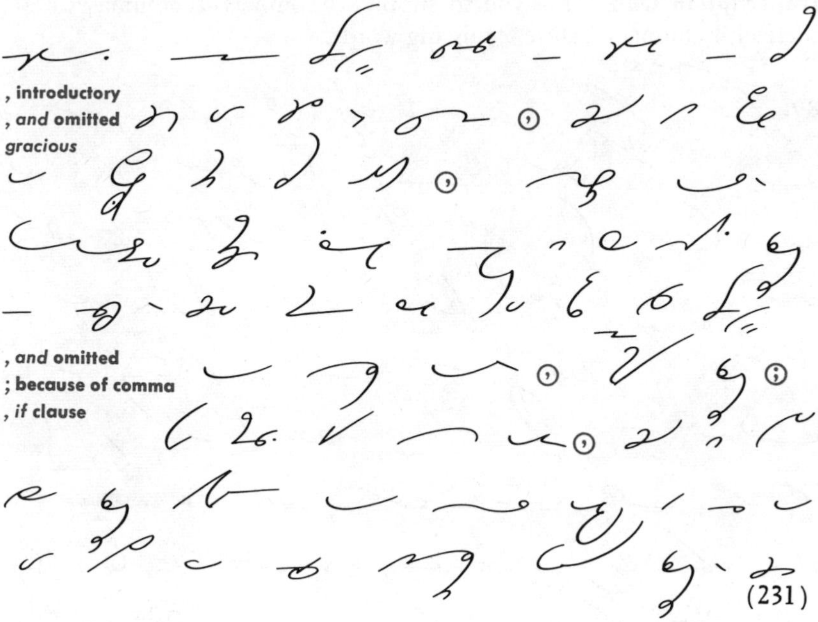

, introductory
, and omitted
gracious

, and omitted
; because of comma
, if clause

(231)

88.

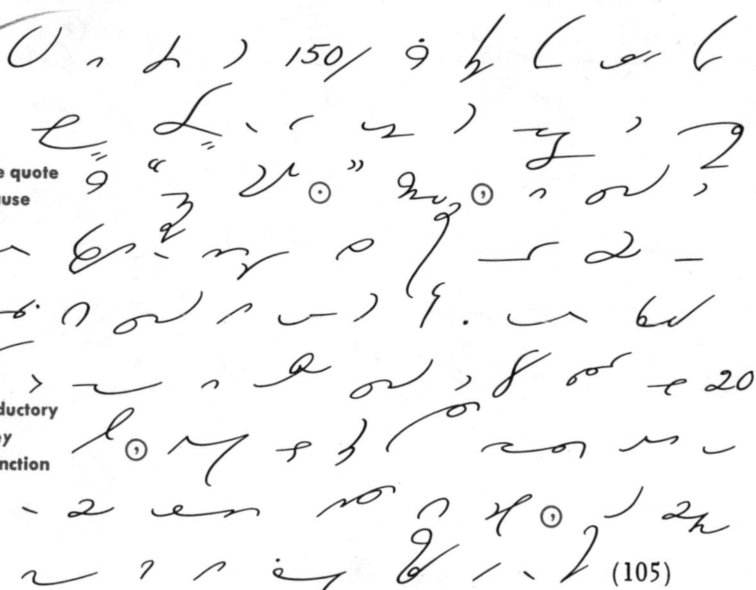

150 ... 20

. inside quote
, as clause

, introductory
attorney
, conjunction

(105)

Transcription Quiz. For you to supply: 7 commas–6 commas parenthetical, 1 comma *if* clause; 2 missing words.

89.

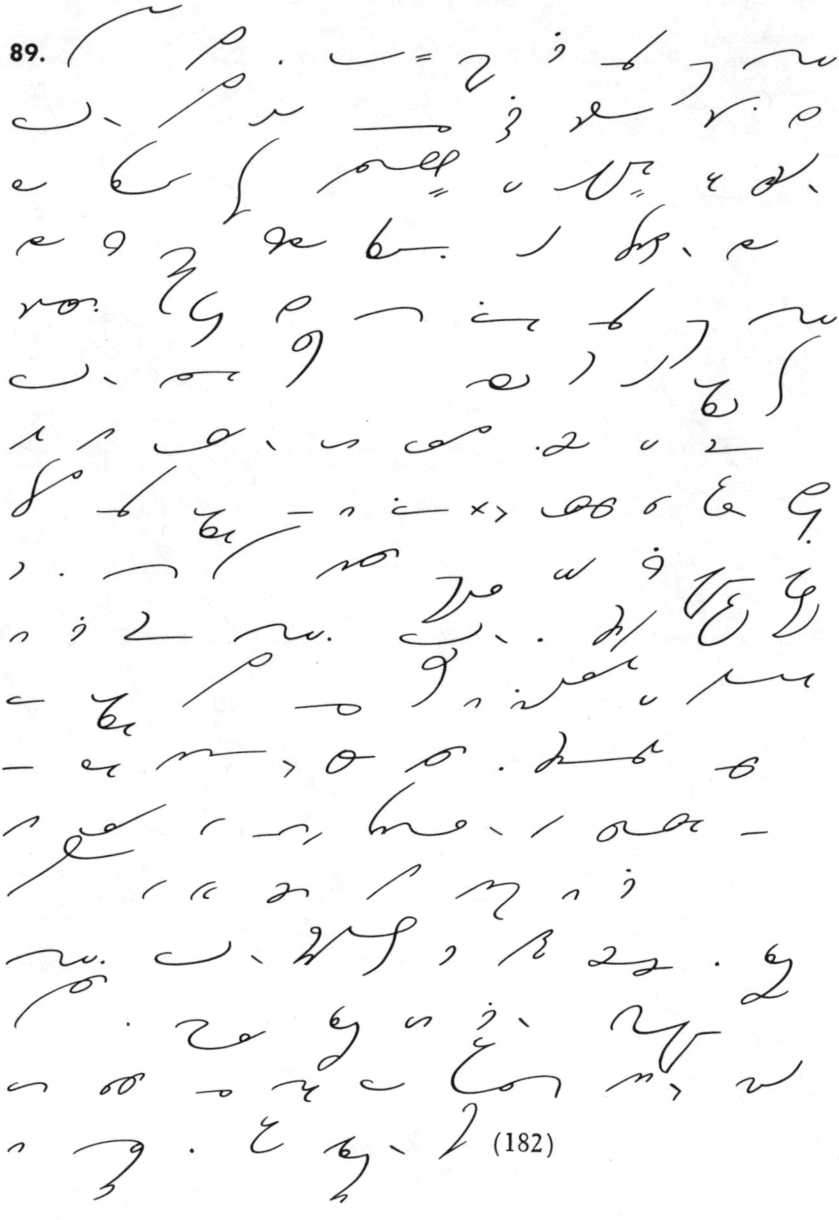

(182)

LESSON 14

Marginal Reminders, 9

; illustrative ,

When an illustration is introduced by some such expression as *namely, that is,* or *for example,* the expression should be preceded by a semicolon and followed by a comma.

Mary has only one ambition; namely, to be a secretary.

90. Word Beginnings and Endings

-lity

1 

-rity

2 

Incl-

3 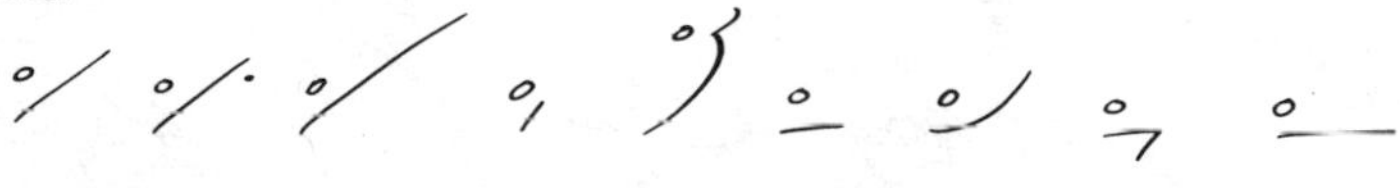

-ward

4 

-ship

5 

1. Quality, ability, inability, liability, reliability, possibility.
2. Authority, minority, majority, sincerity, charity, clarity.
3. Include, including, included, inclusion, inclusive, incline, inclined, inclination, inclement.
4. Forward, backward, afterward, onward, upward, outward, inward, reward.
5. Steamship, relationship, kinship, friendship, hardship, buymanship, courtship.

91. Geographical Expressions

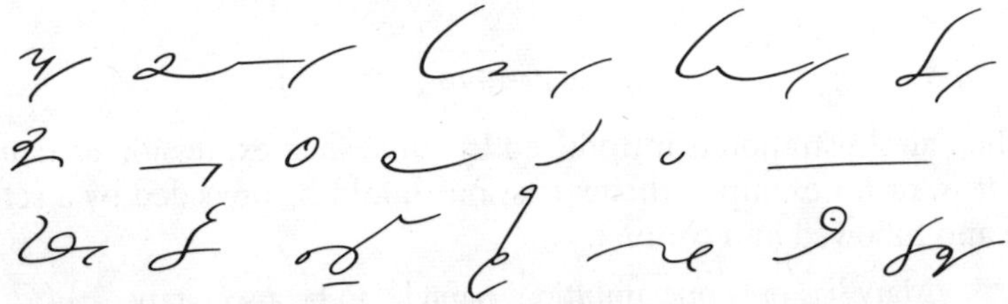

1. Washington, Wilmington, Bloomington, Burlington, Bennington.
2. Wisconsin, Michigan, Iowa, Illinois, Indiana, Ohio, Minnesota.
3. France, Spain, Equador, Egypt, Greece, India, Pakistan.

Reading and Writing Practice

92. Transcription Word Study

primary Main, basic, major.

consumer Buyer, purchaser.

interpret Analyze, understand.

93.

carefully planned no hyphen after *ly*

, introductory

, parenthetical

; illustrative ,

protein
, series
: introducing long quote
, series
fatigue
; no conjunction
. inside quote
, when clause
grocery
, when clause
Bell's

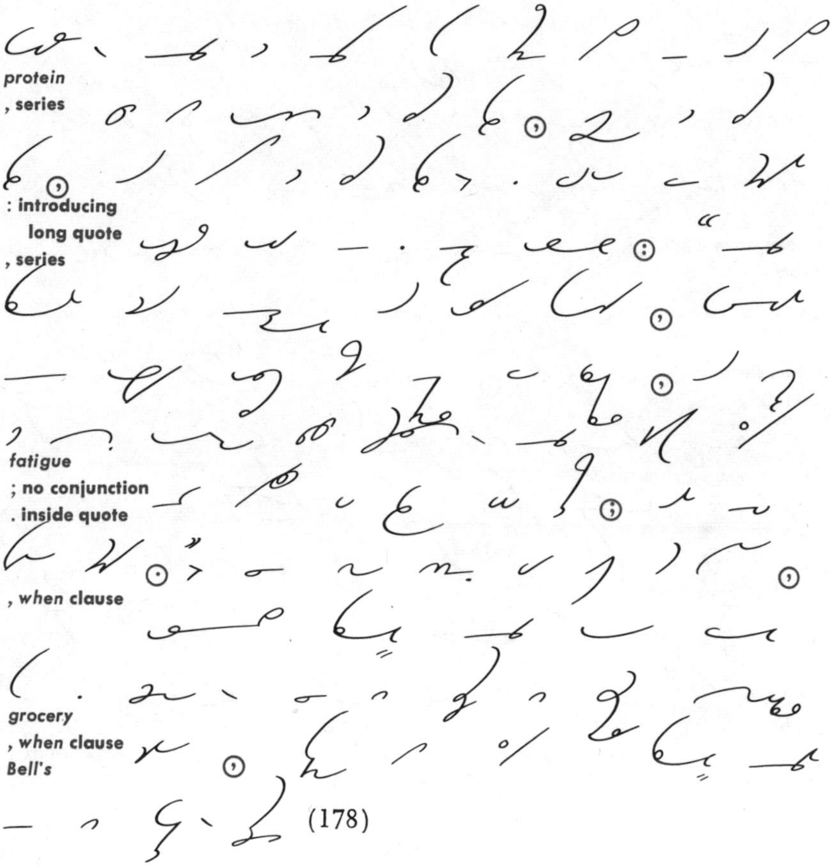

(178)

94.
attractively
, when clause

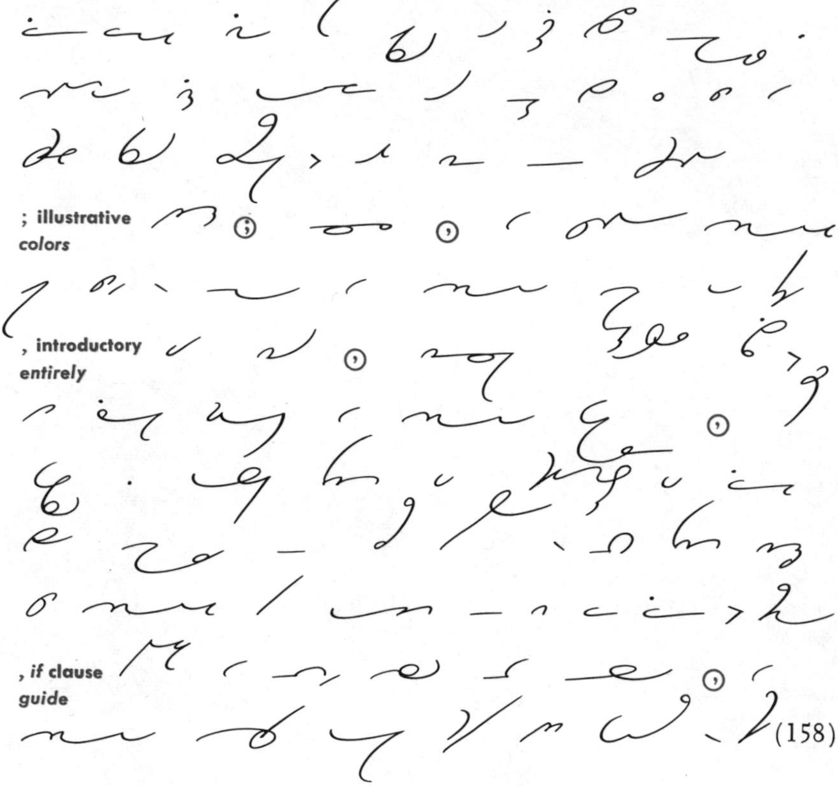

; illustrative
colors

, introductory
entirely

, if clause
guide

(158)

95.

, introductory
: enumeration

, apposition
Buymanship

, *if* clause

(81)

Transcription Quiz. For you to supply: 9 commas—1 comma as clause, 6 commas parenthetical, 1 comma introductory, 1 comma *if* clause; 2 missing words.

96.

(141)

LESSON 15

97. Word-Building Practice — Blends

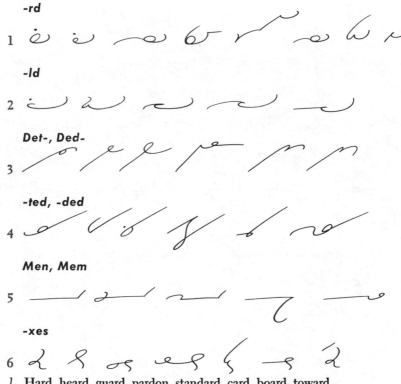

-rd

1 

-ld

2 

Det-, Ded-

3 

-ted, -ded

4 

Men, Mem

5 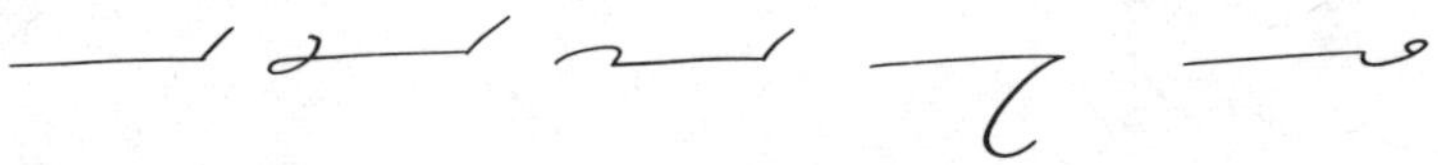

-xes

6 

1. Hard, heard, guard, pardon, standard, card, board, toward.
2. Hold, sold, cold, gold, mold.
3. Detect, deter, detail, detriment, deduct, deduction.
4. Rated, parted, hated, debated, needed, graded.
5. Meant, cement, comment, member, memory.
6. Fixes, taxes, annexes, relaxes, boxes, mixes, transfixes.

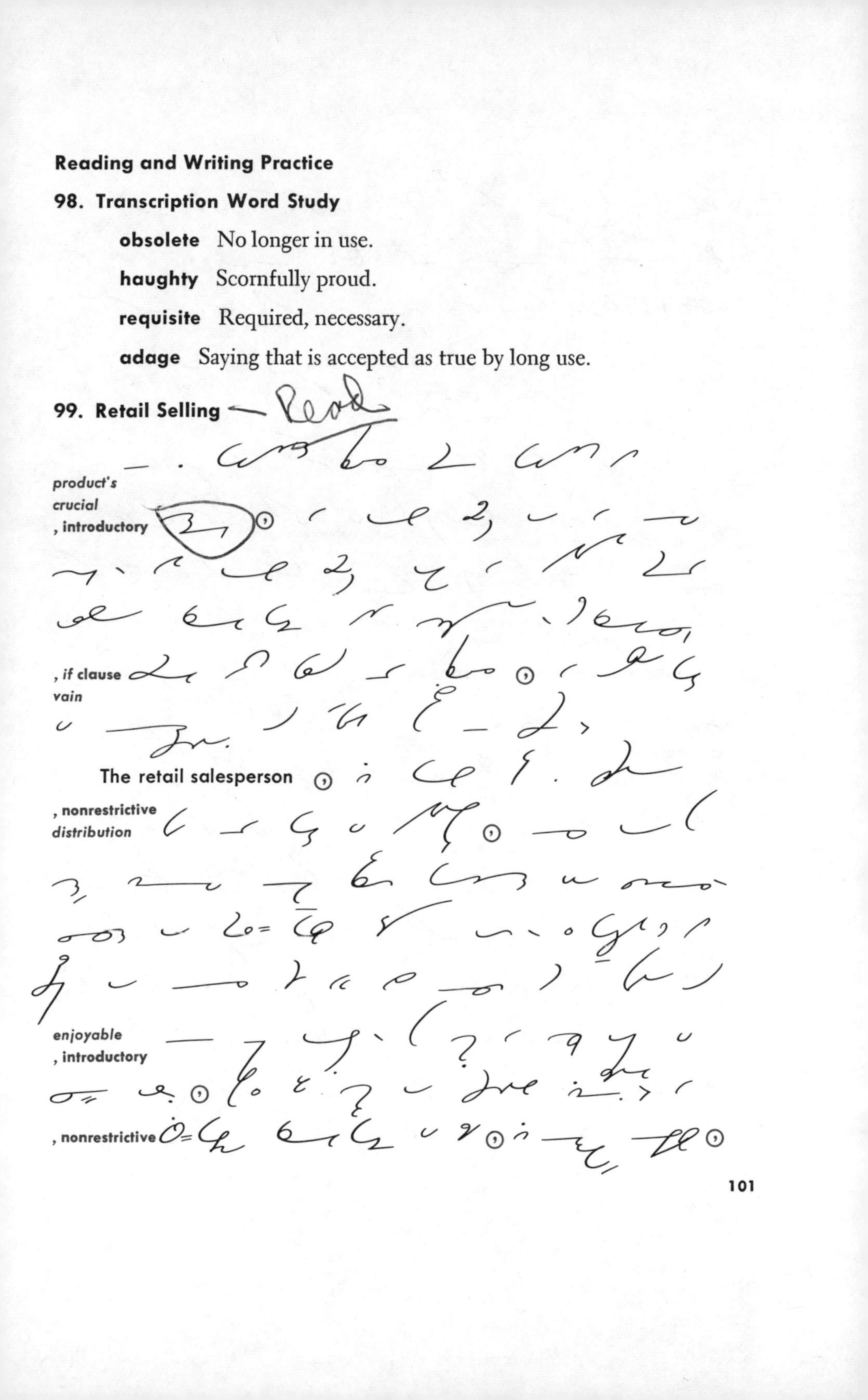

Reading and Writing Practice

98. Transcription Word Study

obsolete No longer in use.

haughty Scornfully proud.

requisite Required, necessary.

adage Saying that is accepted as true by long use.

99. Retail Selling

product's
crucial
, introductory

, if clause
vain

The retail salesperson

, nonrestrictive
distribution

enjoyable
, introductory

, nonrestrictive

, conjunction
firm's

The successful salesperson

customer's
intangible

, introductory
possess

, series
merchandise

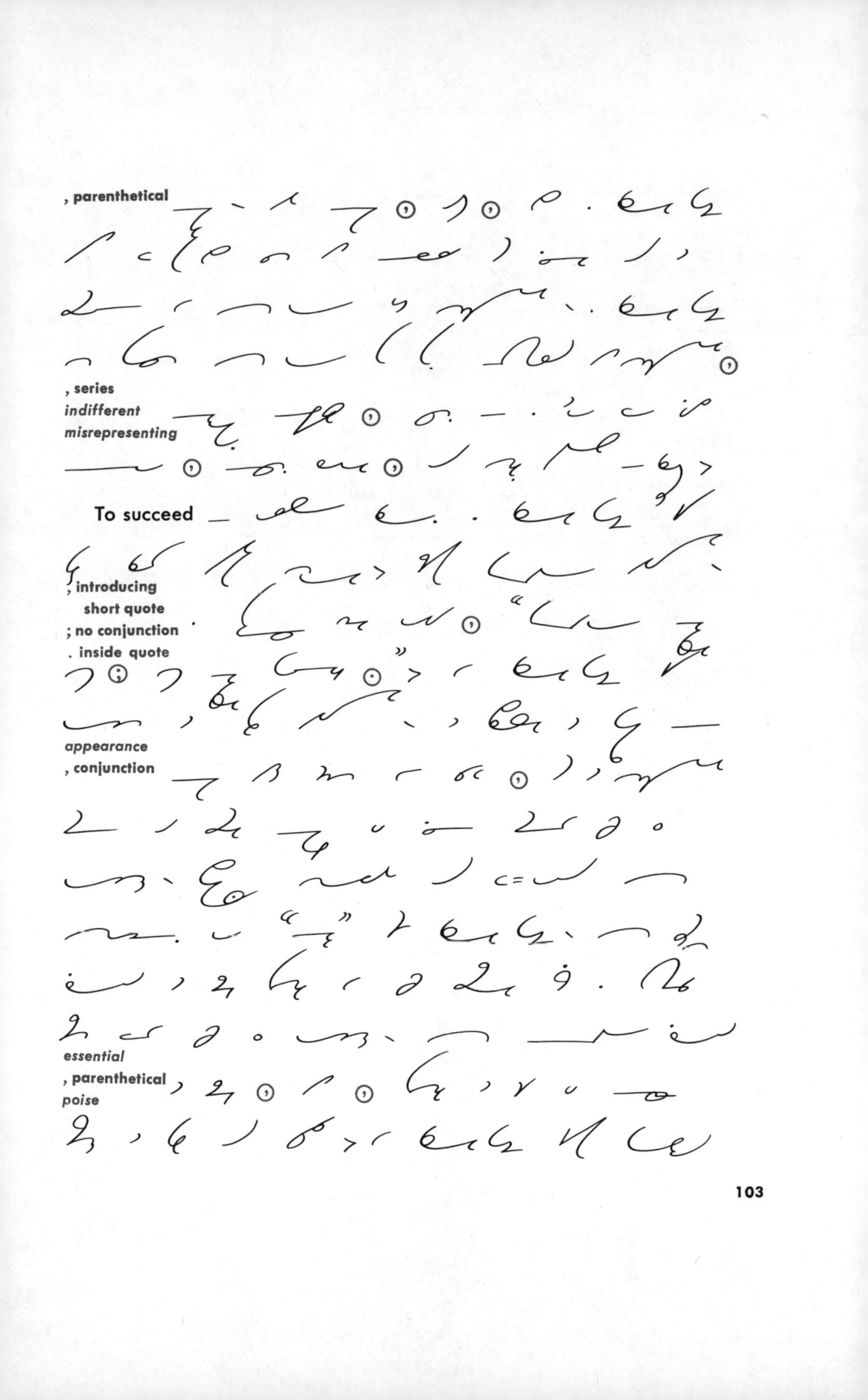

, parenthetical

, series
indifferent
misrepresenting

To succeed

, introducing
short quote
; no conjunction
. inside quote

appearance
, conjunction

essential
, parenthetical
poise

; because of comma
, parenthetical
likely

, parenthetical
actually

friendliness
, series
, apposition

The salesperson's greeting

; illustrative ,
? inside quote

trait
possessed

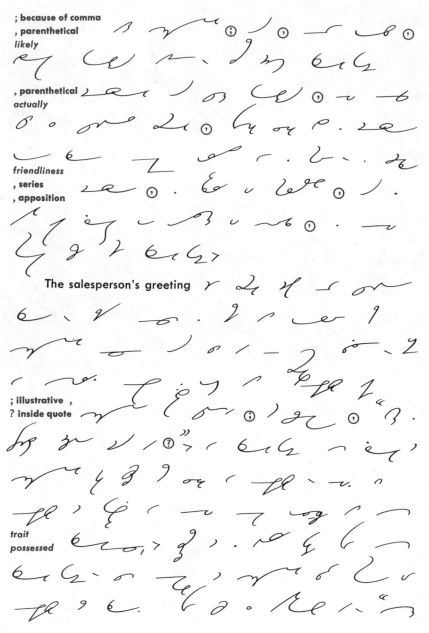

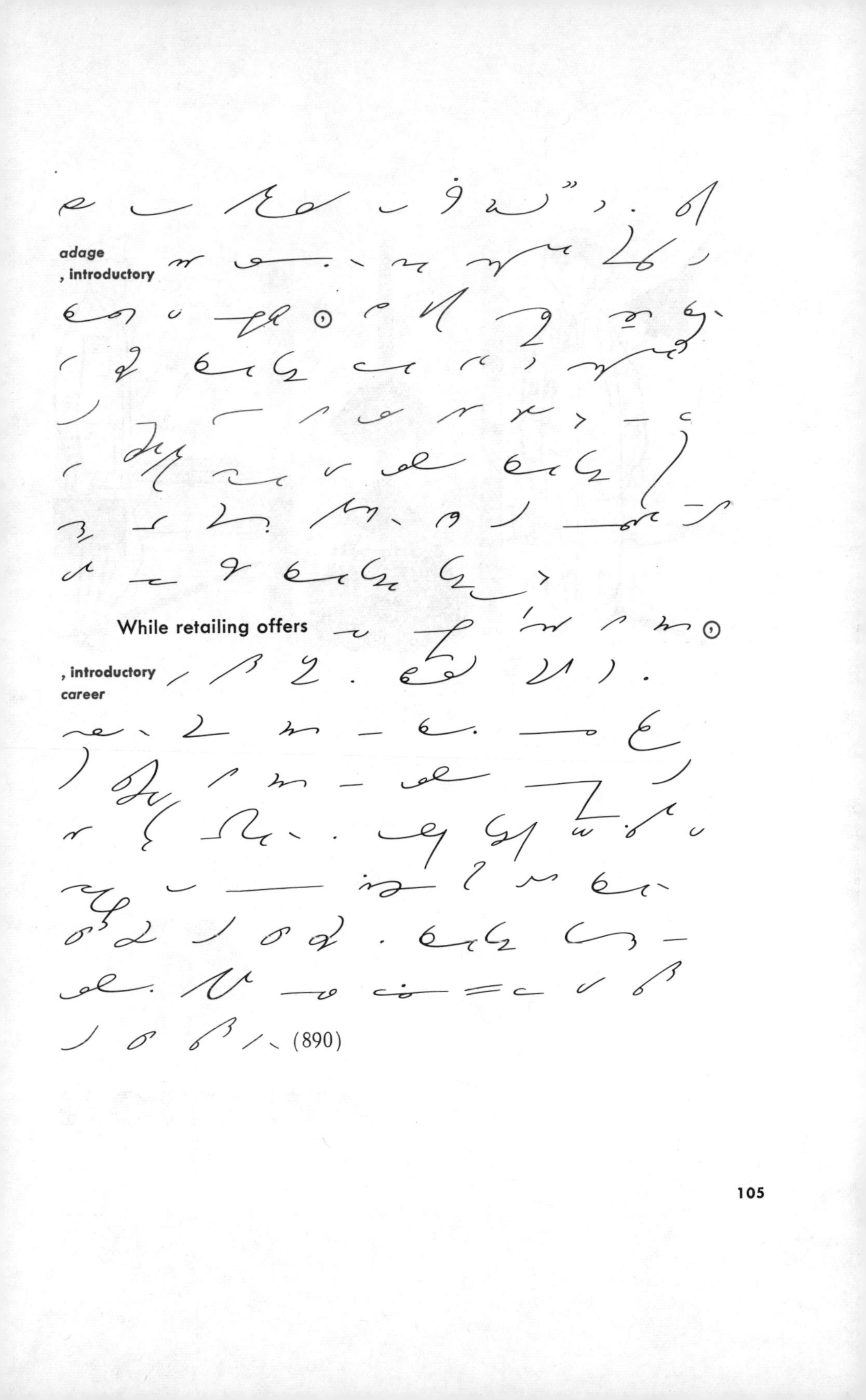

adage
, introductory

While retailing offers

, introductory
career

(890)

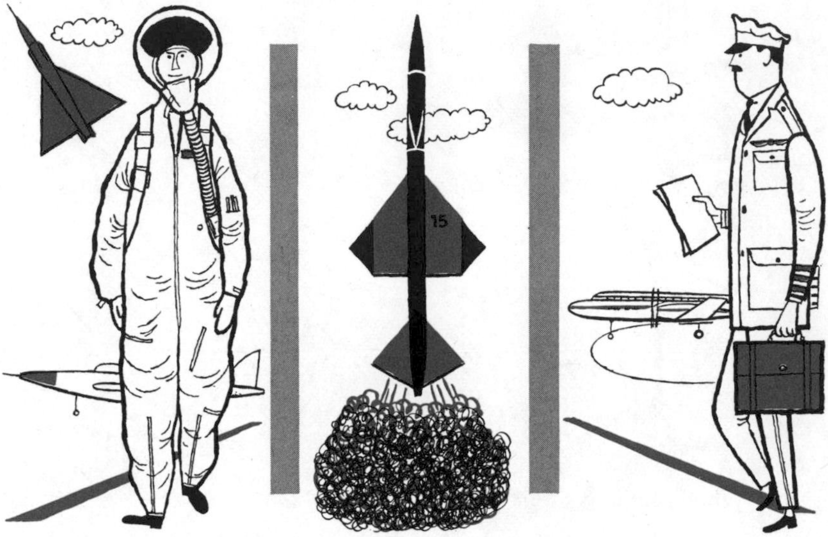

4

AVIATION

LESSON 16

100. Brief Forms and Derivatives

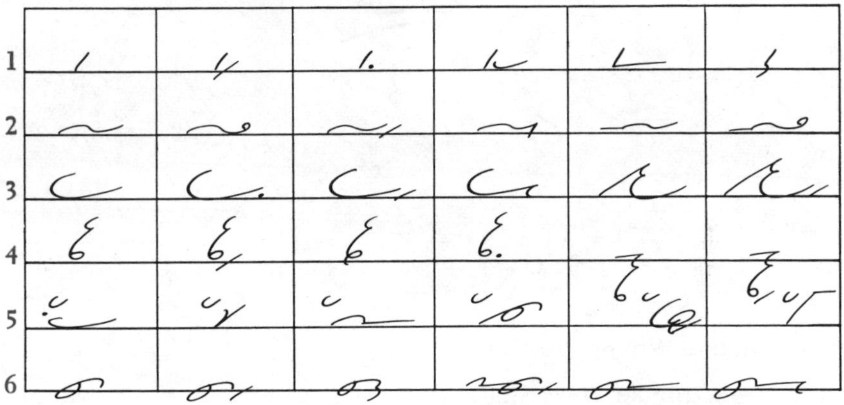

1. Shall-ship, shipped, shipping, shipper, shipment, ships.
2. Correct, correctly, corrected, correction, incorrect, incorrectly.
3. Please, pleasing, pleased, pleases, displease, displeased.
4. Experience, experienced, experiences, experiencing, inexperience, inexperienced.
5. Overhaul, overstate, overcome, overtake, overpriced, overdone.
6. Acknowledge, acknowledged, acknowledges, unacknowledged, acknowledgment, acknowledgments.

101. Brief Form and Phrase Letter

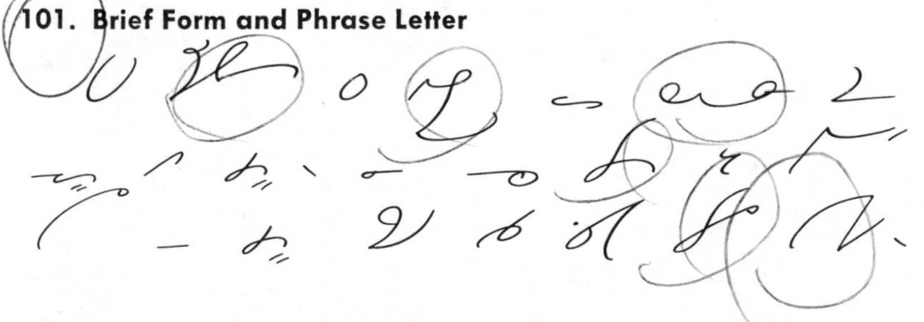

(127)

Reading and Writing Practice

102. Transcription Word Study

custody Care.

brief *(noun)* A short summary of a client's case.

in transit On the way.

103.

, apposition
; illustrative ,
slash

, as clause
mishandled

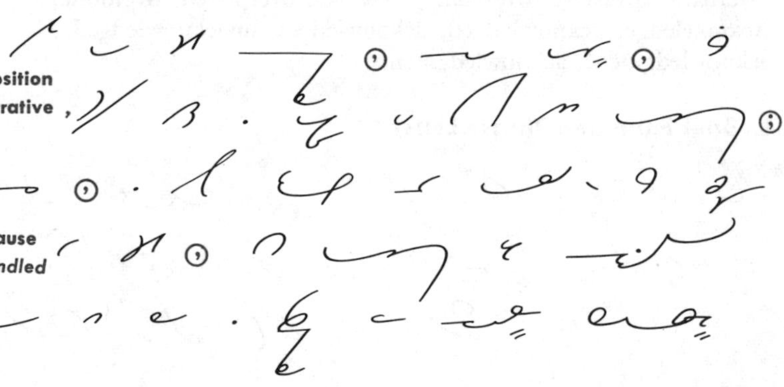

Pittsburgh

, introductory

, parenthetical

air-express

hyphenated before noun

, introductory

assistance

, if clause

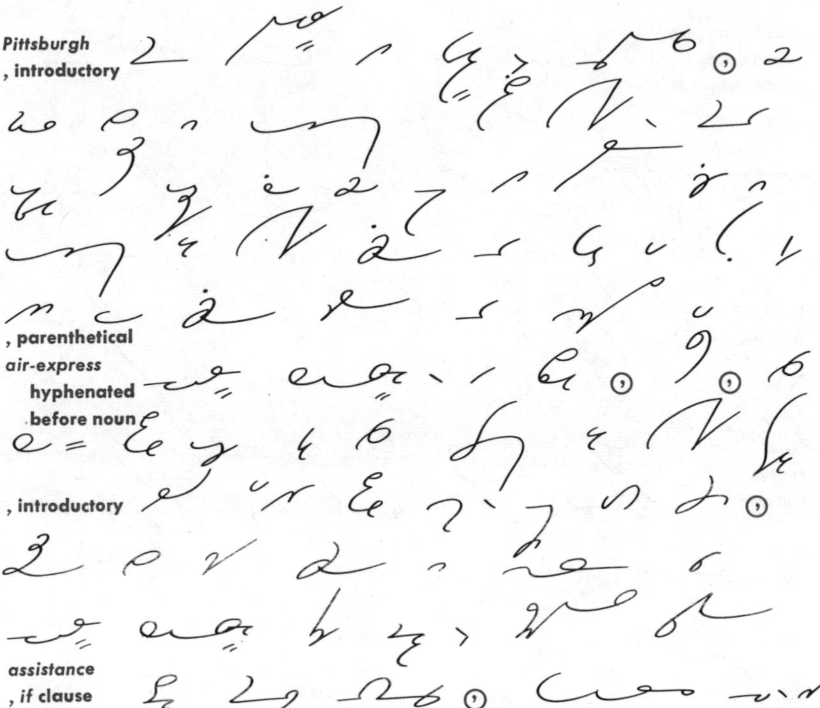

(158)

104.

, introductory

communicated

, parenthetical

experienced

, introducing short quote
. inside quote
; because of comma
, introductory
, conjunction
equitable

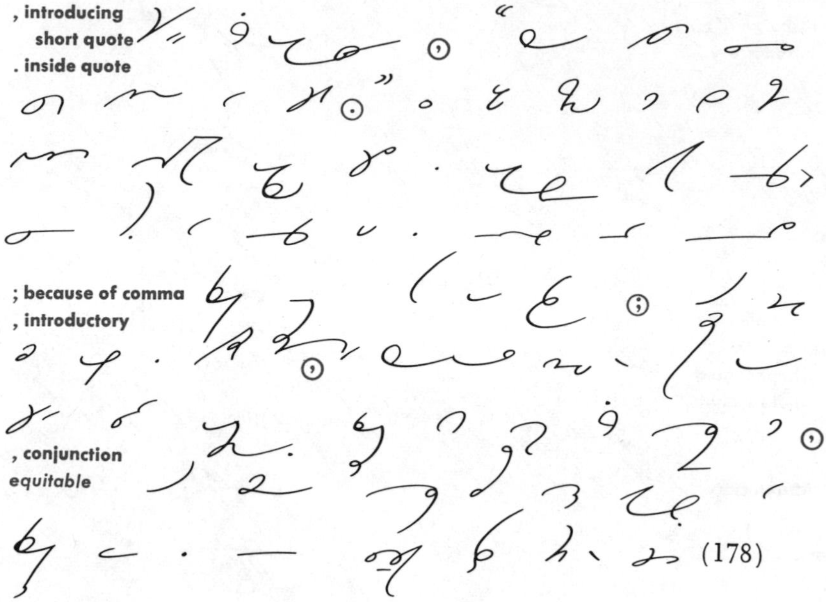

(178)

105.

comprehensive
, conjunction
Commissioner
, apposition
procedure
: enumeration

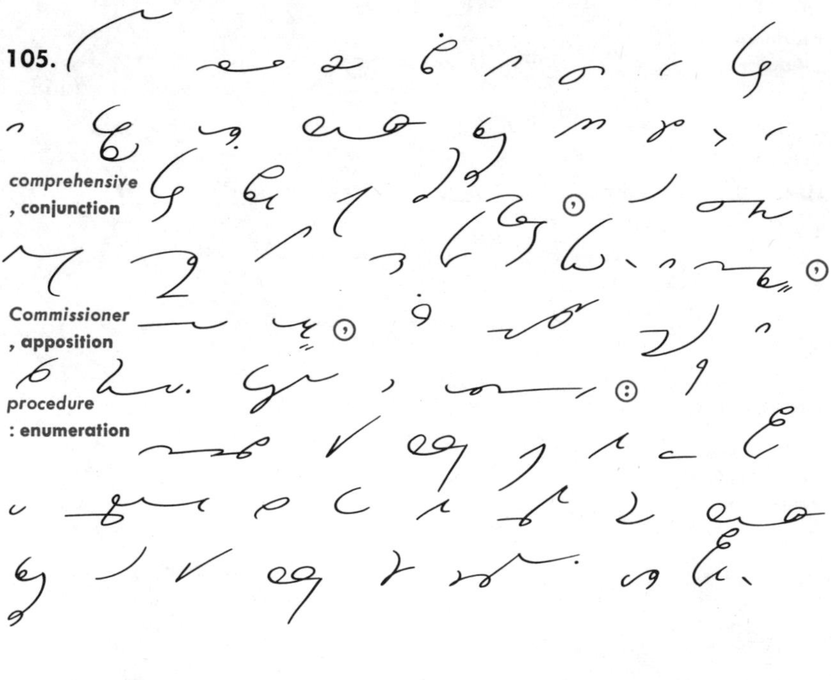

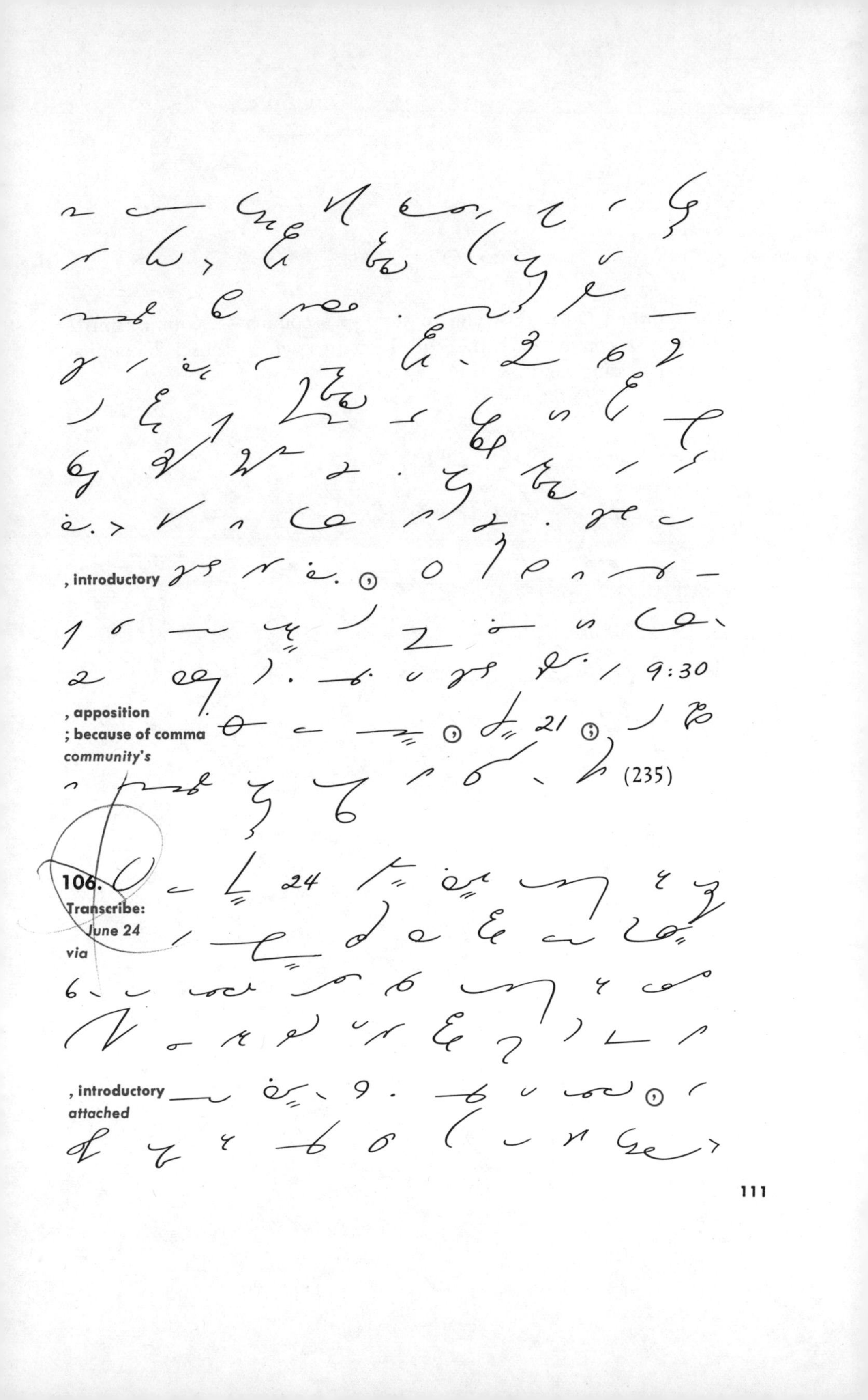

, introductory

9:30

, apposition
; because of comma
community's

21

(235)

106. 24

Transcribe:
June 24
via

, introductory
attached

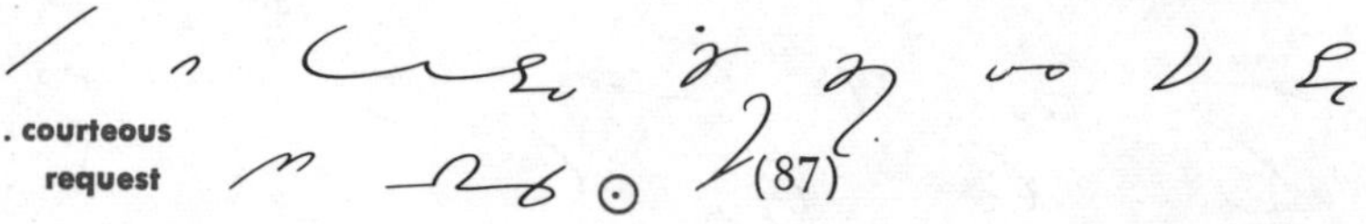

. courteous request (87)

Transcription Quiz. For you to supply: 6 commas—2 commas introductory, 1 comma parenthetical, 1 comma *when* clause, 2 commas series; 2 missing words.

107.

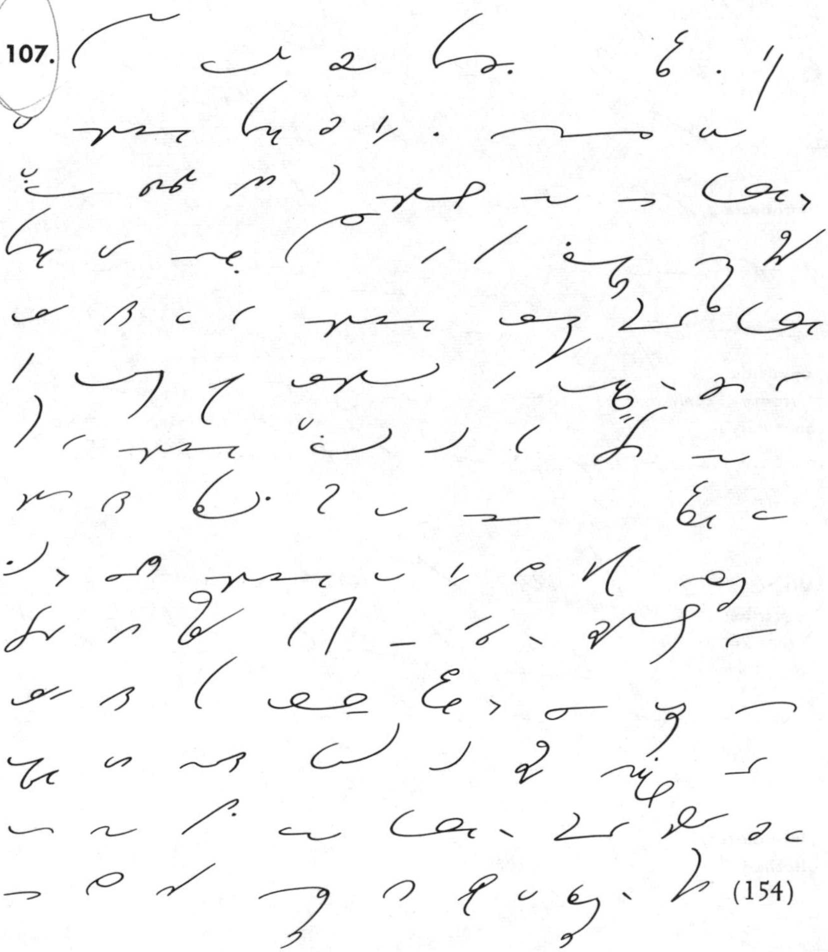

(154)

LESSON 17

108. Useful Business-Letter Phrases

From

1 

Of

2 

On

3 

In

4 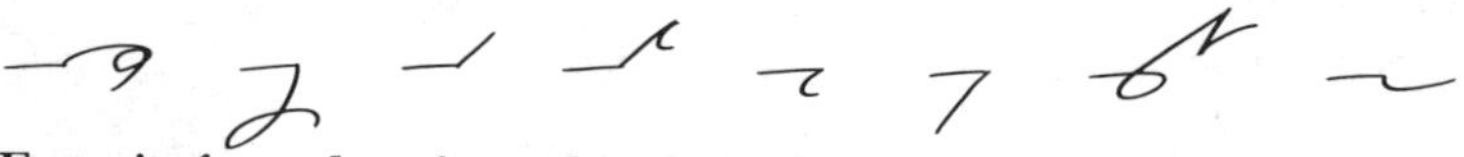

1. From it, from that, from this, from them, from you, from our.
2. Of all, of any, of his, of it, of its, of life, of our, of ours, of their, of the.
3. On his, on it, on our, on that, on the, on these, on this, on which.
4. In case, in fact, in it, in its, in his, in which, in addition to the, in our.

109. Frequent Names

1. Crowley, Daly, Davidson, Davis, Donovan, Doyle.
2. Arthur, Benjamin, Charles, Clarence, Daniel, David.

Reading and Writing Practice

110. Transcription Word Study

personnel department That part of an organization which handles the hiring of employees and looks after their welfare in the organization. (Do not confuse with *personal,* which means "private.")

decentralize To divide and distribute what has been centralized.

aeronautics The science that deals with the operation of aircraft.

111.

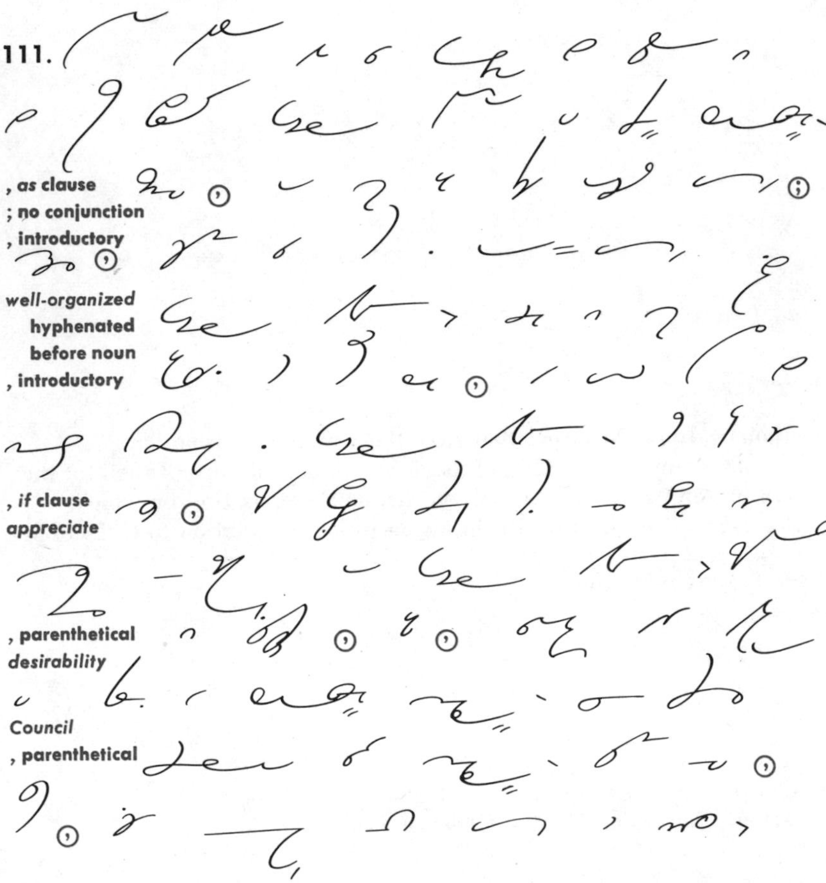

, introductory

(162)

112.

Transcribe:
April 11
appointment

operation
, introductory
, introductory
frequently used
no hyphen
after *ly*
; illustrative ,
, series
inasmuch as
up to date
no noun,
no hyphen

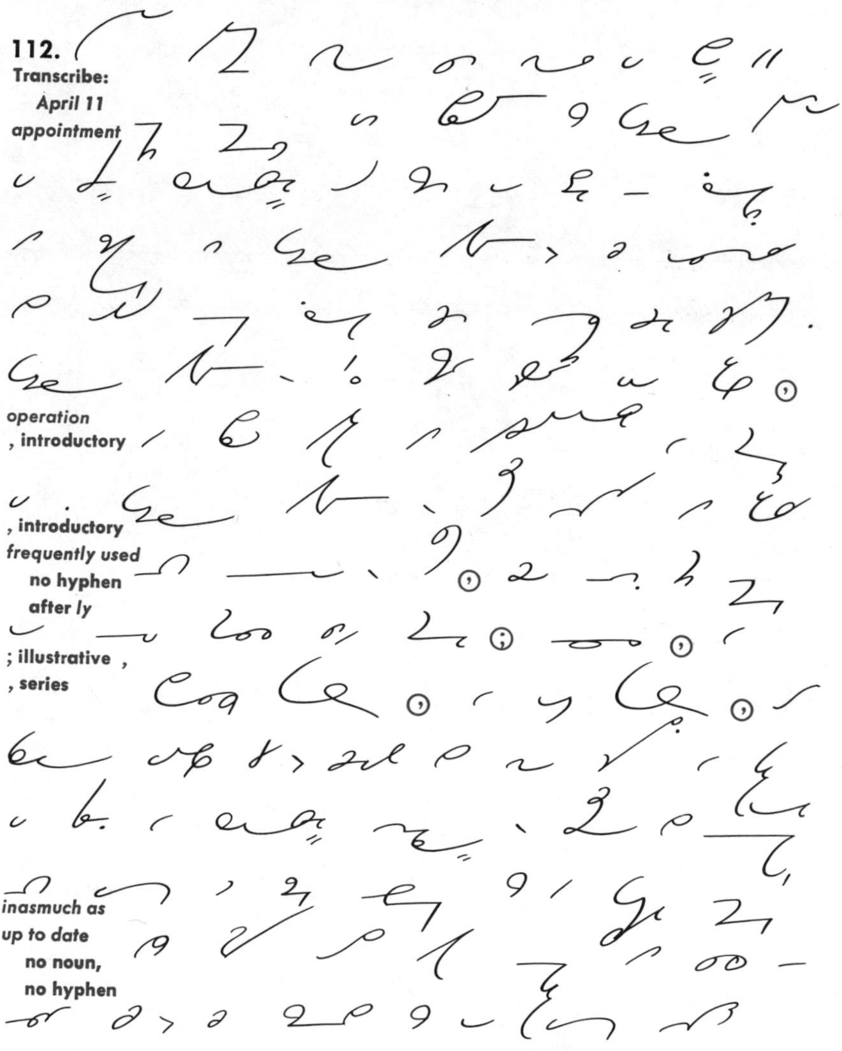

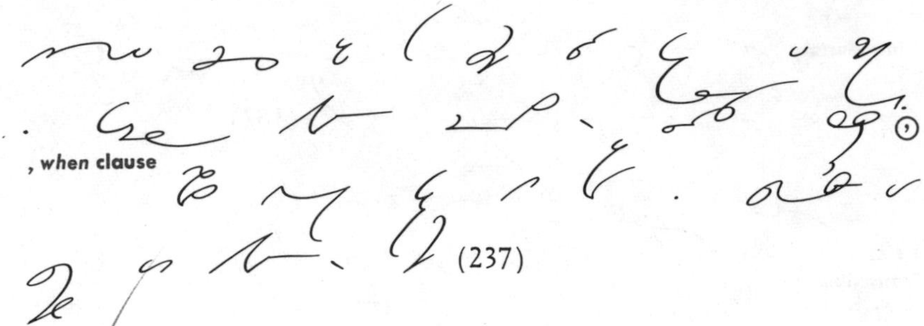

, *when* clause

(237)

113.

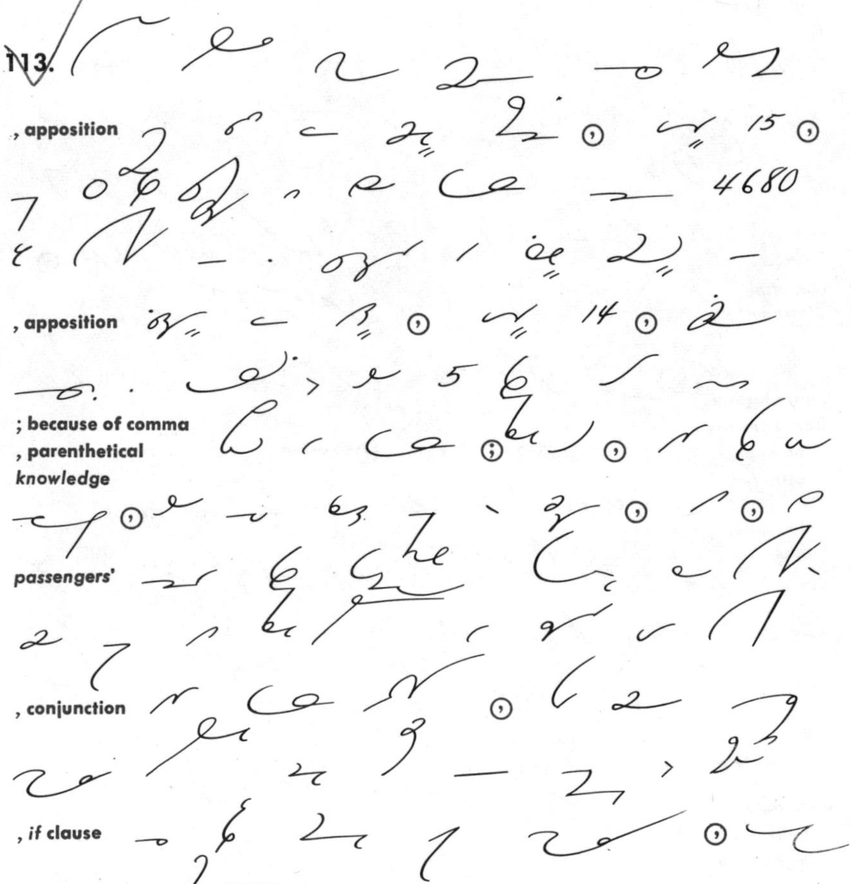

, apposition

, apposition

; because of comma

, parenthetical

knowledge

passengers'

, conjunction

, *if* clause

(137)

114.

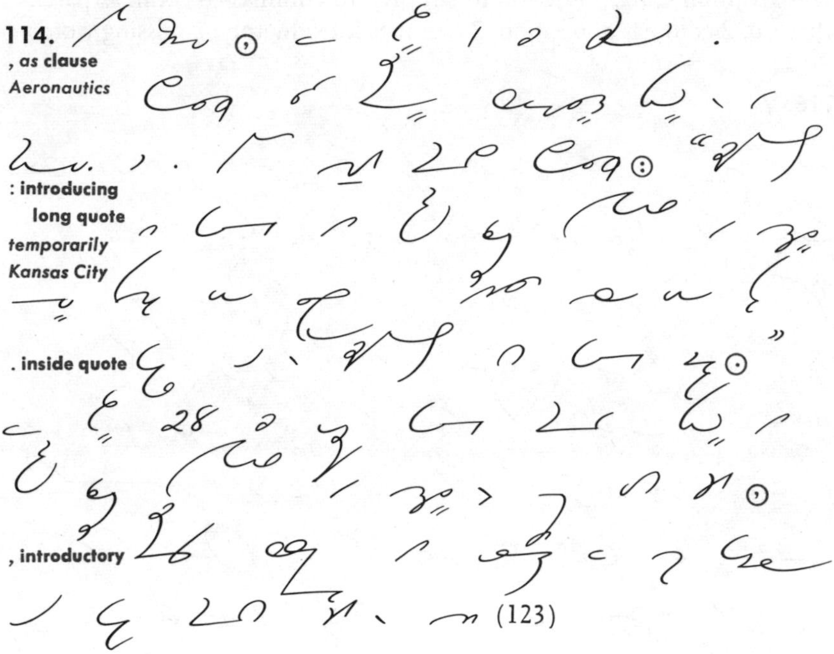

, *as clause*
Aeronautics
: *introducing long quote*
temporarily
Kansas City
. *inside quote*
, *introductory*

(123)

115.

, *nonrestrictive*
, *series*
, *introductory*
accomplishment
; *because of comma*

(90)

Transcription Quiz. For you to supply: 10 commas–6 commas parenthetical, 2 commas apposition, 2 commas introductory; 2 missing words.

116.

(173)

LESSON 18

117. Word Families

-ctive

1 

-most

2 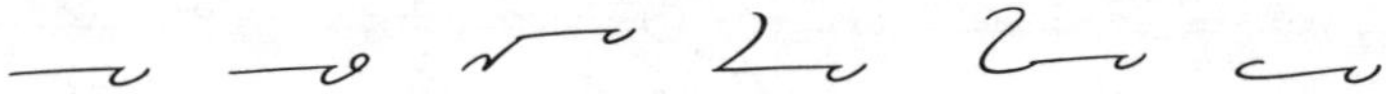

-port

3 

-form

4 

-line

5 

1. **Effective, attractive, prospective, constructive, active, detective, respective.**
2. **Most, mostly, utmost, foremost, uppermost, almost.**
3. **Port, airport, import, export, report, deport, comport, sport.**
4. **Form, conform, reform, uniform, perform, inform, misinform.**
5. **Line, align, outline, airline, deadline.**

Reading and Writing Practice

118. Transcription Word Study

reciprocate Return or exchange something that has been given.

intervene Come in between.

119.

, introducing short quote

franchise

. inside quote

reciprocate

, if clause

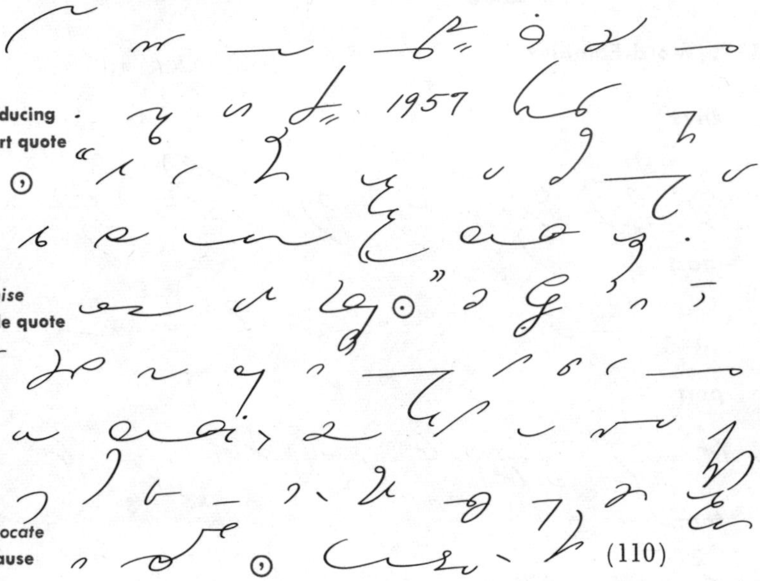

(110)

120.

, nonrestrictive

refueling

facilities

, as clause

; illustrative ,

, series

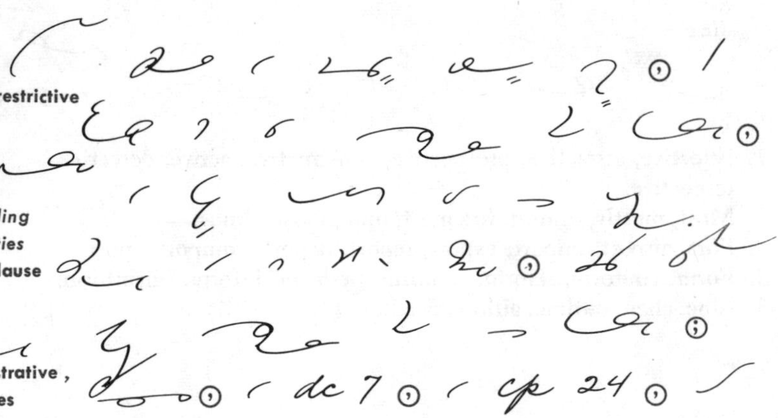

, and omitted
awkward

, when clause
, parenthetical
accordance

diagram
desired

121.

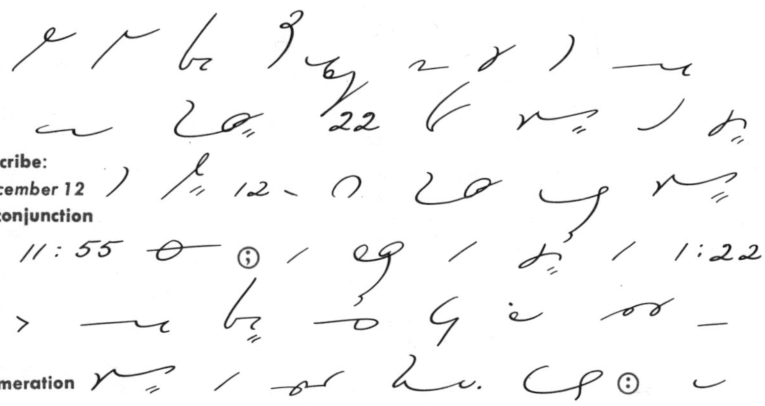

Transcribe:
December 12
; no conjunction

: enumeration

, series
agencies
, when clause

newly revised
no hyphen
after *ly*

(134)

122.

, *and* omitted
, nonrestrictive

person's

; no conjunction

, conjunction

, apposition

; because of comma

, *if* clause

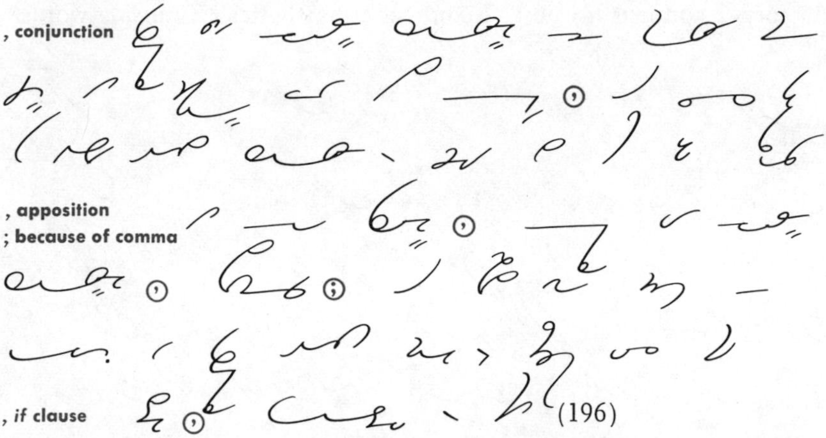

(196)

123.

permission

, parenthetical

, introductory

, parenthetical

procedures

. courteous request

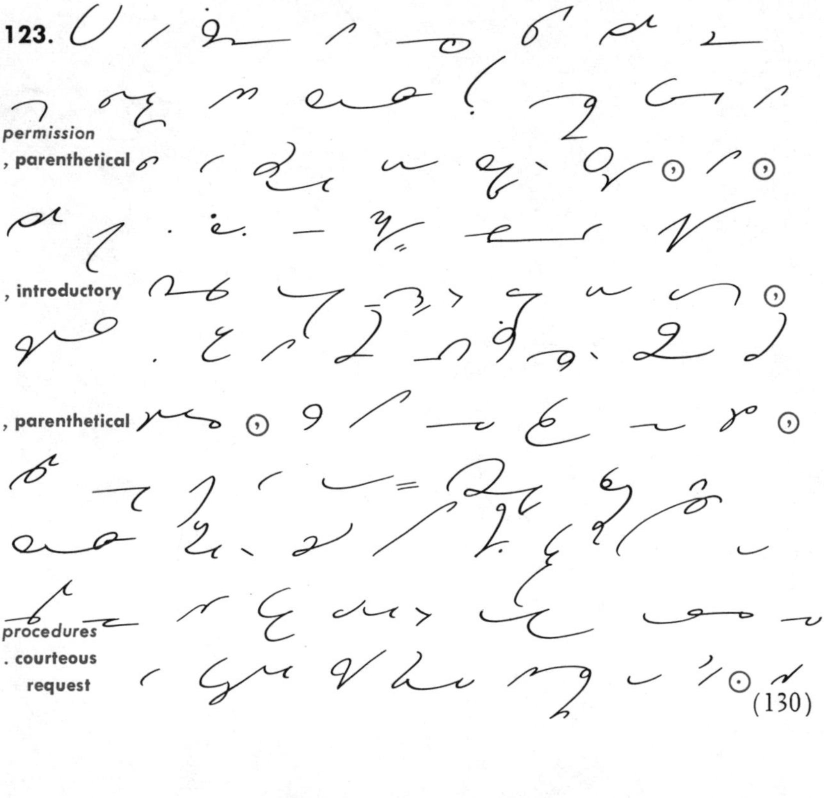

(130)

Transcription Quiz. For you to supply: 5 commas—1 comma introductory, 2 commas *if* clause, 2 commas parenthetical; 2 missing words.

124.

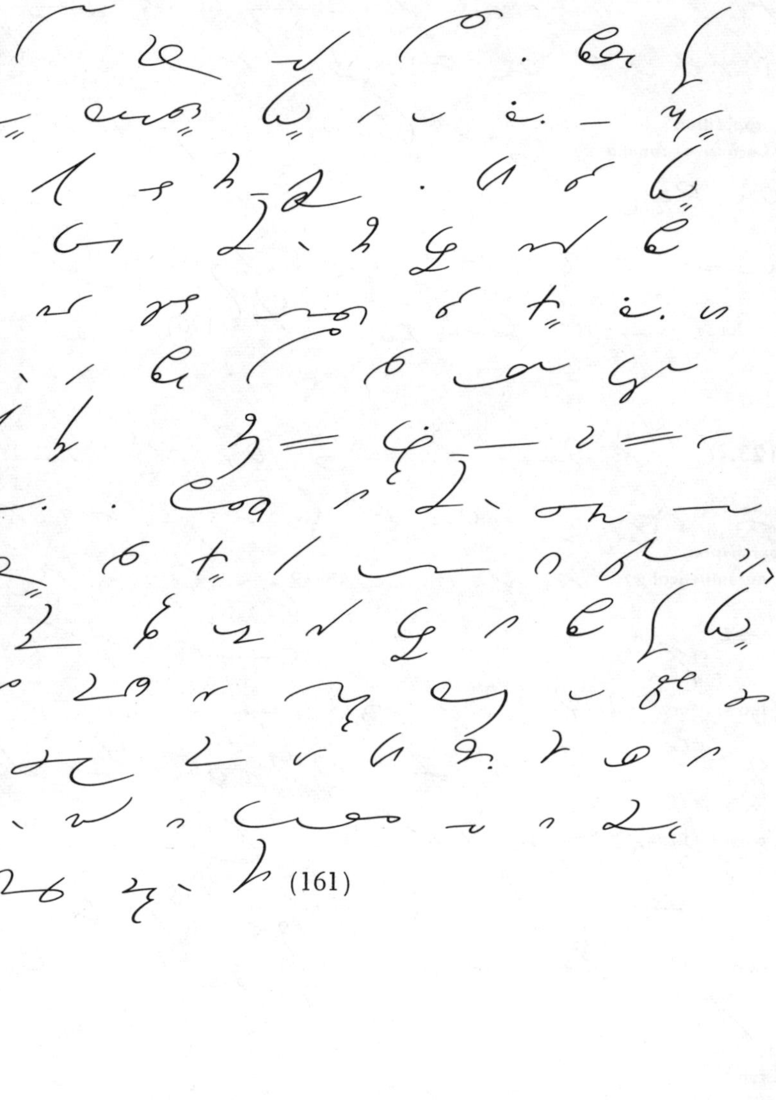

(161)

LESSON 19

125. Word Beginnings

De-

1 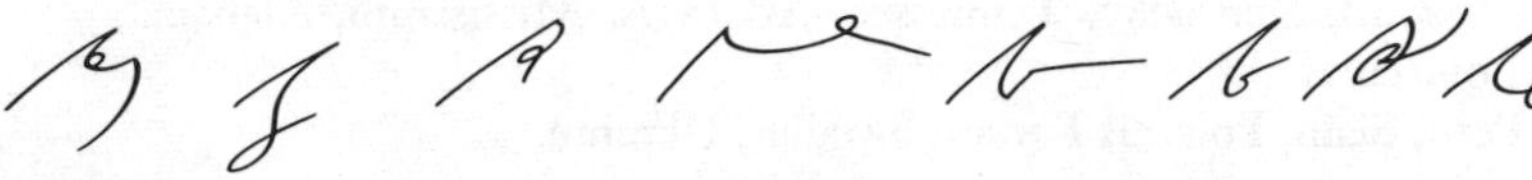

Dis-

2 

Em-

3 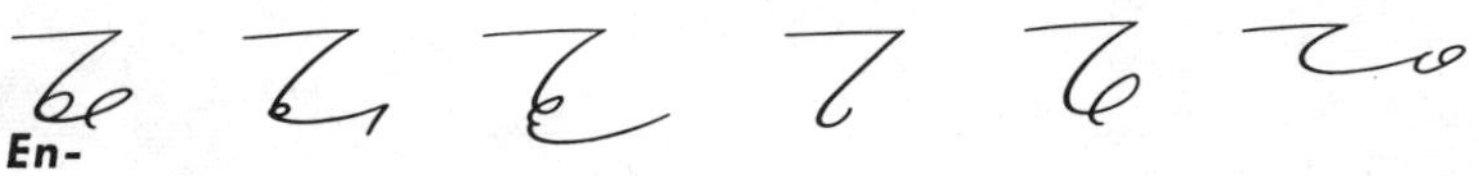

En-

4 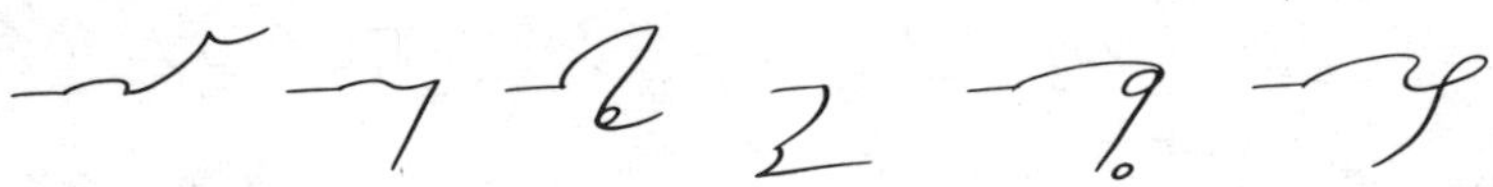

Ex-

5 

Fore-

6 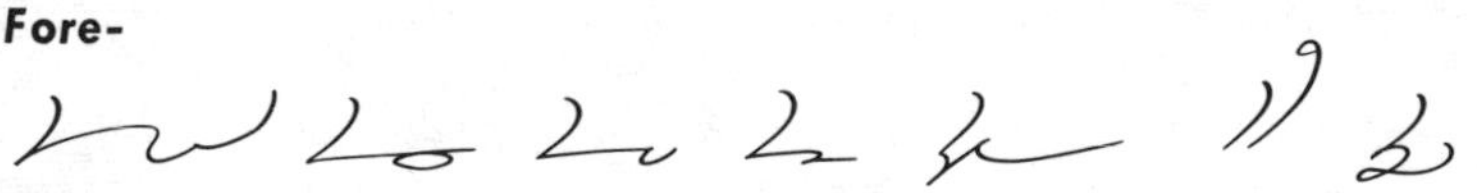

1. **Deserve, debate, decision, delinquent, department, deport, designed, depress.**
2. **Disarm, distress, discussion, dismayed, displeased, disappointment.**
3. **Embarrass, embellish, embezzle, embody, embrace, employ.**
4. **Encounter, encourage, endanger, enforcement, engagingly, engrave.**

5. Exception, exceed, exclaim, exclude, excitement, execute, examine.
6. Foreground, foreman, foremost, forenoon, forestall, forever, foreword.

126. Geographical Expressions

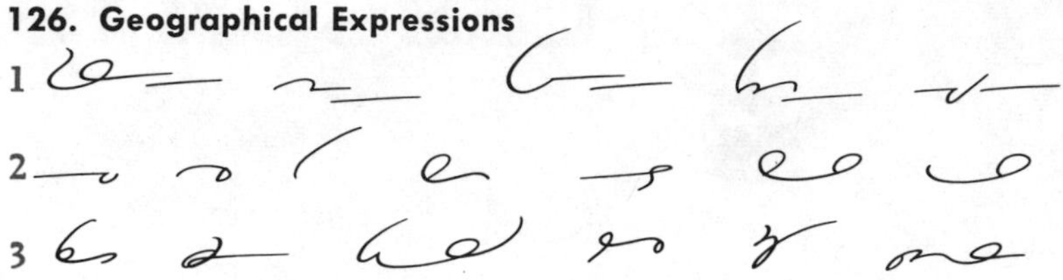

1. Framingham, Cunningham, Birmingham, Buckingham, Nottingham.
2. Missouri, Kentucky, Tennessee, Arkansas, Mississippi, Alabama, Louisiana.
3. Peru, Siam, Poland, Turkey, Sweden, Ukraine.

Reading and Writing Practice

127. Transcription Word Study

reinstated Placed in force or in operation again.

compensate To make an equal return.

128.

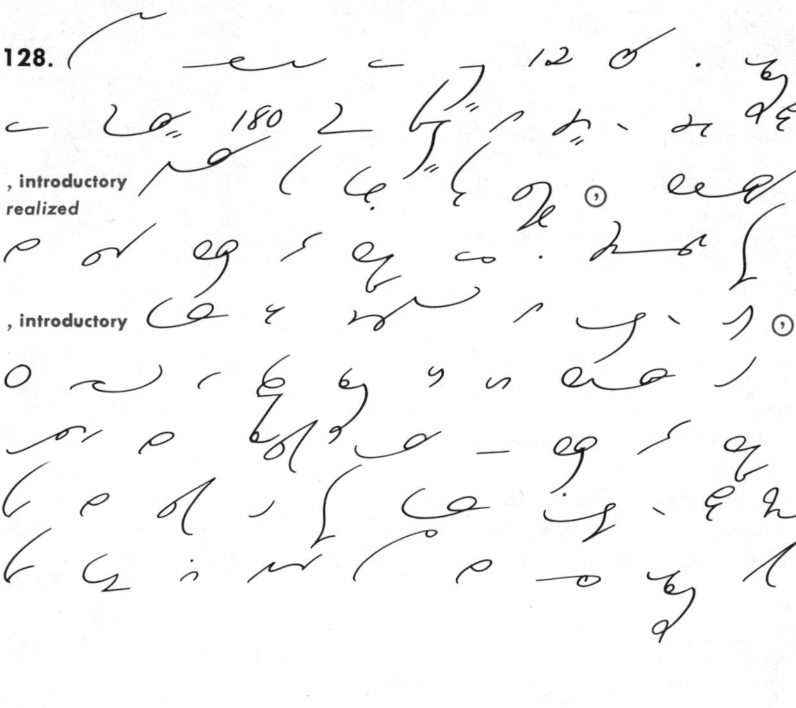

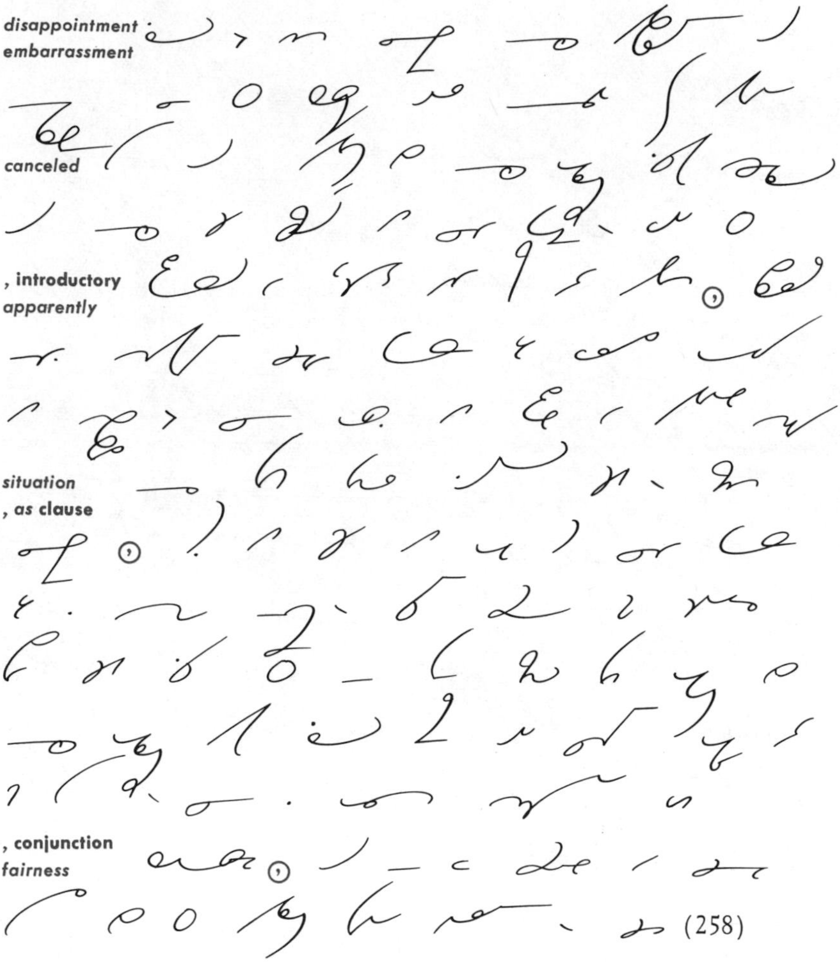
disappointment
embarrassment
canceled
, introductory
apparently
situation
, as clause
, conjunction
fairness
(258)

129.

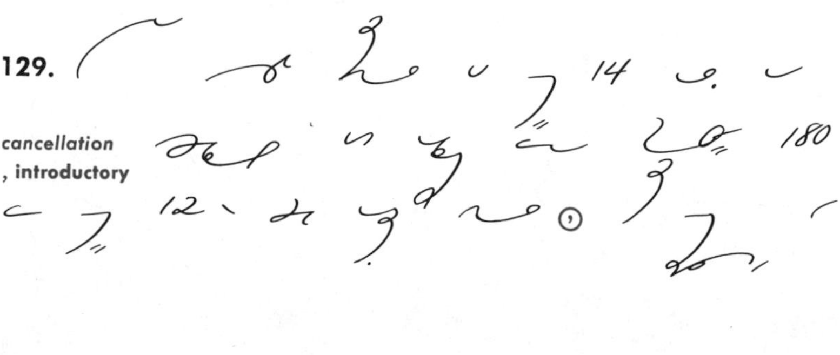
cancellation
, introductory

advise
, apposition

, introducing short quote

10

. inside quote
, parenthetical

, parenthetical

, parenthetical
similar

(201)

130. 1, 1955

Transcribe:
January 1
agreement

temporarily
, introductory
reinstated
, *if* clause
efficient
, *and* omitted

(120)

131.

, introductory
, parenthetical
, nonrestrictive
first-class
hyphenated
before noun
; no conjunction
, introductory

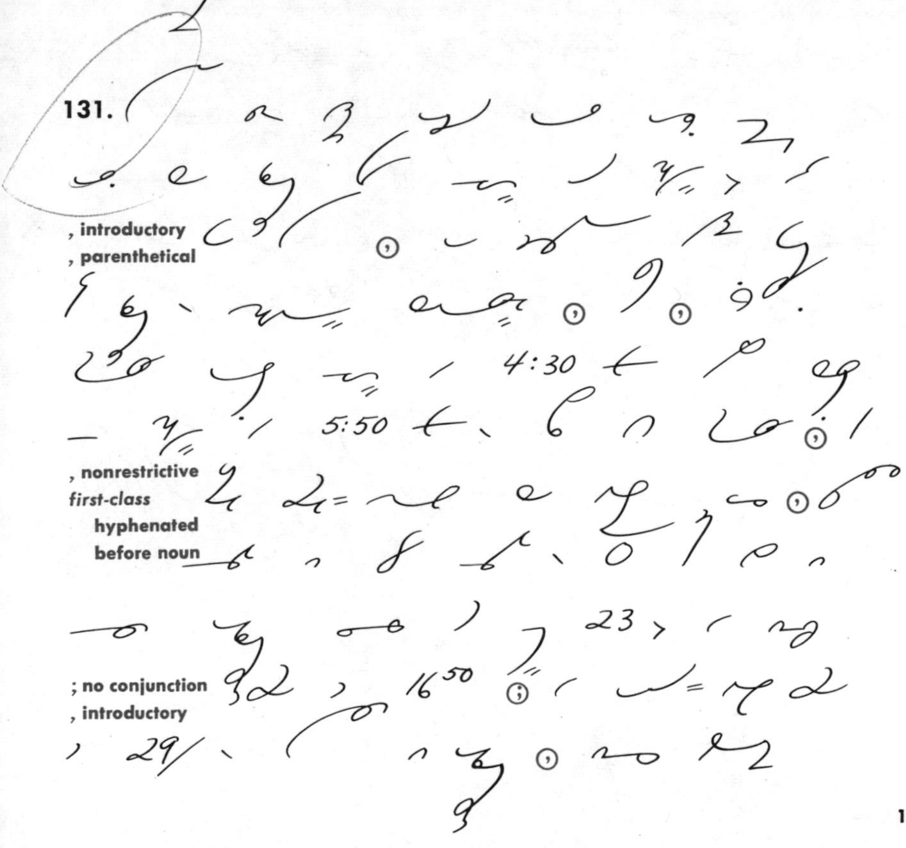

(132)

Transcription Quiz. For you to supply: 4 commas—1 comma *when* clause, 3 commas introductory; 2 missing words.

132.

(124)

LESSON 20

133. Word-Building Practice—Omission of Vowels

Omission of Short U

1 

Omission of Ow

2 

Omission of E in Diphthong U

3 

Omission of Minor Vowel

4 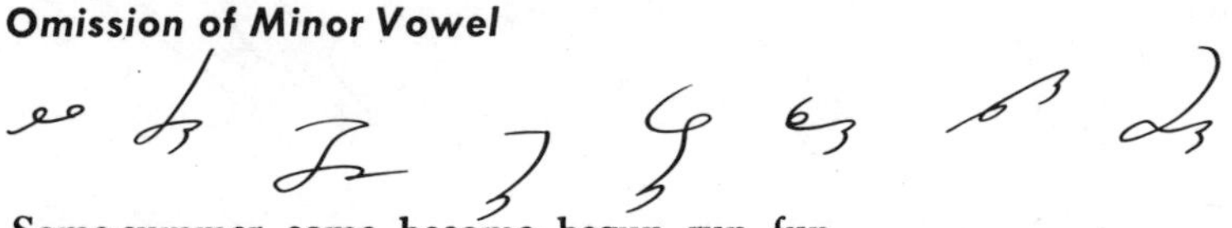

1. Some summer, come, become, begun, run, fun.
2. Count, account, accountant, discount, noun, pronoun, renounce, denounce.
3. New, renew, renewal, menu, manuscript, neutral.
4. Theory, genius, companion, envious, previous, serious, tedious, various.

134. Accuracy Practice—Circles

1 

2 

1. Air, ail; ache, ago, gay; return, rate.
2. Lead; take, tag; teeth, detain.

Reading and Writing Practice

135. Transcription Word Study

pageants An exhibition for public entertainment, such as a parade with floats.

congenial Having similar tastes and interests.

careen Sway from side to side; to tip or incline.

136. A Trip to Europe by Plane

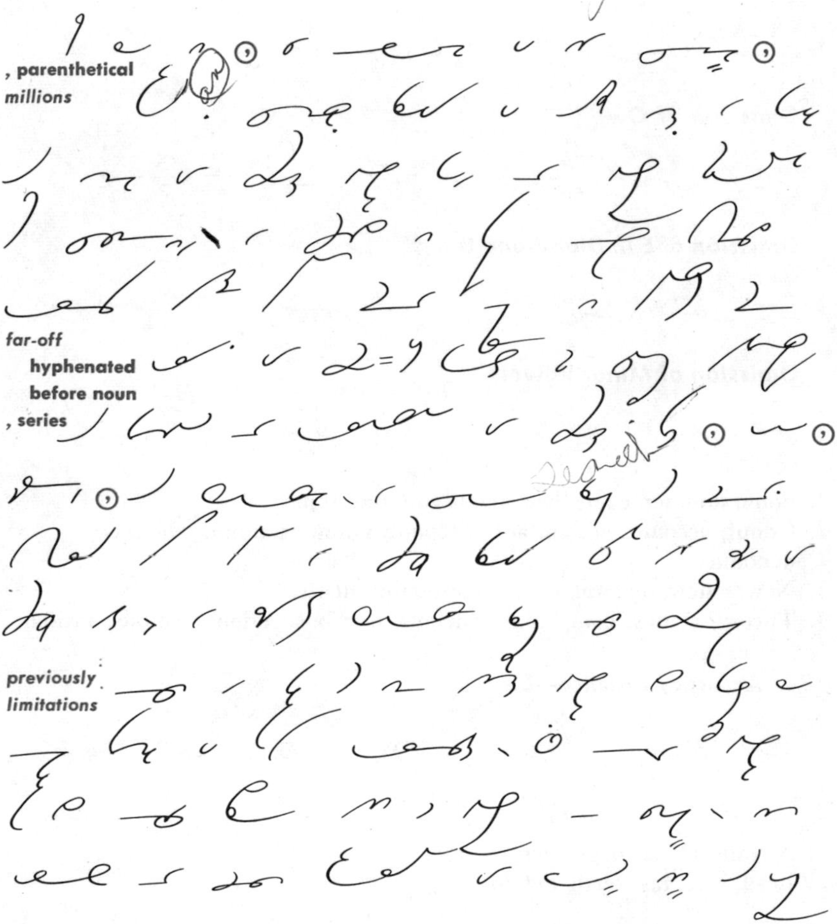

, parenthetical
millions

far-off
hyphenated before noun

, series

previously
limitations

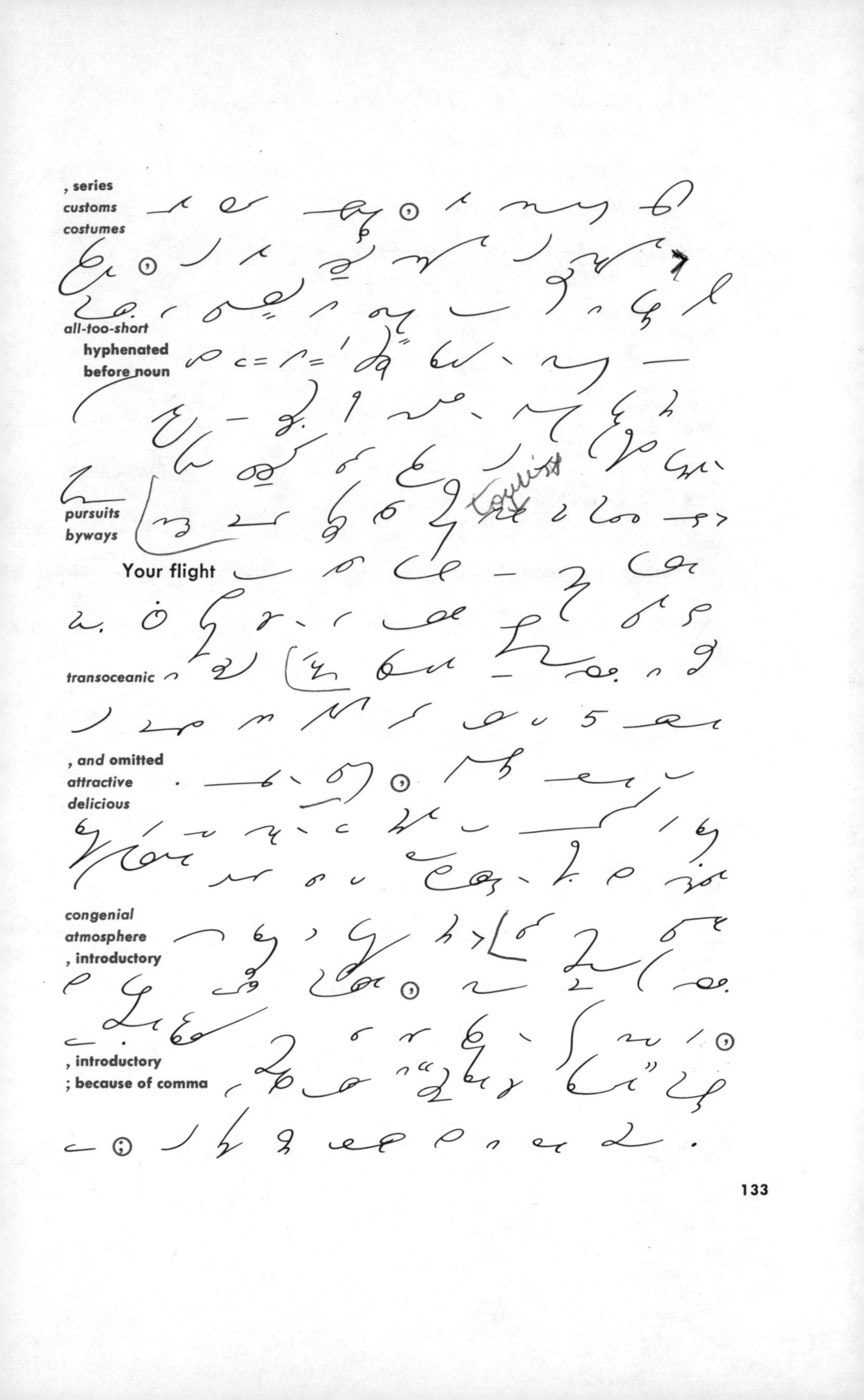

, series
customs
costumes

all-too-short
hyphenated before noun

pursuits
byways

Your flight

transoceanic

, *and omitted*
attractive
delicious

congenial
atmosphere
, *introductory*

, *introductory*
; *because of comma*

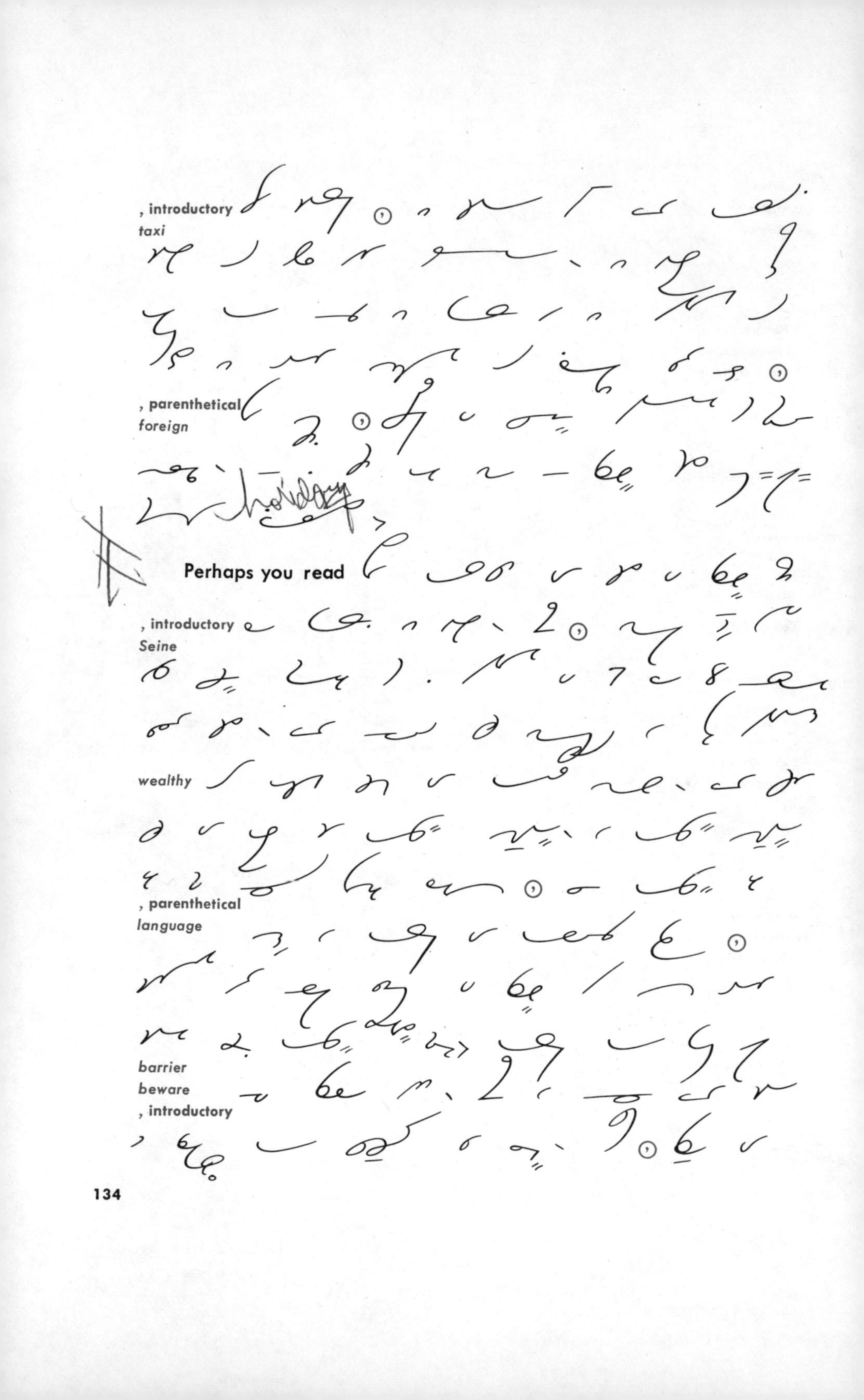

, introductory
taxi

, parenthetical
foreign

Perhaps you read

, introductory
Seine

wealthy

, parenthetical
language

barrier
beware
, introductory

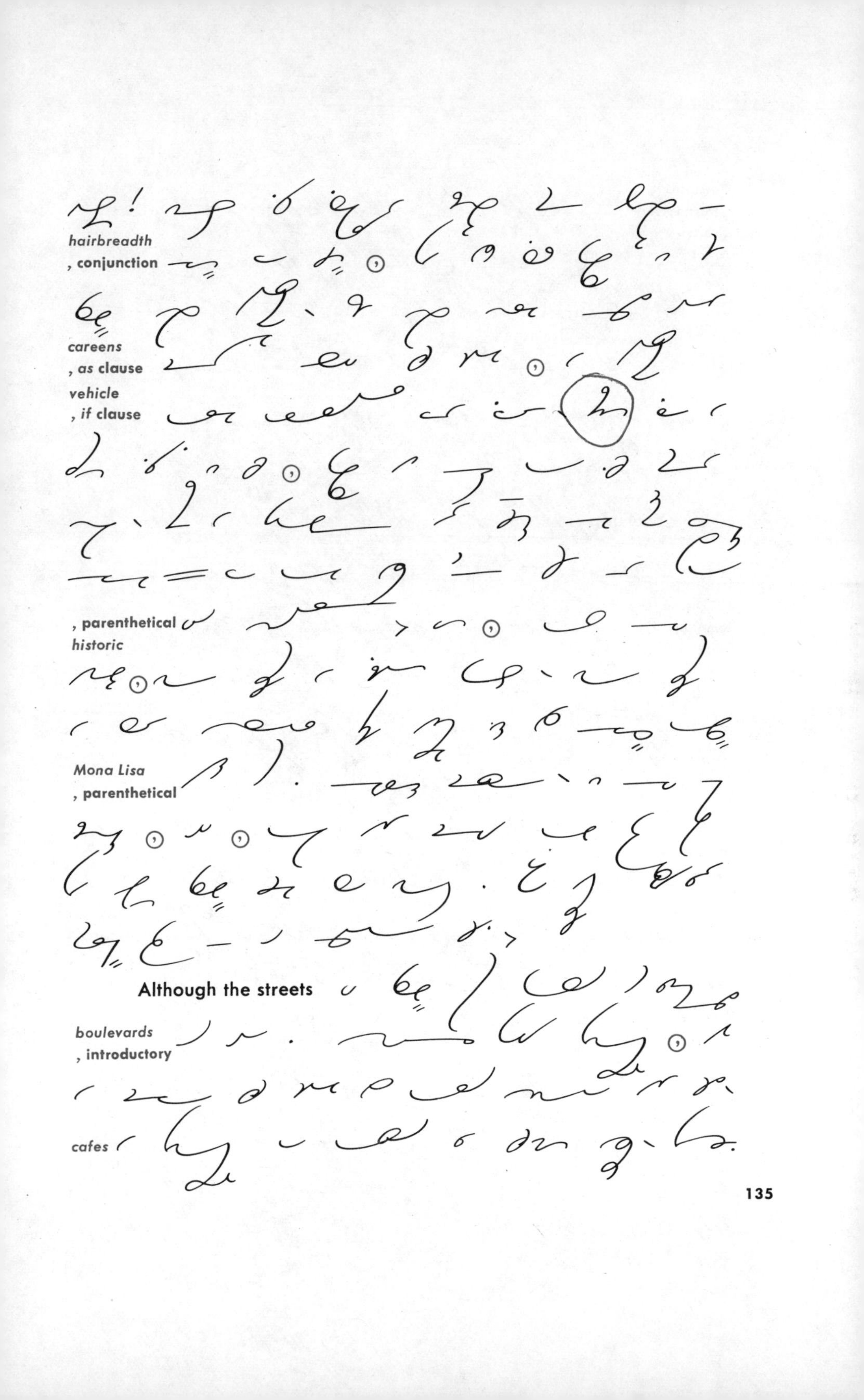

hairbreadth

, conjunction

careens

, *as* clause

vehicle

, *if* clause

, parenthetical

historic

Mona Lisa

, parenthetical

Although the streets

boulevards

, introductory

cafes

Parisians
, introductory
, series

, if clause

Your trip

, if clause
tempted
creation

souvenirs
amazed

, parenthetical

– Flora Stenzel
(974)

PART TWO

automobiles
general transportation
hotels
banking

MARTIN J. DUPRAW

World's Champion Shorthand Writer

One of the greatest shorthand writers of all time is Martin J. Dupraw, who has won more shorthand trophies than any other person in the long history of shorthand. When Mr. Dupraw won the World's Shorthand Championship, he established amazing records of speed and accuracy. For example, on a speech dictated at 200 words a minute for 5 minutes (1,000 words) he made only one minor error; on court testimony dictated at 280 words a minute for 5 minutes (1,400 words) he made only two errors.

These and the many other records that he established are due in large measure to the extremely legible style of shorthand that he writes, no matter how high the speed.

Look for a moment at his shorthand notes, written from dictation at about 100 words a minute, on the opposite page. One outstanding fact will immediately impress you: his careful attention to proportion.

Notice, for example, the size of his circles. The *a* circles are huge; the *e* circles are tiny. There is never any question whether any given circle is an *a* or *e*. Notice, too, that his *r*'s are considerably shorter than his *l*'s; his *n*'s considerably shorter than his *m*'s.

Another thing that will strike you as you examine Mr. Dupraw's notes is the way he rounds off angles. He does not do this consciously; rounding angles comes naturally to him as a result of his high speed. He is very careful, however, not to let this rounding off of angles distort the shape of an outline. As your speed increases, you, too, will round off angles naturally.

Mr. Dupraw has definite convictions on the size of shorthand notes. He explains these convictions to you in his own beautiful shorthand on the opposite page. Mr. Dupraw writes a large style of shorthand just as he writes a large style of longhand. If you have been wondering whether your notes are too large or too small, you will find some valuable advice in his article "How Big Should My Shorthand Notes Be?"

How Big Should My Shorthand Notes Be?

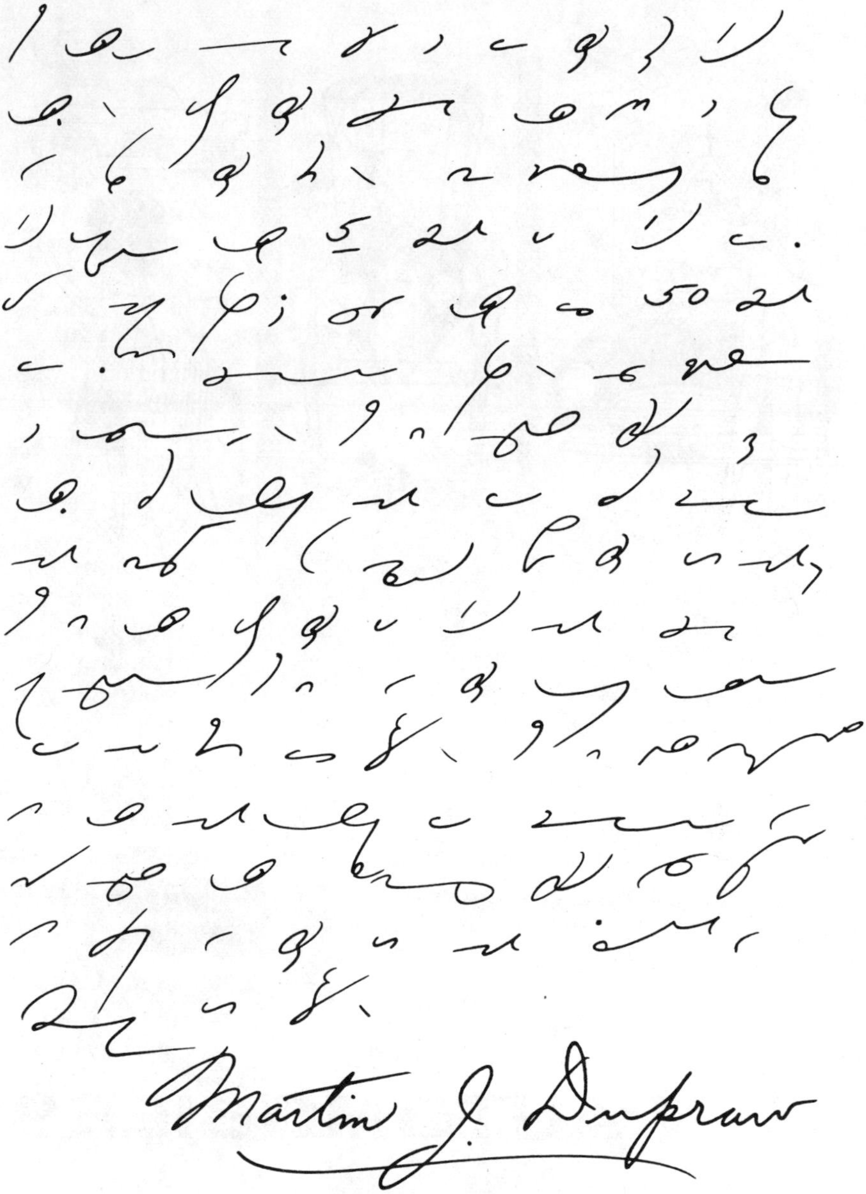

5
AUTOMOBILES

LESSON 21

137. Brief Forms and Derivatives

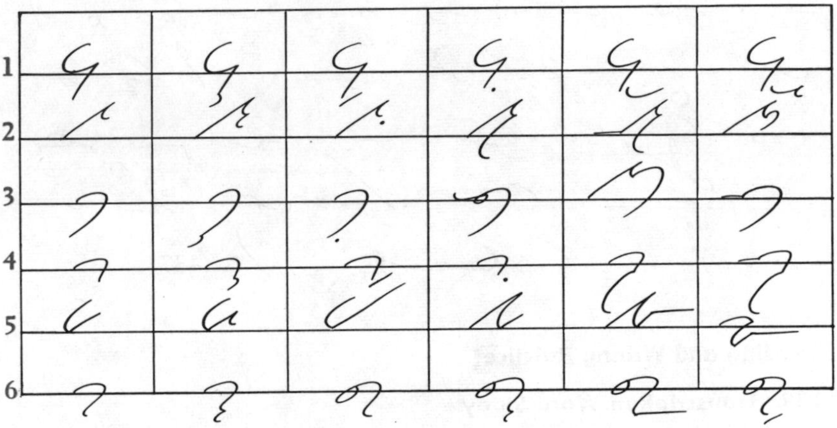

1. Purchase, purchases, purchased, purchasing, purchaser, purchasers.
2. Dear Sir-desire, desires, desiring, desirable, undesirable, desirous.
3. Cover, covers, covering, recover, discover, uncover.
4. Question, questions, questioned, questioning, questionable, unquestionable.
5. Part, parts, parted, depart, department, compartment.
6. Keep-company, keeps-companies, accompany, accompanies, accompaniment, accompanied.

138. Brief Form and Phrase Letter

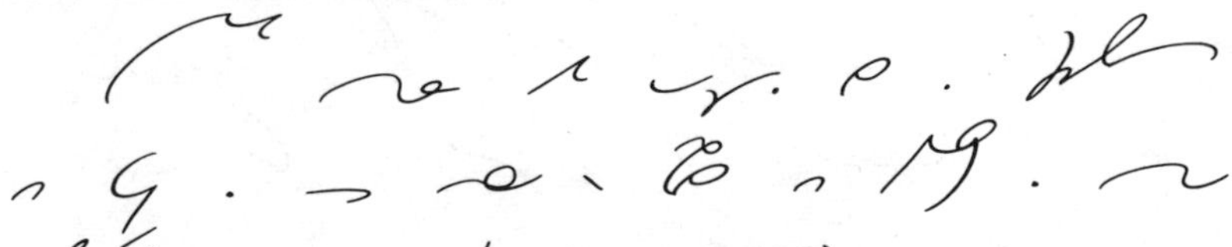

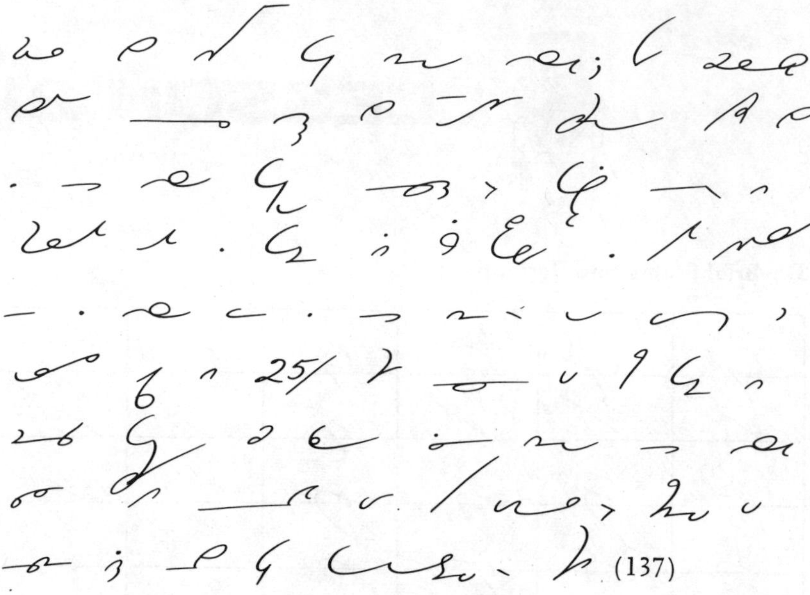

(137)

Reading and Writing Practice

139. Transcription Word Study

ensuing Following, coming afterward as a consequence.

solace Comfort.

secondary schools High schools.

140.

driveway

, conjunction

collision

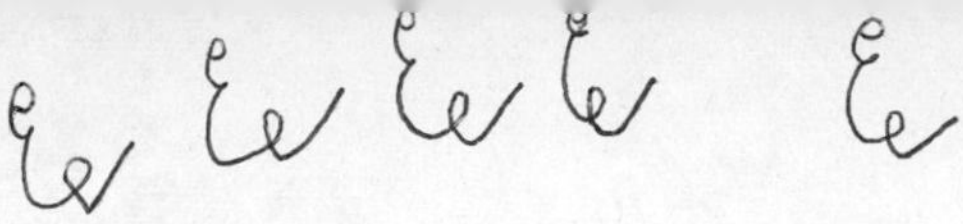

, introductory
agency

, as clause
expires
ensuing

(134)

141.

; no conjunction
decision

permanent
, conjunction

(96)

142.

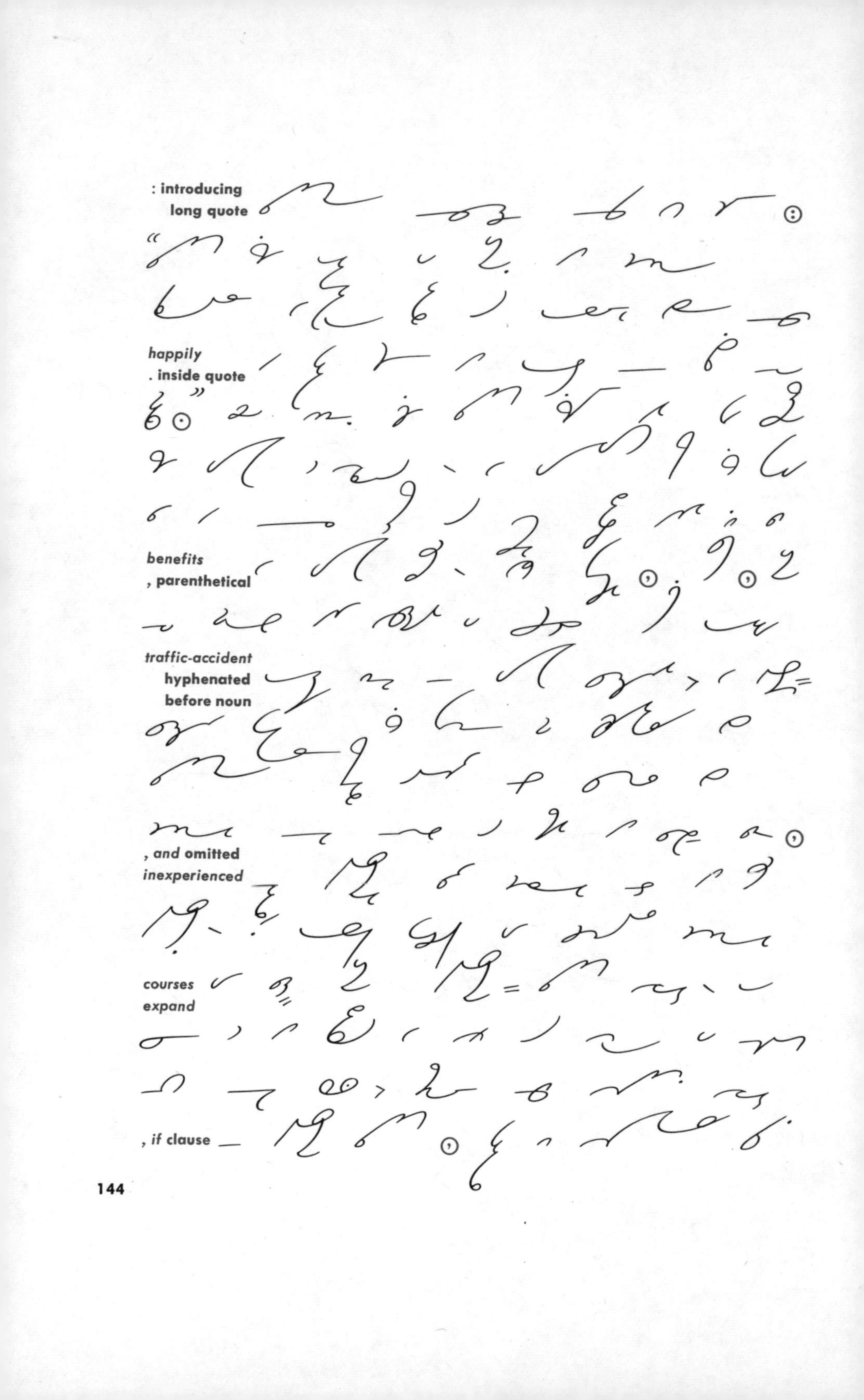

: introducing
long quote

happily
. inside quote

benefits
, parenthetical

traffic-accident
hyphenated
before noun

, and omitted
inexperienced

courses
expand

, if clause

curriculum

, if clause

; illustrative ,

badly needed no hyphen after *ly*

, introductory

self-satisfied

(334)

Transcription Quiz. The Transcription Quiz in this lesson and succeeding lessons will be a greater challenge to you in two ways:

1. Up to this stage you have had to supply only commas in order to punctuate a letter correctly; hereafter, you will also have to supply semicolons and colons.

2. Up to this point you have had to supply missing words in the shorthand that were obvious; hereafter, any one of a number of words will make sense. It will be your job to supply the word that you think fits best in the sentence. For example.

In the spot where there has been an omission, any one of the following words would be considered correct: *plain, obvious, apparent.* Assuming that the word *obvious* makes the sentence read most smoothly, you would write it in your notebook thus:

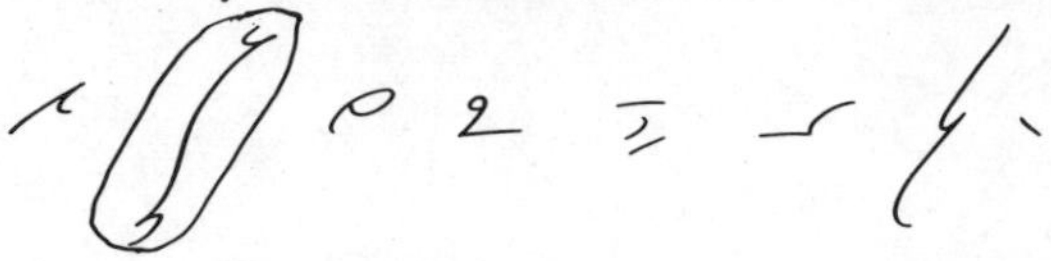

For you to supply: 4 commas—3 commas introductory, 1 comma *when* clause; 1 semicolon no conjunction; 1 colon enumeration; 2 missing words.

143.

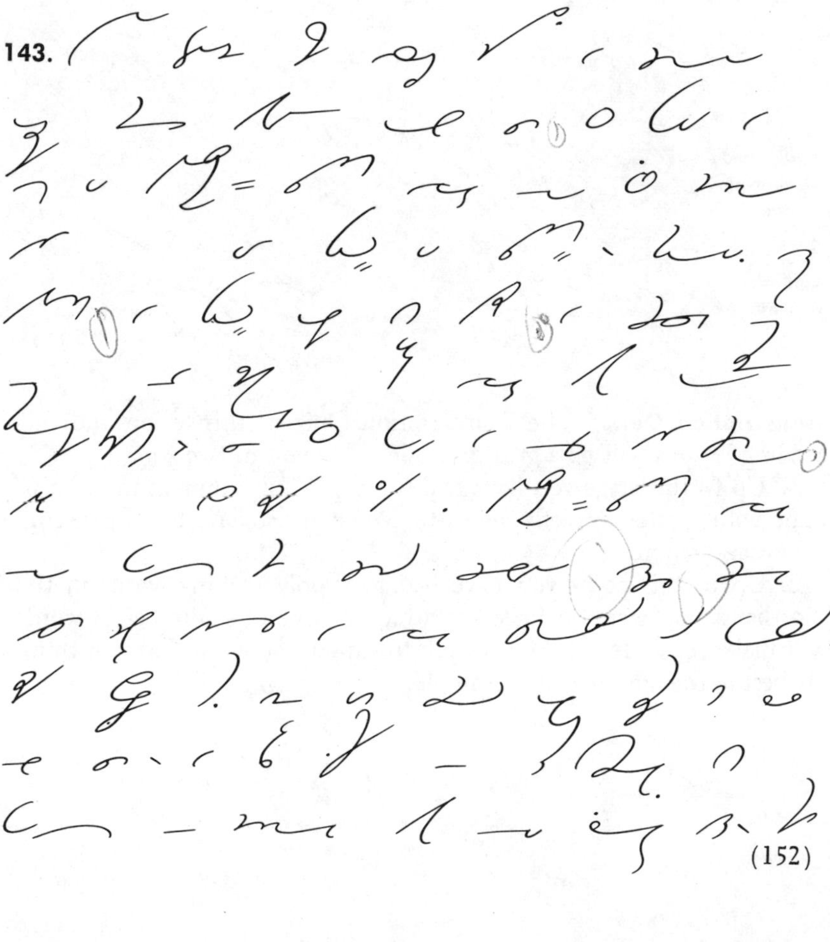

(152)

LESSON 22

144. Useful Business-Letter Phrases

So

1 

Very

2 

As

3 

About

4 

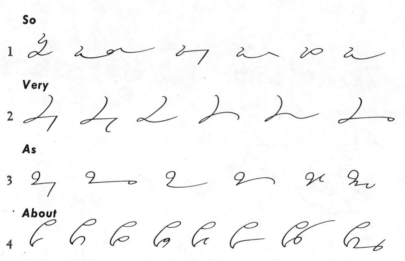

1. So far, so little, so much, so long, so that, so well.
2. Very much, very important, very well, very good, very glad, very many.
3. As much, as many, as well, as good, as it is, as you know.
4. About the, about this, about that, about these, about those, about them, about that time, about this matter.

145. Frequent Names

1. Driscoll, Duffy, Duncan, Dunne, Edwards, Evans, Farrell.
2. Charlotte, Clara, Constance, Cora, Cynthia, Delia.

Reading and Writing Practice

146. Transcription Word Study

lubrication The application of oil.

unsurpassed Having no superior in quality or performance.

reputable Enjoying a good reputation; held in esteem.

147.

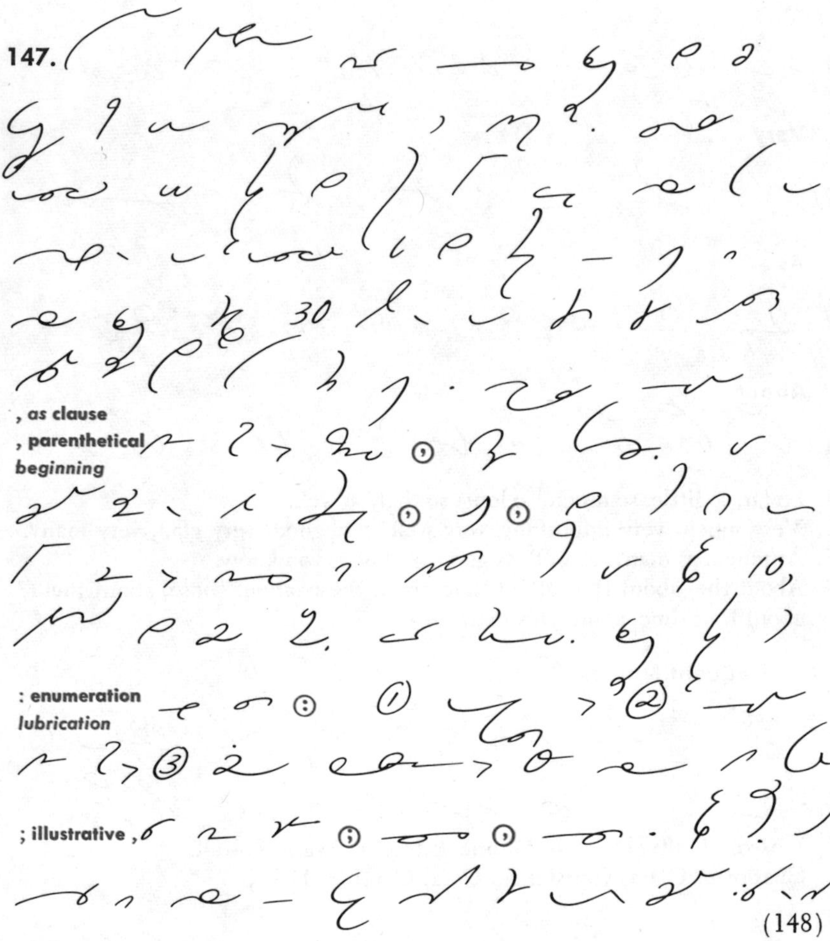

, as clause

, parenthetical

beginning

: enumeration

lubrication

; illustrative ,

(148)

148.

crowd

; because of comma

, introductory

, parenthetical

It's

, introductory

winning

economical

Its

durability

; no conjunction

unsurpassed

, and omitted

, series

amazing

, introductory
, introducing
short quote
. inside quote

(185)

149.

, series
weeks'

, when clause
Today's

, introductory
assurance

Transcribe:
82 per cent

82,

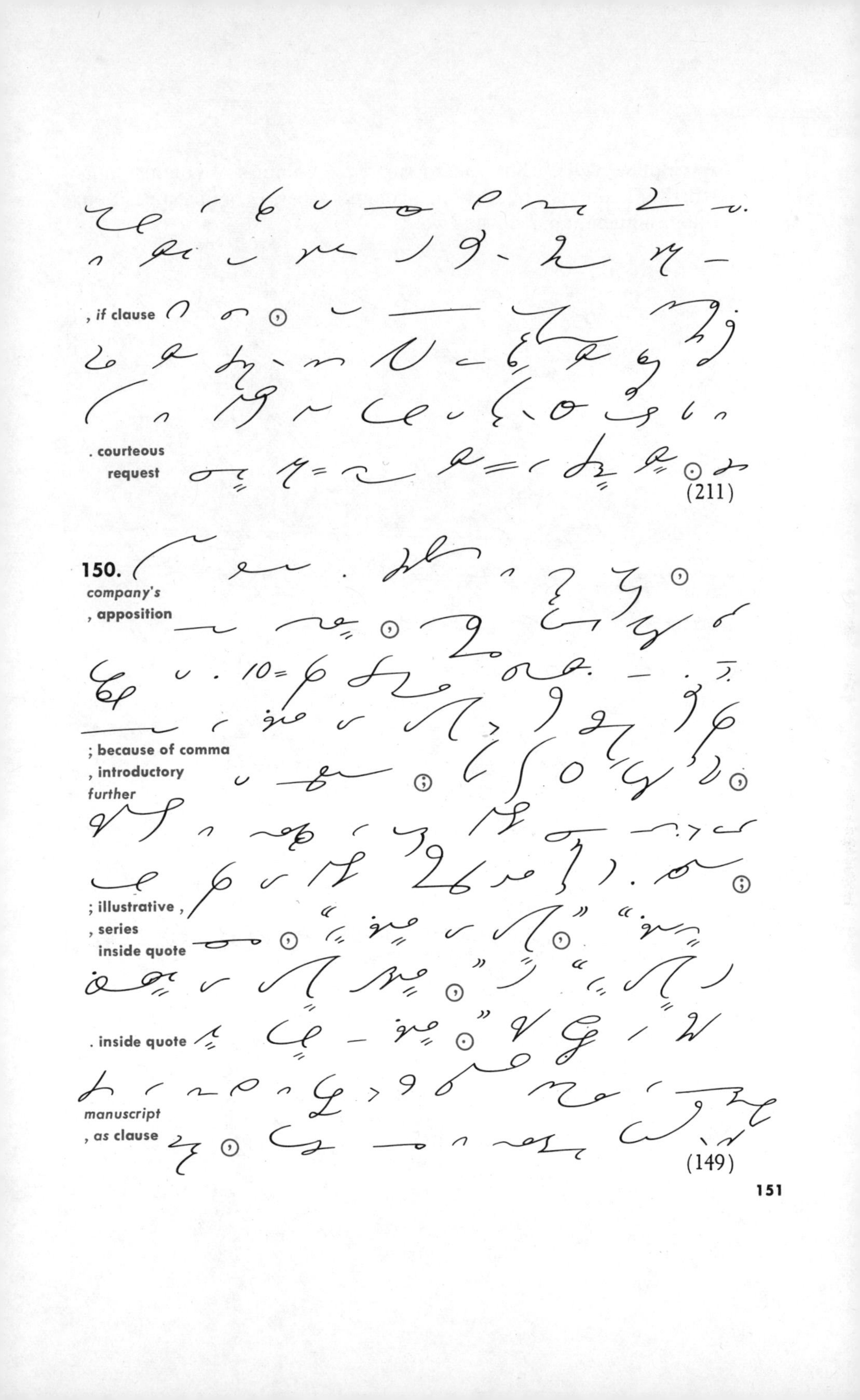

, *if clause*

. courteous request

(211)

150.

company's

, apposition

; because of comma

, introductory

further

; illustrative ,

, series

inside quote

. inside quote

manuscript

, as clause

(149)

Transcription Quiz. For you to supply: 6 commas—2 commas nonrestrictive, 1 comma conjunction, 2 commas series, 1 comma apposition; 1 colon enumeration; 2 missing words.

151.

LESSON 23

152. Word Families

-er

1 

-or

2 

-ery

3 

-ory

4 

-ary

5 

1. Rocker, locker, thicker, baker, striker, blacker.
2. Tailor, sailor, parlor, color, councilor.
3. Robbery, bribery, refinery, cannery, flattery, bravery, slavery.
4. Memory, advisory, supervisory, accessory, explanatory.
5. Secondary, customary, primary, contrary, secretary, notary.

Reading and Writing Practice

153. Transcription Word Study

incredibly Unbelievably.

enhance To increase in value or desirability.

warranty A guarantee.

154.

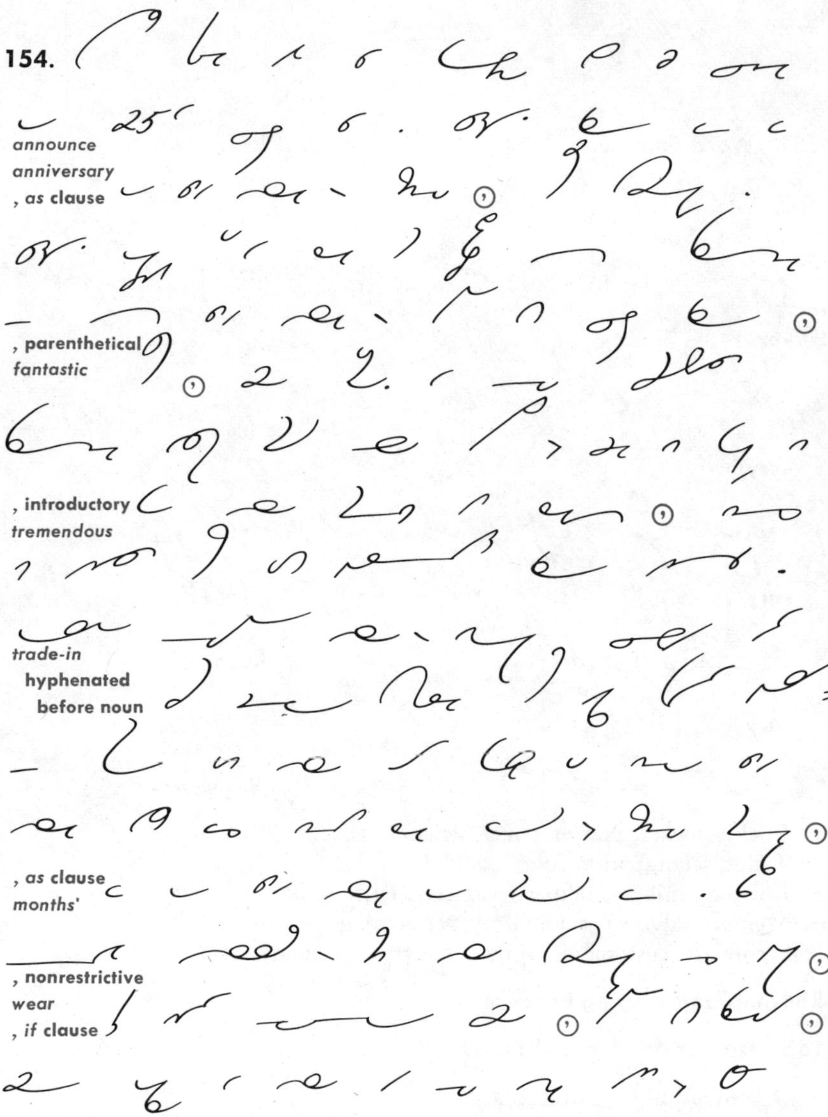

announce
anniversary
, as clause
, parenthetical
fantastic
, introductory
tremendous
trade-in
hyphenated
before noun
, as clause
months'
, nonrestrictive
wear
, if clause

. courteous request

(206)

155.

license

, when clause

, conjunction

ph=1305

ph=13005

wife's

, apposition

1956

clarify

, introductory

(117)

156.

, as clause

notary

, introductory
; because of comma
, parenthetical

assistance
, if clause

(107)

157.

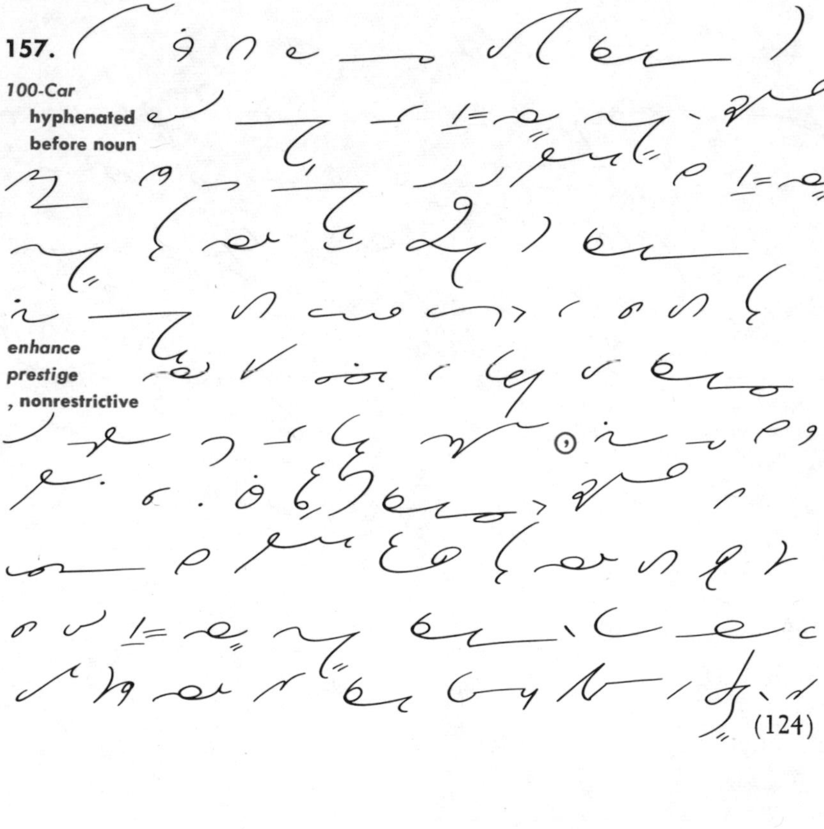

100-Car
hyphenated before noun

enhance
prestige
, nonrestrictive

(124)

Transcription Quiz. For you to supply: 6 commas—1 comma introductory, 2 commas parenthetical, 2 commas series, 1 comma *and* omitted; 2 missing words.

158.

(201)

LESSON 24

159. Word Beginnings

Im-

1 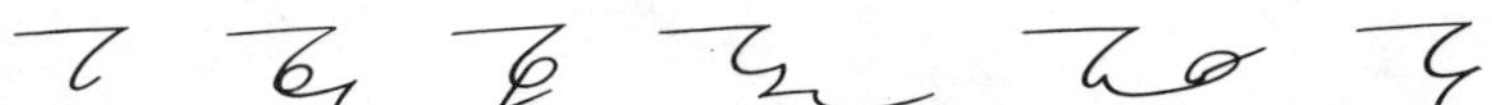

In-

2 

Mis-

3 

Per-

4 

Pro-

5 

Re-

6 

1. Impose, impartial, impatient, impersonal, impolite, improper.
2. Incident, incite, income, inconsistent, incredible, injure, inspect.
3. Misconception, misconduct, misdirect, misguided, misinform.
4. Persist, persuade, permit, perspire, perplex, perfume, perhaps.

5. Procedure, professor, profound, project, pronounce, prosper, professional, profane.
6. Refute, refresh, refuse, reflect, repel, reprint, replenish.

160. Geographical Expressions

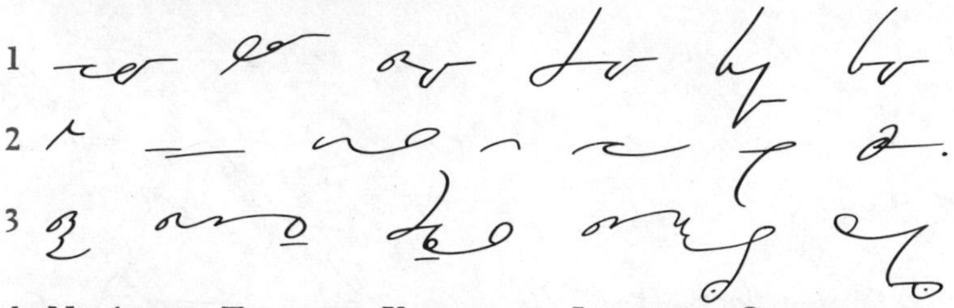

1. Norristown, Tarrytown, Youngstown, Jamestown, Georgetown, Johnstown.
2. Texas, New Mexico, Oklahoma, Kansas, Colorado, Nebraska, Wyoming.
3. U.S.S.R., Uruguay, Venezuela, Yugoslavia, Albania.

Reading and Writing Practice

161. Transcription Word Study

transmission The gear that carries the power from an automobile engine to the axle.

brake The mechanism that stops a car. (Do not confuse with *break,* which means "to separate into parts.")

title Ownership.

162.

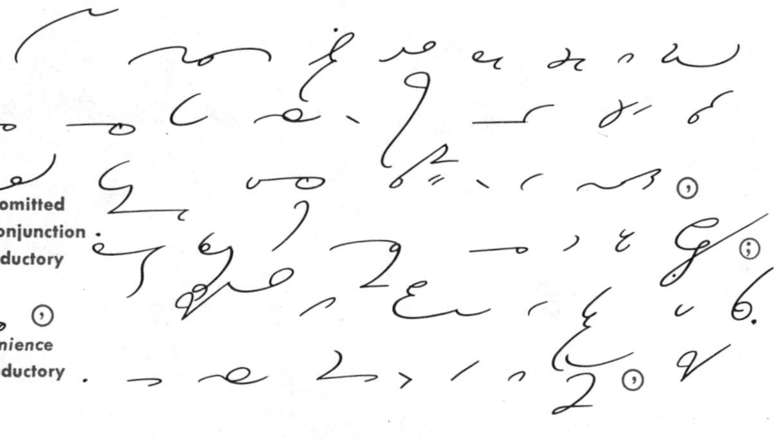

, *and* omitted
; no conjunction
, introductory
convenience
, introductory

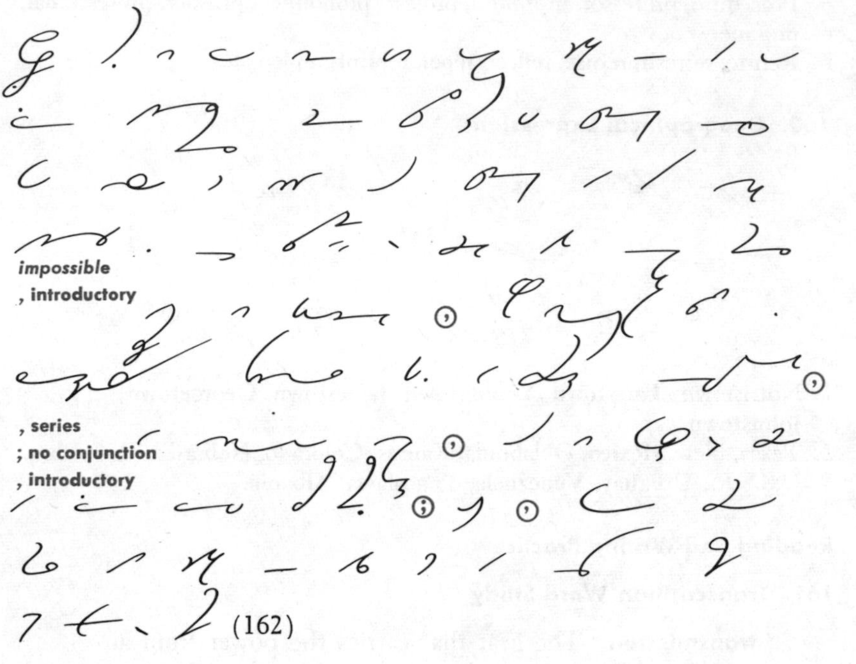

impossible

, introductory

, series

; no conjunction

, introductory

(162)

163.

Edison's

, parenthetical

, introductory

, parenthetical

, apposition

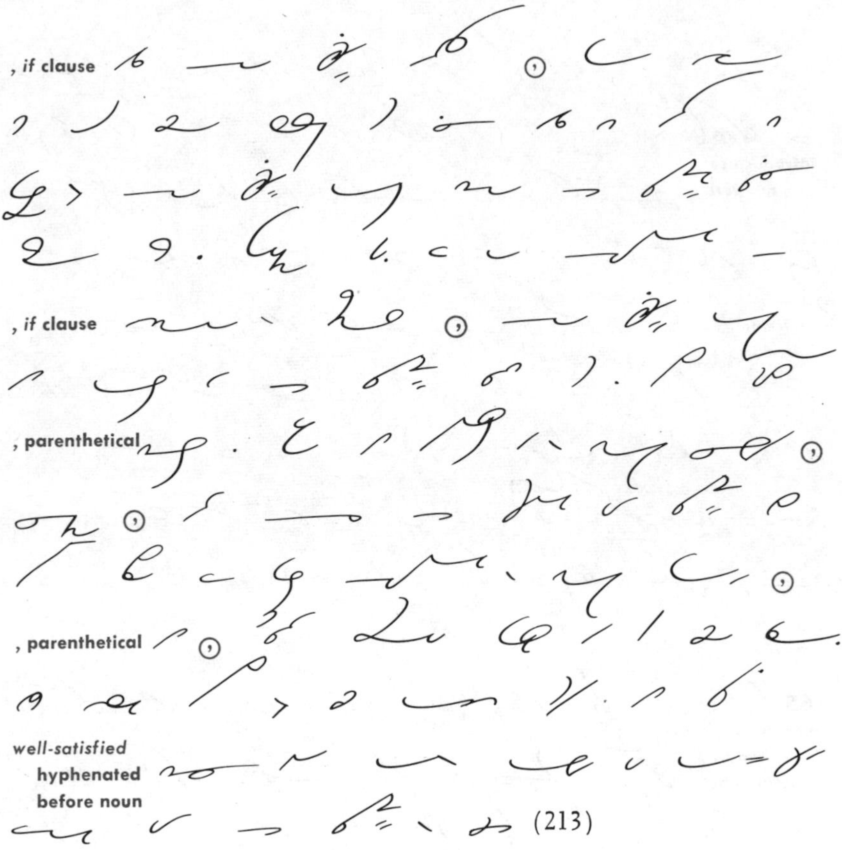

, if clause

, if clause

, parenthetical

, parenthetical

well-satisfied
hyphenated before noun

(213)

164.

, introductory
, *and* omitted

requirements
, introductory

, nonrestrictive

(138)

165. 15, 1952

two-door
hyphenated
before noun

30, 1953

title
, introductory

, introducing
short quote
canceled
. inside quote

, *if* clause

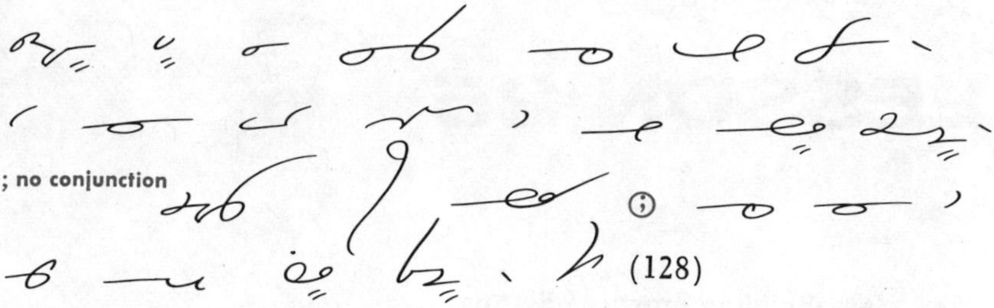

; no conjunction

(128)

Transcription Quiz. For you to supply: 2 commas—1 comma introductory, 1 comma *when* clause; 1 semicolon because of comma; 1 colon enumeration; 2 missing words.

166.

(117)

LESSON 25

167. Word-Building Practice—Blends

Nt

1 

Md

2 

Gent, Pend

3 

Tive

4 

Ten

5 

Tem

6 

1. Sent, consent, convent, prevent, disappoint, current, printer.
2. Informed, dreamed, named, disarmed, farmed, claimed.
3. Gentle, gentleman, spend, expend, opened, ripened, legend.
4. Native, captive, sensitive, motive, positive, restive.

5. Tension, attention, intention, intent, tentative, tender, tenant, tennis.
6. Temper, temperament, temperature, contemplate, temptation, temporary.

Reading and Writing Practice

168. Transcription Word Study

trundled Rolled along, as a hoop.

grievance Complaint.

dominion Supreme authority or control.

169. The Boy Who Put the World on Wheels

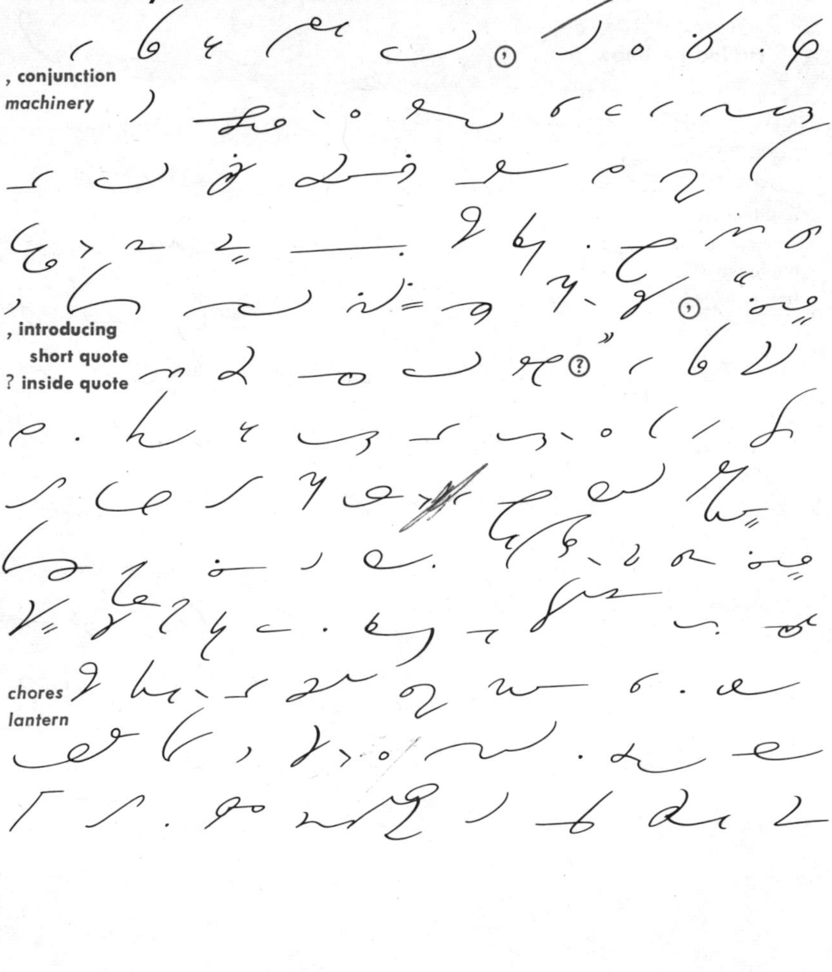

, conjunction
machinery

, introducing short quote
? inside quote

chores
lantern

knitting

, *and* omitted

, conjunction
idea

He learned how

, series

, parenthetical
two-passenger
hyphenated
before noun

cylinders
; because of comma

, parenthetical
. inside quote
, conjunction

inside quote (297)

170. Let's Tell the Worker Why

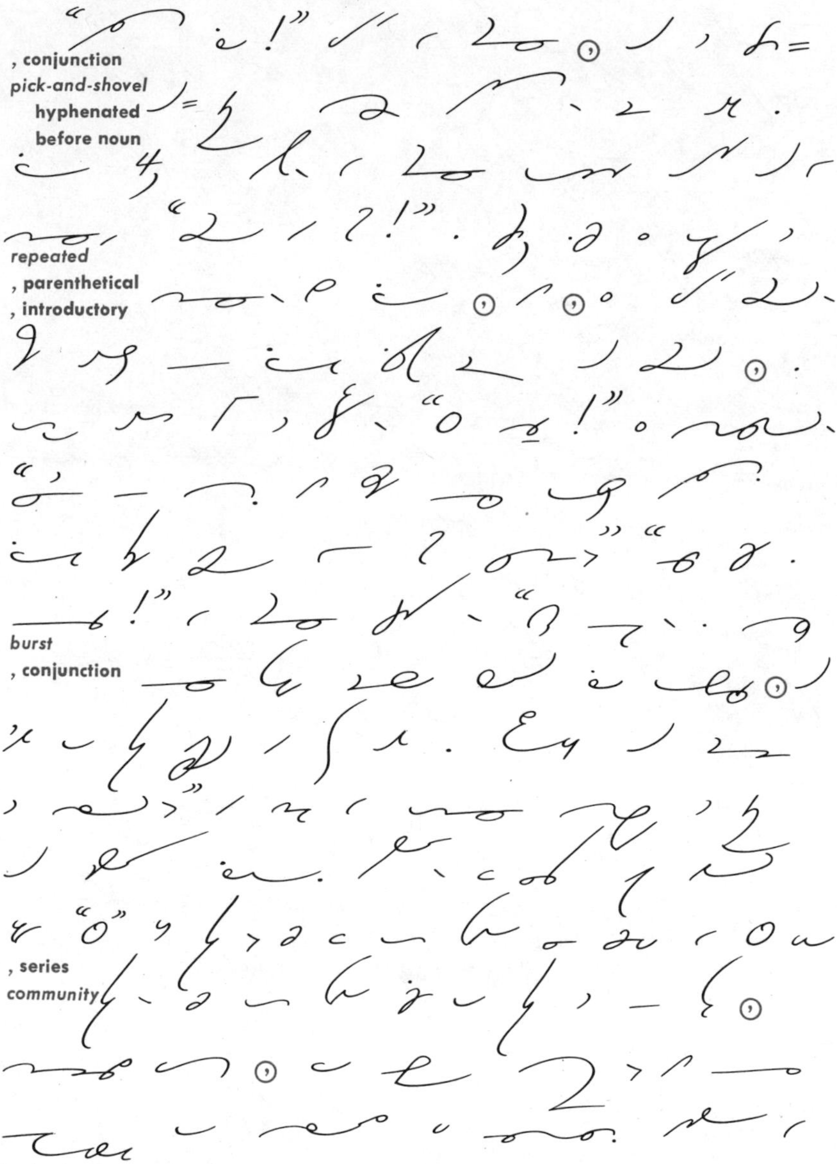

, conjunction
pick-and-shovel hyphenated before noun

repeated
, parenthetical
, introductory

burst
, conjunction

, series
community

Recently

, series
freely

, and omitted

, introductory
grievance
procedure

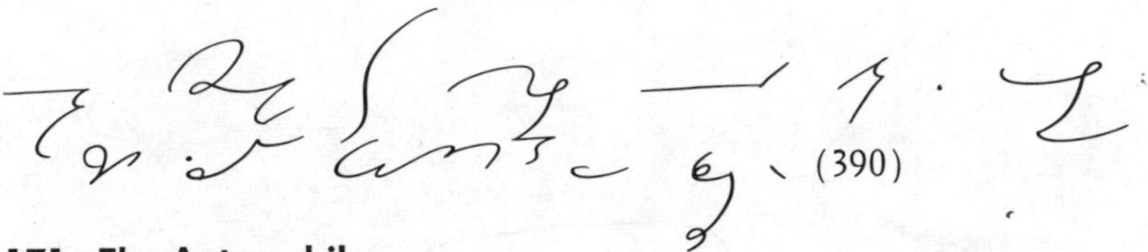

(390)

171. The Automobile

dominion
humanity
subtle

, conjunction
isolated

, series
adventure
recreation

stifling

reunion

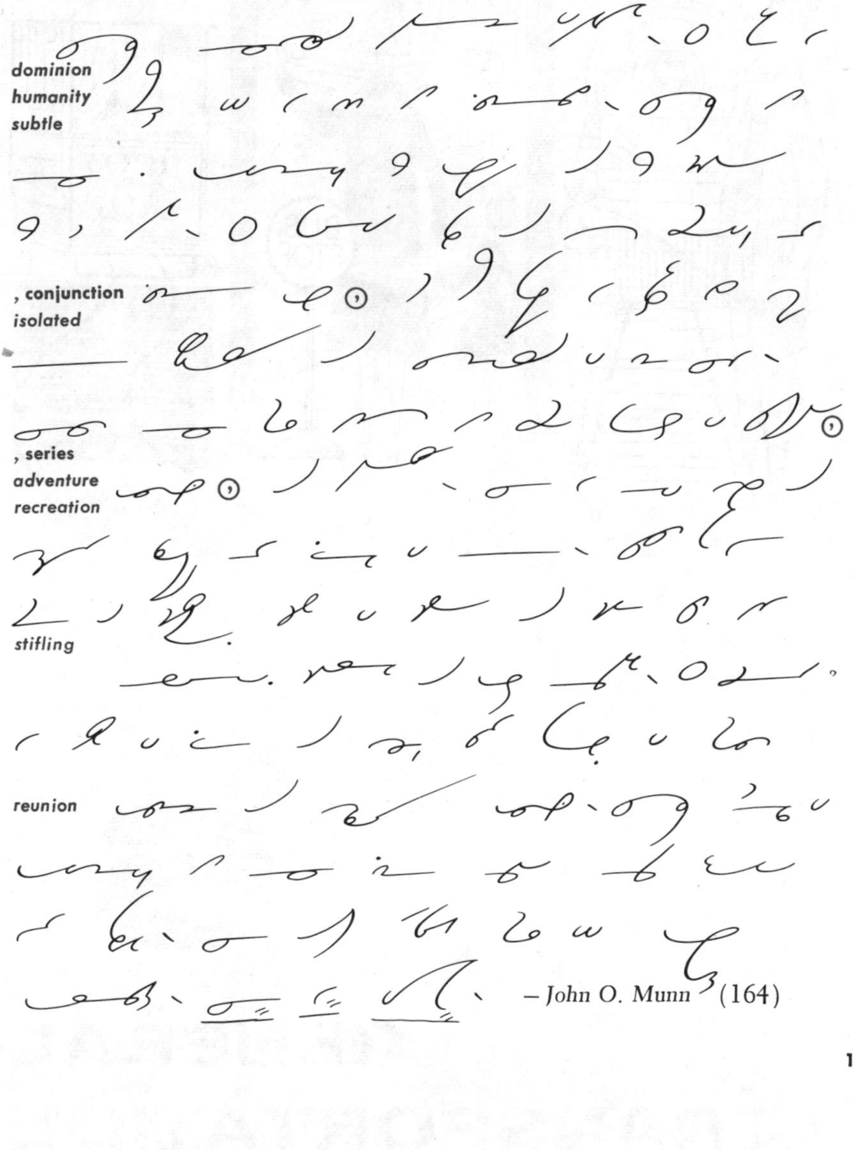

– John O. Munn (164)

6

GENERAL TRANSPORTATION

LESSON 26

172. Brief Forms and Derivatives

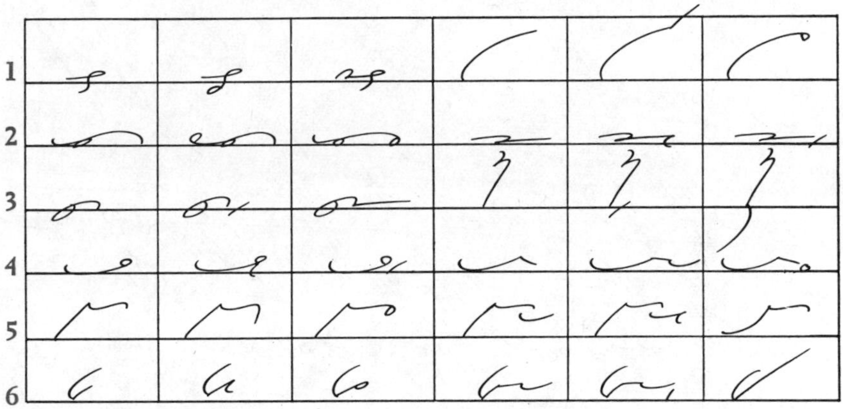

1. Necessary, necessarily, unnecessary; time, timed, timely.
2. Regular, irregular, regularly; number, numbers, numbered.
3. Acknowledge, acknowledged, acknowledgment; suggest-suggestion, suggested, suggestive.
4. Let-letter, letters, lettered; long, longer, longingly.
5. Direct, direction, directly, director, directors, indirect.
6. Part, parts, partly, partner, partnership, parted.

173. Brief Form and Phrase Letter

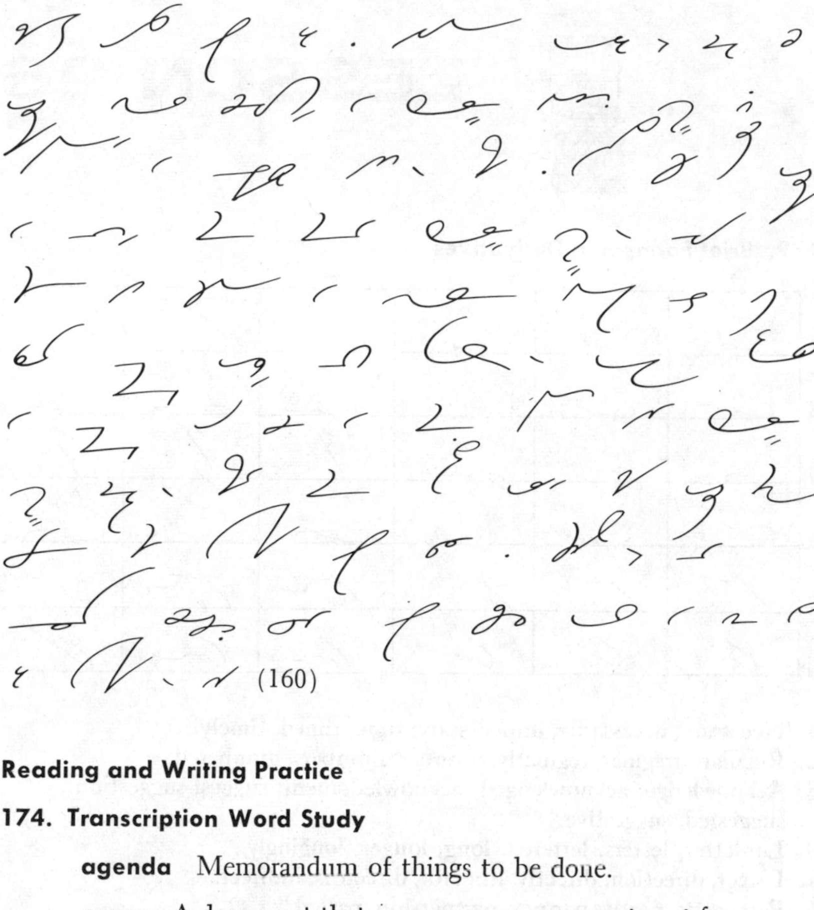

(160)

Reading and Writing Practice

174. Transcription Word Study

agenda Memorandum of things to be done.

proxy A document that empowers one person to act for another.

suburban train A train serving residential districts on the outskirts of a city.

175.

Transcribe:
No. 13

, parenthetical
unnecessary

, introductory
, parenthetical

, introductory

courteous
, and omitted

(145)

176.

, introductory

, as clause

, if clause
schedule
, as clause

, introductory

arrangements

, conjunction

(144)

177.

, apposition

: enumeration

four-year

hyphenated before noun

, *if clause*

proxy
, series
authorizing

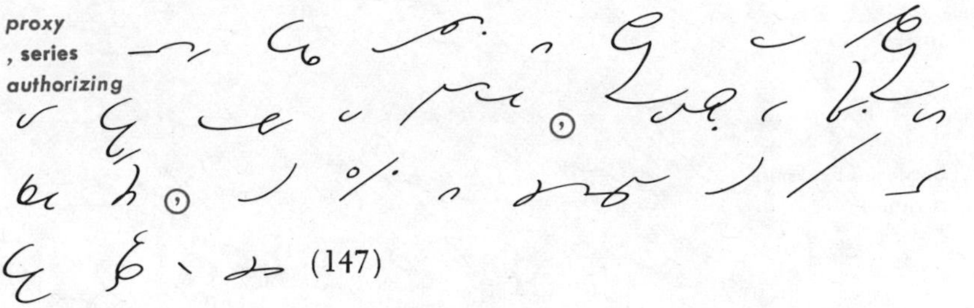

(147)

178.

, introductory
occurs
; because of comma
; illustrative ,
specially

(111)

179.

, nonrestrictive
, introducing
short quote

? inside quote

; because of comma

, if clause

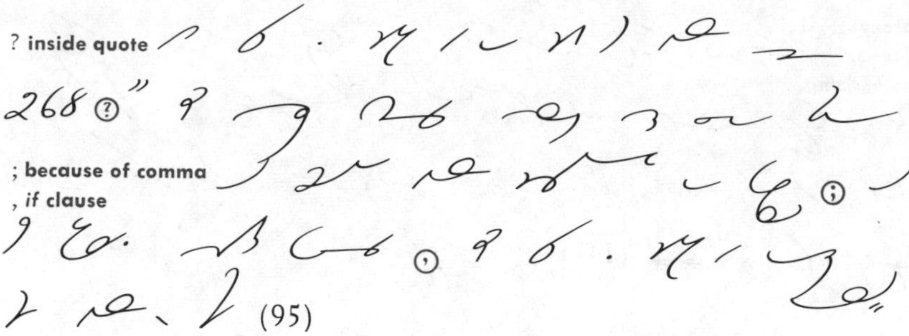

(95)

Transcription Quiz. For you to supply: 4 commas—3 commas introductory, 1 comma *when* clause; 1 semicolon no conjunction; 2 missing words.

180.

(122)

LESSON 27

181. Useful Business-Letter Phrases

Any

1 

Each

2 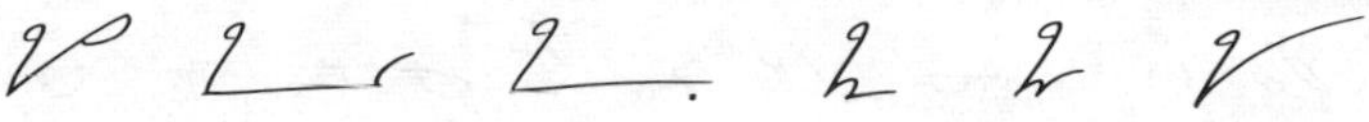

Few

3 

Many

4 

1. Any more, any more than, any one of the, anyone else, any other, any time.
2. Each day, each month, each morning, each one, each other, each time.
3. Few minutes, few minutes ago, few months, few days, few days ago.
4. Many other, many others, many thousands, many times, many days.

182. Frequent Names

1
2 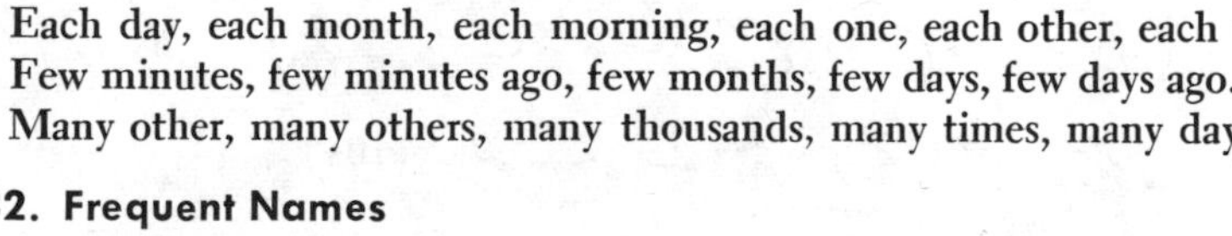

1. Fisher, Fitzgerald, Foley, Fox, Fraser, Gordon.
2. Duncan, Edgar, Edmond, Edward, Ernest, Eugene.

Reading and Writing Practice

183. Transcription Word Study

Kentucky Derby A famous horse race that is run annually at Churchill Downs in Kentucky.

reclining seat A seat that can be tilted backward for greater comfort.

depot Station.

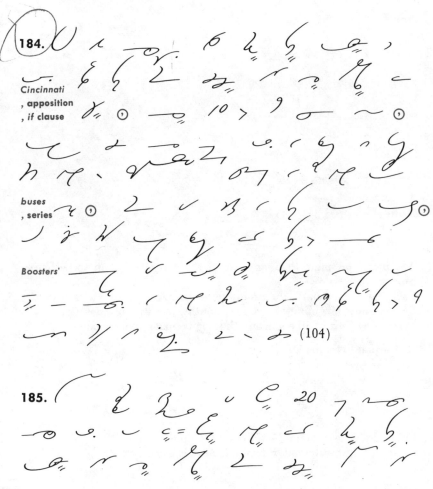

184.

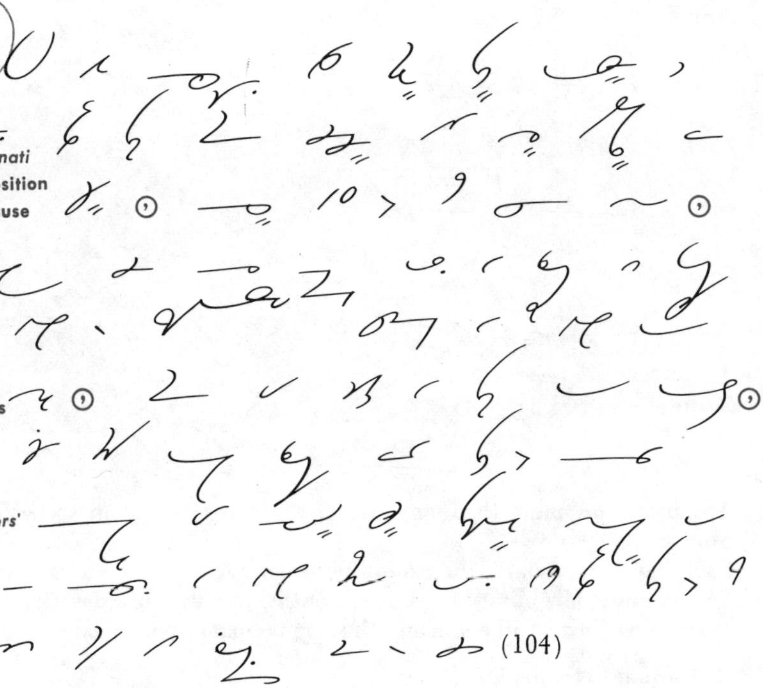

Cincinnati

, apposition

, if clause

buses

, series

Boosters'

(104)

185.

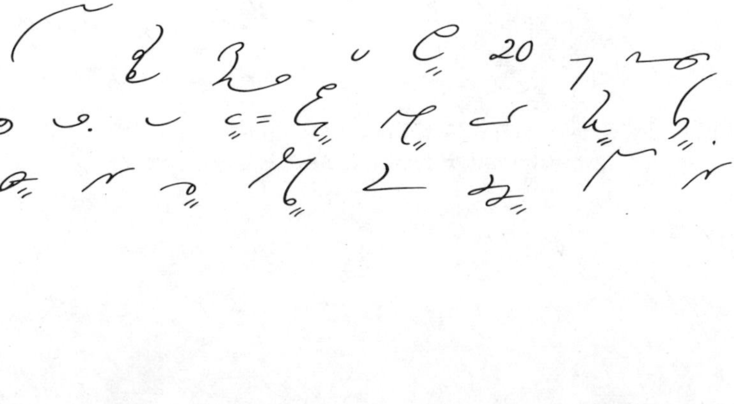

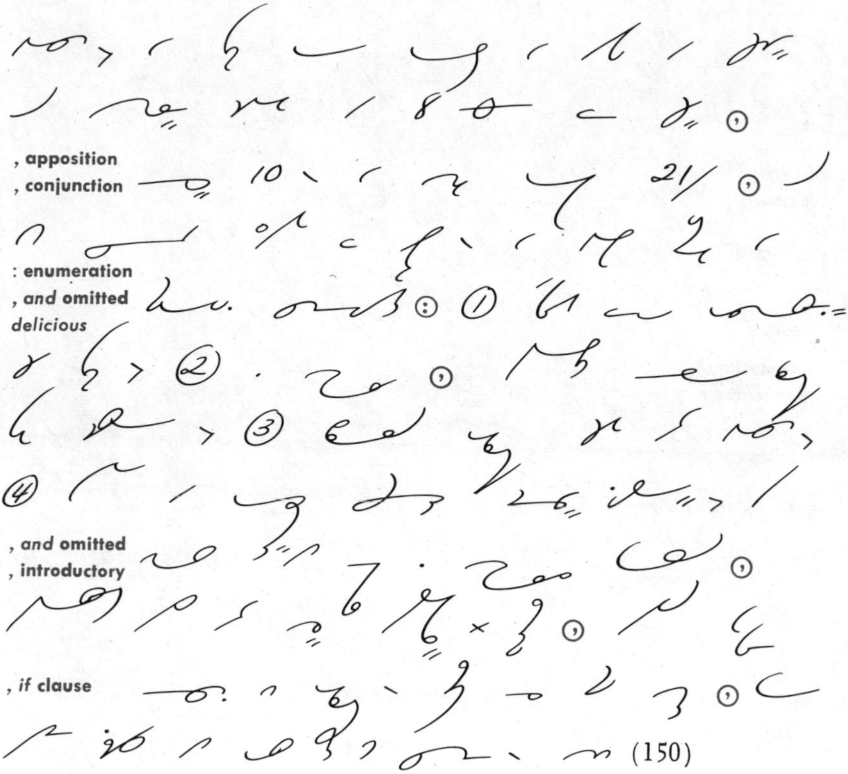

, apposition
, conjunction
: enumeration
, and omitted
delicious
, and omitted
, introductory
, if clause

(150)

186.

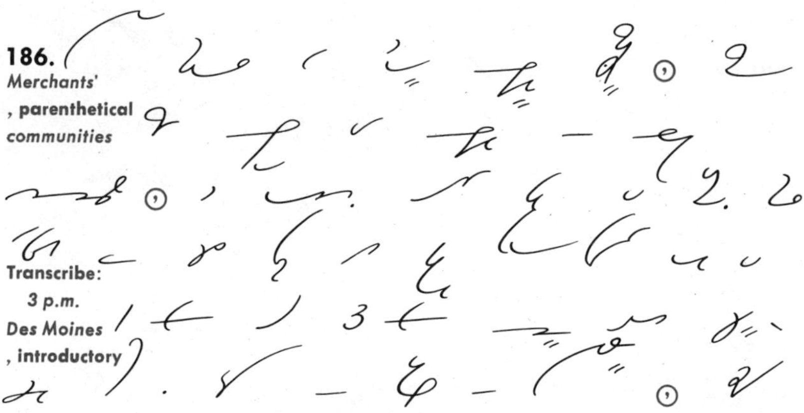

Merchants'
, parenthetical
communities

Transcribe:
3 p.m.
Des Moines
, introductory

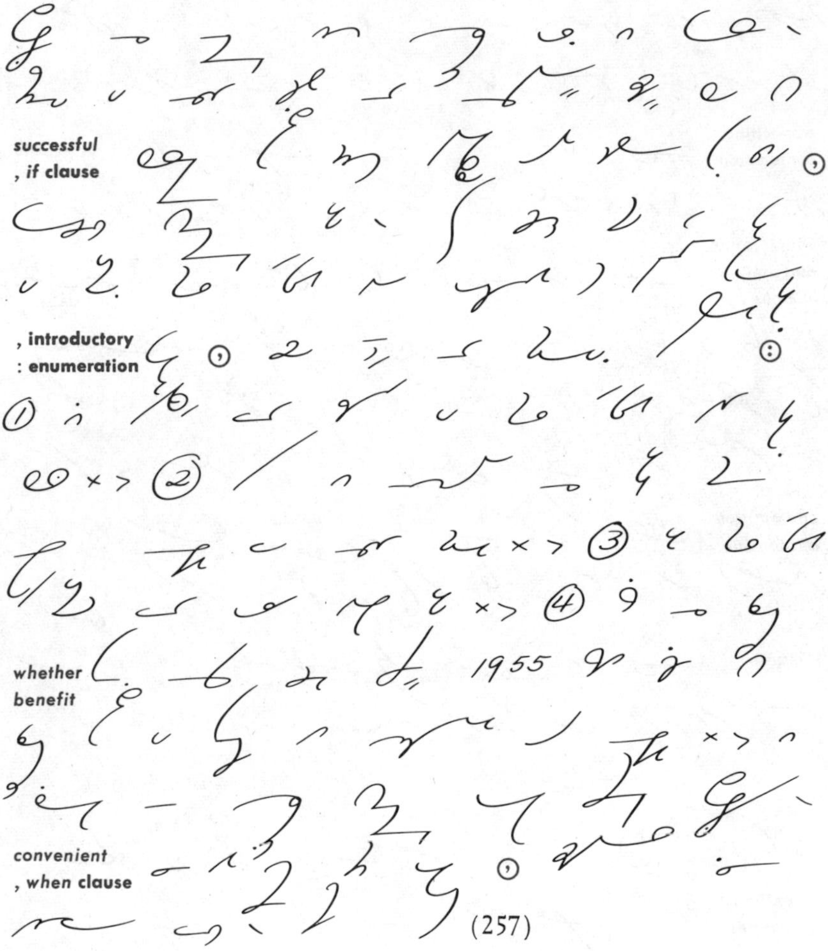

successful
, if clause
, introductory
: enumeration
whether
benefit
convenient
, when clause

(257)

187.

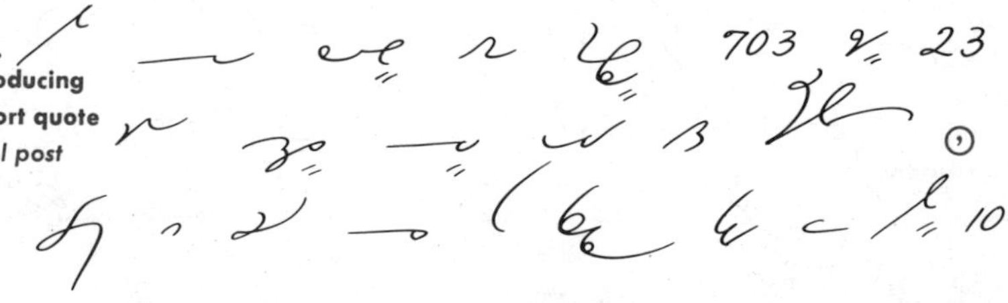

, introducing
short quote
parcel post

Transcription Self-Check

Remember, you can never become an efficient stenographer unless you can spell and punctuate correctly; therefore, be sure that you

1. Know the reason for the use of each punctuation mark in your Reading and Writing Practice.

2. Look in the margin of your shorthand page if there is any doubt in your mind about the reason for the use of a punctuation mark.

3. Spell aloud at least once each word in the margin.

received
? inside quote
, *if clause*
, introductory

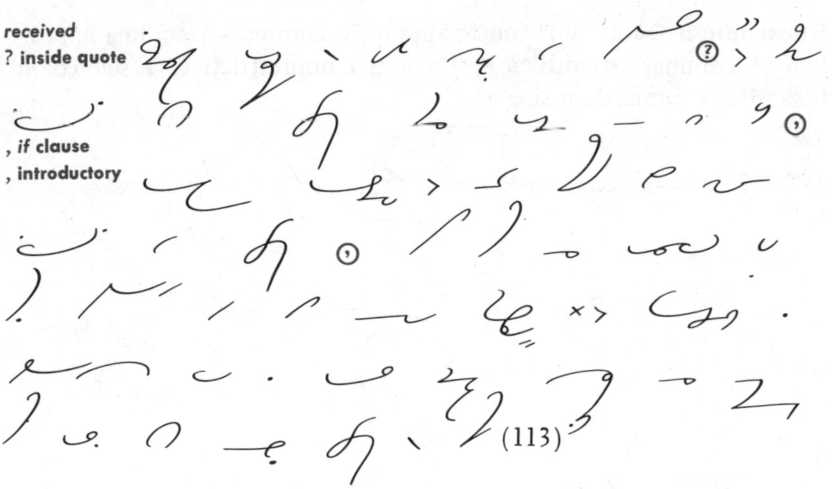

188.

, introductory
helpful

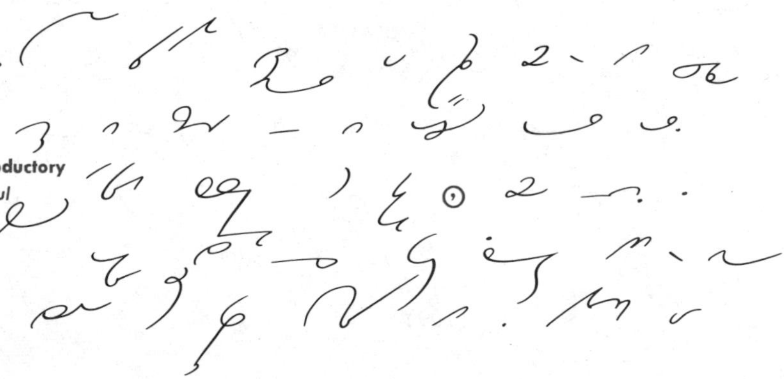

; illustrative ,
, series
, nonrestrictive
familiar
, apposition

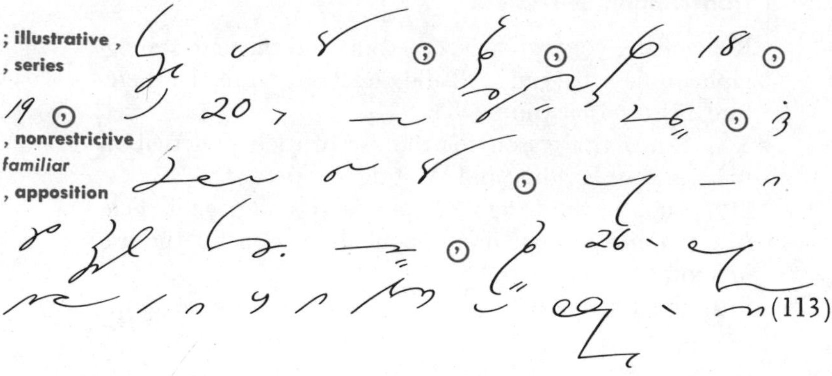

Transcription Quiz. For you to supply: 6 commas—1 comma apposition, 4 commas parenthetical, 1 comma nonrestrictive; 1 semicolon because of comma; 2 missing words.

189.

LESSON 28

190. Word Families

-ish

1 

-age

2 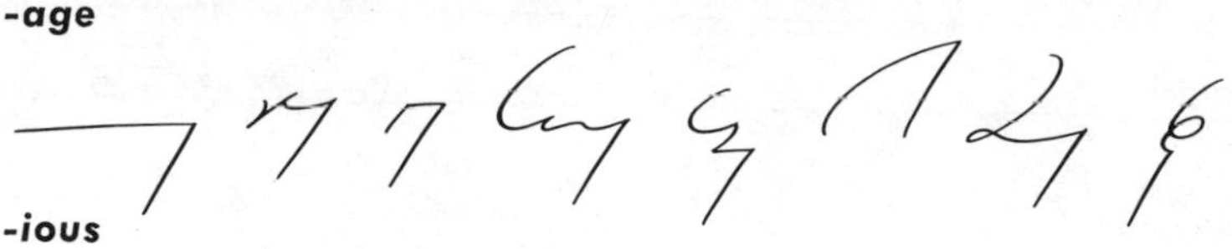

-ious

3 

-al

4 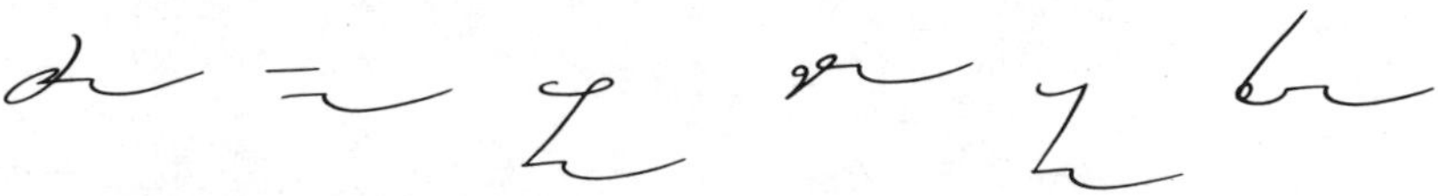

1. **Polish, abolish, stylish, foolish, banish, finish, varnish, vanish.**
2. **Manage, storage, tonnage, brokerage, personage, damage, village, passage.**
3. **Tedious, obvious, serious, various, envious, harmonious, devious.**
4. **Final, internal, original, external, regional, journal.**

Reading and Writing Practice

191. Transcription Word Study

10 Downing Street The home of the Prime Minister of England.

excursion A pleasure trip.

capital A city that is the seat of a nation's government. (Do not confuse with *capitol,* which is the building in which Congress or a state legislature meets.)

192.

well-known
hyphenated before noun

, conjunction
counselors

, parenthetical

, introductory

(159)

193.

co-operate
accommodations

, inside quote
accommodates

, series

: enumeration
, series
Eiffel

length
, series
, introductory

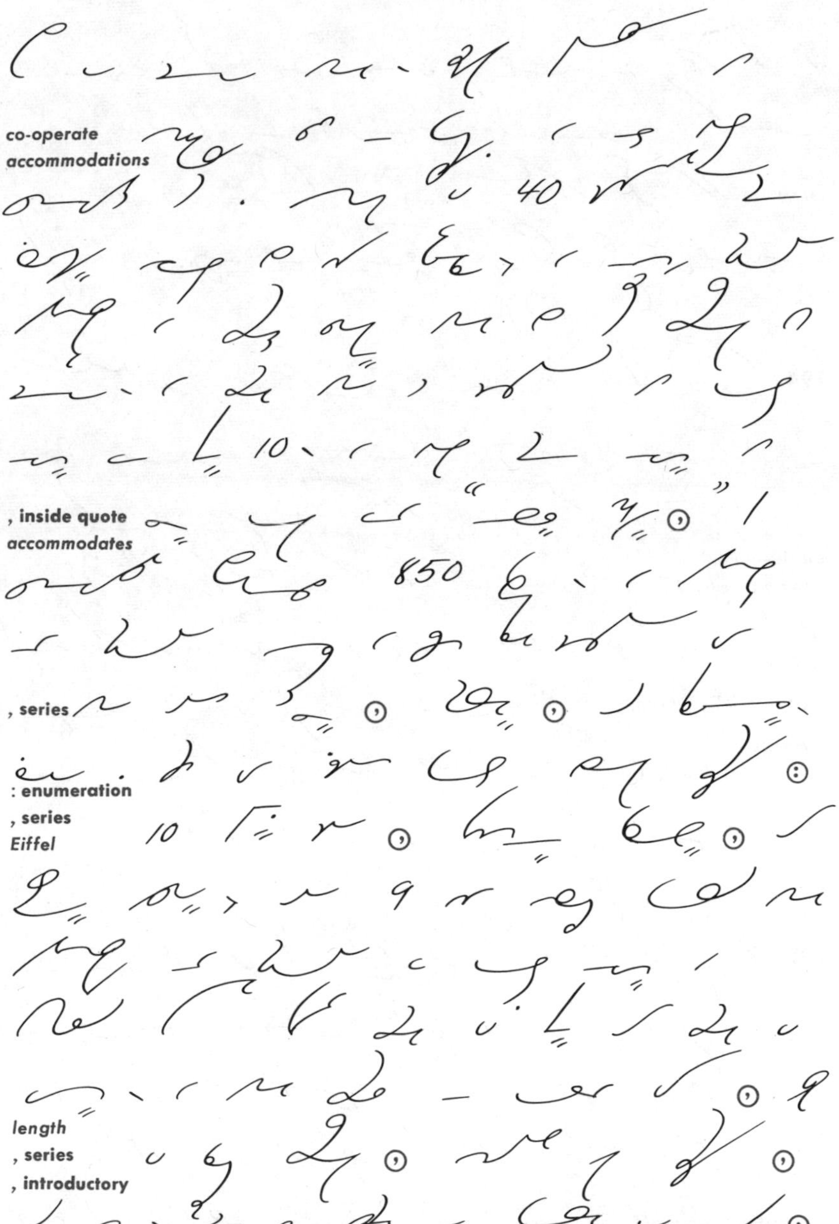

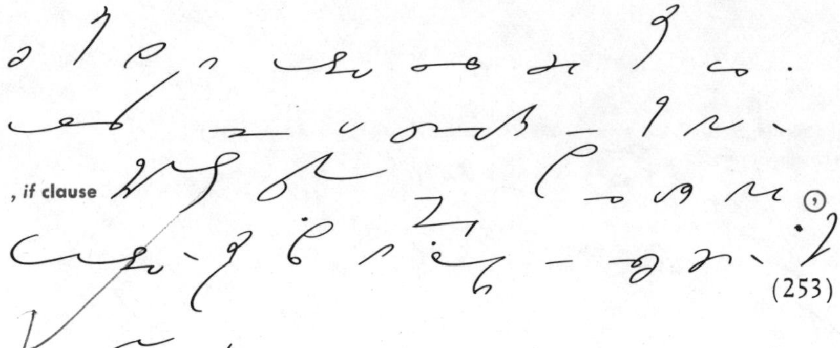

, *if clause*

(253)

194.

, **inside quote**

, *and* **omitted**

successful

; **because of comma**

(92)

195.

, **introductory**

nation's

capital

, **apposition**

; no conjunction

, introductory

further

, apposition

(119)

Transcription Quiz. For you to supply: 8 commas—2 commas nonrestrictive, 4 commas parenthetical, 2 commas series; 1 semicolon because of comma; 2 missing words.

196.

(124)

LESSON 29

197. Word Endings

-tion

1 

-sume, -sumption

2 

-tern, -term, -thern

3 

-ther

4 

-ual

5 

-ture

6 

1. Mention, action, fashion, detention, prevention, nation, national, nationally.
2. Resume, presume, assume, consume, consumer, resumption, assumption.
3. Stern, lantern, attorney, fraternal, eternal, determine, southern.
4. Mother, brother, father, bother, other, gather, gathered.

5. Annual, manual, manually, gradual, schedule.
6. Nature, creature, feature, mature, matured, immature.

198. Geographical Expressions

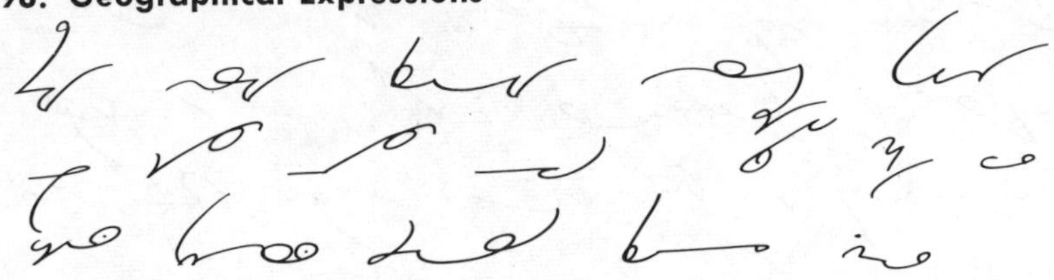

1. Evanston, Cranston, Charleston, Galveston, Brockton.
2. Nebraska, South Dakota, North Dakota, Montana, Idaho, Washington, Oregon.
3. Austria, Bulgaria, Finland, Germany, Hungary.

Reading and Writing Practice

199. Transcription Word Study

debris Rubbish.

itineraries Outlines of travel routes.

200.

, as clause

, conjunction

managers

efficiently run

no hyphen after *ly*

, parenthetical

, introductory
acceptable

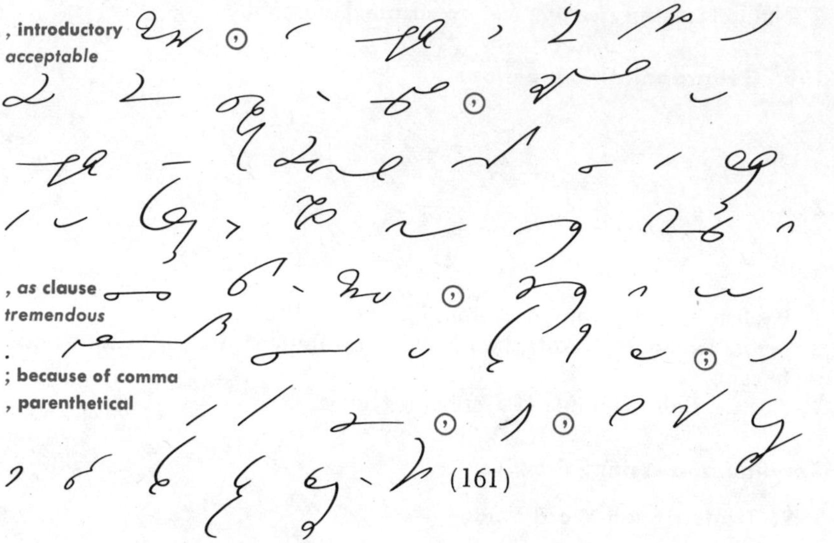

, as clause
tremendous

.
; because of comma
, parenthetical

(161)

201.

, introductory
co-operation

, *and* omitted

; illustrative ,
, series

, introductory

adjustments

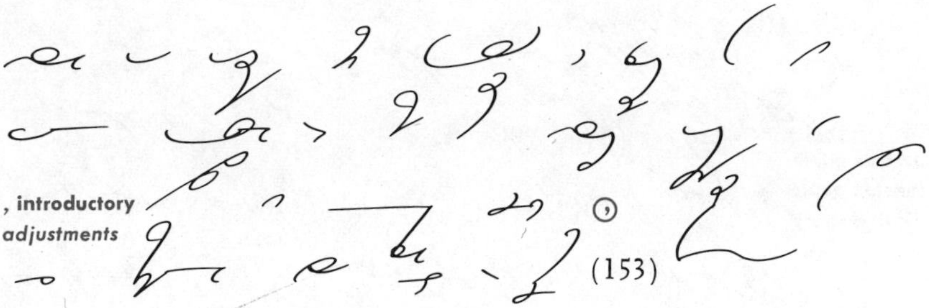

(153)

202.

itineraries

, introductory

, nonrestrictive

up-to-date

hyphenated before noun

. courteous request

, parenthetical

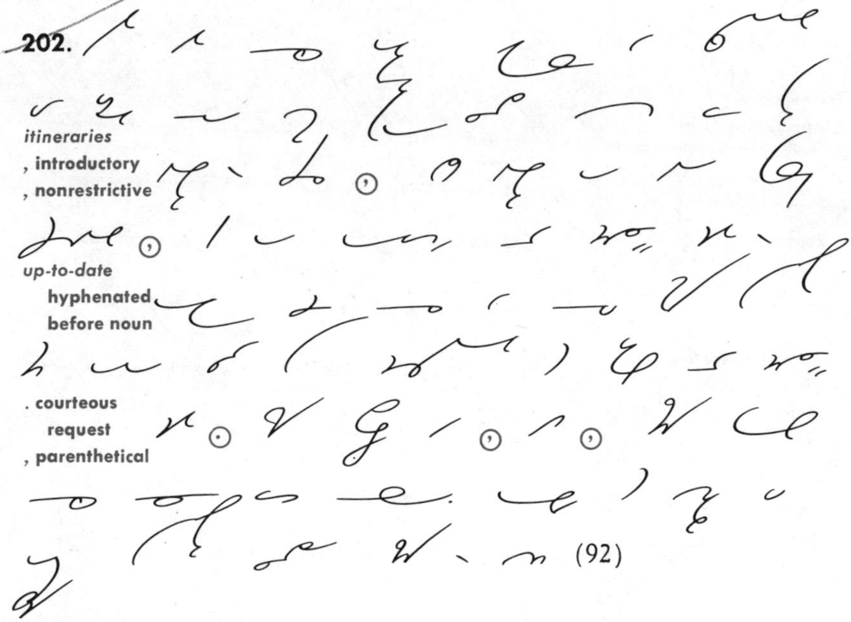

(92)

203.

: introducing long quote

, apposition

, *if* clause

Transcribe:

May 30

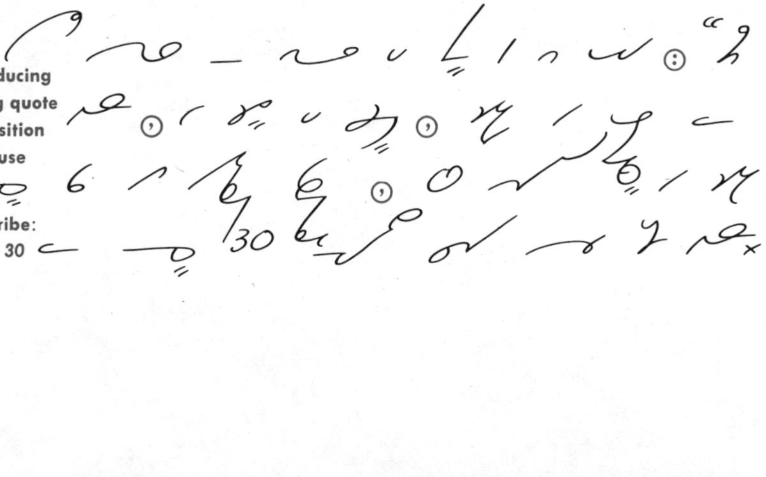

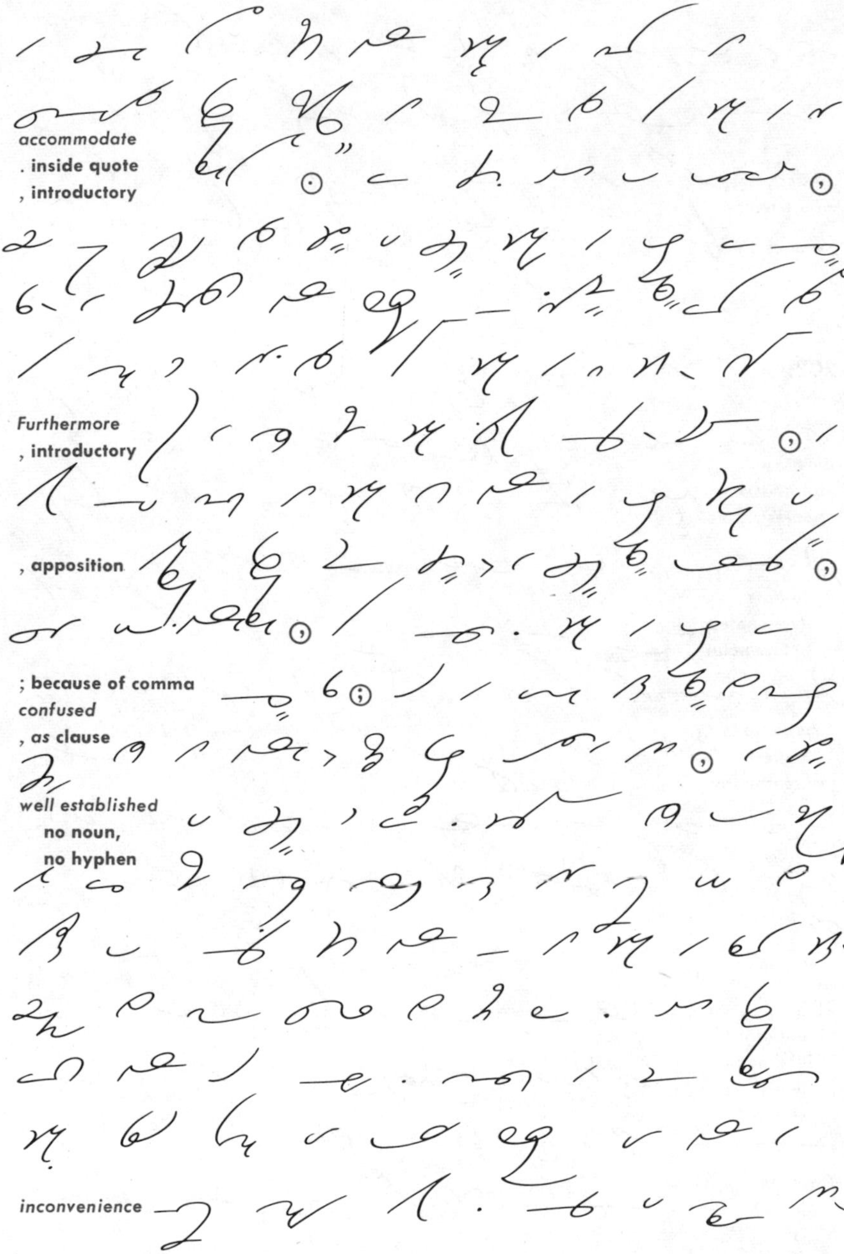

accommodate
. inside quote
, introductory
Furthermore
, introductory
, apposition
; because of comma
confused
, as clause
well established
no noun,
no hyphen
inconvenience

, parenthetical

, if clause

hesitate

(303)

Transcription Quiz. For you to supply: 5 commas—1 comma apposition, 1 comma *when* clause, 3 commas parenthetical; 1 semicolon because of comma; 2 missing words.

204.

(158)

LESSON 30

205. Word-Building Practice—Vowel Combinations

Ia, Ea

1 

Ye, Ya

2 

Double Circle

3 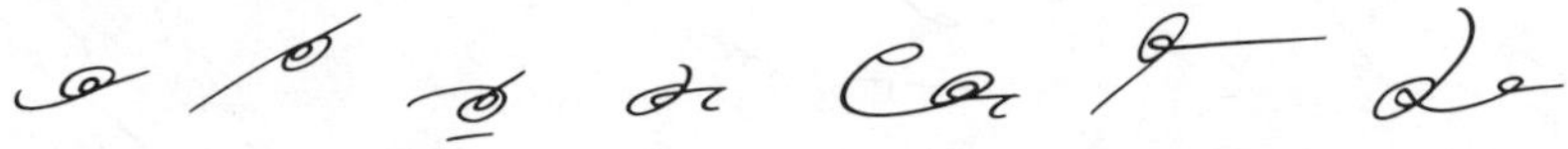

Oe, Eo

4 

1. Area, create, bacteria, cafeteria, aviation, appreciate, civilian.
2. Yell, yellow, yield, yearn, Yale, yarn.
3. Riot, diet, quiet, science, appliance, diamond, violin.
4. Poem, poet, poetry, folio, portfolio, radio.

206. Accuracy Practice—Proportion

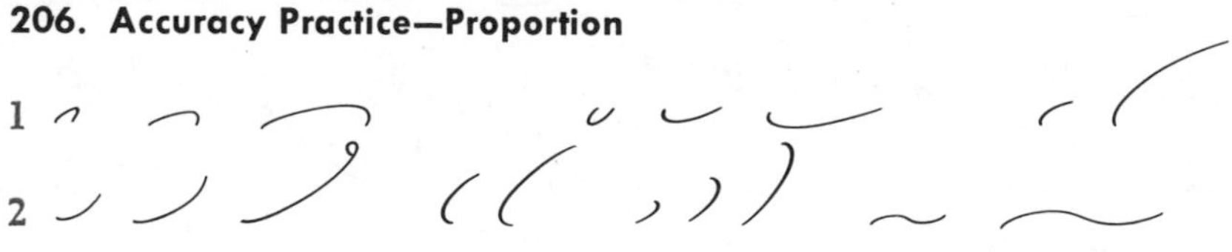

1. You-your, can, go-good; of, our-are-hour, will-well; the, time.
2. There-their, and-end, empty; put, be-by; is-his, for, have; correct, glad.
3. Of all, of our; world, you can, you go; can go, can you.

Reading and Writing Practice

207. Transcription Word Study

curt Rudely brief.

pompous Self-important.

eradicating Eliminating.

pervading Spreading throughout.

208. Telephone Manners

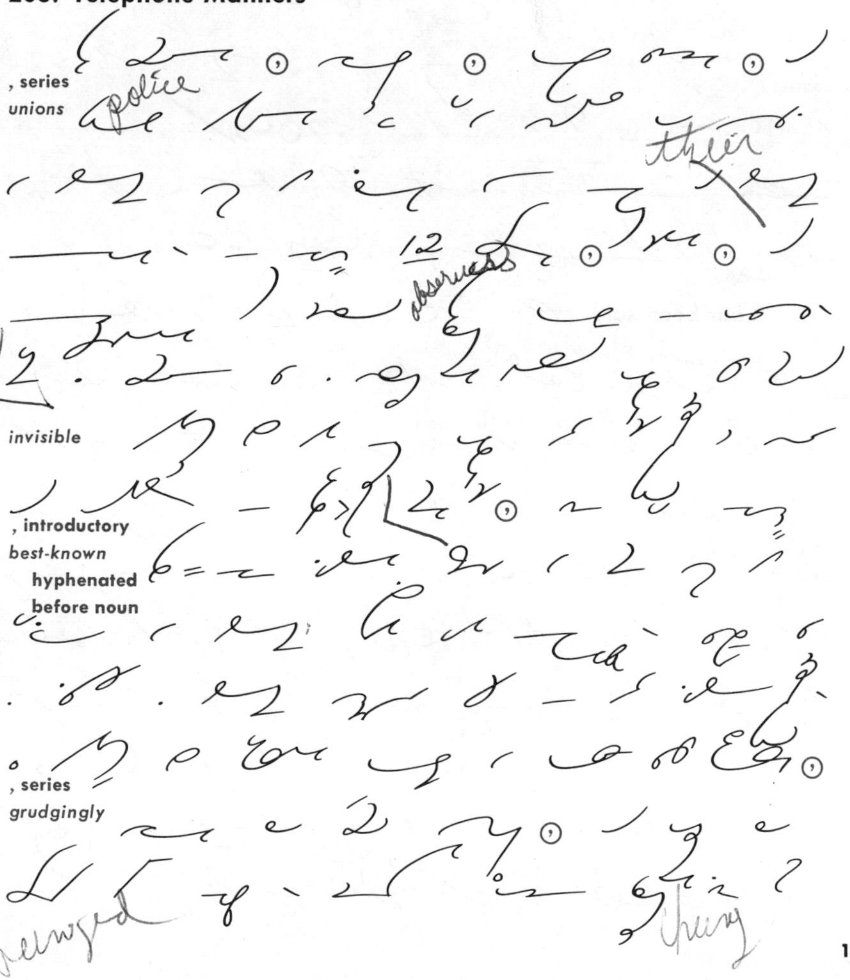

, series
unions

invisible

, introductory
best-known
hyphenated
before noun

, series
grudgingly

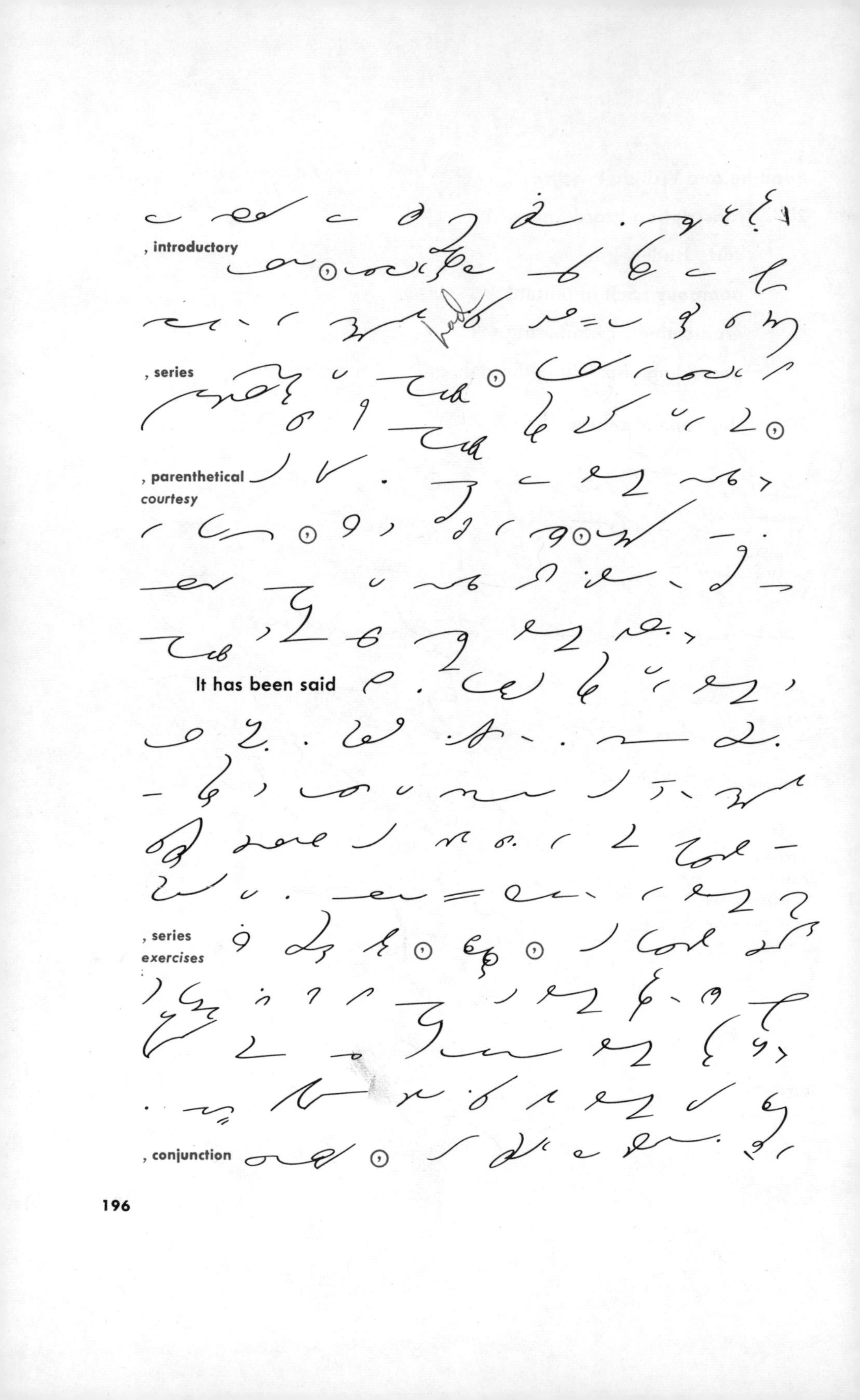

, introductory

, series

, parenthetical
courtesy

It has been said

, series
exercises

, conjunction

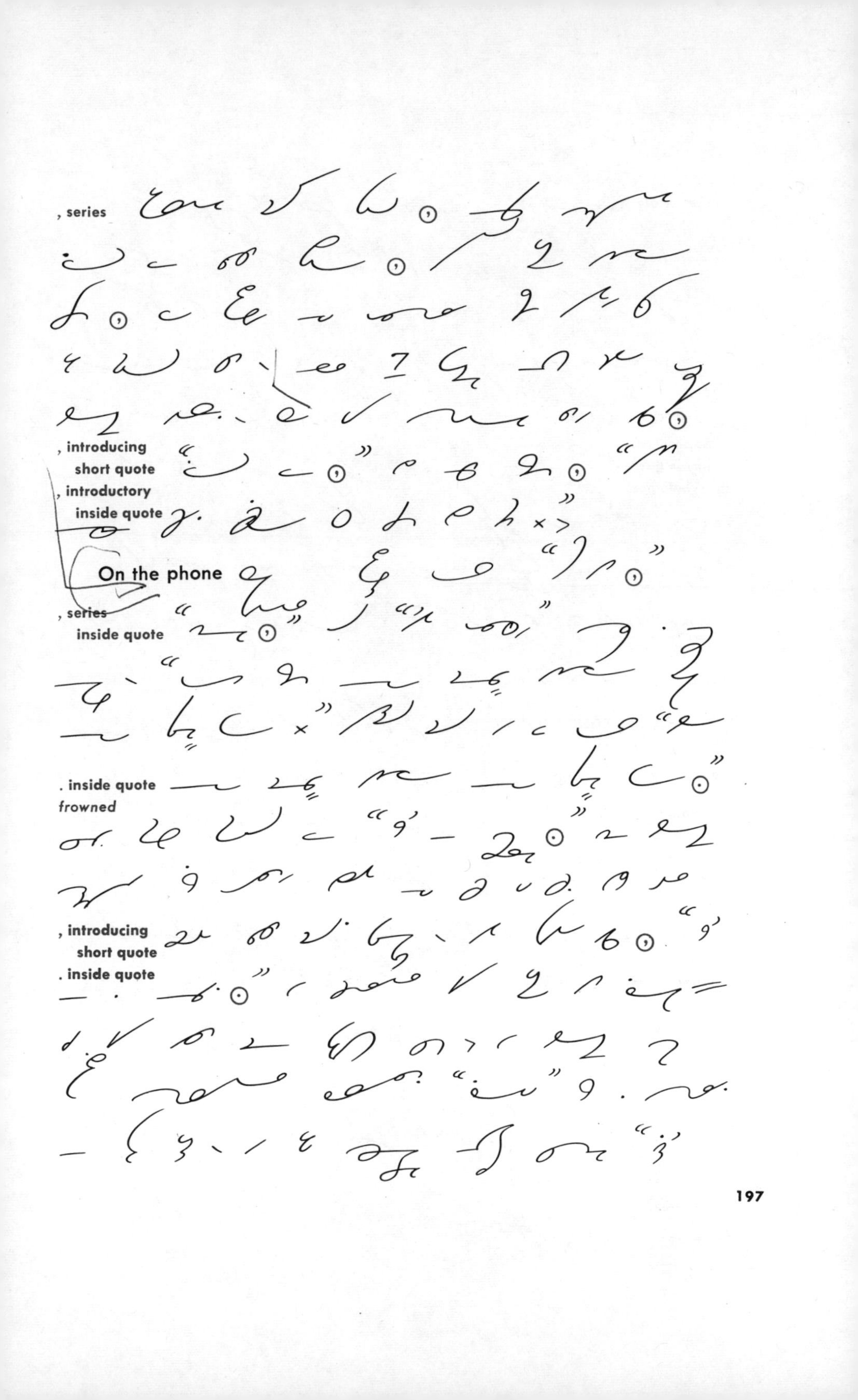

, series

, introducing short quote

, introductory inside quote

On the phone

, series inside quote

. inside quote

frowned

, introducing short quote

. inside quote

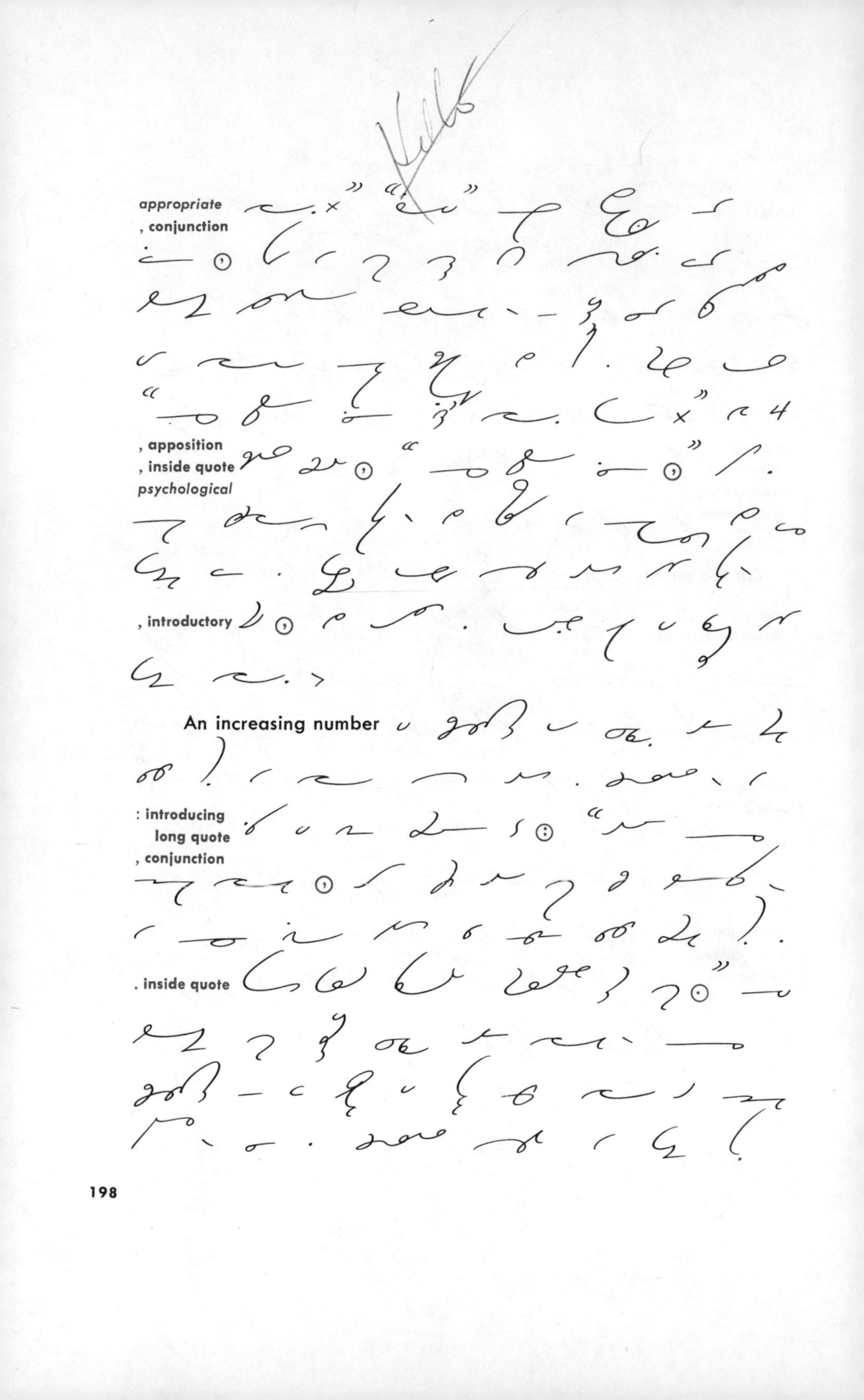

appropriate
, conjunction

, apposition
, inside quote
psychological

, introductory

An increasing number

: introducing long quote
, conjunction

. inside quote

, when clause
frequently
transferred
System's
operators
courteous
supervisor
chief
, series

Operators often record

discs
, series
girl's
, introductory

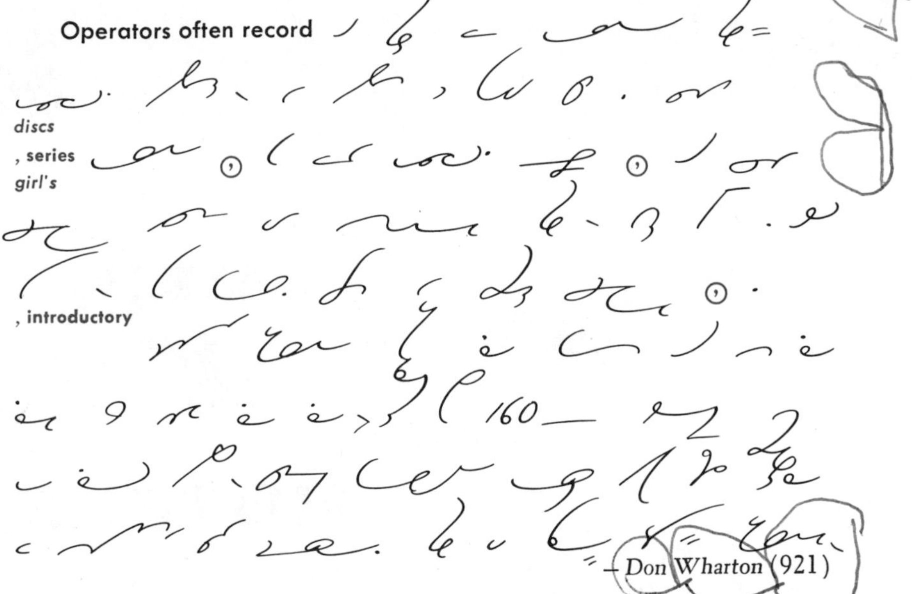

—Don Wharton (921)

7

HOTELS

LESSON 31

209. Brief Forms and Derivatives

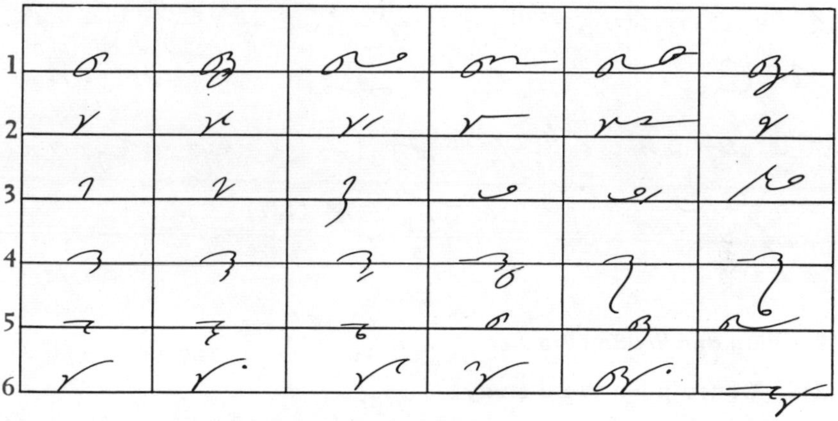

1. How-out, outside, outlet, outcome, outline, outfit.
2. State, states, stated, statement, stateroom, estate.
3. Usual-wish, wished, wishful; regard, regarded, disregard.
4. Consider-consideration, considers-considerations, considered, inconsiderate, considerable, inconsiderably.
5. Instant-instance, instances, instantly; use, useful, useless.
6. Stand, standing, stands, understand, outstanding, misunderstand.

210. Brief Form and Phrase Letter

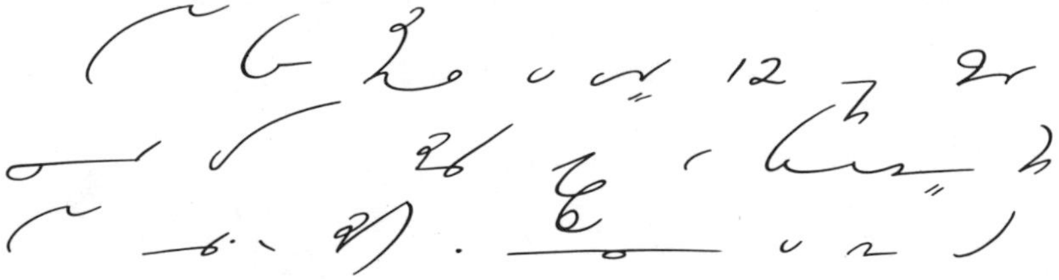

(127)

Reading and Writing Practice

211. Transcription Word Study

ascertaining Finding out.

delinquent Failing in one's duty.

impair To diminish in value.

212

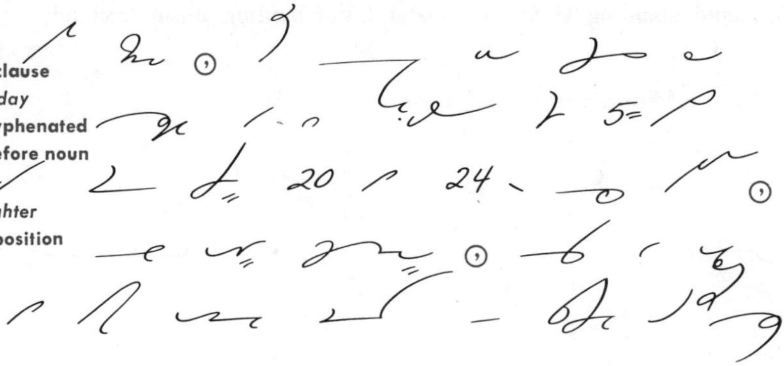

as **clause**

five-day
hyphenated before noun

daughter
, apposition

, when clause
occurred

, introductory
ascertaining

, conjunction
courtesy
pleasant

(176)

213.

Transcribe:
$25

, apposition

, introductory

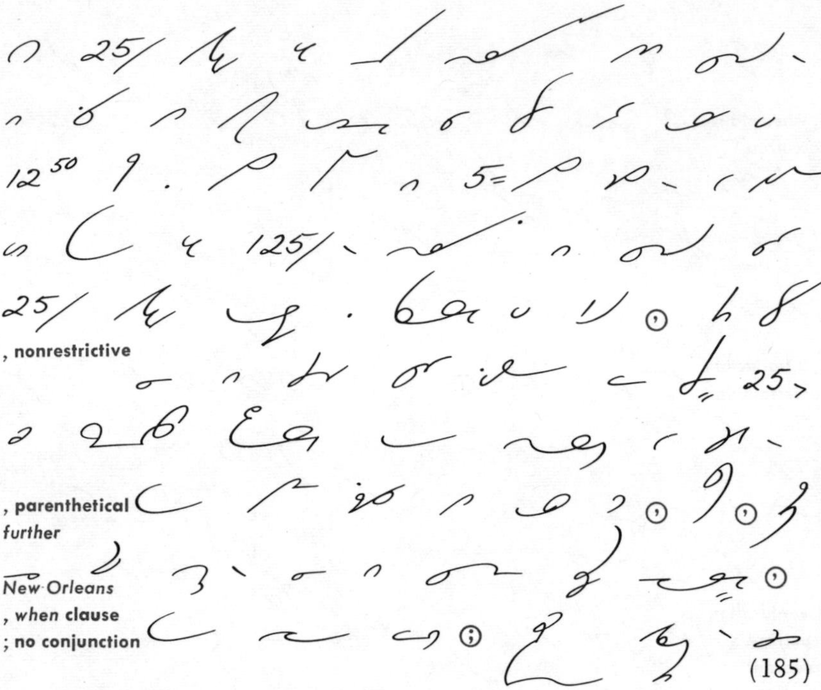

, nonrestrictive

, parenthetical

further

New Orleans

, when clause

; no conjunction

(185)

214.

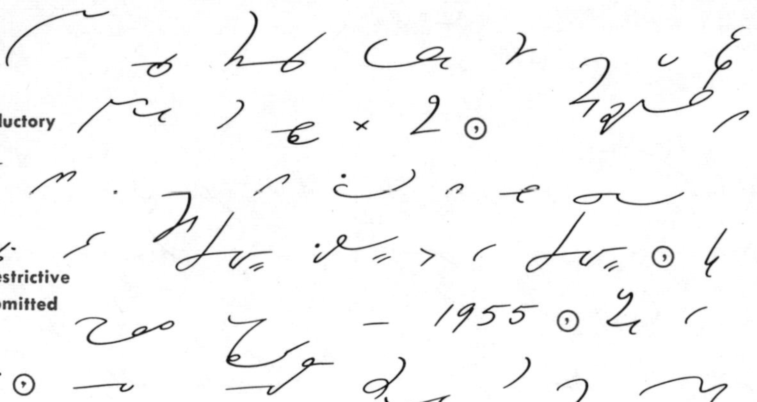

, introductory

annual

, nonrestrictive

, and omitted

, introductory

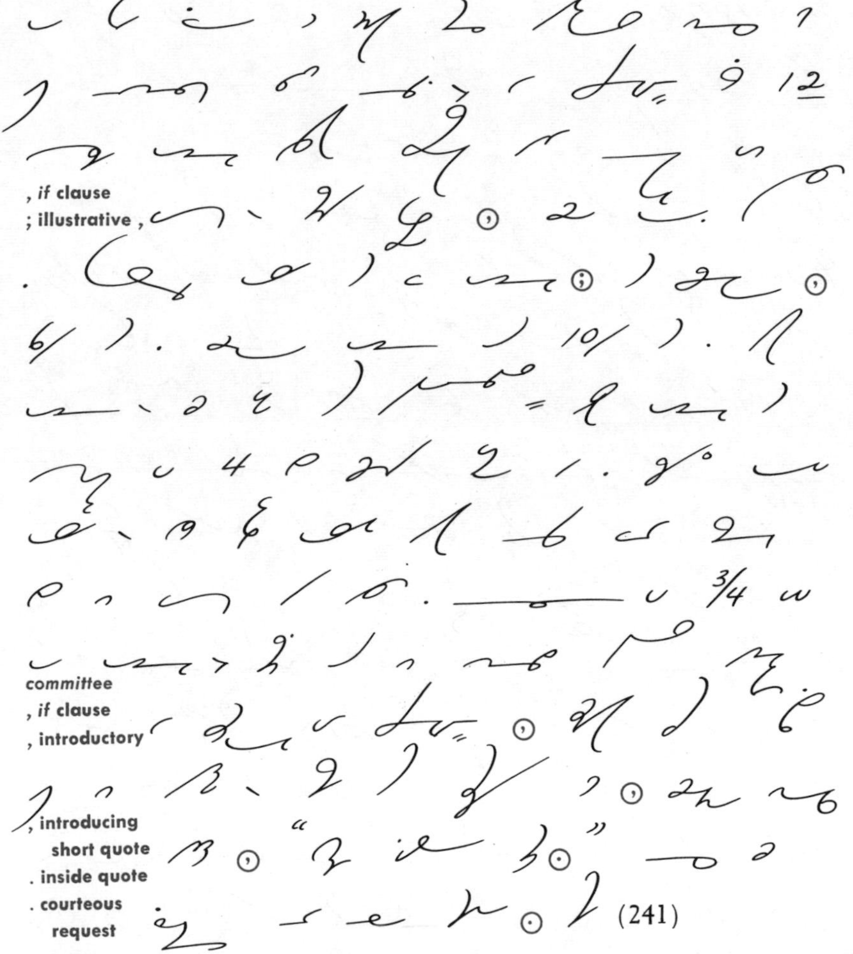

Transcription Quiz. For you to supply: 6 commas—1 comma parenthetical, 2 commas conjunction, 2 commas introductory, 1 comma *if* clause; 1 semicolon because of comma; 2 missing words.

215.

(192)

LESSON 32

216. Useful Business-Letter Phrases

At

1 

With

2 

To

3 

For

4 

1. At this, at this time, at the time, at all times, at last, at least.
2. With the, with this, with that, with those, with them, with which, with which the, with our, with reference.
3. To be, to be able, to be sure, to build, to change, to feel, to find, to fit, to have.
4. For the, for that, for these, for those, for them, for it, for their, for our, for my, for which.

217. Frequent Names

1
2
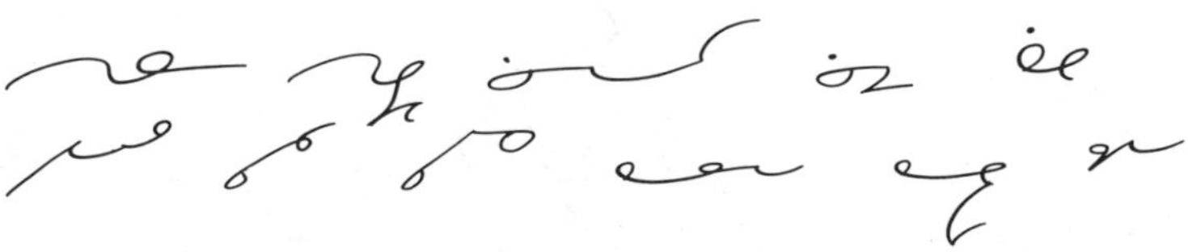

1. Graham, Griffiths, Hamilton, Hanson, Harris.
2. Dorothy, Edith, Edna, Eleanor, Elizabeth, Esther.

Reading and Writing Practice

218. Transcription Word Study

accessible Easy to reach.

forthcoming Approaching.

219.

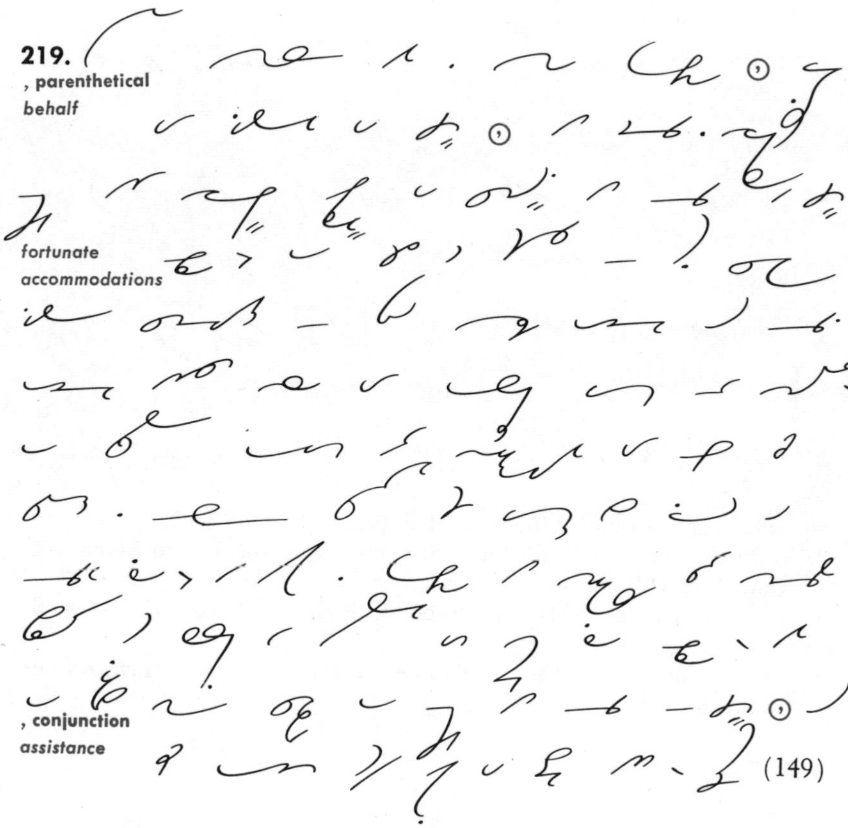

, parenthetical
behalf

fortunate
accommodations

, conjunction
assistance

(149)

220.

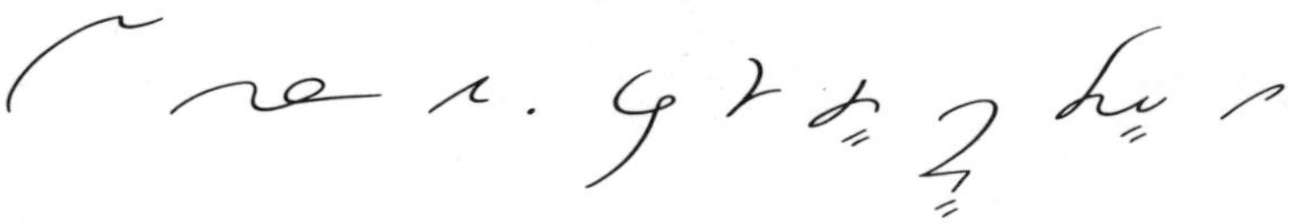

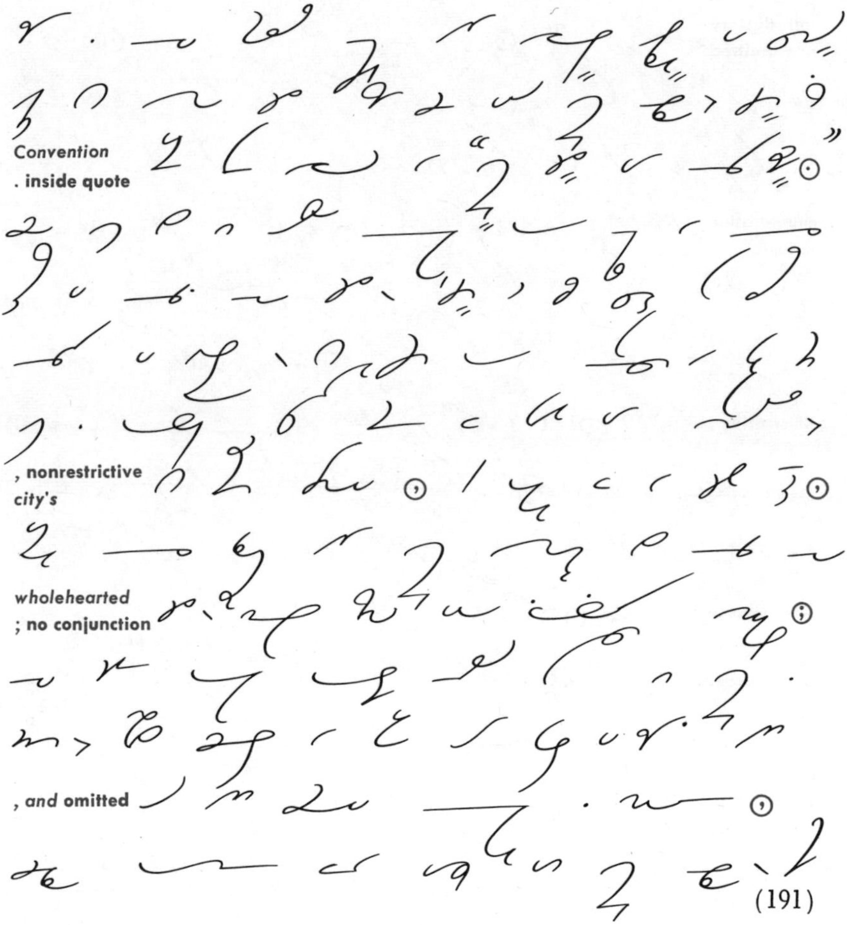

Convention

. inside quote

, nonrestrictive

city's

wholehearted

; no conjunction

, and omitted

(191)

221.

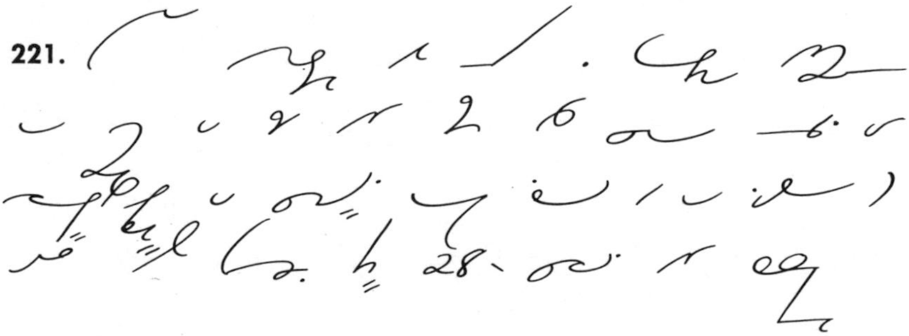

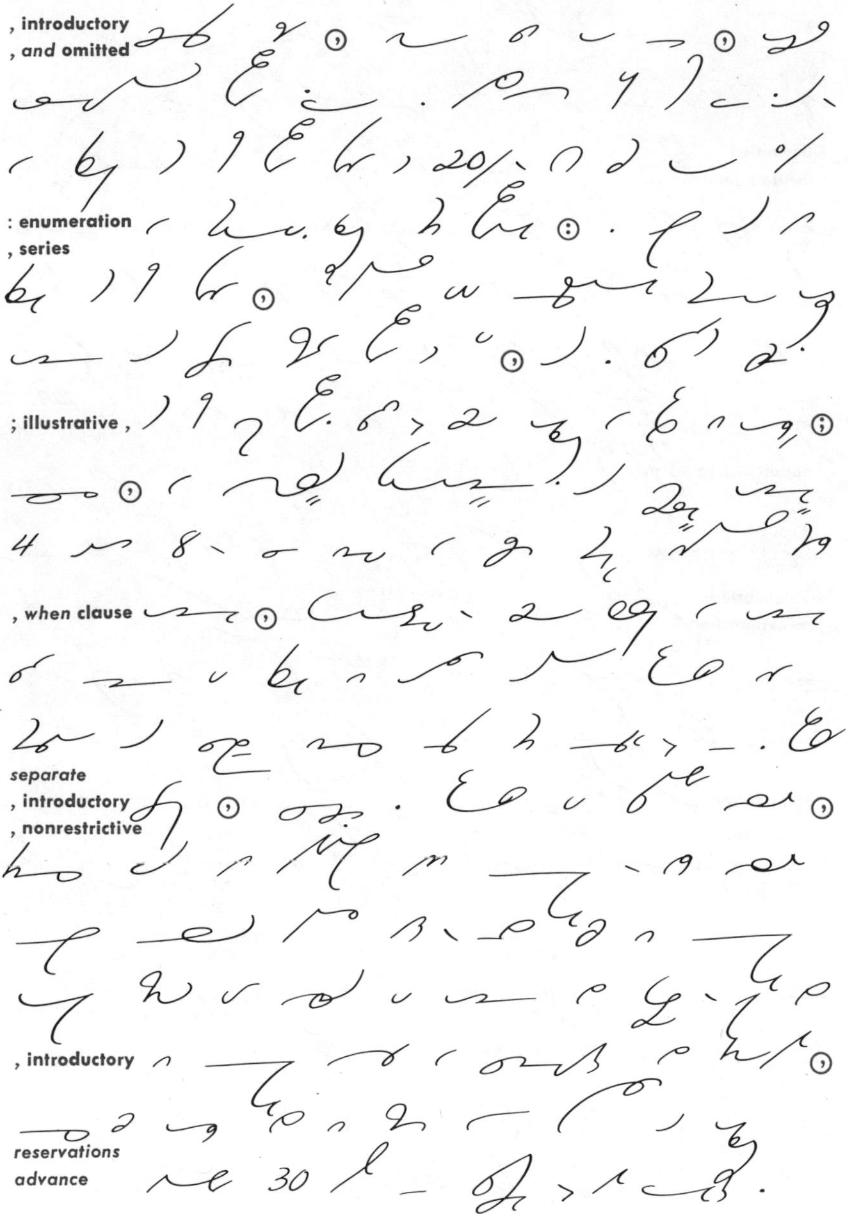
, introductory
, *and* omitted
: enumeration
, series
; illustrative ,
, *when* clause
separate
, introductory
, nonrestrictive
, introductory
reservations
advance

, parenthetical
; because of comma

(289)

222.

textbooks
, if clause
, apposition

; no conjunction
, introducing
short quote
V
. inside quote
Black's

; no conjunction
, introductory

likelihood
, if clause

, as clause
Suite

(210)

Transcription Quiz. For you to supply: 4 commas—1 comma apposition, 1 comma as clause, 2 commas introductory; 1 semicolon no conjunction; 2 missing words.

223.

(167)

LESSON 33

224. Word Families

-ciate, -tiate

1 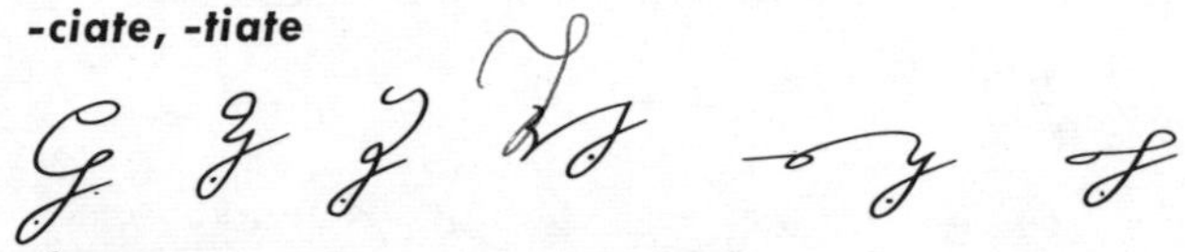

-iance

2 

-ial

3 

-like

4 

-cy, -sy

5 

1. Appreciate, associate, officiate, substantiate, negotiate, initiate.
2. Alliance, appliance, reliance, compliance, self-reliance.
3. Serial, material, aerial, burial, industrial.
4. Sportsmanlike, businesslike, childlike, unlike, dislike.
5. Secrecy, diplomacy, fallacy, lunacy, accuracy, courtesy.

Reading and Writing Practice

225. Transcription Word Study

compliance Act of yielding, conforming, acting upon.

confirm Verify.

excerpt Extract.

226.

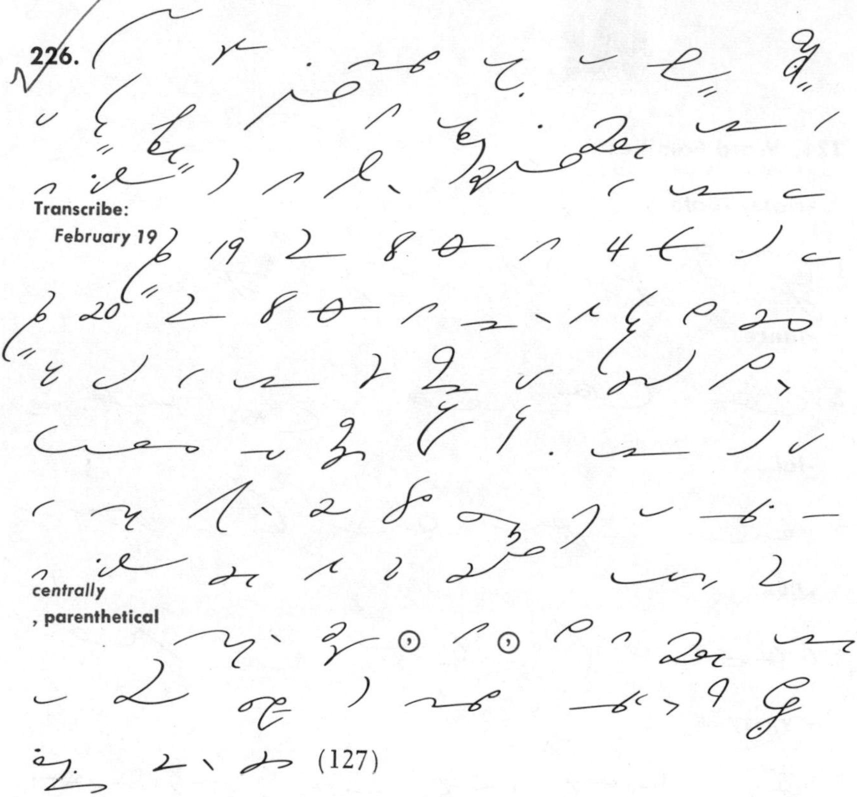

Transcribe:
February 19

centrally

, parenthetical

(127)

227.

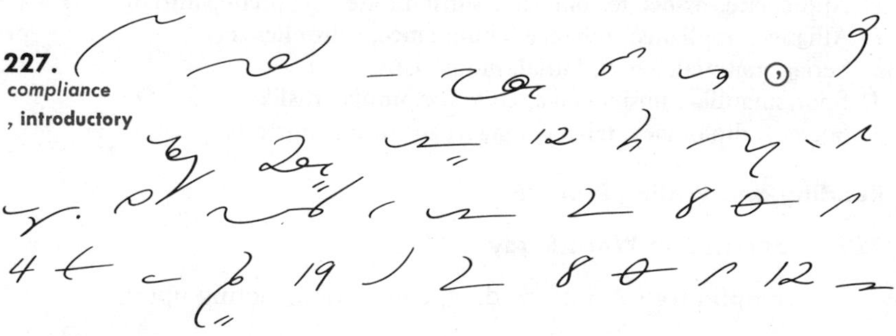

compliance

, introductory

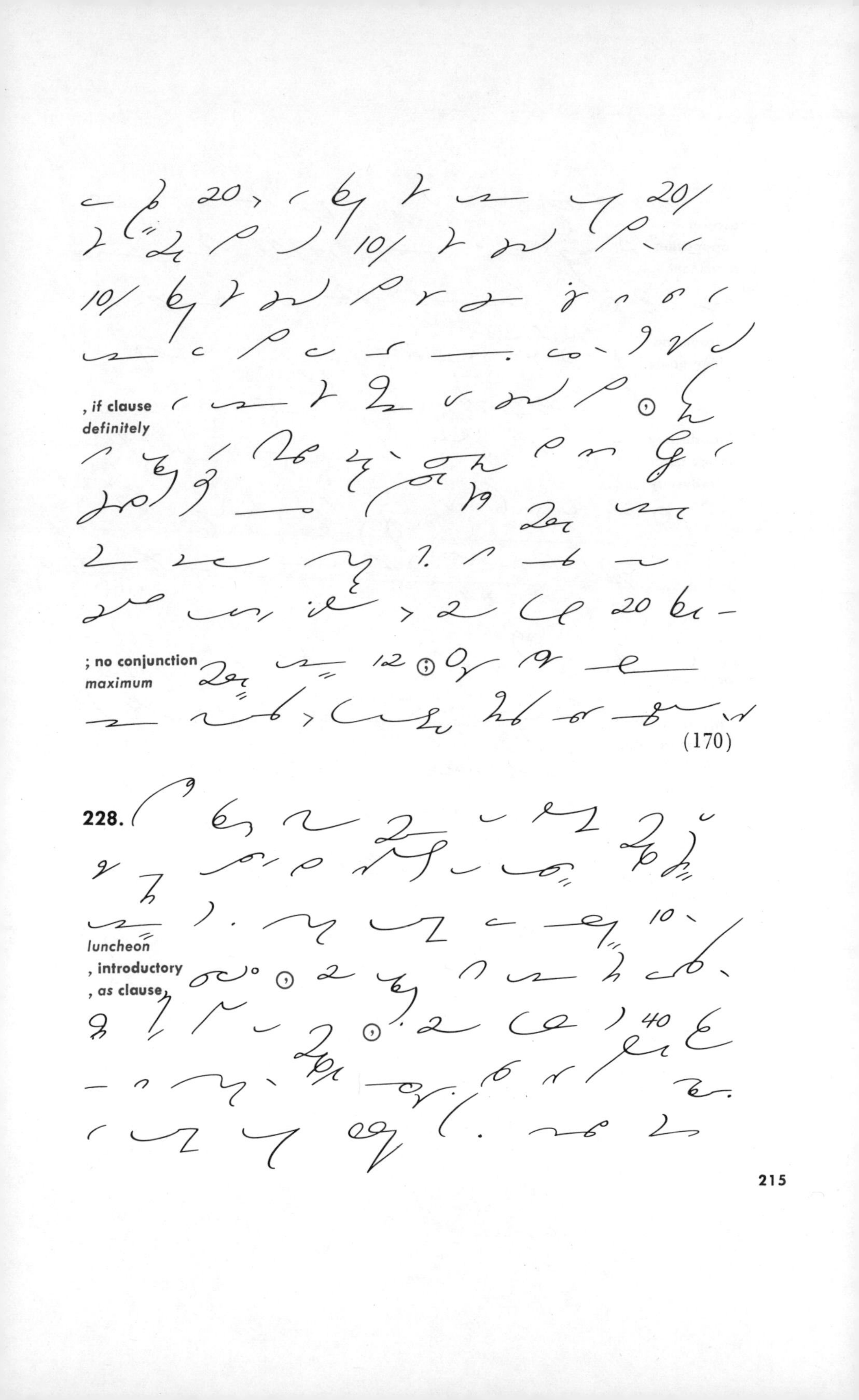

, if clause
definitely

; no conjunction
maximum

(170)

228.

luncheon
, introductory
, as clause

excerpt
, apposition
prominent
: introducing long quote
, introductory
. inside quote
, introductory

(164)

229.

, *as* clause
three-year hyphenated before noun
, conjunction
disappointed
, parenthetical
, *and* omitted
revenue
, introductory
questionnaire

(120)

Transcription Quiz. For you to supply: 4 commas—1 comma introductory, 1 comma apposition, 2 commas series; 1 semicolon because of comma; 2 missing words.

230.

(204)

LESSON 34

231. Word Beginnings

Sub-

1 

Tern-, Term-

2 

Un-

3 

Des-

4 

Pur-

5 

Ul-

6 

1. Submit, substantial, sublease, subway, subdue, substitute, subeditor.
2. Turn, turned, turning, terminate, termination, terminal.
3. Unconscious, unchecked, unfriendly, unlock, unpolished, unwise, unwittingly.
4. Despair, desperate, despise, despondent, destined, destitute, destiny.

5. Purport, purported, purple, pursue, pursuance, pursued, purvey, purveyor.
6. Ulterior, ultimate, ultimately, ultimatum, ultramodern.

232. Geographical Expressions

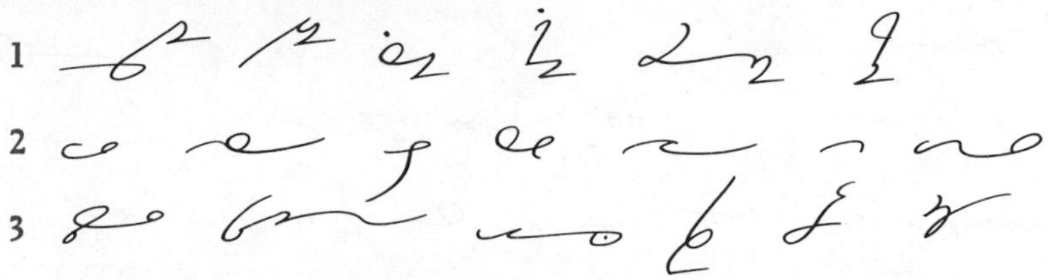

1. Madison, Dawson, Harrison, Hutchinson, Ferguson, Atchison.
2. Oregon, California, Nevada, Arizona, Colorado, Kansas, Oklahoma.
3. Italy, Portugal, Romania, Japan, Spain, Sweden.

Reading and Writing Practice

233. Transcription Word Study

flexible Capable of being modified or changed.

booked to capacity Full.

palate Taste.

234.

, introductory
secure

(154)

235.
requested
, as clause

booked
, parenthetical

, introductory
brochure

, series

, *when* clause

up-to-date hyphenated before noun

, apposition

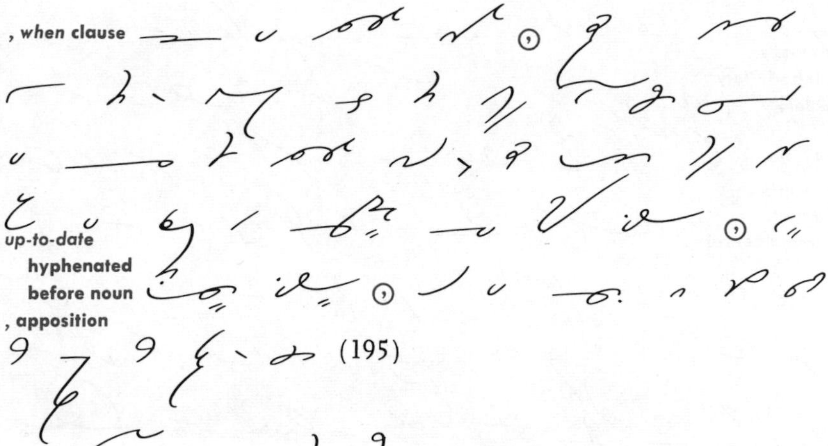

(195)

236.

, conjunction

hazard

, introductory

employees

, nonrestrictive

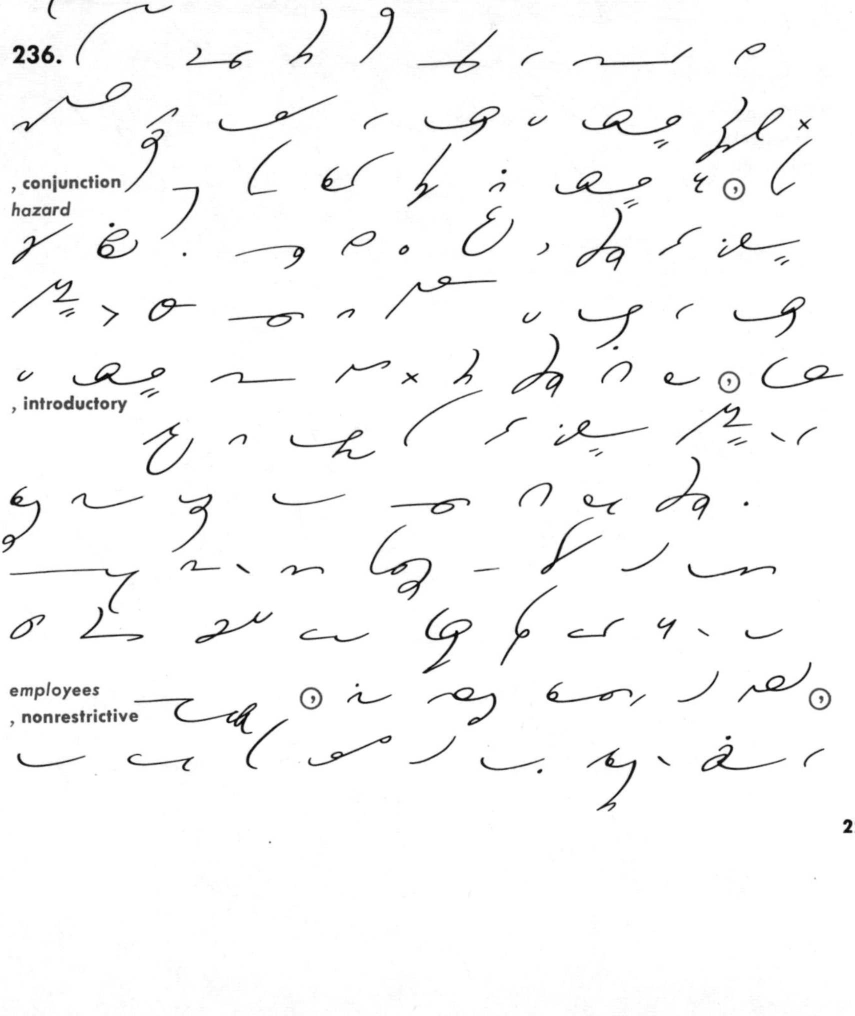

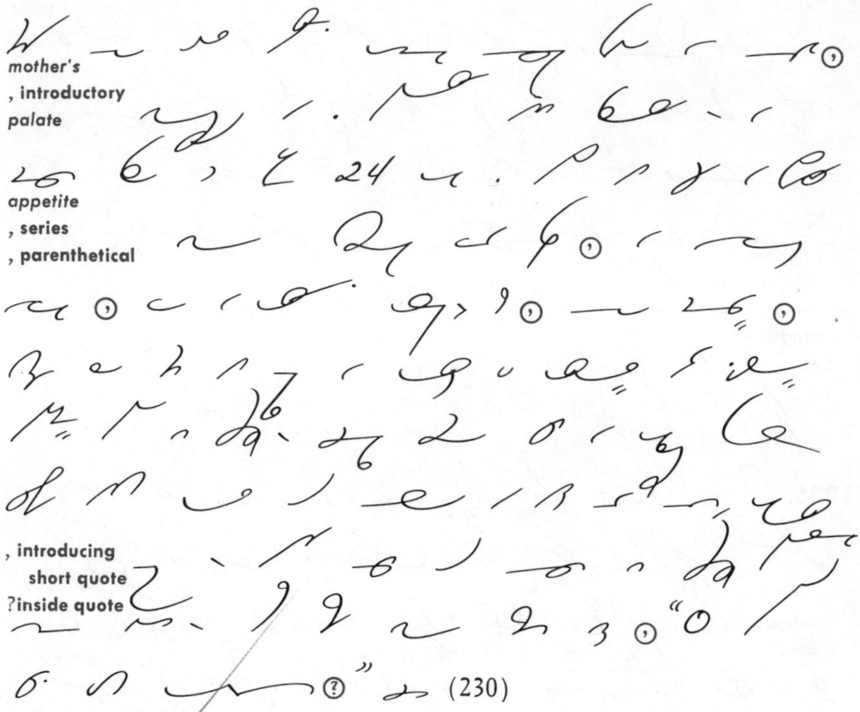

mother's
, introductory
palate
appetite
, series
, parenthetical
, introducing short quote
?inside quote

(230)

237.

five-day hyphenated before noun
, introductory
, series
Teddy bear
, apposition
developed

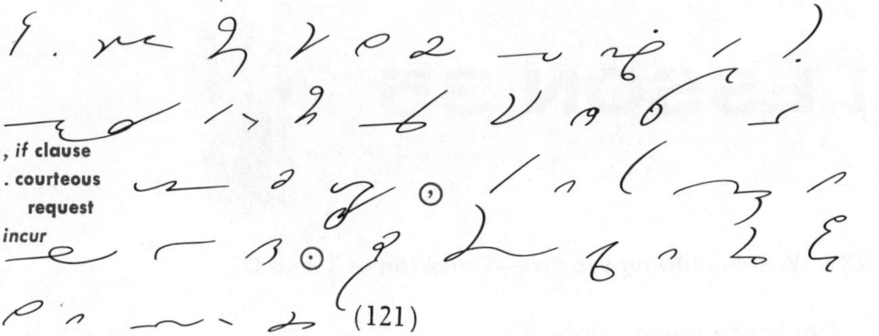

, *if* clause

. courteous request

incur

(121)

Transcription Quiz. For you to supply: 4 commas—2 commas introductory, 1 comma introducing short quote, 1 comma *if* clause; 1 semicolon because of comma; 2 missing words.

238.

(121)

LESSON 35

239. Word-Building Practice—Omission of T and D

T in Seven Monosyllables

1 

-ct

2 

-est, -ist

3 

Omission of D

4 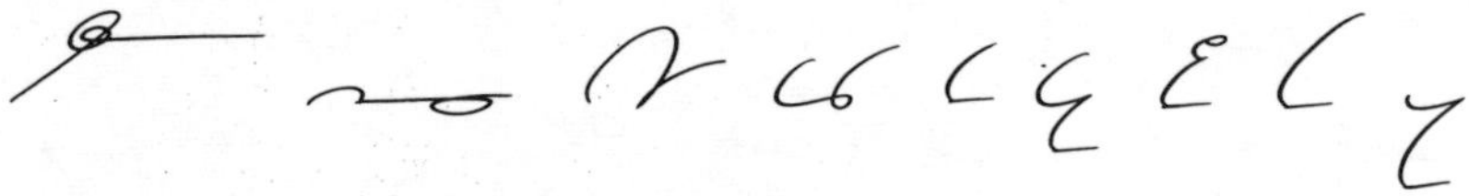

1. Test, rest, best, first, past, last, tested, lasting.
2. Fact, contract, attract, collect, act, reflect, conflict.
3. Kindest, longest, nearest, fairest, capitalist, chemist, humorist.
4. Diamond, command, dividend, pretend, pound, propound, expound, bound, rebound.

Reading and Writing Practice

240. Transcription Word Study

forerunner Predecessor.

commodious Large and comfortable.

migration Movement from one place or country to another.

grandeur Magnificence, greatness.

241. Speaking of United States Hotels

Oddly

, introductory

The explanation for this

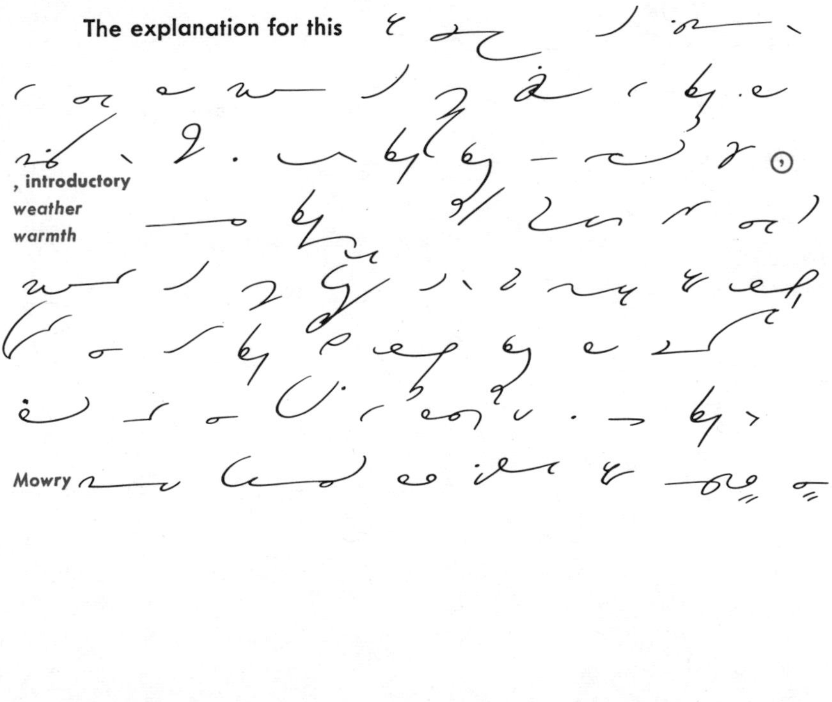

, introductory

weather

warmth

Mowry

, nonrestrictive
colonial

Council
, series

After the Revolution,

, series
Philadelphia

Fraunces
hotel's
bade

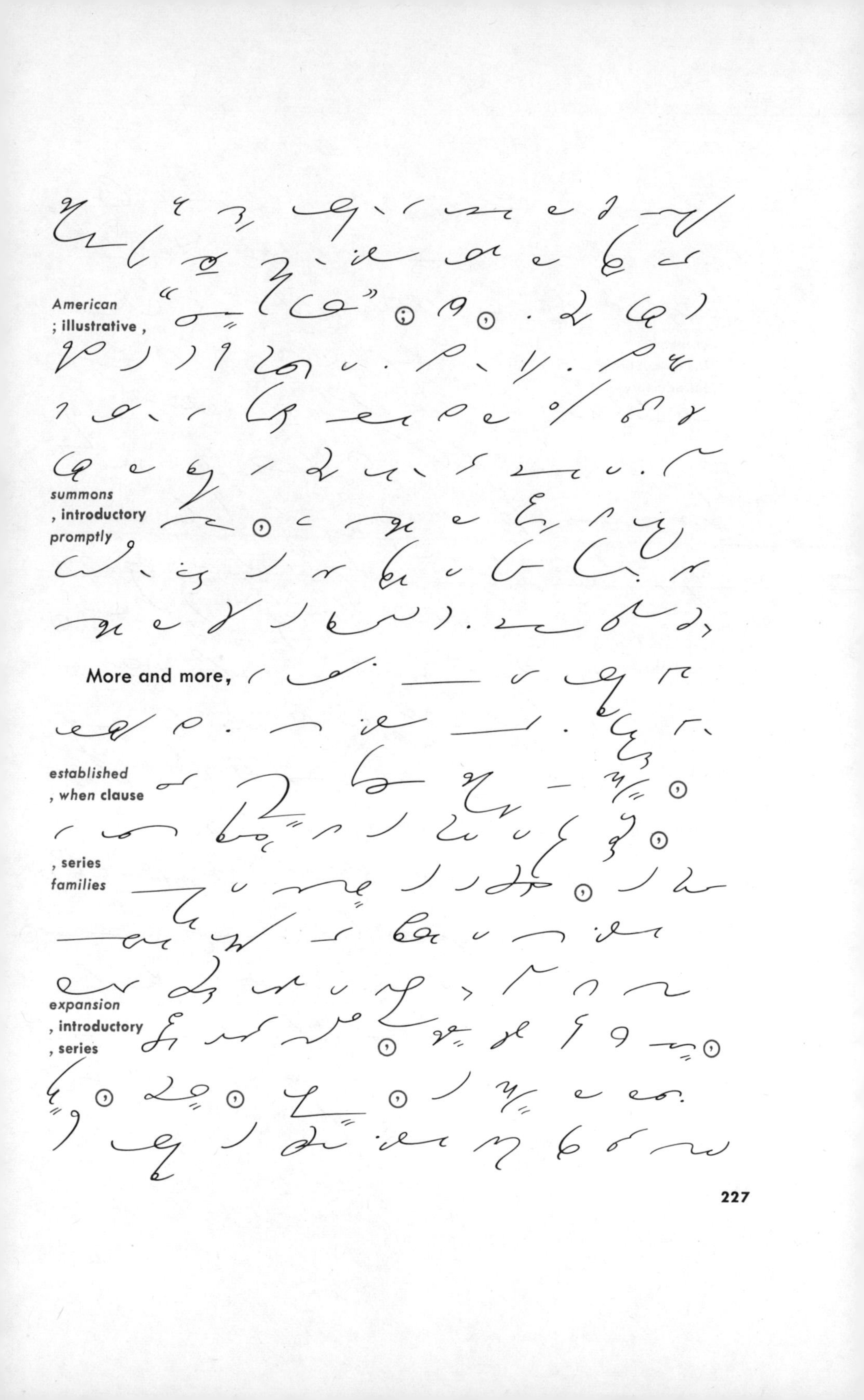

American
; illustrative ,

summons
, introductory
promptly

More and more,

established
, when clause

, series
families

expansion
, introductory
, series

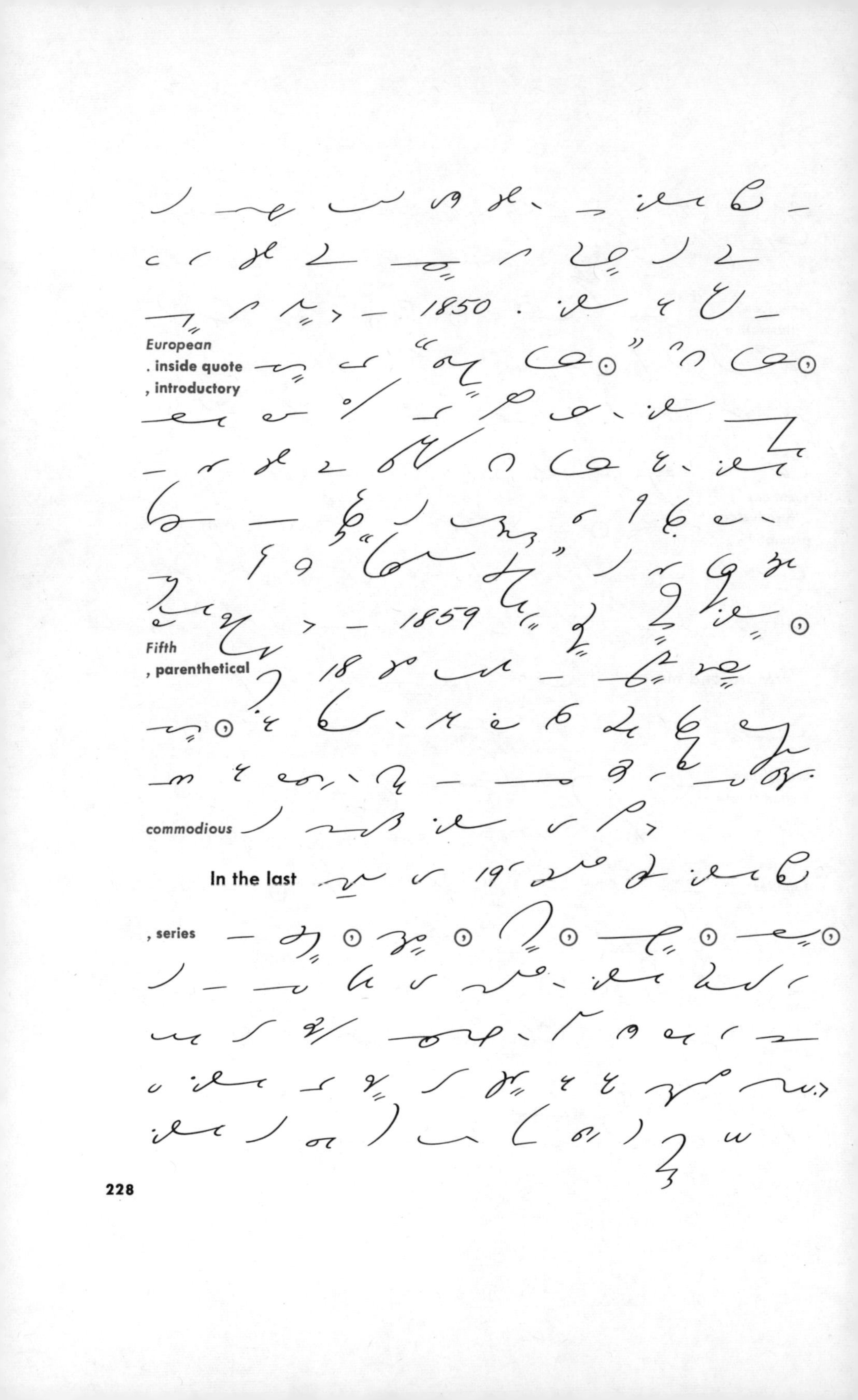

European

. inside quote

, introductory

Fifth

, parenthetical

commodious

In the last

, series

, series
diplomacy
economic

discussed
Waldorf-Astoria

1893-
1929

; because of comma
, apposition

present-day
hyphenated
before noun

The new 50

22

restaurants
, series

(962)

8

BANKING

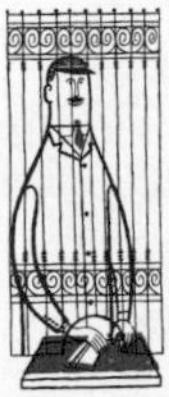

LESSON 36

242. Brief Forms and Derivatives

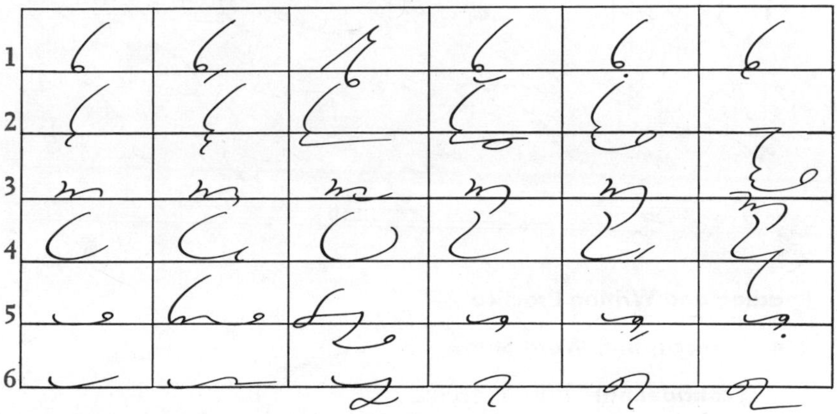

1. Belief-believe, believed, disbelief-disbelieve, believer, believing, beliefs-believes.
2. Business, businesses, businessmen, businessman, businesslike, unbusinesslike.
3. Success, successes, successor, successful, successive, unsuccessful.
4. Bill, bills, billed; value, valued, valuable.
5. Let-letter, booklet, pamphlet; request, requested, requesting.
6. Will-well, welcome, welfare; keep-company, accompany, accompaniment.

243. Brief Form and Phrase Letter

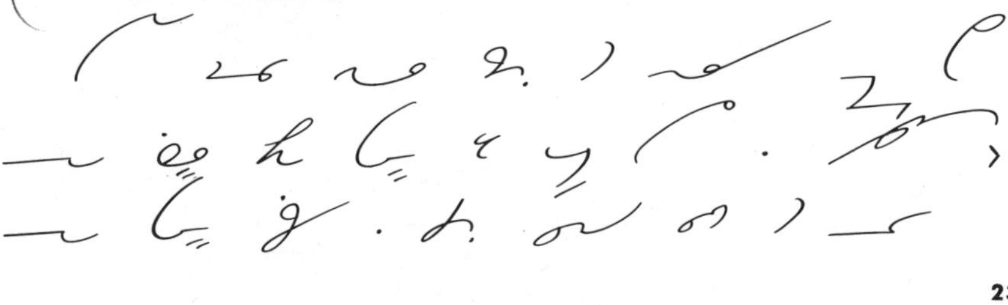

(130)

Reading and Writing Practice

244. Transcription Word Study

confidential Private, secret.

red tape Official routine.

modest Unpretentious.

245.

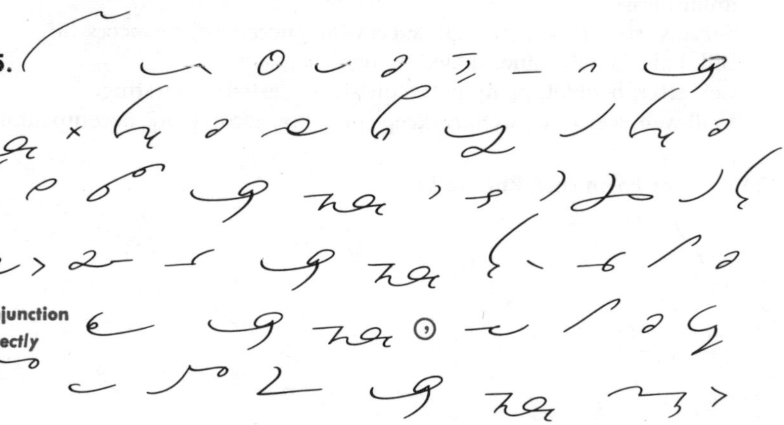

, conjunction

indirectly

National's
, introductory

, introductory

, introductory
, *if* clause
advise

(201)

246.

withdraw

, introductory
balance

pleasant
, and omitted

, if clause
reopen

(110)

247.
, when clause
inside quote

neighborhood
, apposition
, if clause

, introductory
accumulated
; illustrative ,

, series
children's

, when clause
cosigners
indorsers

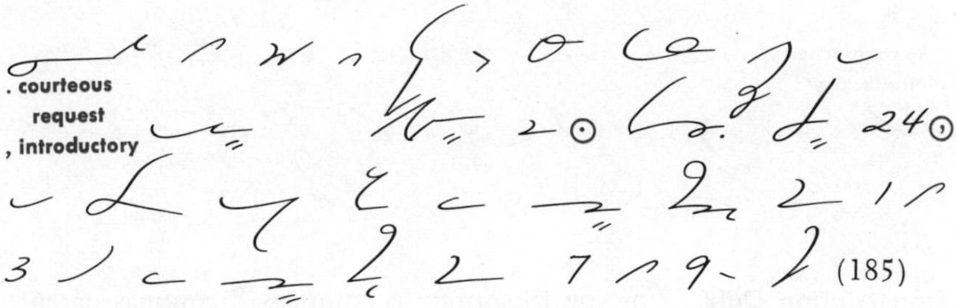

. courteous request
, introductory

(185)

248.

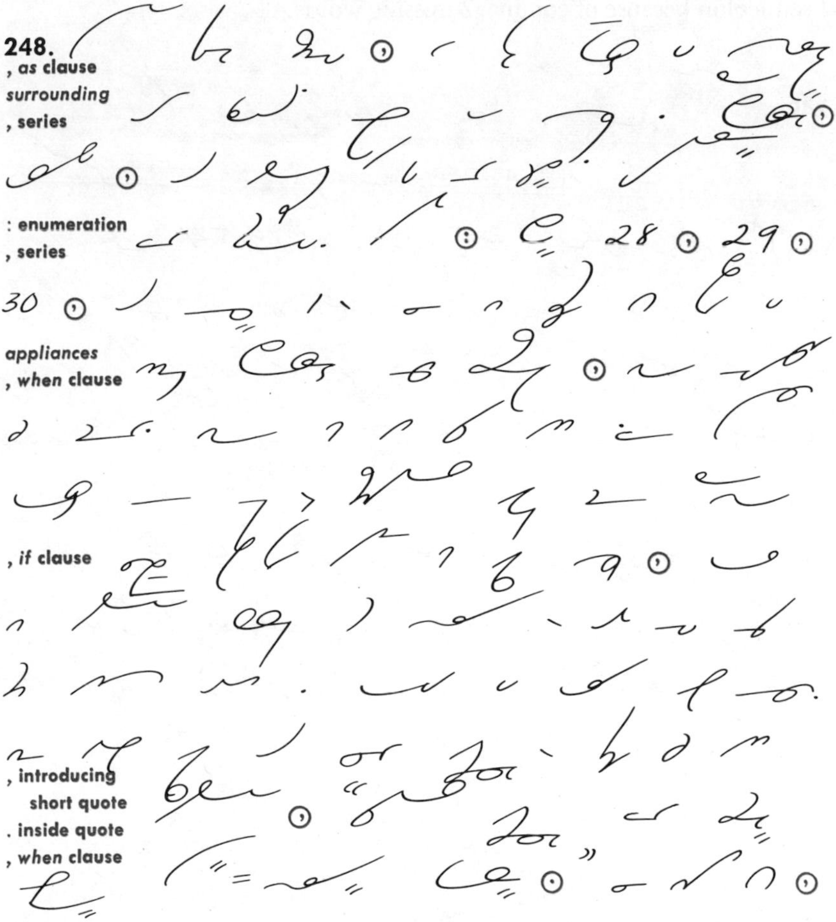

, as clause
surrounding
, series
: enumeration
, series
appliances
, when clause
, *if* clause
, introducing short quote
. inside quote
, when clause

; no conjunction
, introductory

(172)

Transcription Quiz. For you to supply: 6 commas—2 commas parenthetical, 1 comma *when* clause, 1 comma introductory, 2 commas series; 1 semicolon because of comma; 2 missing words.

249.

(112)

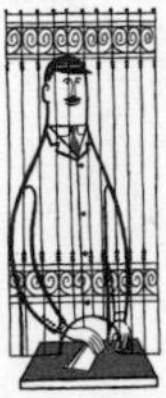

LESSON 37

250. Useful Business-Letter Phrases

To

1 

And

2 

There

3 

If

4 

1. To consider, to cover, to get, to carry, to collect, to go, to the.
2. And are, and will, and is, and say, and that, and the, and let, and will be.
3. There is, there is not, there was, there was not, there wasn't, there are, there are not, there will, there will be.
4. If you, if you are, if you are not, if you can, if you cannot, if you have, if you will, if you will not.

251. Frequent Names

1 

2 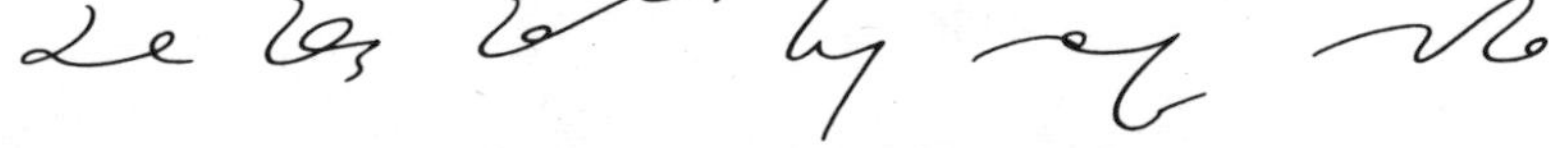

1. Henderson, Hoffman, Hughes, Hunter, Jackson, Johnson, Johnston.
2. Felix, Francis, Frederick, George, Gilbert, Godfrey.

Reading and Writing Practice

252. Transcription Word Study

reconciling Adjusting.

discrepancy Difference, disagreement.

executor A person appointed by the maker of a will to carry out the terms of the will.

253.

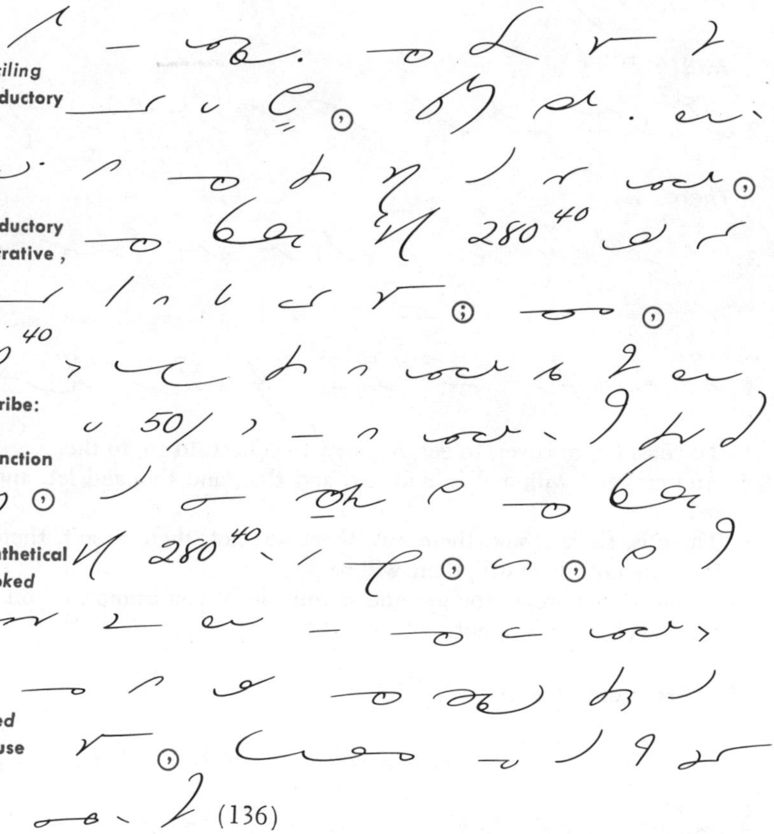

reconciling
, introductory
stubs
, introductory
; illustrative ,
Transcribe:
$50
, conjunction
, parenthetical
overlooked
canceled
, if clause

(136)

254.

, introductory
difference

exists
rechecking
, introductory

(107)

255.

, parenthetical
, nonrestrictive

473897

principal

(95)

256.

Transcribe:
$40,000

patronage
, introductory

(98)

257.

, nonrestrictive
premium

: introducing
long quote

, series
; because of comma

; no conjunction
, introductory
. inside quote
, *as* clause

, parenthetical

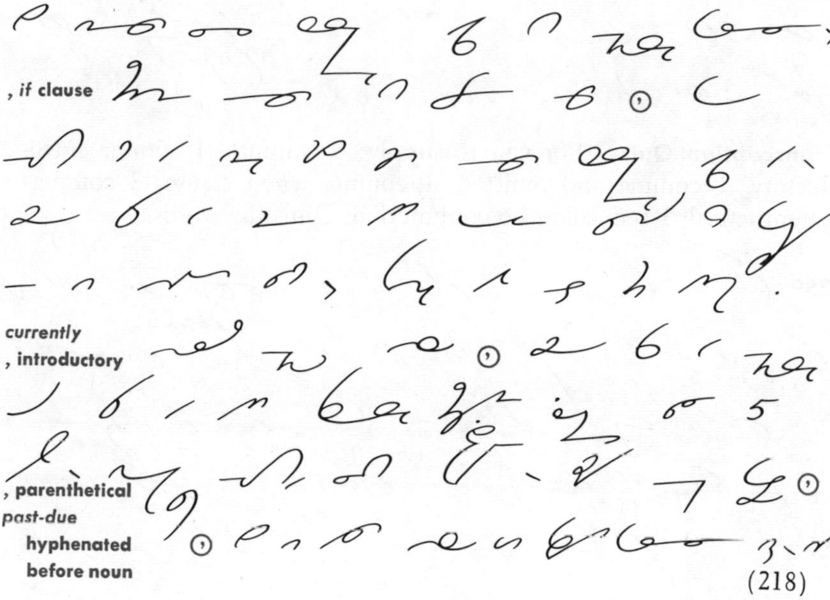

, *if clause*

currently

, *introductory*

, *parenthetical*

past-due
hyphenated before noun

(218)

258.

, *as clause*

Felix

resources

, *introductory*

(136)

Transcription Quiz. For you to supply: 5 commas—1 comma introductory, 1 comma *and* omitted, 1 comma *when* clause, 2 commas parenthetical; 1 semicolon no conjunction; 2 missing words.

259.

(174)

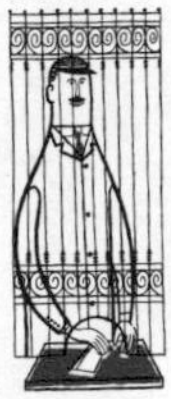

LESSON 38

260. Word Families

-minate

1 

-cate

2 

-mentation

3 

Past Tense

4 

1. Eliminate, discriminate, incriminate, terminate.
2. Duplicate, abdicate, educate, indicate, certificate, allocate.
3. Experimentation, instrumentation, argumentation, implementation, regimentation.
4. Examined, remained, determined, mended.

Reading and Writing Practice

261. Transcription Word Study

severe Extreme, harsh. (Do not confuse with *sever*, which means "to cut.")

liquidated Discharged, paid off.

262.

severe
, introductory

, parenthetical
modernizing

encourage
, series
, *if* clause

, nonrestrictive

(107)

263.

; illustrative ,
features
: enumeration

, and omitted

, apposition

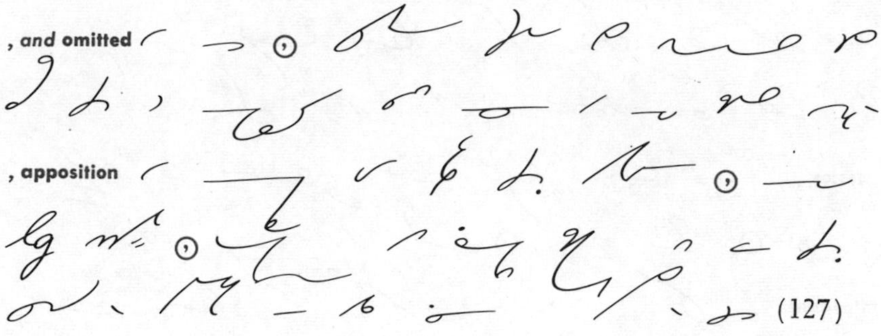

(127)

264.

, parenthetical

, apposition

Transcribe:

86 Street

, introductory

; no conjunction

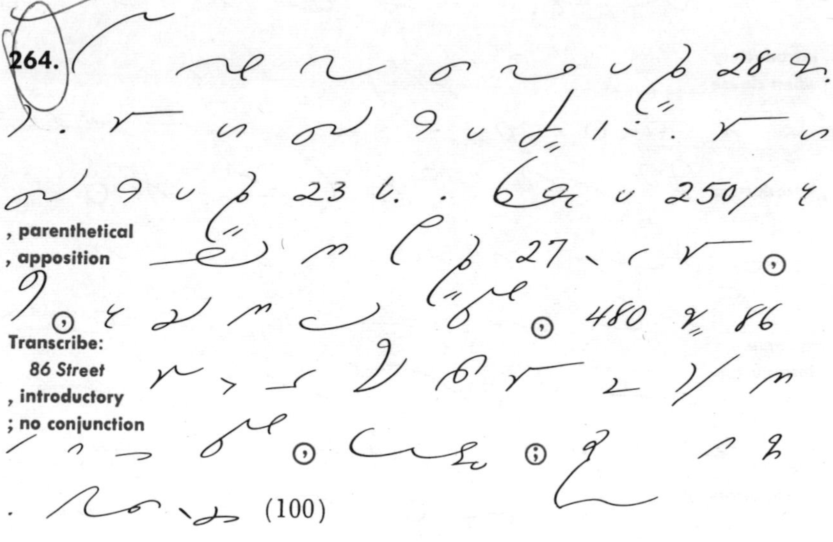

(100)

265.

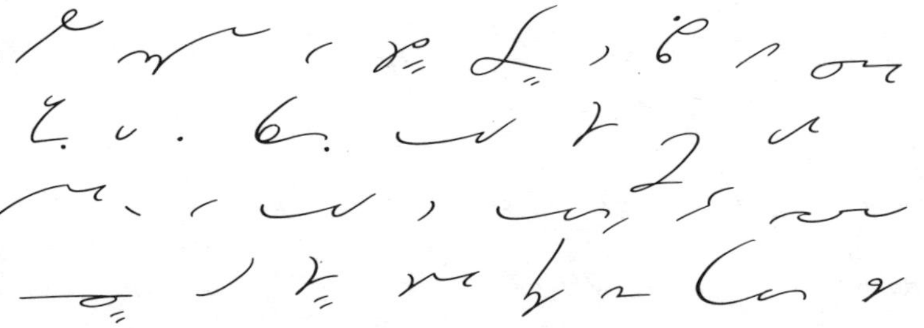

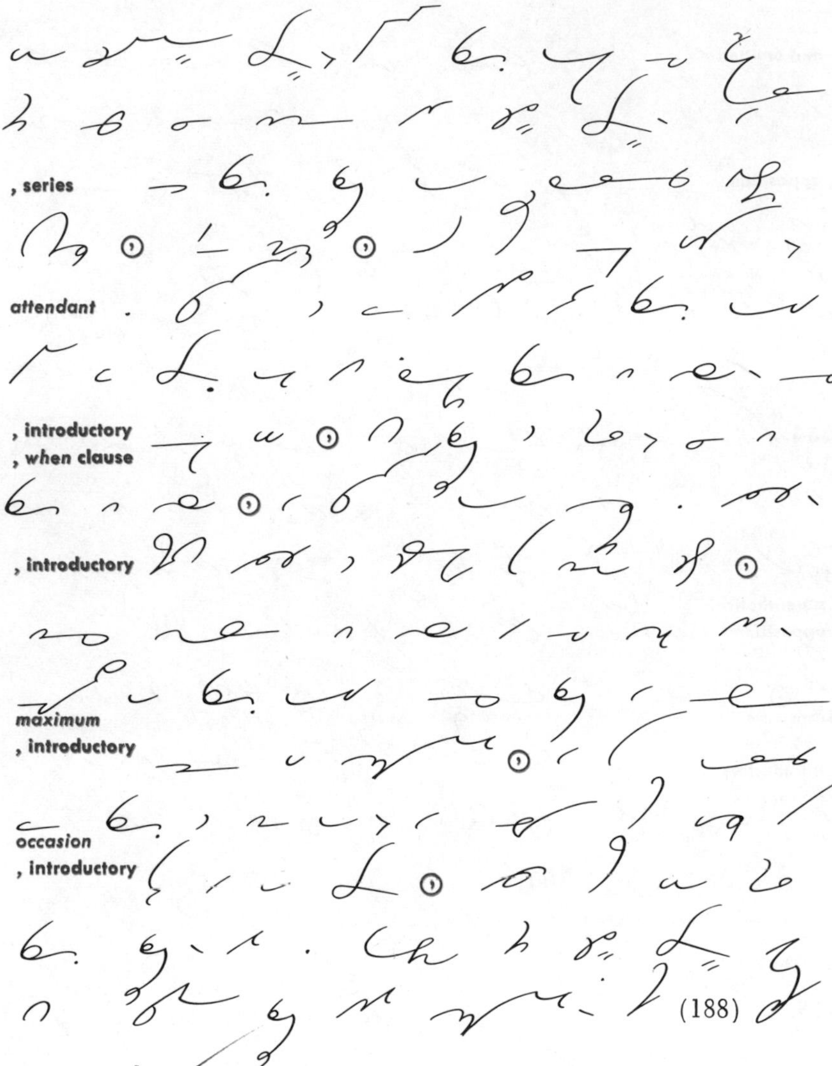

266. 

Transcribe:
No. 49783

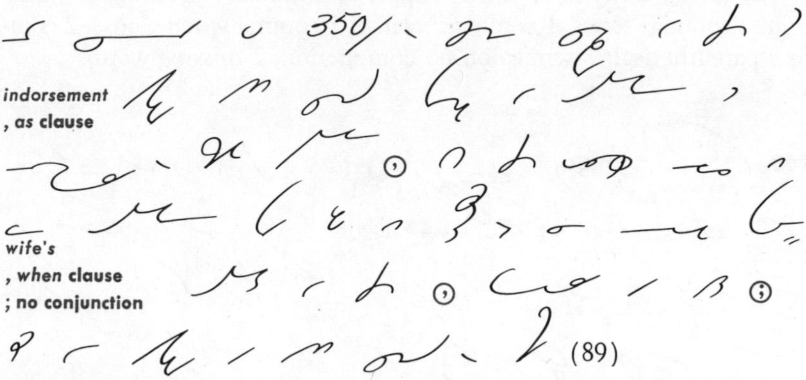

indorsement
, as clause
wife's
, when clause
; no conjunction

(89)

267.

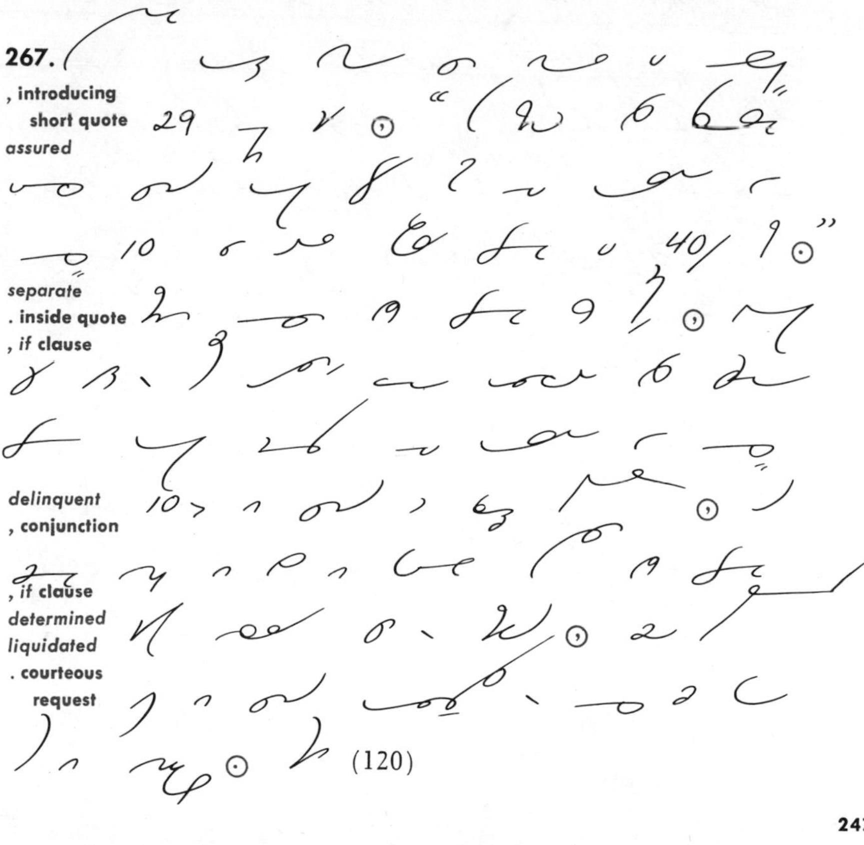

, introducing short quote
assured
separate
. inside quote
, if clause
delinquent
, conjunction
, if clause
determined
liquidated
. courteous request

(120)

Transcription Quiz. For you to supply: 7 commas—1 comma conjunction, 2 commas series, 1 comma *if* clause, 1 comma *when* clause, 2 commas parenthetical; 1 semicolon no conjunction; 2 missing words.

268.

(171)

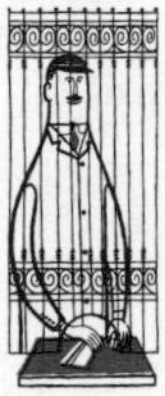

LESSON 39

269. Word Endings

-gram

1 

-hood

2 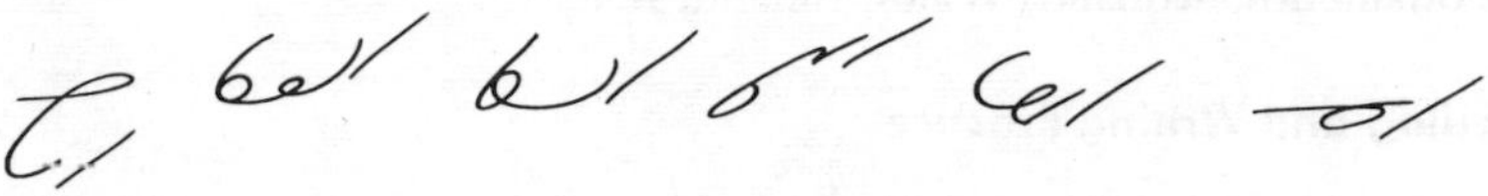

-ification

3 

-ingly

4 

-ings

5 

-lity

6 

1. Program, diagram, monogram, radiogram, telegram.
2. Neighborhood, parenthood, childhood, adulthood, priesthood, manhood.
3. Notification, modification, fortification, gratification, ratification, specification, specifications.

4. Willingly, seemingly, surprisingly, entertainingly, grudgingly, jokingly.
5. Feelings, engravings, shavings, greetings, castings, mornings.
6. Facility, ability, dependability, probability, sensibilities, possibilities.

270. Geographical Expressions

1. New Orleans, New York, New London, New Bedford, New Britain, Newark.
2. Alaska, Arizona, Arkansas, California, Colorado, Connecticut, Delaware.
3. Portsmouth, Scotland, Wales, Ireland, Belfast.

Reading and Writing Practice

271. Transcription Word Study

statutes Laws enacted by a legislature.

rebate Repayment.

272.

, introductory

, introductory

: introducing long quote

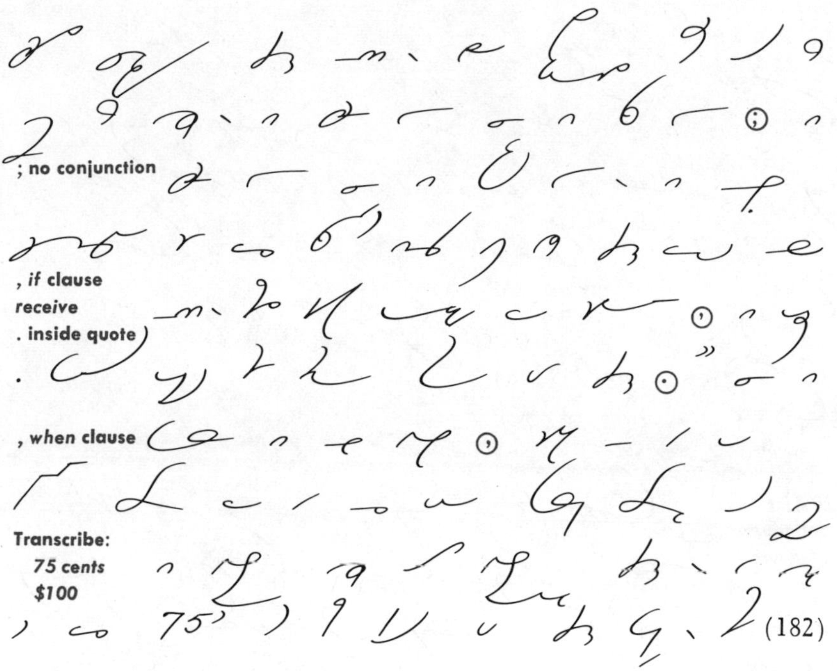

; no conjunction

, *if* clause

receive

. inside quote

, *when* clause

Transcribe:

75 cents

$100

(182)

273.

devoted

, introductory

, introductory

, series

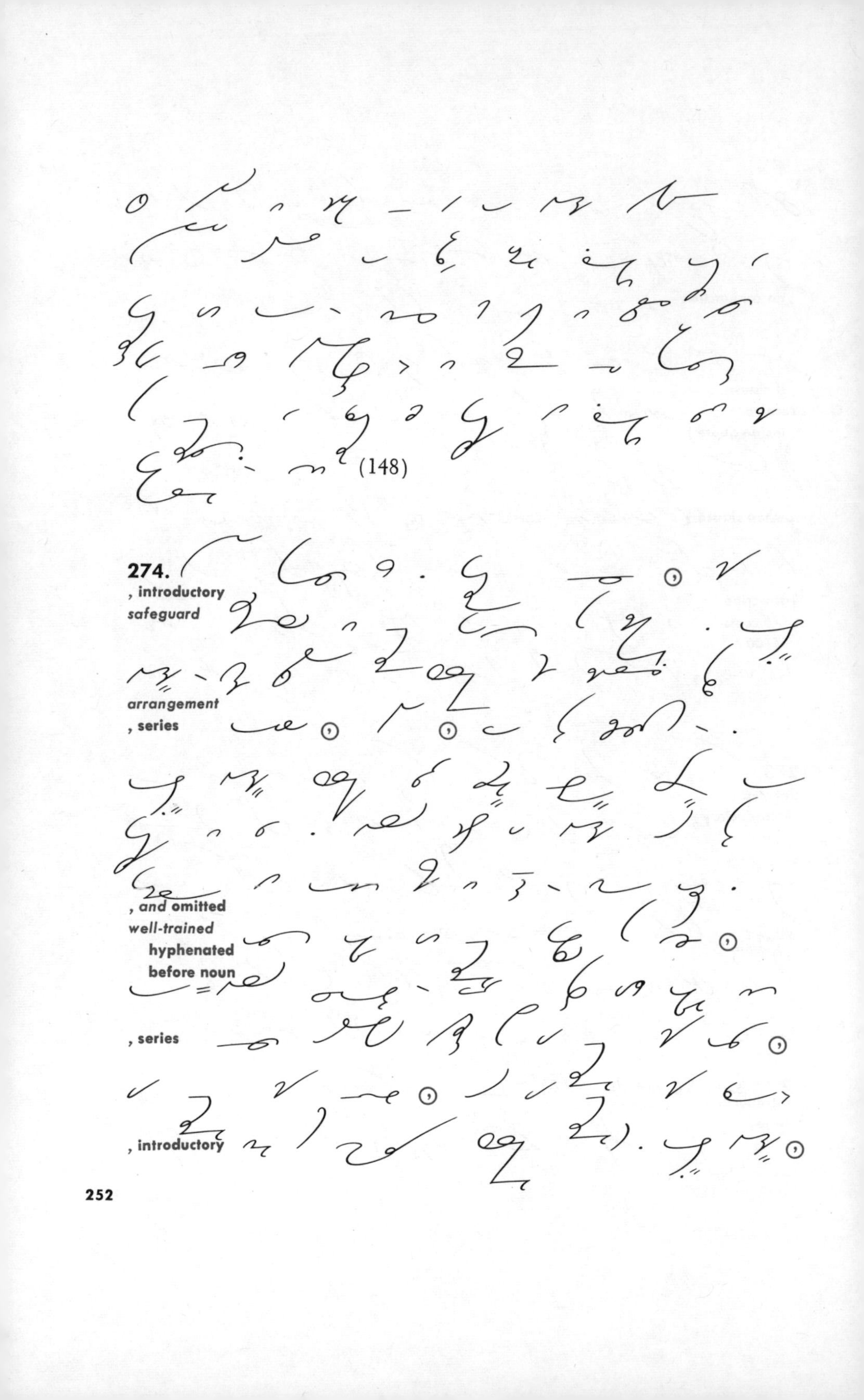

(148)

274.

, introductory

safeguard

arrangement

, series

, *and* omitted

well-trained

hyphenated before noun

, series

, introductory

(152)

275.

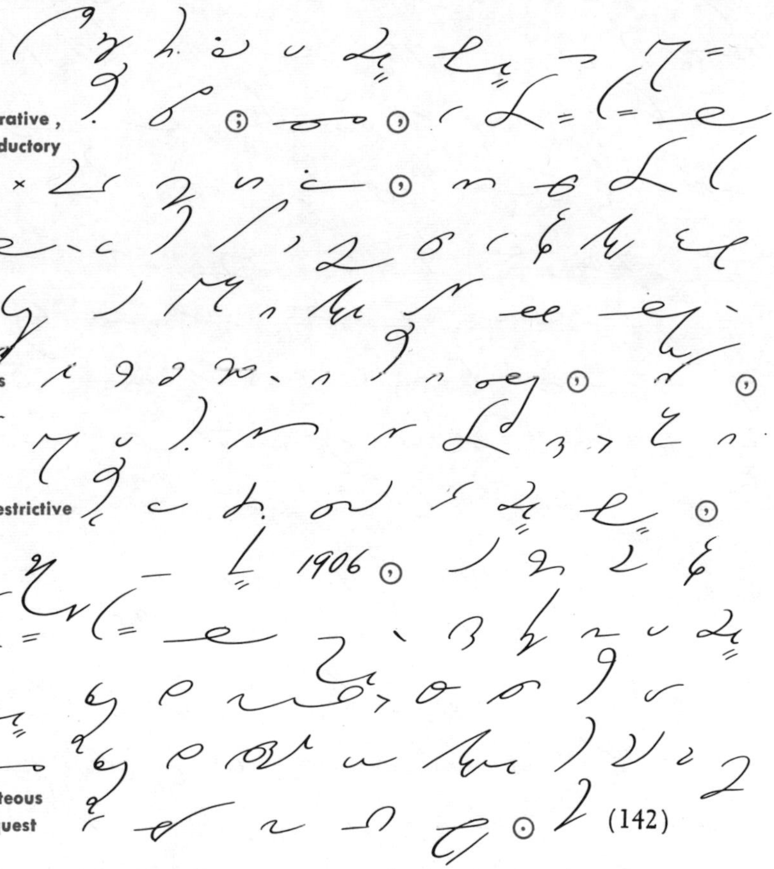

; illustrative ,
, introductory
, series
, nonrestrictive
. courteous request

(142)

Transcription Quiz. For you to supply: 7 commas–4 commas parenthetical, 1 comma *if* clause, 1 comma *when* clause, 1 comma conjunction; 1 semicolon because of comma; 2 missing words.

276.

(217)

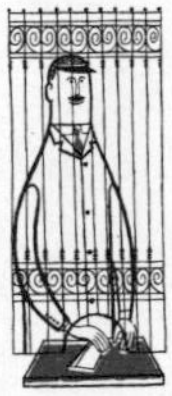

LESSON 40

277. World-Building Practice—Omission of Vowels

-tation, Etc.

1 

-est, -ist Following a Vowel

2 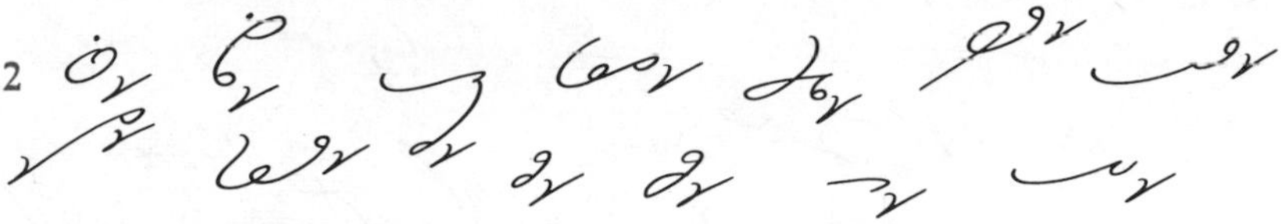

Omission of Ow

3 

1. Station, sanitation, interpretation, condition, expedition, addition, foundation, inclination, termination, condemnation, summation, formation, information.
2. Highest, happiest, loveliest, prettiest, fanciest, daintiest, wealthiest, steadiest, friendliest, easiest, essayist, newest, lowest.
3. Announce, announcement, council, councilor, sound, found.

278. Accuracy Practice—O Hook

1 

2 

1. Of, was, hope, object; row, low; toe, no, most.
2. What, order; or, coal; body, saw; of course, organize.

Reading and Writing Practice

279. Transcription Word Study

crusaders Those who try with zeal and enthusiasm to bring about a change.

servitude Slavery.

earmarks Distinctive identifying marks.

280. The Typewriter

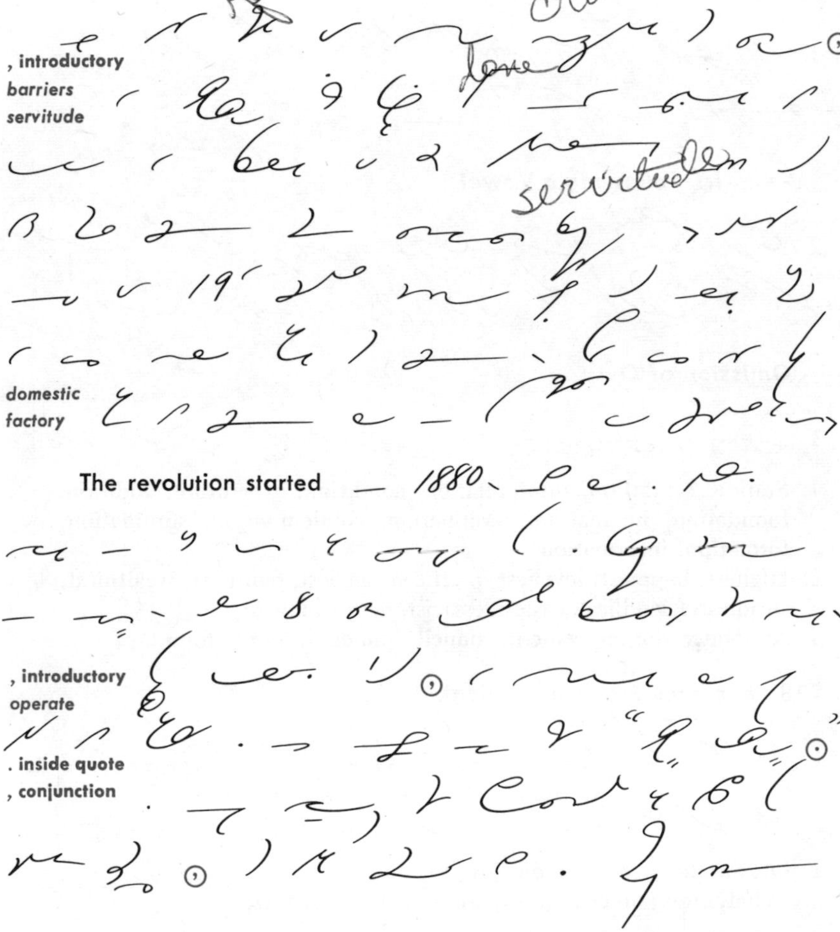

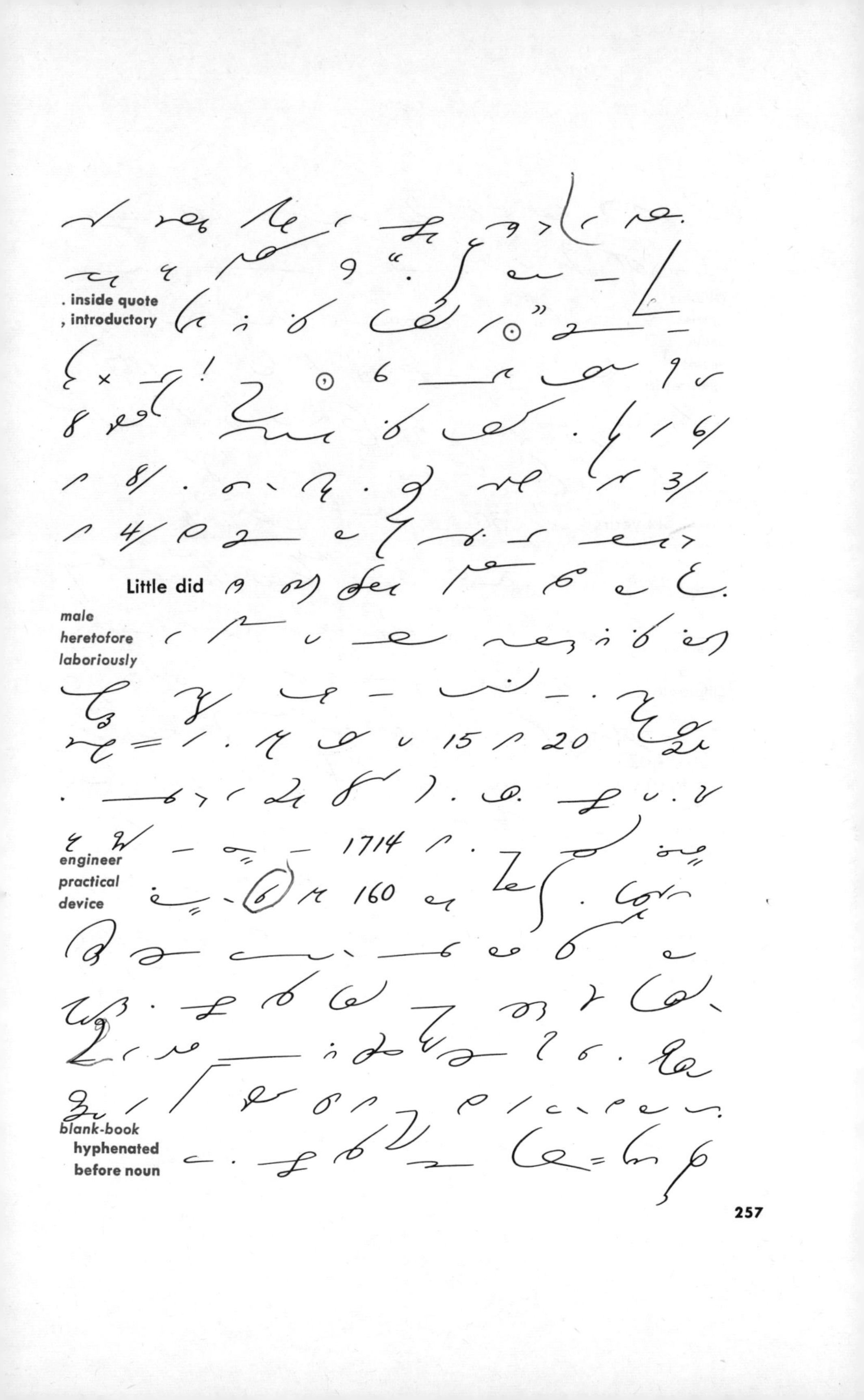

. inside quote
, introductory

Little did

male
heretofore
laboriously

engineer
practical
device

blank-book
hyphenated
before noun

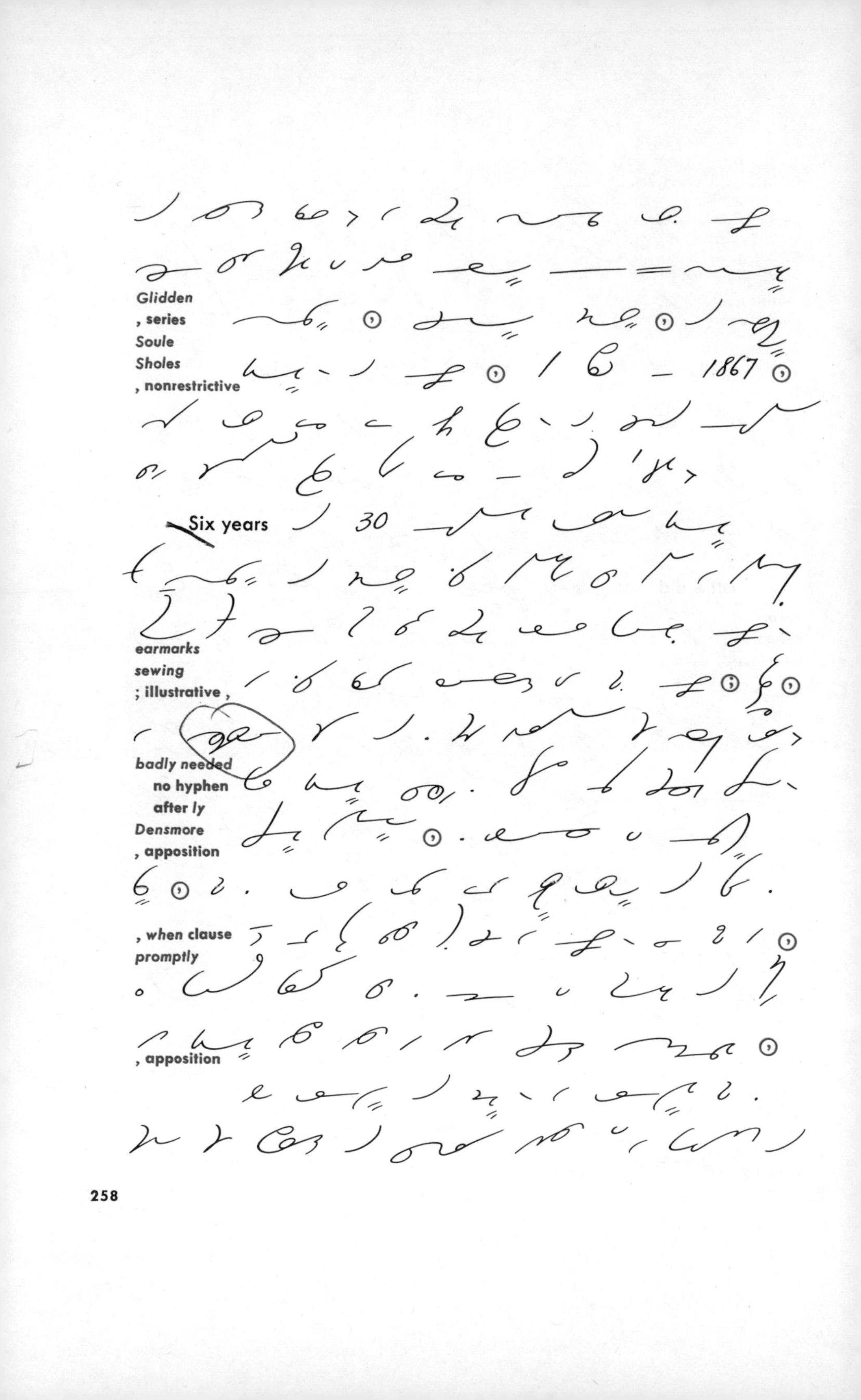

Glidden
, series
Soule
Sholes
, nonrestrictive

Six years

earmarks
sewing
; illustrative ,

badly needed
no hyphen
after *ly*
Densmore
, apposition

, when clause
promptly

, apposition

, introductory
Transcribe:
No. 1

; no conjunction
, introductory
steel

, introductory

The machine

, introductory
reflection

: introducing long quote
, introductory

. inside quote
; no conjunction

Tiffany's
, parenthetical

, nonrestrictive
technique
boost
McGurrin
, nonrestrictive
; no conjunction
Presently
various
, introductory
blacksmith's
, conjunction
, conjunction
break

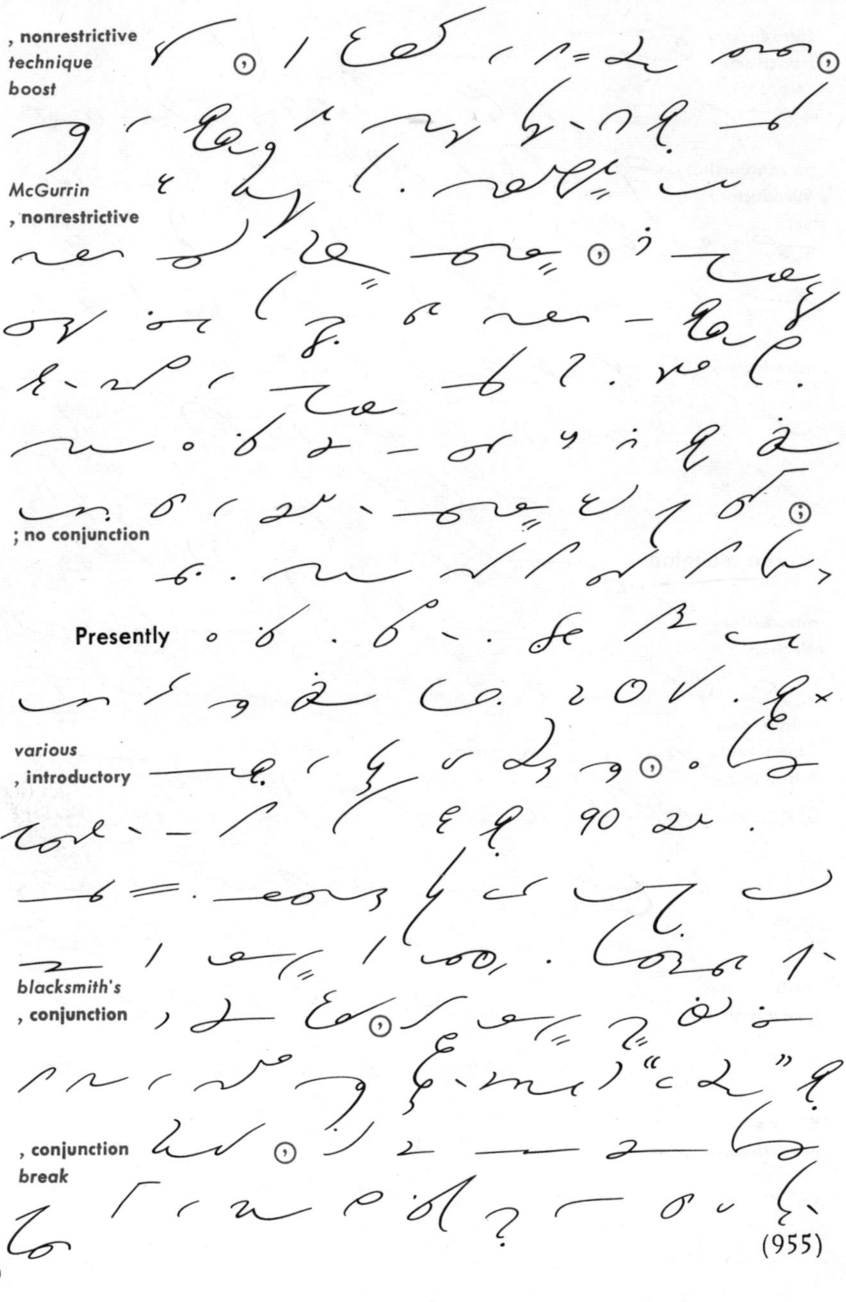

(955)

PART THREE

insurance
real estate
office machines
publishing

DICTATION PROBLEMS

In developing speed on new material – material that has not been previously practiced – every shorthand writer at one time or another encounters three problems. Perhaps you have already faced them in your dictation practice.

1. He falls behind.
2. He is called upon to write an unfamiliar word.
3. He does not hear, or mis-hears, a word.

What does the experienced writer do when he meets these problems?

He falls behind

1. He "hangs on" as long as he can. He realizes that the dictator may come to his rescue by stopping a few moments to take a breath, to cough, or to clear his throat. Often these few moments enable him to catch up.
2. When he falls hopelessly behind, he drops the words he has not written and skips a line or two. This blank space indicates to him the point at which he has a break.
3. He picks up the dictation at the new point.
4. When he transcribes he tries, with the help of context, to supply the missing words.

He encounters an unfamiliar word

1. He tries to write it alphabetically, in full.

2. If he cannot write it in full, he tries to write at least the beginning of the word. This beginning often helps him to locate the word in a dictionary when he transcribes.

3. If the word completely escapes him, he leaves a space in his notes and continues writing; he does not waste precious moments trying to build an outline for it because he knows that the dictator will not wait for him.

4. When he transcribes, he substitutes for the word he missed a synonym that will not change the meaning of the dictated material.

He does not hear, or mis-hears, a word

1. When he does not hear a word, either because the dictator did not enunciate clearly or because some noise interfered, he leaves a space in his notes and supplies the word later, with the help of context. He does not stop writing!

2. If he thinks he heard a word but knows from context that it could not possibly be the correct one, he writes the word he thinks he heard and encircles it. If he is pressed for time to encircle it, he skips a line in his notes. Often, the outline for the word that he thought he heard will help him supply the correct one.

3. On some occasions the word that he did not hear, or mis-heard, will occur to him later during the dictation. He does not take time to insert it in its proper place; he knows that this may cause him to fall behind. He does, however, try to hold the word in his mind and fill it in immediately upon the completion of the dictation.

These suggestions, of course, apply to your work on speed development. On the job, however, you would stop the dictator tactfully when one of these situations arises rather than risk the possibility of turning in an inaccurate transcript.

9

INSURANCE

LESSON 41

281. Brief Forms and Derivatives

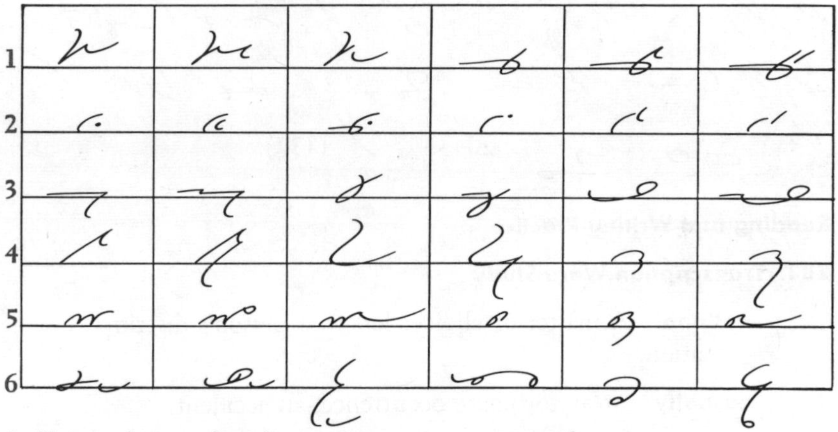

1. Future, futures, futurity; matter, matters, mattered.
2. Thing-think, things, anything; thank, thanks, thanked.
3. Important-importance, unimportant-unimportance; satisfy-satisfactory, unsatisfactory; like, unlike.
4. Dear-Sir-desire, desirable; value, valuable; consider-consideration, considerable.
5. Worth, worthy, worthless; use, useful, useless.
6. Sender, writer, publisher; regularly, confidently, probably.

282. Brief Form and Phrase Letter

(137)

Reading and Writing Practice

283. Transcription Word Study

optional A matter of choice; left to a person's discrimination.

casualty An unfortunate occurrence; an accident.

involuntary Not done willingly or through choice.

284.

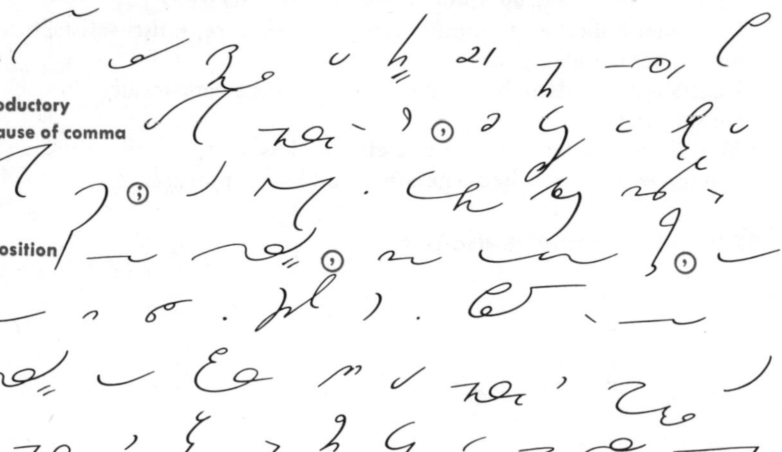

, introductory

; because of comma

local

, apposition

, *if* clause

(139)

285.

facilities

, parenthetical

, *when* clause

peak

, introductory

; no conjunction

(153)

286.

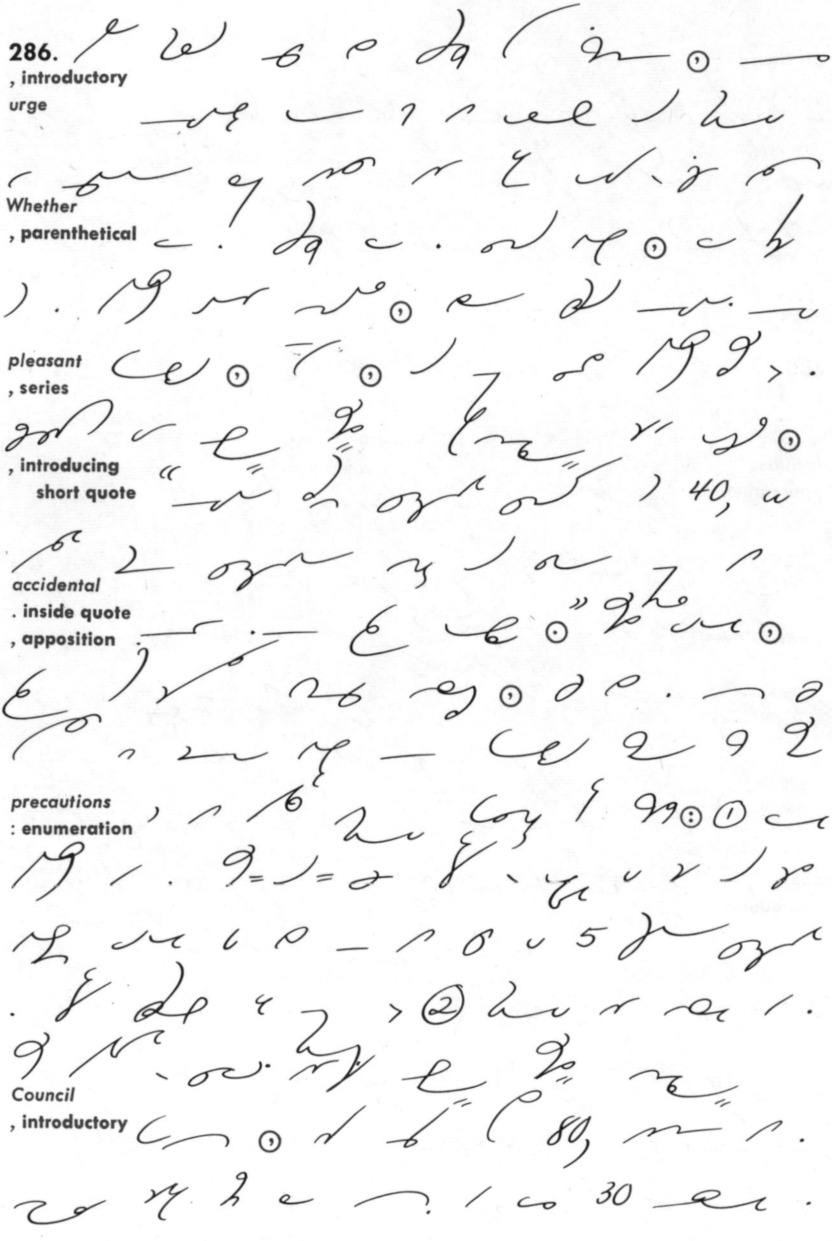

, introductory
urge
Whether
, parenthetical
pleasant
, series
, introducing short quote
accidental
. inside quote
, apposition
precautions
: enumeration
Council
, introductory

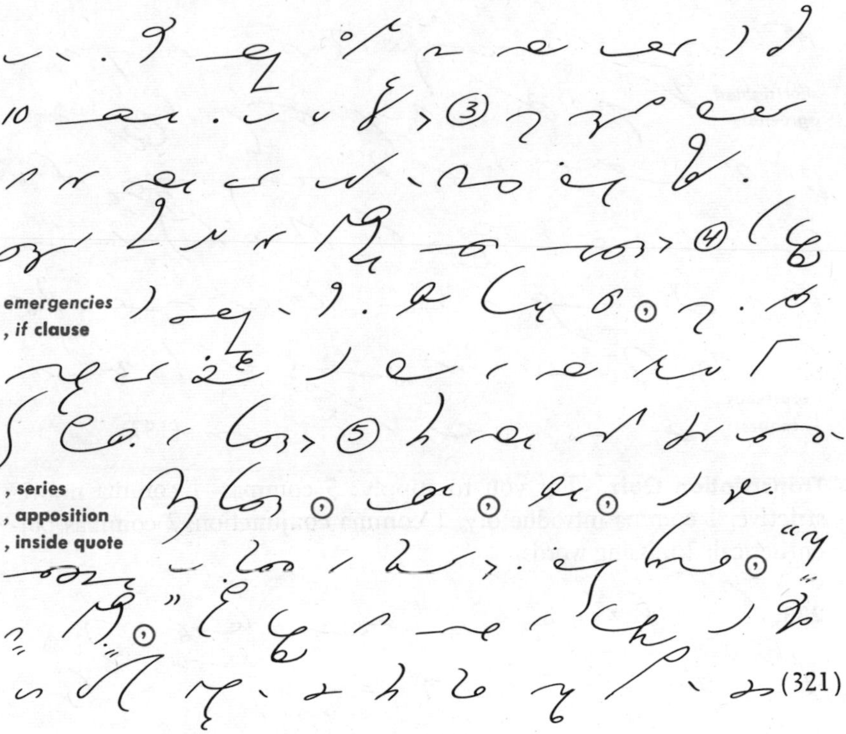

emergencies
, if clause
, series
, apposition
, inside quote

(321)

287.

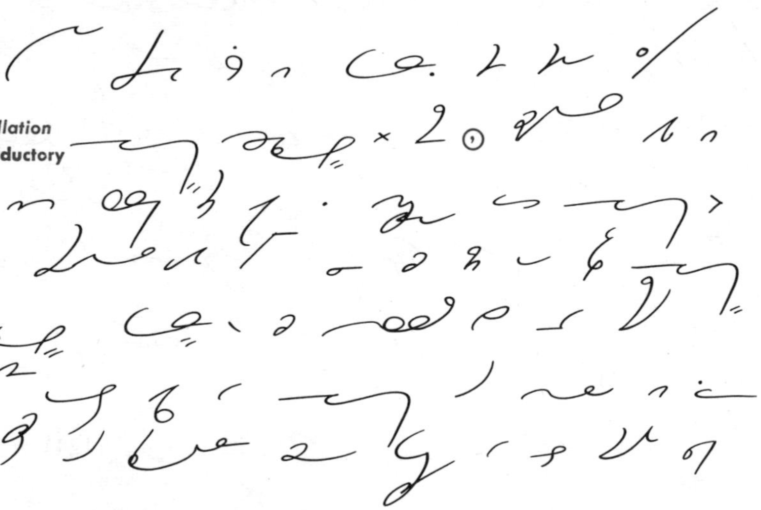

Cancellation
, introductory

shortsighted
agreeably

. courteous
request

(157)

Transcription Quiz. For you to supply: 5 commas—1 comma nonrestrictive, 1 comma introductory, 1 comma conjunction, 2 commas parenthetical; 2 missing words.

288.

(124)

LESSON 42

289. Useful Business-Letter Phrases

Do

1 

Has

2 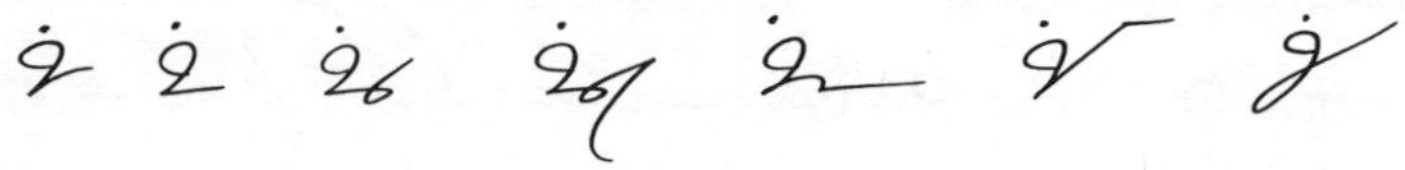

Is

3 

Please

4 

1. Do you, do you think, do you know, do not, do not have, do this, do so.
2. Has the, has not, has not yet, has not yet been, has come, has done, has had.
3. Is the, is that, is that the, is this, is not, isn't, is made, is to be.
4. Please see, please pay, please send, please write, please write me, please rush.

290. Frequent Names

1 

2 

1. Kerr, King, Klein, Larsen, Levy, Lynch.
2. Flora, Florence, Georgiana, Gertrude, Harriet, Henrietta.

Reading and Writing Practice

291. Transcription Word Study

grossly Shamefully.

substantiate Verify.

292.

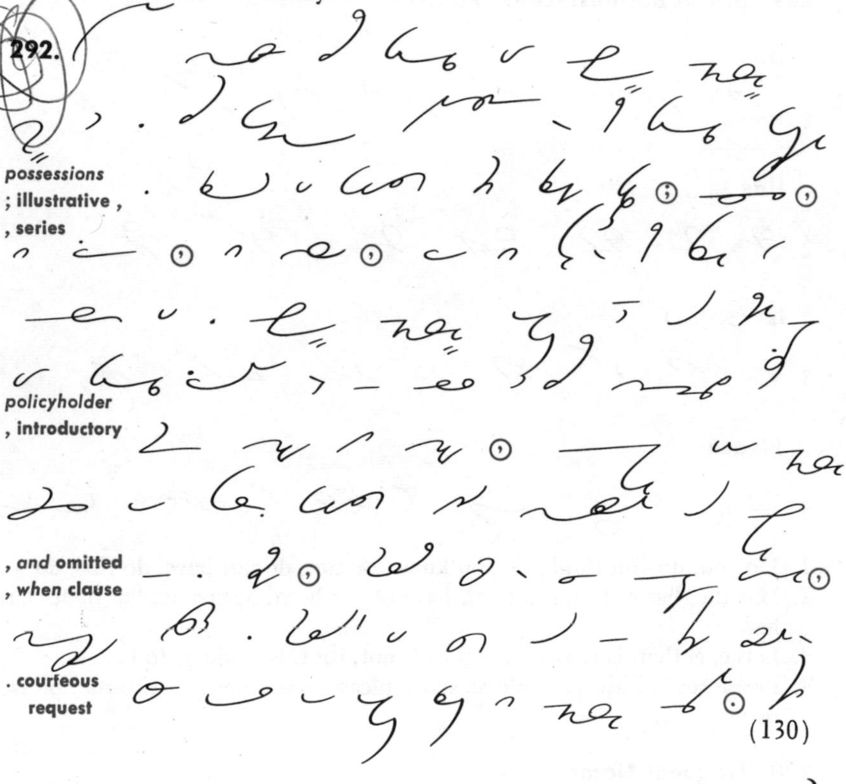

possessions
; illustrative ,
, series
policyholder
, introductory
, *and* omitted
, *when* clause
. courfeous request

(130)

293.

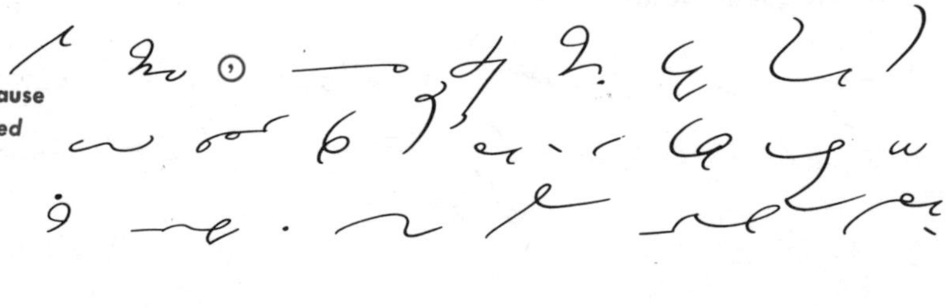

, *as* clause
occurred

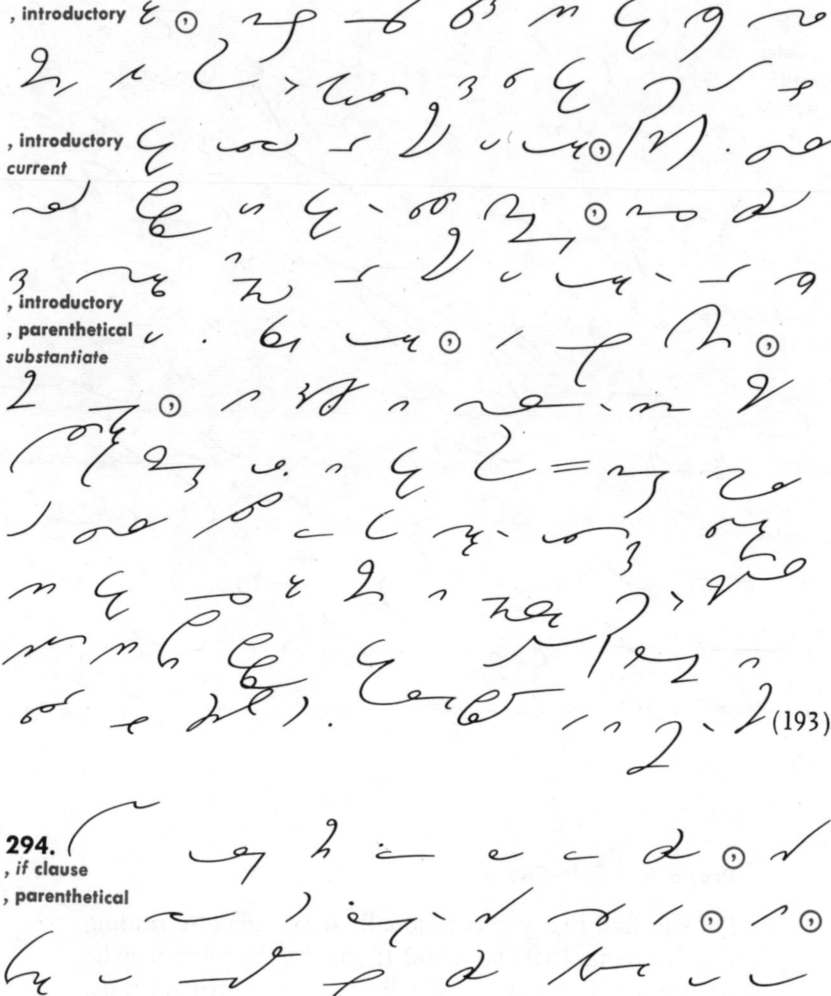

, introductory

, introductory
current

, introductory
, parenthetical
substantiate

(193)

294.

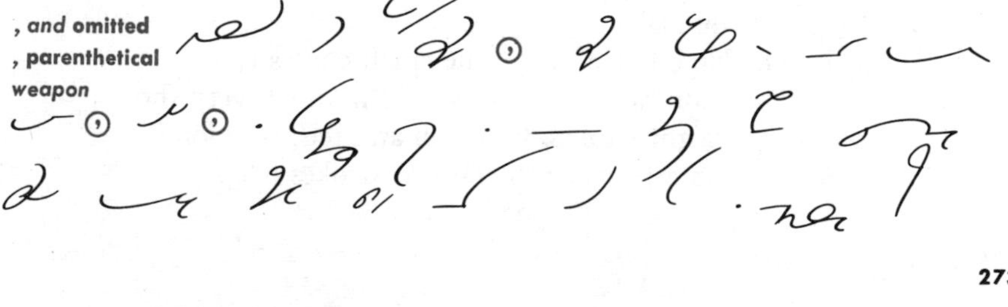

, *if clause*
, parenthetical

, *and omitted*
, parenthetical
weapon

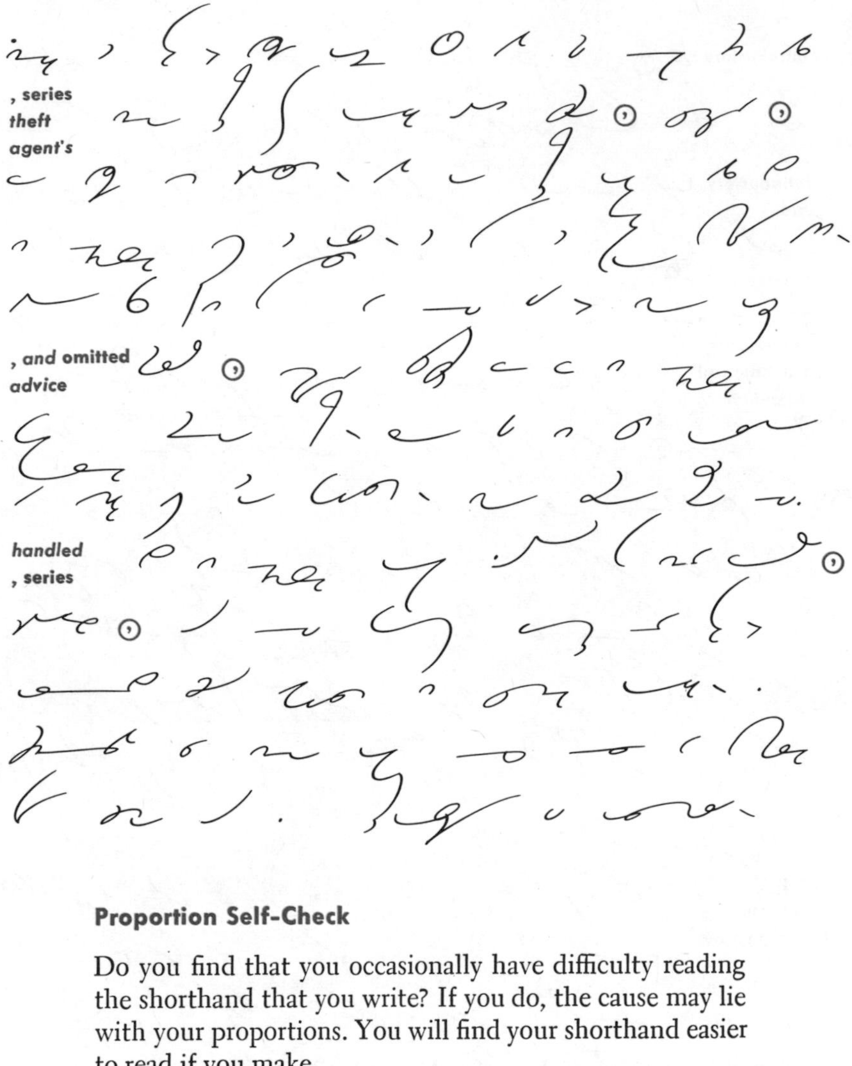

Proportion Self-Check

Do you find that you occasionally have difficulty reading the shorthand that you write? If you do, the cause may lie with your proportions. You will find your shorthand easier to read if you make

1. The large circles *huge;* the small circles *tiny.*

2. The short straight strokes, like *n* and *t, very* short; the long straight strokes, like *men* and *ted, very* long.

Also, be sure to make the curved strokes deep.

won't
. courteous request

(226)

295.
year-by-year
hyphenated before noun
, *as clause*

nation's
, *and omitted*
, parenthetical

, nonrestrictive

, introductory

(165)

Transcription Quiz. For you to supply: 5 commas–4 commas series, 1 comma conjunction; 1 colon enumeration; 2 missing words.

296.

(187)

LESSON 43

297. Word Families

-tent

1 

-dence

2 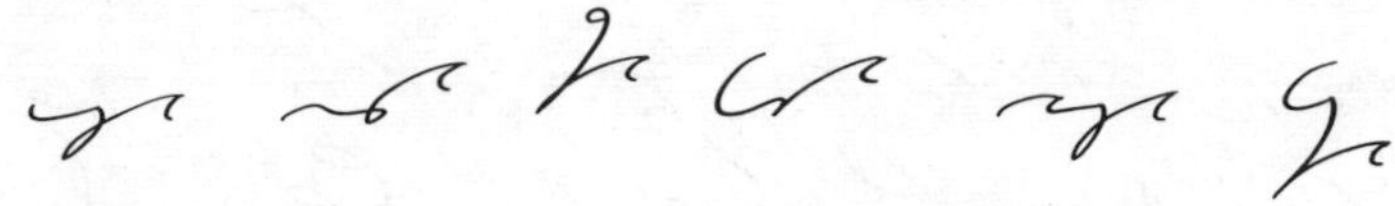

-hand

3 

-spect

4 

-signed

5 

1. Content, intent, patent, extent, discontent, competent.
2. Residence, credence, evidence, prudence, coincidence, providence.
3. Hand, handle, shorthand, longhand, backhand, beforehand, secondhand.
4. Inspect, respect, self-respect, aspect, prospect, expect, disrespect.
5. Signed, assigned, designed, resigned, countersigned, unsigned, redesigned.

Reading and Writing Practice

298. Transcription Word Study

devastate To lay waste.

irrefutable Incapable of being disproved.

premium The cost of an insurance policy.

299.

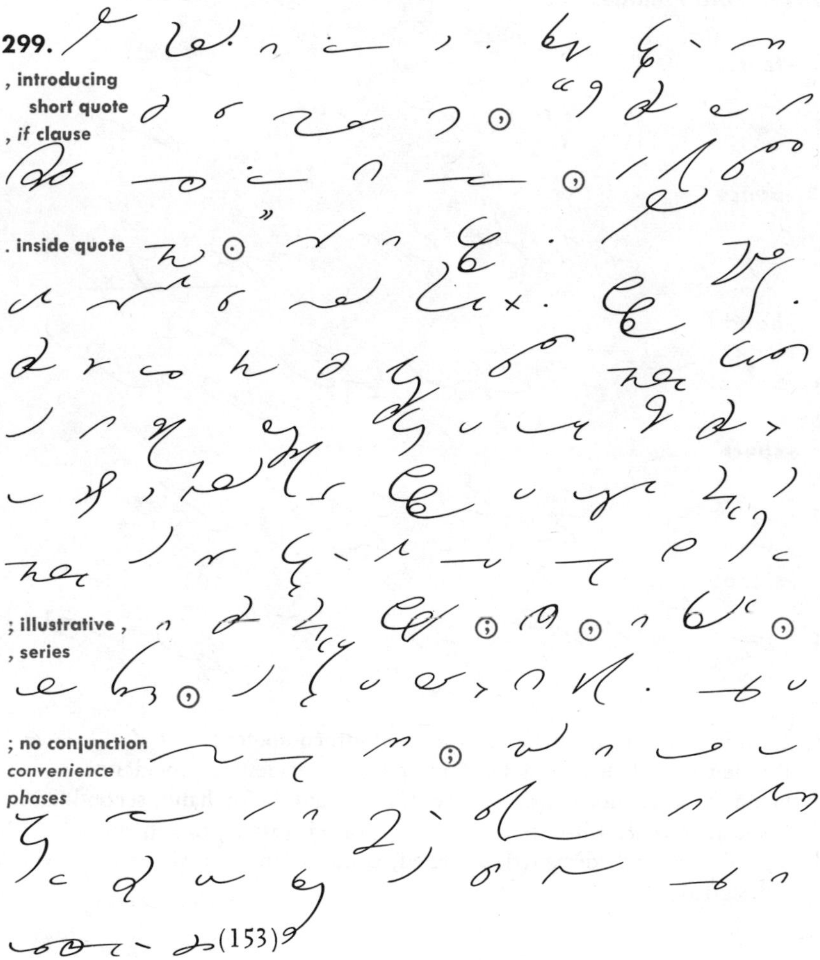

, introducing short quote

, *if* clause

. inside quote

; illustrative ,

, series

; no conjunction

convenience

phases

(153)

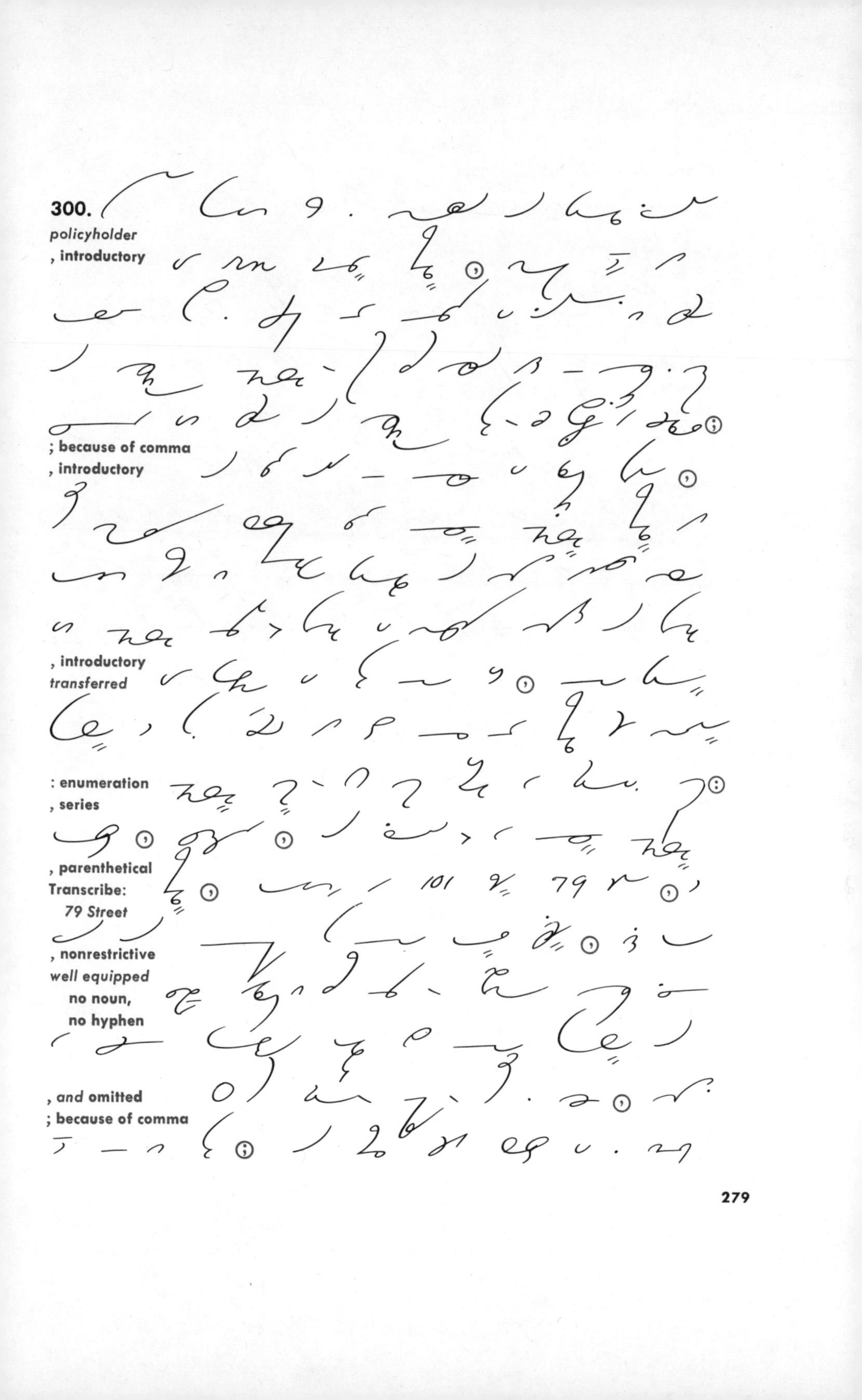

300.

policyholder

, introductory

; because of comma

, introductory

, introductory

transferred

: enumeration

, series

, parenthetical

Transcribe:

79 Street

, nonrestrictive

well equipped

no noun,

no hyphen

, *and* omitted

; because of comma

, *if* clause 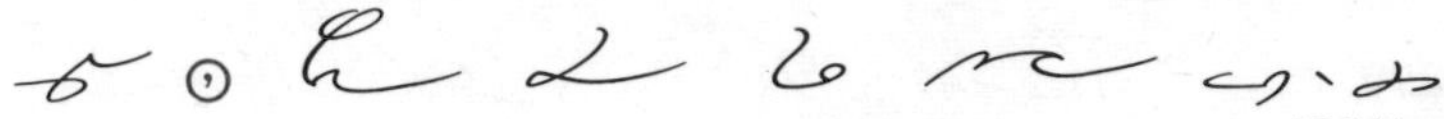

(234)

301. 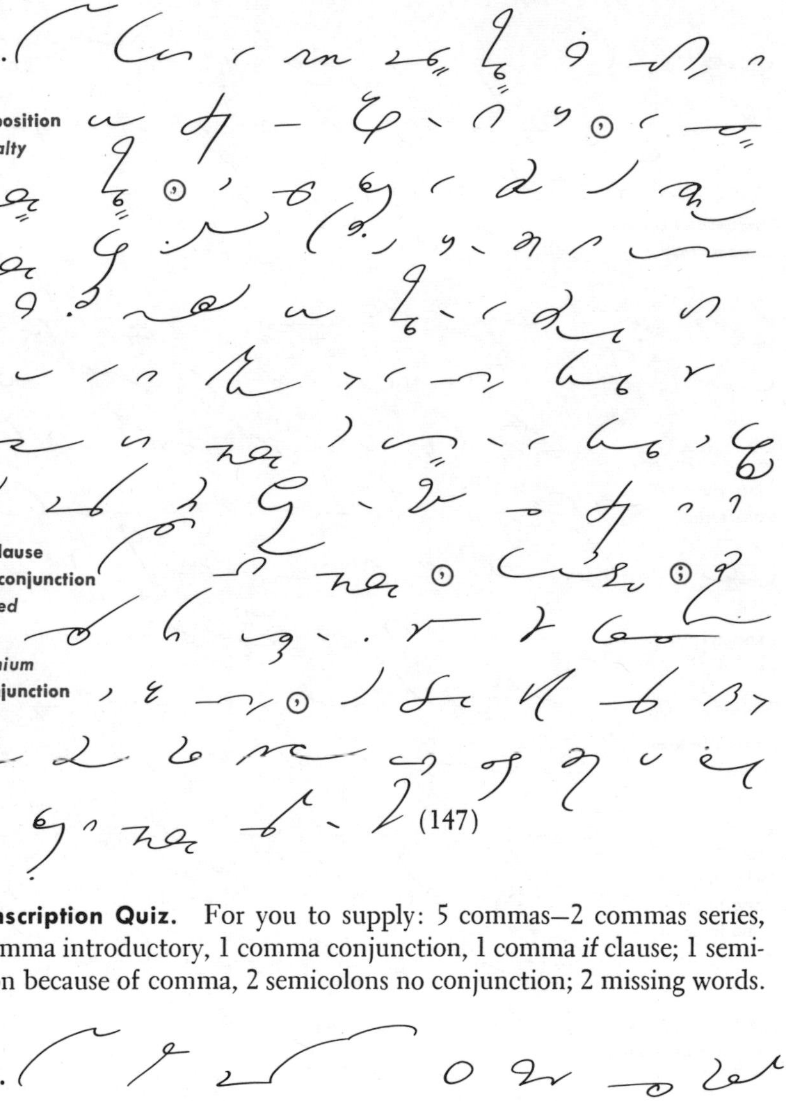

, apposition
casualty
, *if* clause
; no conjunction
guided
premium
, conjunction

(147)

Transcription Quiz. For you to supply: 5 commas–2 commas series, 1 comma introductory, 1 comma conjunction, 1 comma *if* clause; 1 semicolon because of comma, 2 semicolons no conjunction; 2 missing words.

302.

(212)

LESSON 44

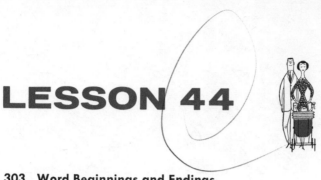

303. Word Beginnings and Endings

Post-

1 

-ically

2 

-sult

3 

-ship

4 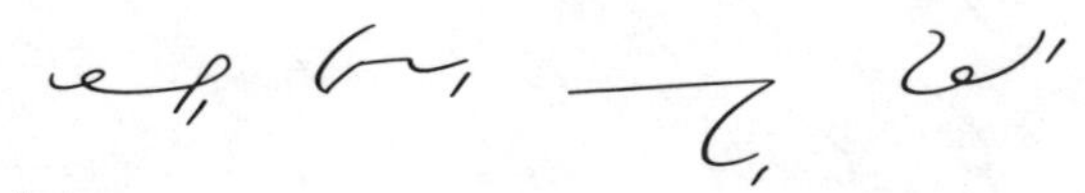

Intr-

5 

1. Postage, postman, postmaster, postal, postcard, postpone, postponement.
2. Specifically, periodically, technically, mechanically, practically, critically.
3. Result, results, resulted, resultant, consult, consultation, consulted, insult.
4. Relationship, partnership, membership, friendship.
5. Introduce, introduced, introduction, intrude, introvert, intrigue, intricate.

304. Geographical Expressions

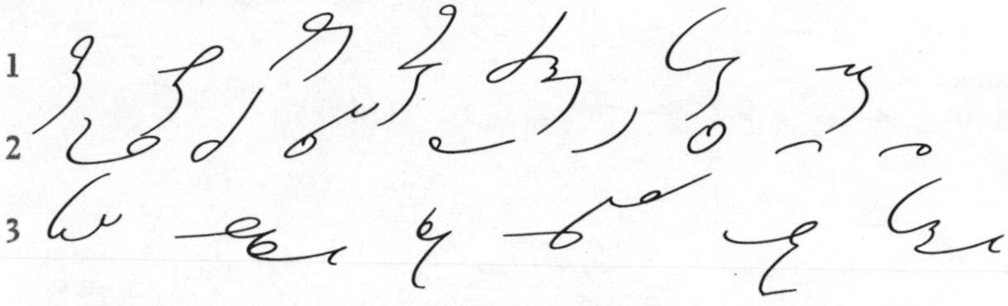

1. Ashville, Nashville, Danville, Evansville, Jacksonville, Brownsville, Knoxville.
2. Florida, Georgia, Idaho, Illinois, Indiana, Iowa, Kansas, Kentucky.
3. Bordeaux, Marseilles, Cherbourg, Madrid, Lisbon, Brussels.

Reading and Writing Practice

305. Transcription Word Study

judiciously Exercising sound judgment.

authenticated Proven.

static Not active.

306.

. courteous request

(124)

307.

authenticated

, conjunction

, introductory

static

, as clause

, series

affect

, and omitted

, apposition

, series *qualified*

(251)

308.

: introducing long quote

, parenthetical

. inside quote

, parenthetical

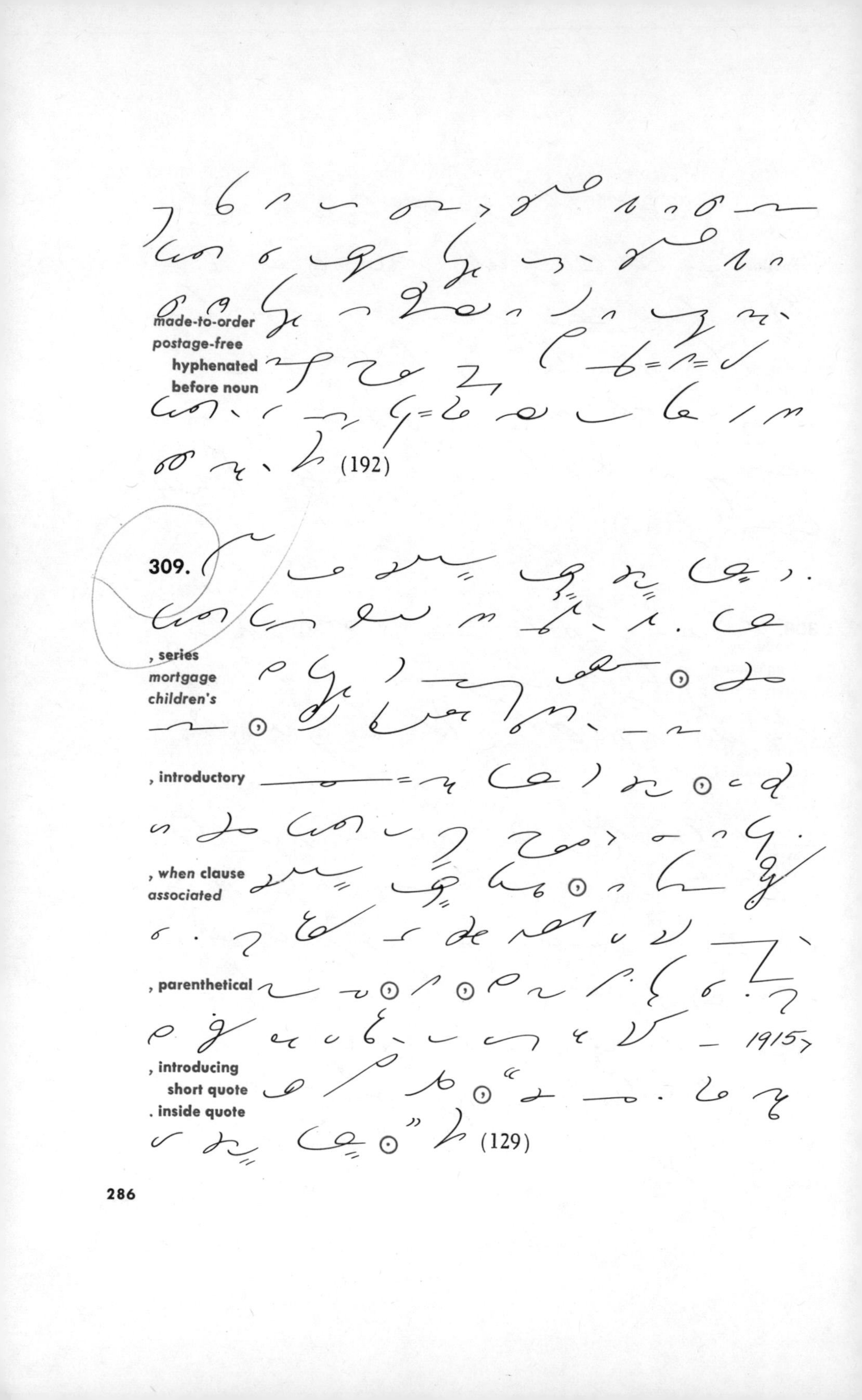

made-to-order
postage-free
hyphenated before noun

(192)

309.

, series
mortgage
children's

, introductory

, *when* clause
associated

, parenthetical

1915

, introducing short quote
. inside quote

(129)

Transcription Quiz. For you to supply: 4 commas—2 commas introductory, 2 commas nonrestrictive; 1 semicolon because of comma; 2 missing words.

310.

(214)

LESSON 45

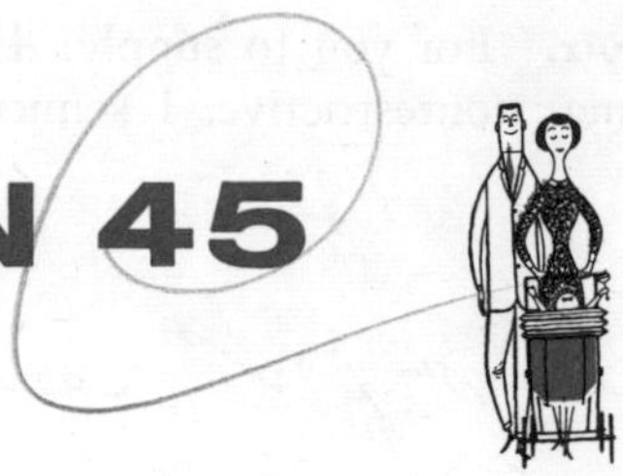

311. Word-Building Practice—Diphthongs

I

1 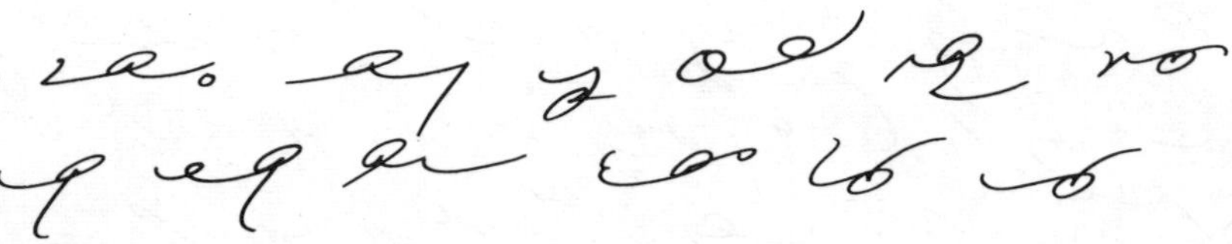

Oi

2 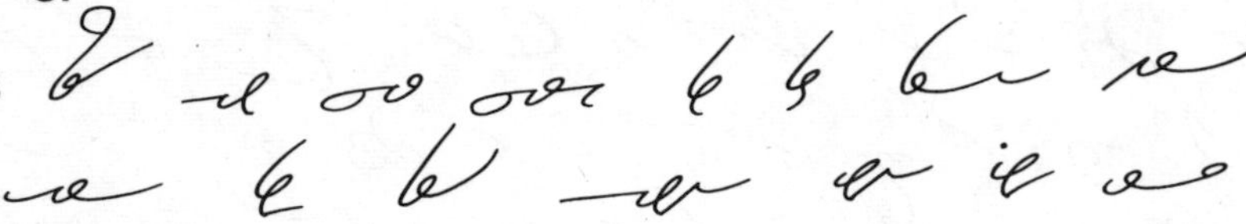

Ow

3 

Ū

4 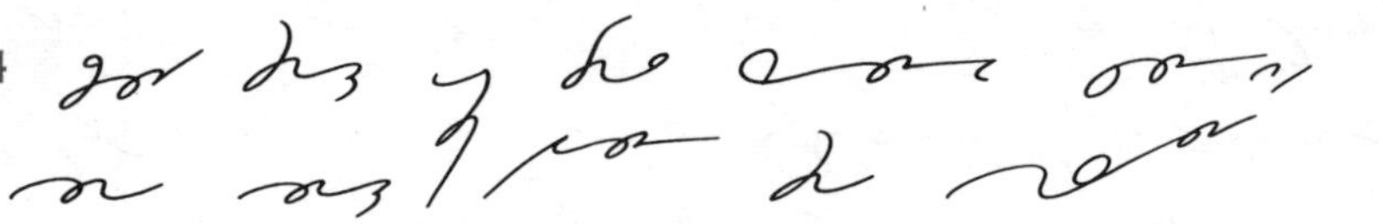

1. Smilingly, mileage, resign, island, trifle, strike, liable, reliable, tireless, slightly, frighten, lighten.
2. Avoid, noise, annoy, annoyance, choice, choices, boiler, toiled, royal, poison, joined, moisture, oyster, hoist, oily.

3. Power, powerful, south, doubtless, crowd, vouch, scouted, powdered, proudly, undoubtedly, clouds, shower, mouths.
4. Execute, furious, refuge, purely, arguments, accumulated, cure, curious, document, fewer, graduate.

Reading and Writing Practice

312. Transcription Word Study

vowed Solemnly promised.

impelling Urging forward, driving.

recipient One who receives.

313. Why Does a Man Buy Life Insurance?

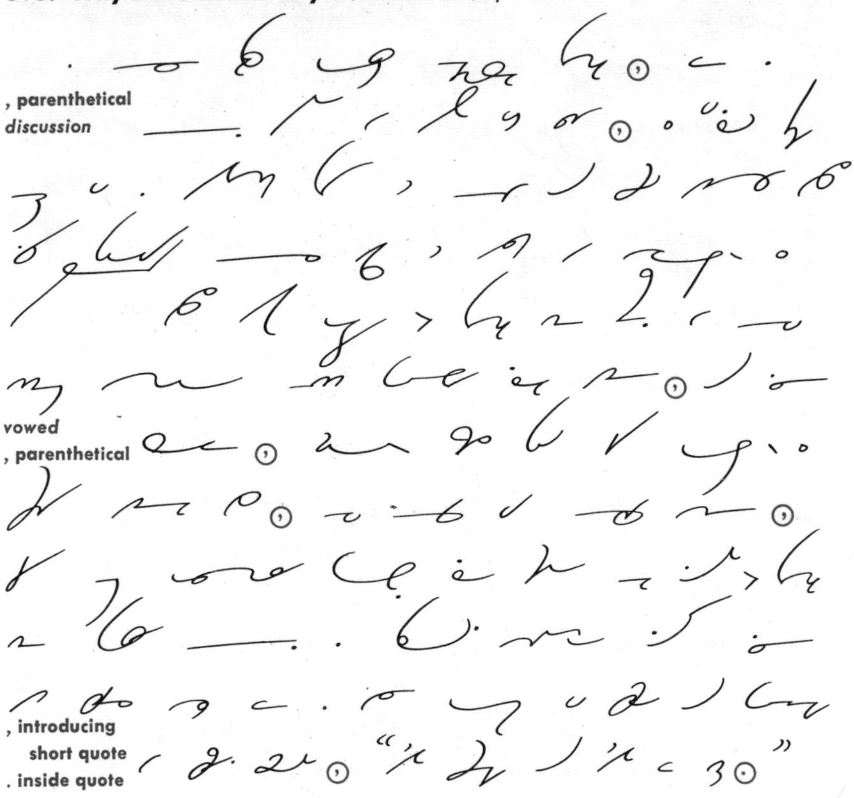

, apposition
dawn

Because

reassure
deceased
wholly

, introductory

, parenthetical

, and omitted
elemental

; no conjunction

honored

recipient

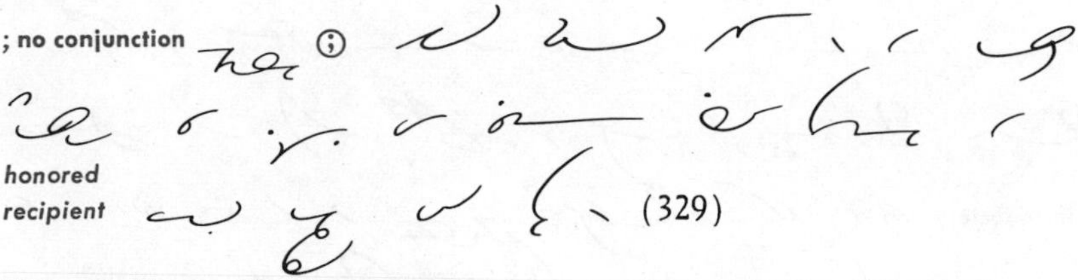

(329)

314. Ordinary Life Insurance

conceivable

stake

, introductory

grown

children's

People use

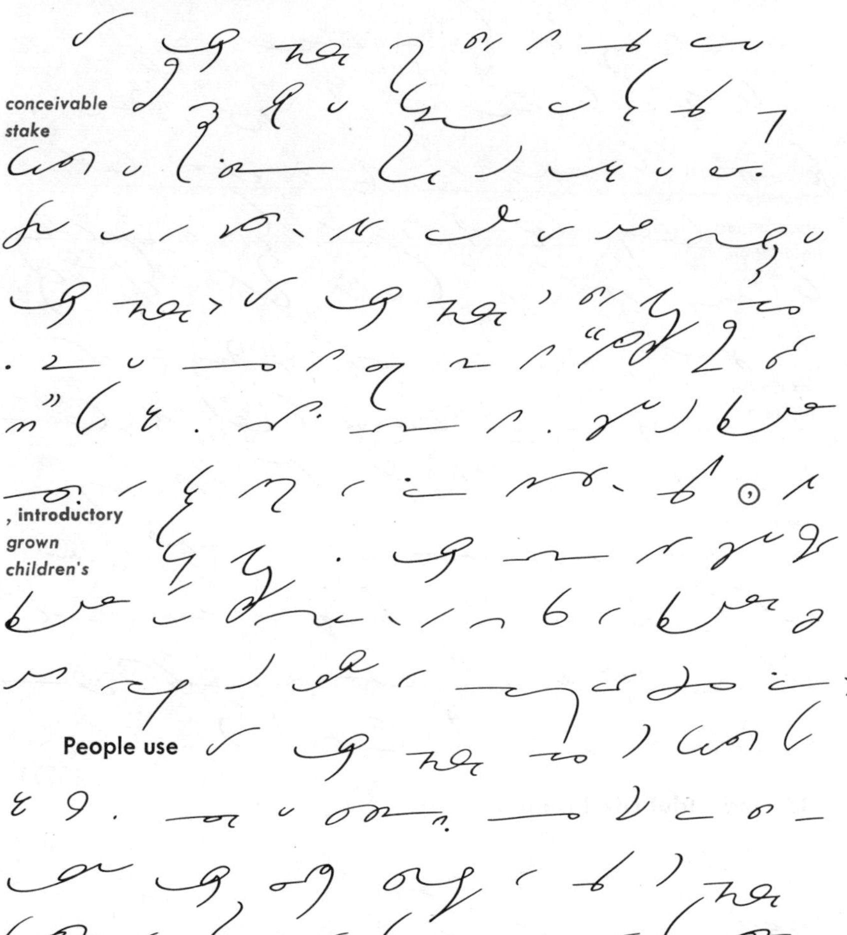

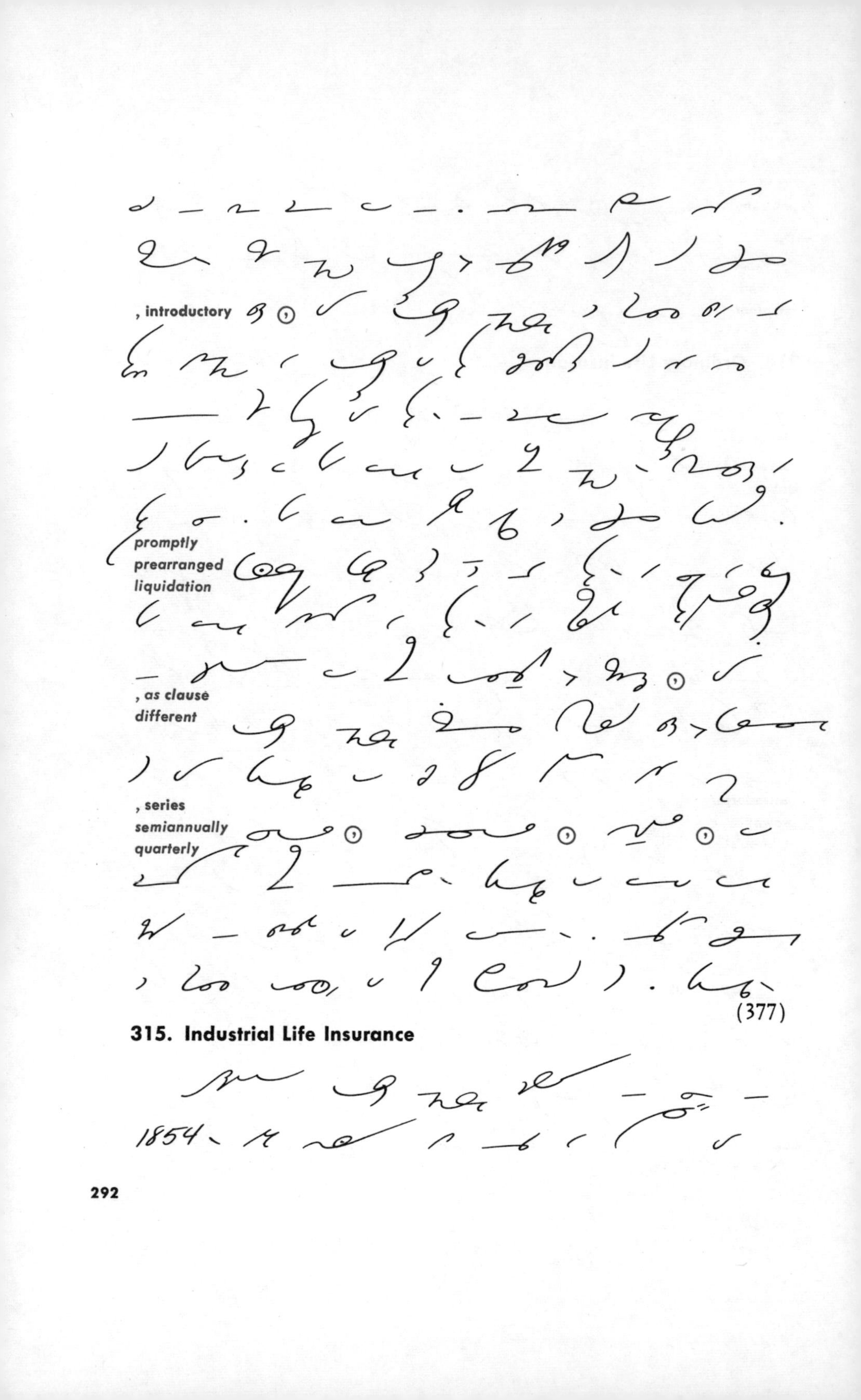

, introductory

promptly
prearranged
liquidation

, as clause
different

, series
semiannually
quarterly

(377)

315. Industrial Life Insurance

1854

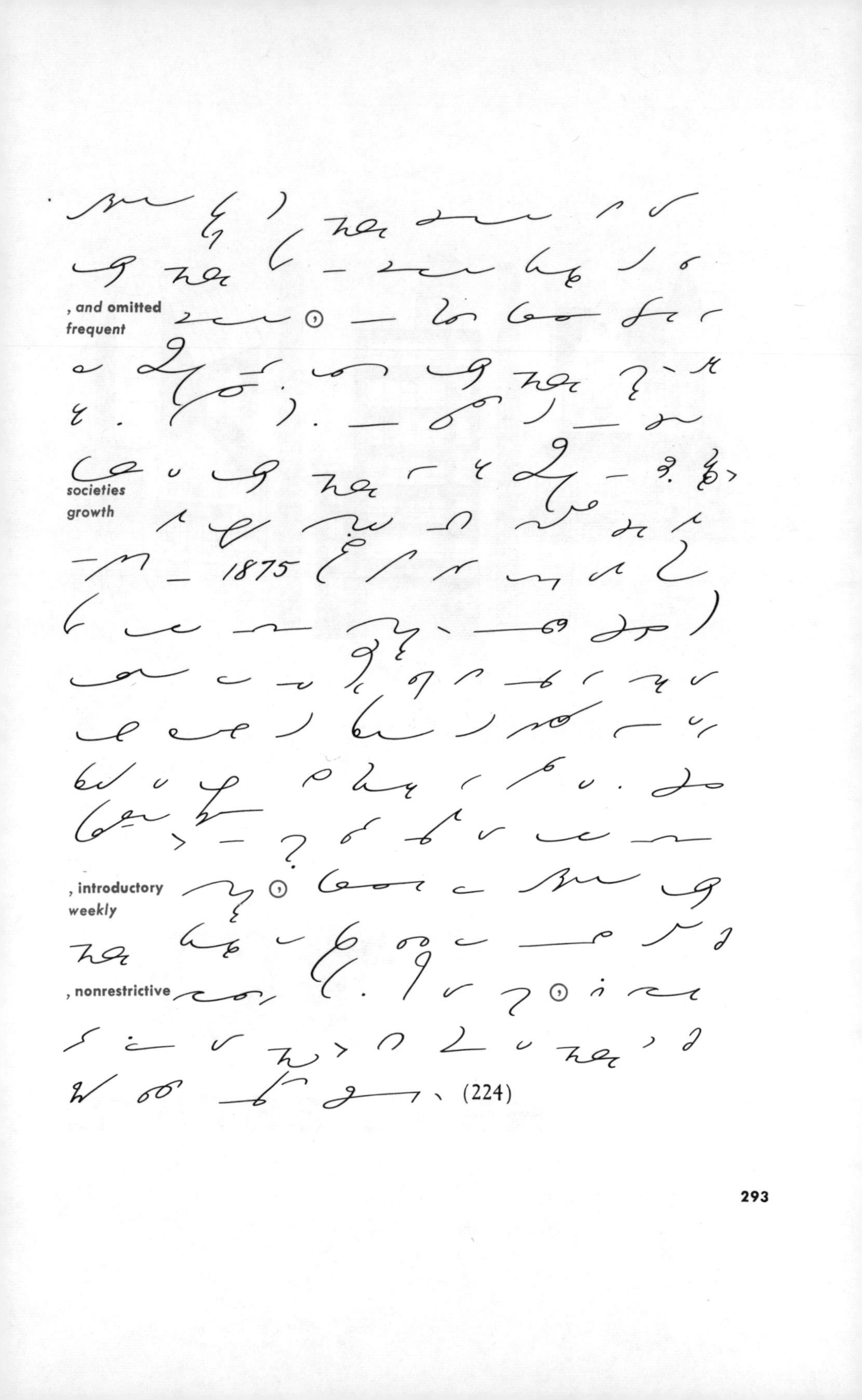

, and omitted
frequent

societies
growth

1875

, introductory
weekly

, nonrestrictive

(224)

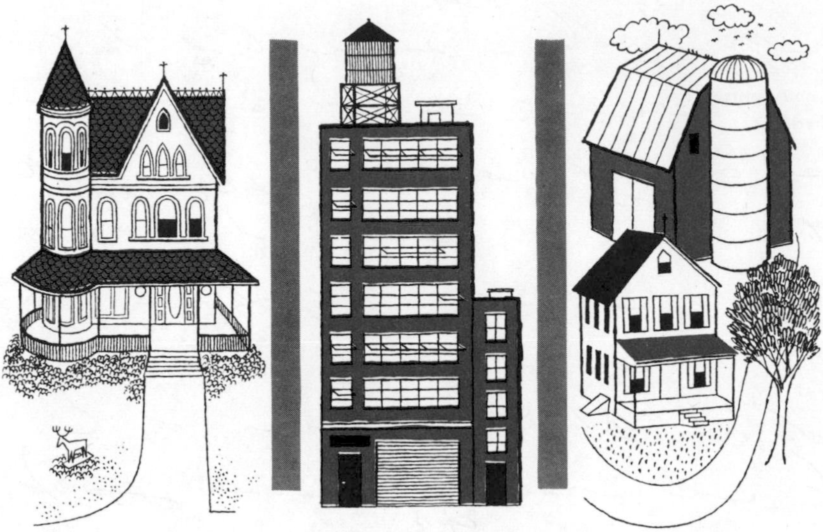

10

REAL ESTATE

LESSON 46

316. Brief Forms and Derivatives

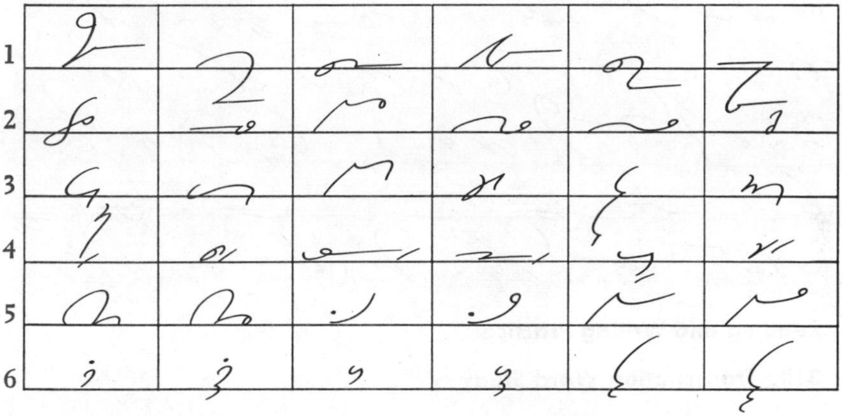

1. Advertisement, government, acknowledgment, department, accompaniment, embodiment.
2. Particularly, mostly, directly, greatly, gladly, usually.
3. Presentation, organization, direction, situation, publication, succession.
4. Suggested, used, remembered, numbered, referred, stated.
5. Difficult, difficulty; hand, handy; deliver, delivery.
6. House, houses; office, offices; business, businesses.

317. Brief Form and Phrase Letter

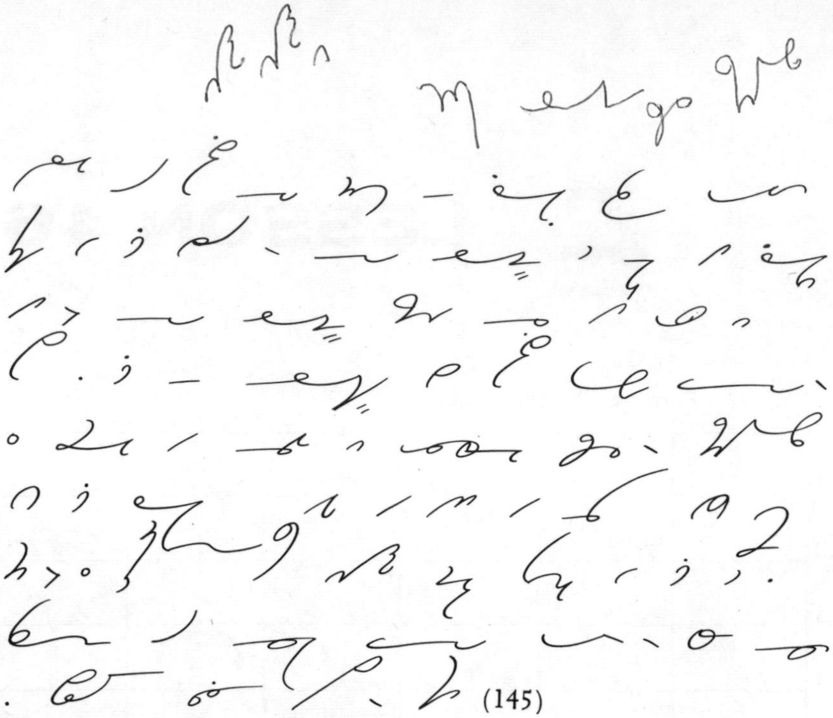

(145)

Reading and Writing Practice

318. Transcription Word Study

tract An area of land not specifically bounded.

frame house A house constructed mainly of wood.

barracks Buildings used for housing soldiers.

319.

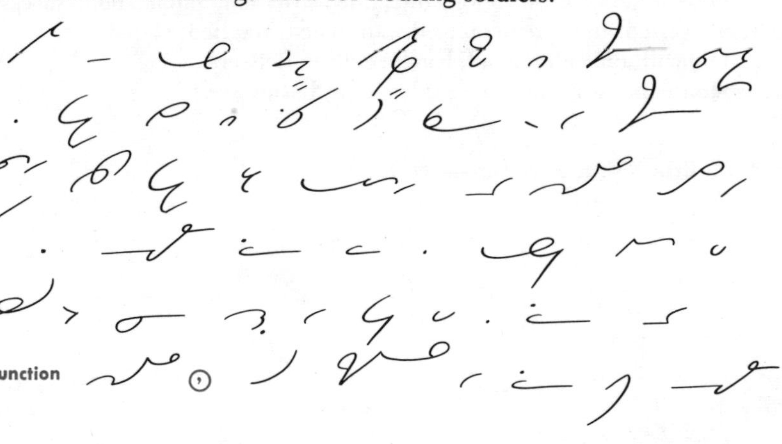

, conjunction

. courteous request

, series

conveniences

, if clause

, as clause

; because of comma

(166)

320.

, apposition

two-story hyphenated before noun

, as clause

area

acreage
, nonrestrictive

beginning
, nonrestrictive

: enumeration
, conjunction
carefully planned
no hyphen
after *ly*

; because of comma
, apposition

(268)

321.

, introductory
, *as* clause
; because of comma

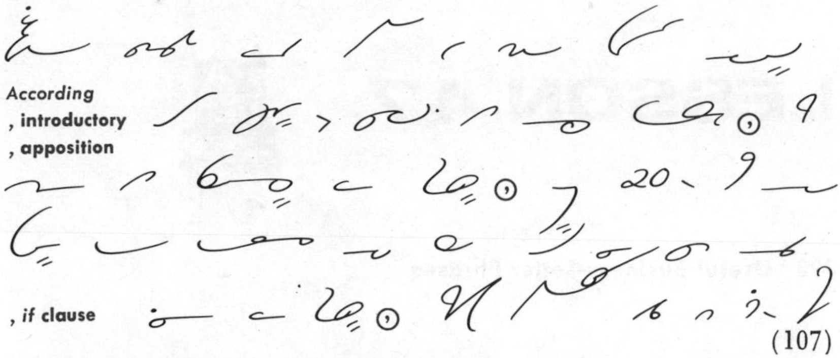

According
, introductory
, apposition
, if clause

(107)

Transcription Quiz. For you to supply: 3 commas–2 commas introductory, 1 comma *when* clause; 1 semicolon because of comma, 1 semicolon no conjunction; 2 missing words.

322.

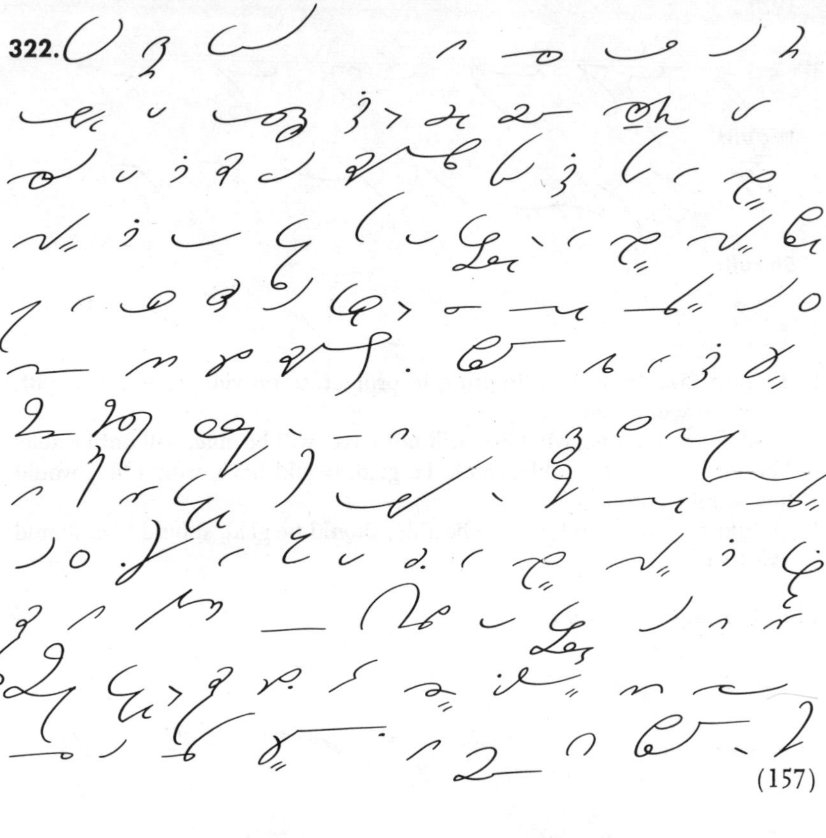

(157)

LESSON 47

323. Useful Business-Letter Phrases

To

1 

Will

2 

Would

3 

Should

4 

1. To purchase, to prepare, to print, to protect, to provide, to brush, to put, to say, to see, to sell.
2. Will be, will not be, will have, will not have, will be able, will not be able.
3. Would be, would be able, would be glad, would have, would like, would not, would not be.
4. Should be, should not, should be able, should be glad, should like, should like to have.

324. Frequent Names

1

2

1. Martin, McCarthy, McDonald, McKenzie.
2. Harold, Herbert, Howard, Hugh, Hugo, Isaac, Jacob.

Reading and Writing Practice

325. Transcription Word Study

realtor A person who deals in the buying and selling of homes.

residential sections Areas occupied by homes.

site Location. (Do not confuse with *cite*, which means "to state," or *sight*, which relates to vision.)

326.

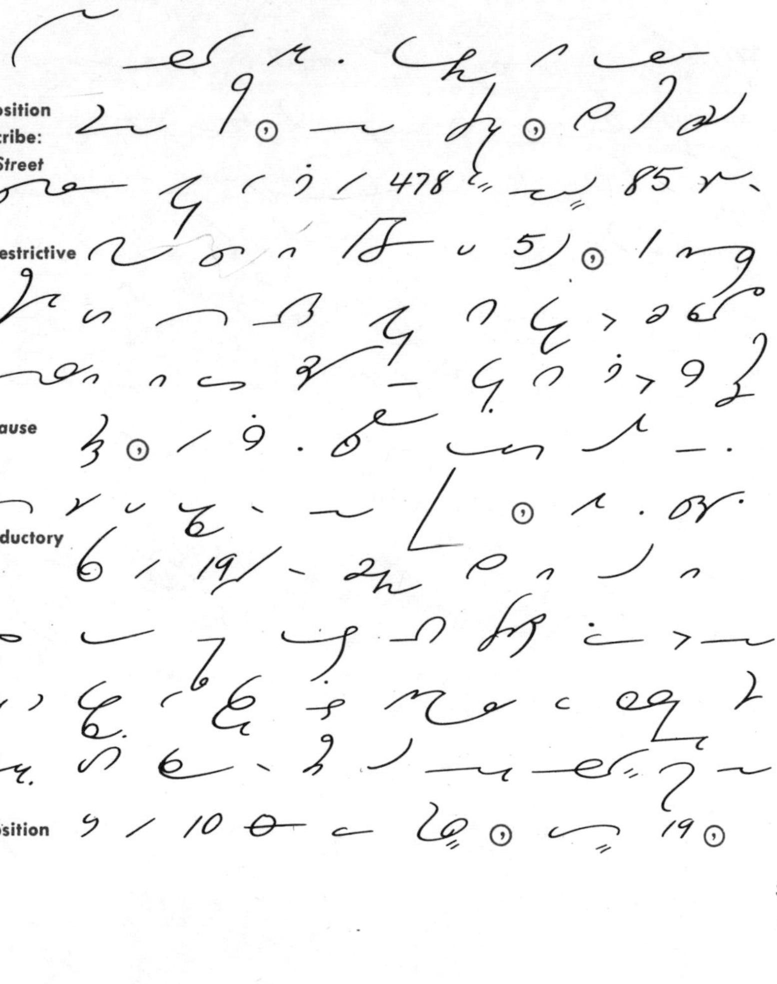

, apposition
Transcribe:
85 Street
, nonrestrictive
, as clause
ideal
, introductory
, apposition

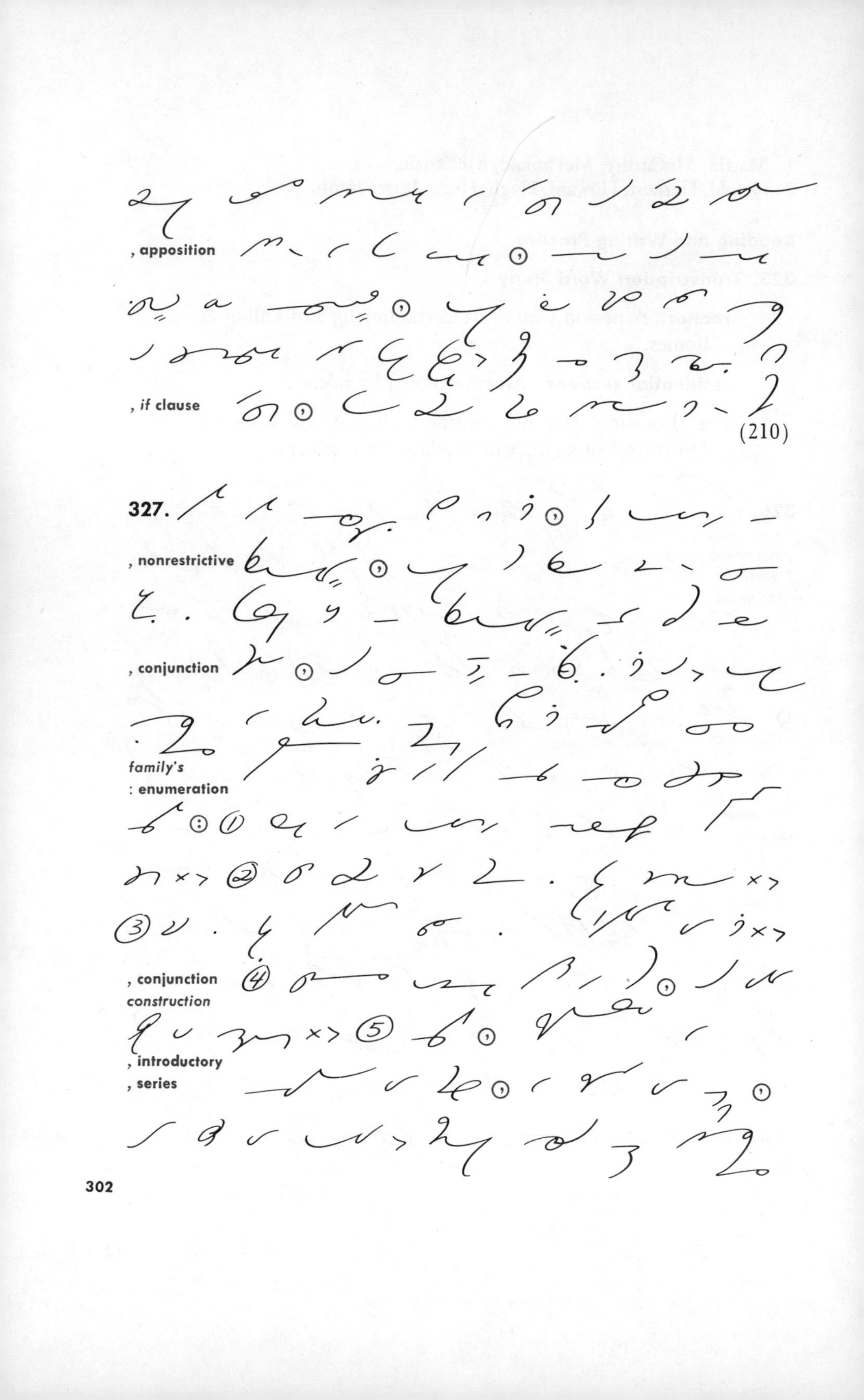

, apposition

, if clause

(210)

327.

, nonrestrictive

, conjunction

family's

: enumeration

, conjunction
construction

, introductory
, series

, *if* clause

, introductory

. courteous request

, *and* omitted

. (195)

328.

, introductory

; because of comma

, apposition

residential

4702

; no conjunction

15-minute hyphenated before noun

15=

two-story hyphenated before noun

1948

, series

, conjunction
operating

, and omitted
; because of comma

, nonrestrictive
landscaped

, if clause
arrangements

realtor
, conjunction

(297)

329.

convenient
, apposition

(62)

Transcription Quiz. For you to supply: 4 commas—3 commas introductory, 1 comma *and* omitted; 1 semicolon no conjunction; 2 missing words.

330.

(177)

LESSON 48

331. Word Families

-scription

1 

-ple

2 

-quent

3 

-son

4 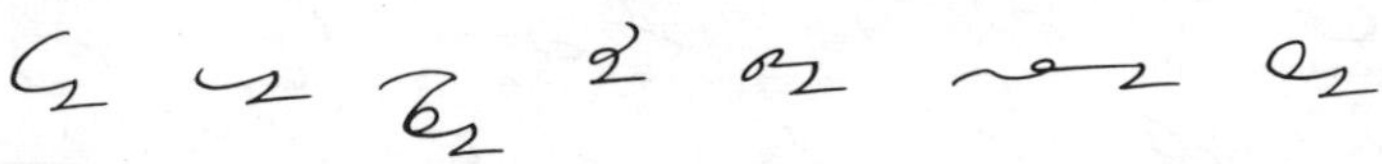

-cation

5 

1. Description, prescription, inscription, conscription, transcription, subscription.
2. Ample, sample, example, triple, disciple.
3. Consequent, frequent, subsequent, eloquent, infrequent, delinquent.
4. Person, reason, comparison, season, unison, crimson, arson.
5. Location, allocation, complication, indication, education, implication.

Reading and Writing Practice

332. Transcription Word Study

project (*noun*) A planned undertaking.

confirming Verifying.

specific Definite.

333.

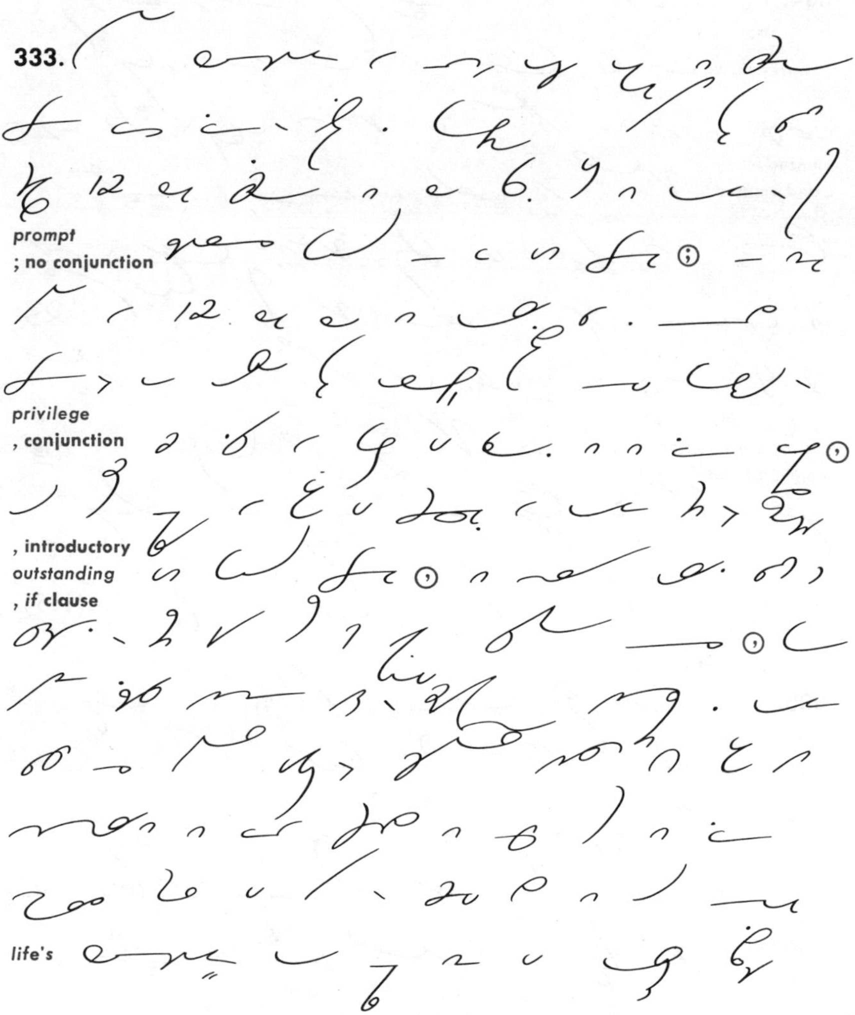

prompt

; no conjunction

privilege

, conjunction

, introductory

outstanding

, *if* clause

life's

; illustrative ,

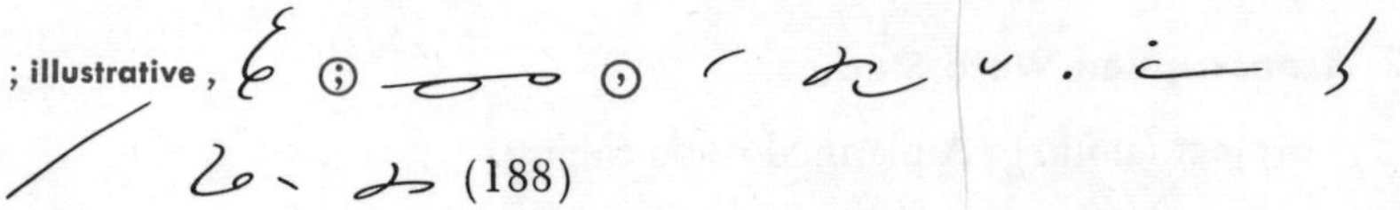

(188)

334.

, nonrestrictive

, introductory

, *and* omitted

, *as* clause

neighborhood

(115)

335.

, parenthetical

, introductory

, apposition

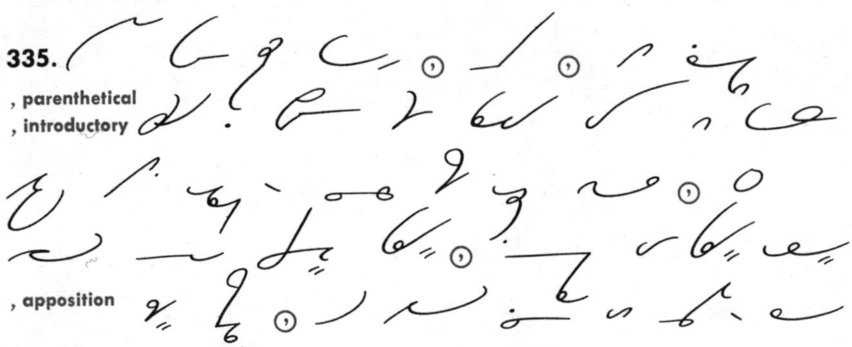

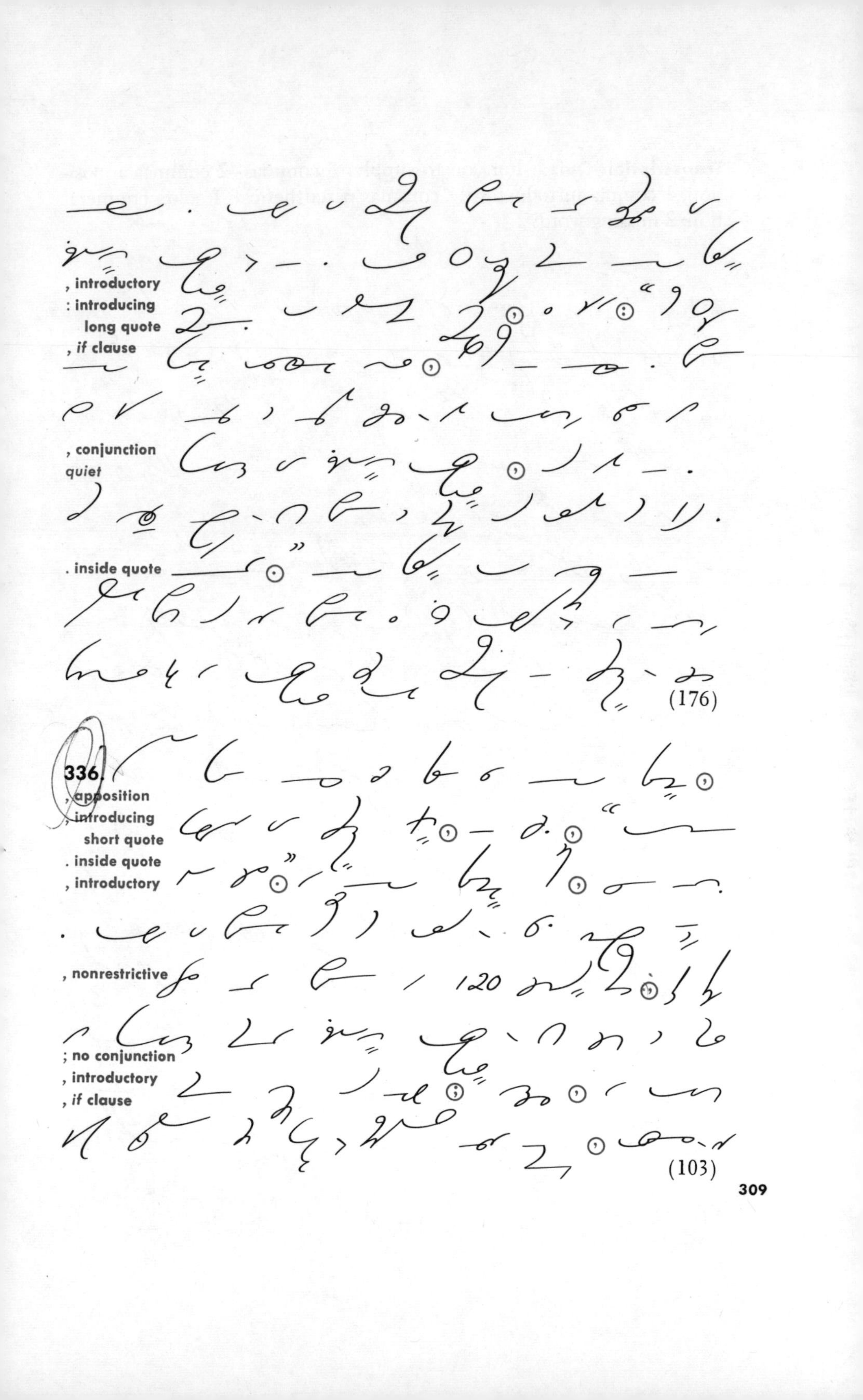

, introductory
: introducing long quote
, *if* clause

, conjunction
quiet

. inside quote

(176)

336.
, apposition
, introducing short quote
. inside quote
, introductory

, nonrestrictive
120

; no conjunction
, introductory
, *if* clause

(103)

Transcription Quiz. For you to supply: 5 commas—2 commas apposition, 1 comma introductory, 2 commas parenthetical; 1 colon enumeration; 2 missing words.

337.

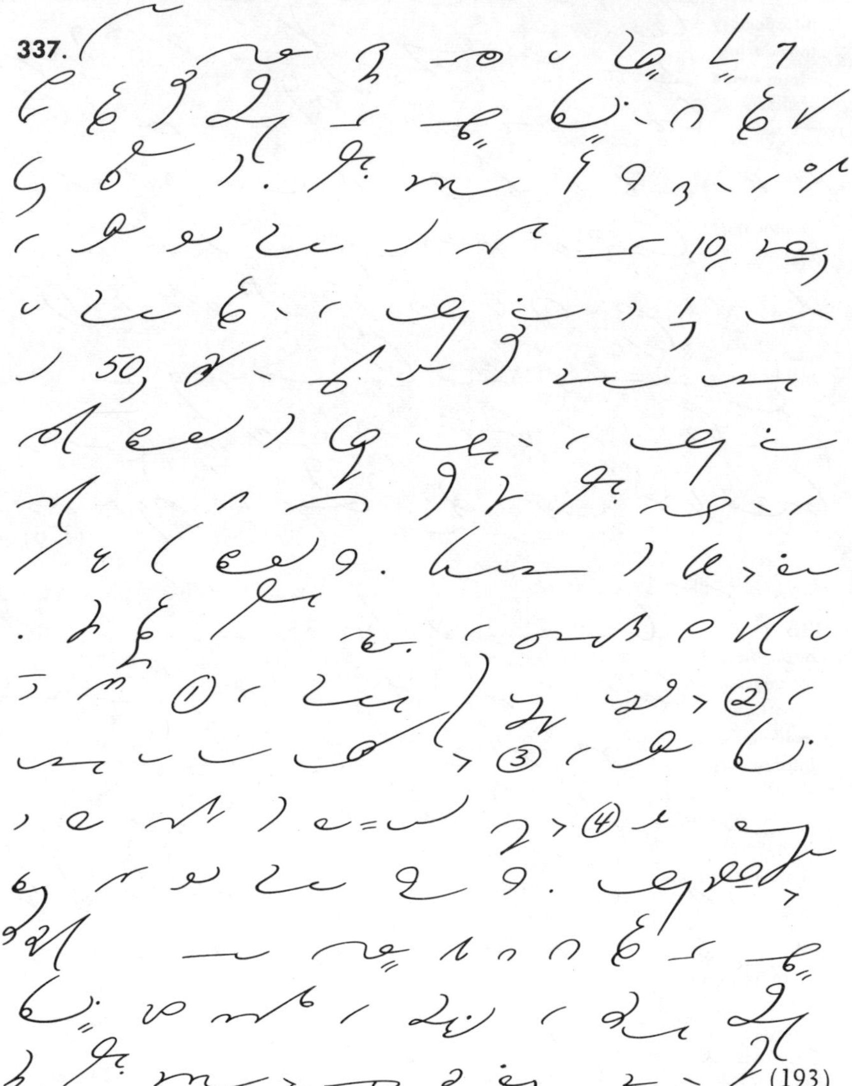

(193)

LESSON 49

338. Word Beginnings and Endings

Super-

1 

Electric-

2 

Incl-

3 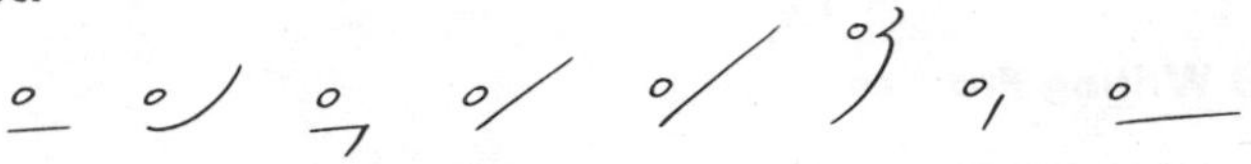

-ulate

4 

-ulation

5 

-ical

6 

1. Supervise, superintend, superhuman, supervisory, supervision, superior, supernatural.

2. Electric motor, electric light, electric fan, electric razor, electric switch, electric wire.

3. Incline, inclined, inclination, include, included, inclusive, inclusion, inclement.
4. Regulate, stimulate, formulate, speculate, stipulate, tabulate, congratulate.
5. Regulation, stimulation, formulation, speculation, stipulation, tabulation, congratulation.
6. Economical, technical, chemical, vertical, logical, medical.

339. Geographical Expressions

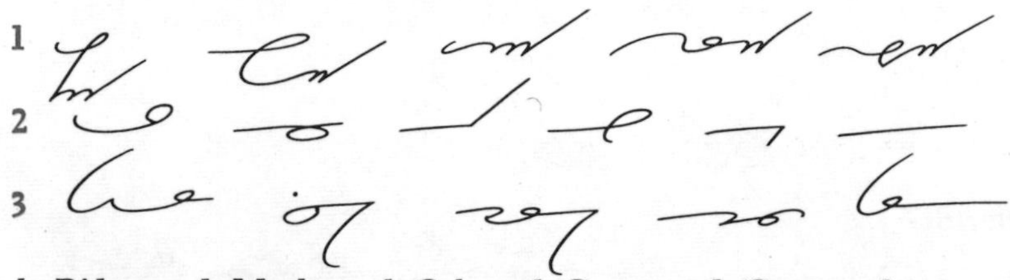

1. Ridgewood, Maplewood, Oakwood, Greenwood, Crestwood.
2. Louisiana, Maine, Maryland, Massachusetts, Michigan, Minnesota.
3. Berlin, Hamburg, Nuremburg, Munich, Bremen.

Reading and Writing Practice

340. Transcription Word Study

occupancy The act of taking possession of a house.

vibrating Moving back and forth; shaking.

redecorate To repair and beautify.

thermostat A device for regulating temperature.

341.

occupancy
, as clause
; because of comma

, nonrestrictive
, apposition
, introductory
responsibility
, introductory
anxious
, conjunction
, as clause
redecorated
well pleased
no noun,
no hyphen

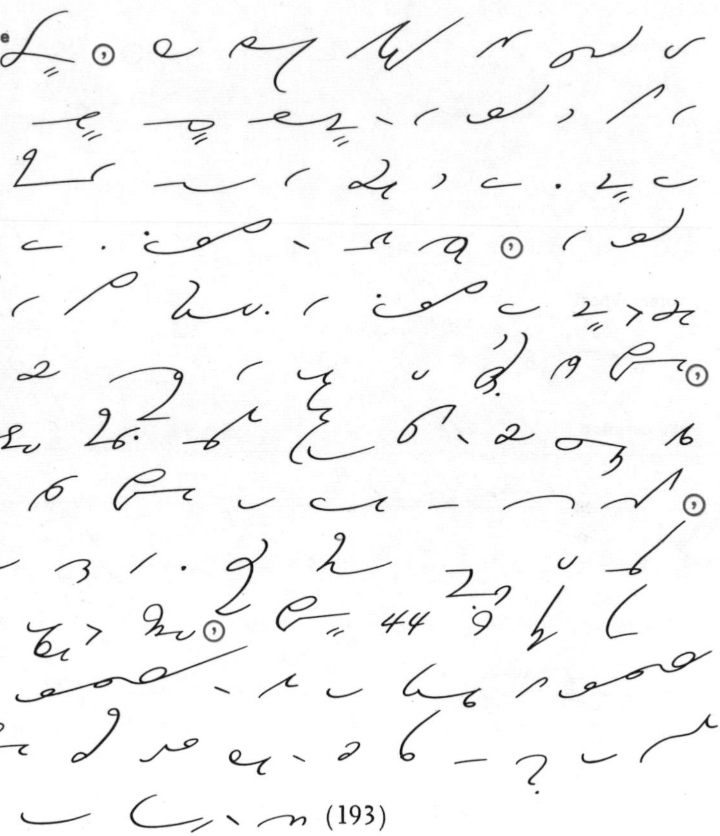

342. Transcribe:
January 1
$90
raise
, conjunction

, as clause

(86)

343.

, parenthetical

: enumeration
gauge

, as clause
thermostat
, nonrestrictive

; illustrative ,

, introductory
, series

(179)

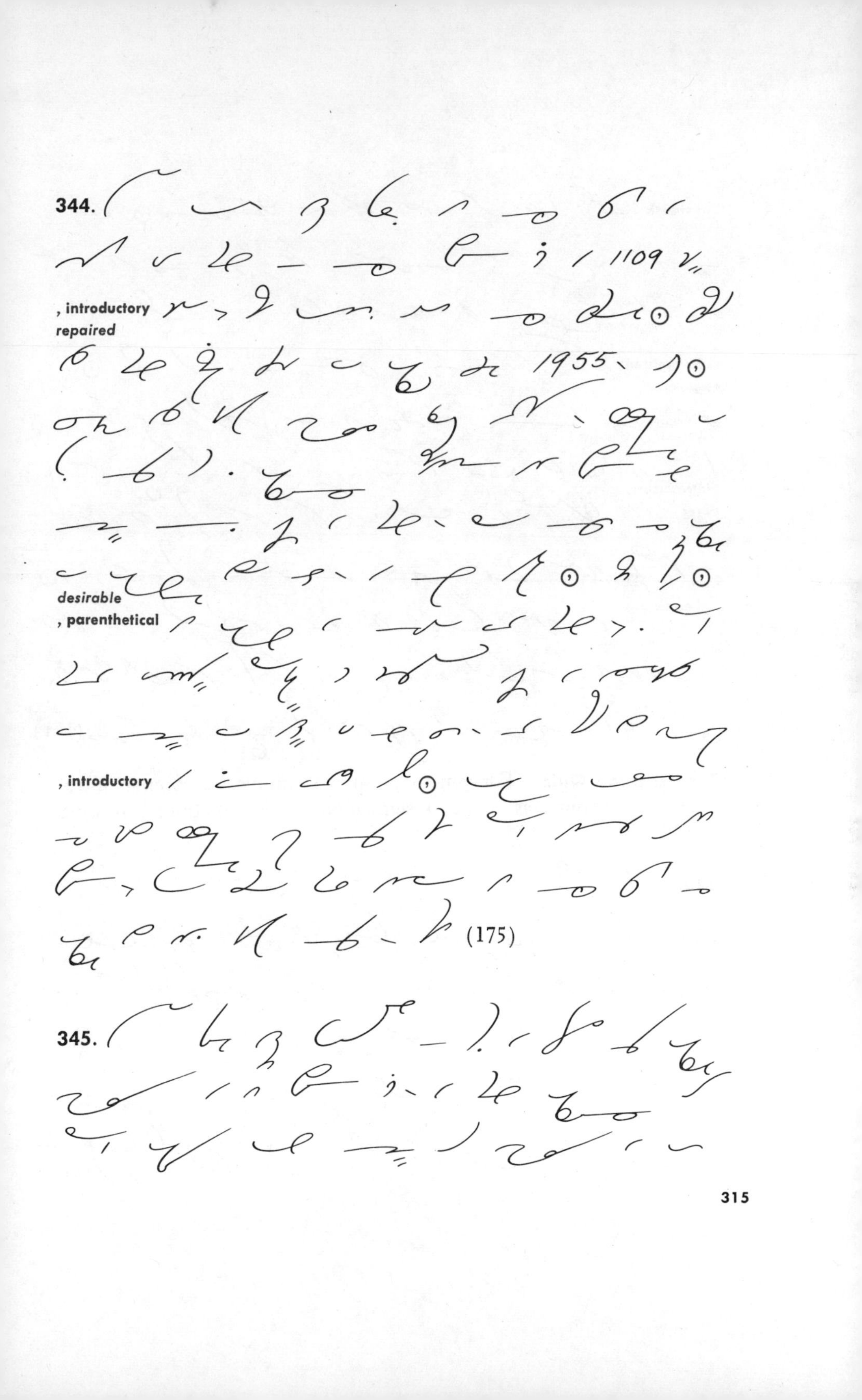

344.

1109

, introductory
repaired

1955

desirable
, parenthetical

, introductory

(175)

345.

, *as* clause

, *and* omitted

economical

, introductory

eaves

, *when* clause

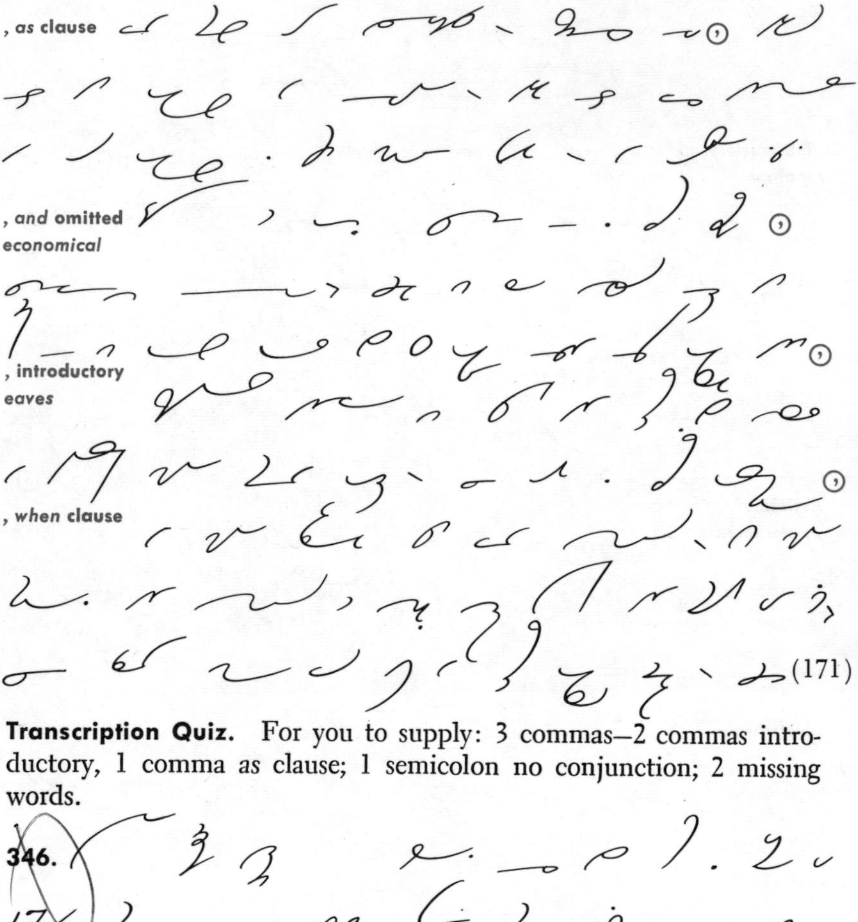

(171)

Transcription Quiz. For you to supply: 3 commas—2 commas introductory, 1 comma *as* clause; 1 semicolon no conjunction; 2 missing words.

346.

(87)

LESSON 50

347. Word-Building Practice—Expression of W

Wa-

1 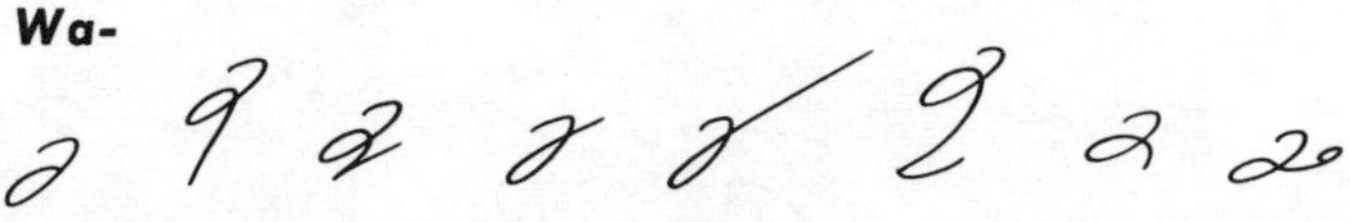

We-

2 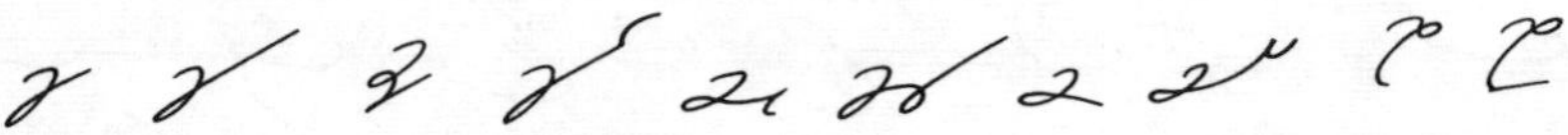

Wo-

3 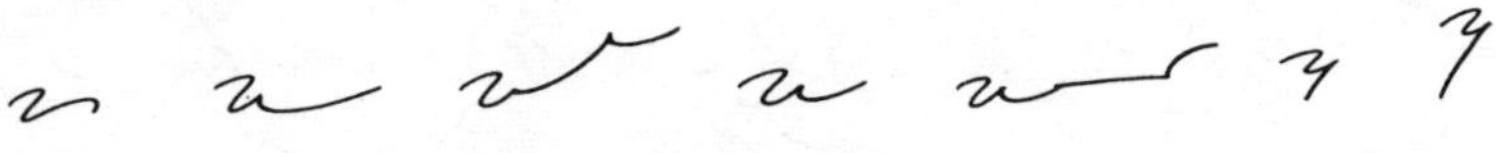

W in the Body of a Word

4 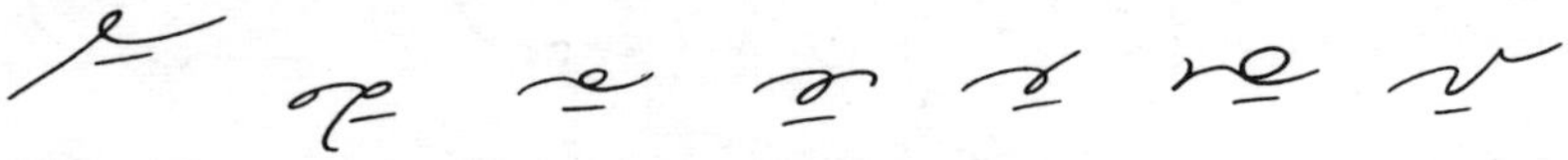

1. Way, wage, waste, wait, waited, waver, wax, wary.
2. Wet, weed, west, width, worse, wicked, wing, window, weep, weapon.
3. Walk, wall, wander, war, warmth, wash, watch.
4. Dwell, equip, queer, quick, quit, square, quarter.

348. Accuracy Practice—OO Hook

1 

2 

1. You, yours truly, you would; other, you want; shoe, woman, do, knew.
2. Into, are you, will you; noon, number, monument.

Reading and Writing Practice

349. Transcription Word Study

compact Pressed closely together.

conveyance A means of carrying; a vehicle.

contraption A gadget.

350. Rolling Homes Gather No Mortgages

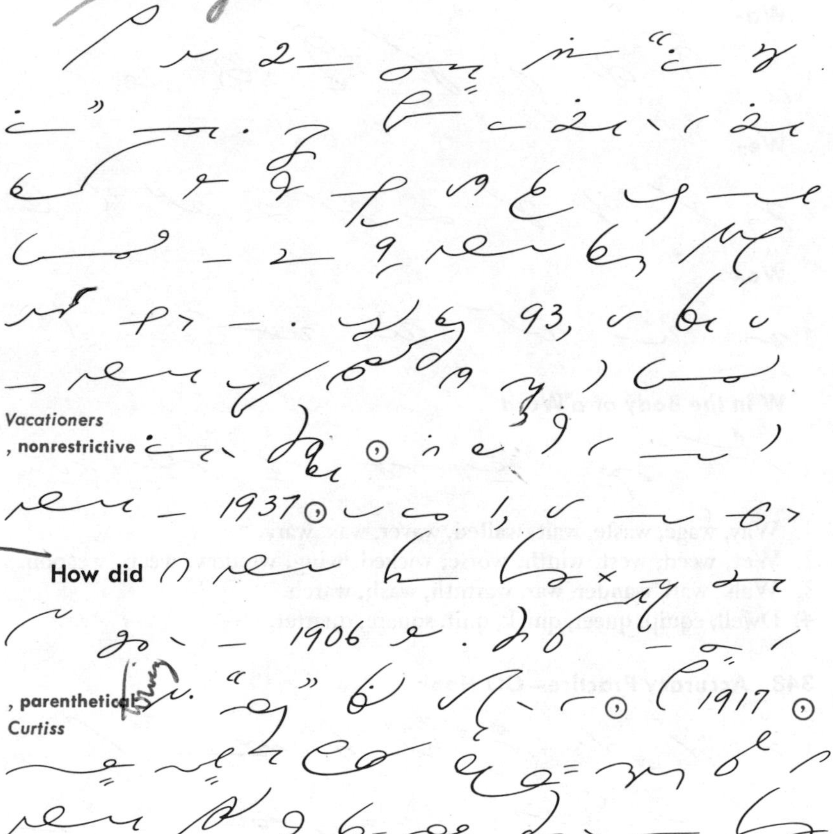

Vacationers

, nonrestrictive

How did

, parenthetical

Curtiss

; because of comma

1920

, series

, inside quote

, introductory

breaking

Sherman's first

conveyance

, parenthetical

garage

, series

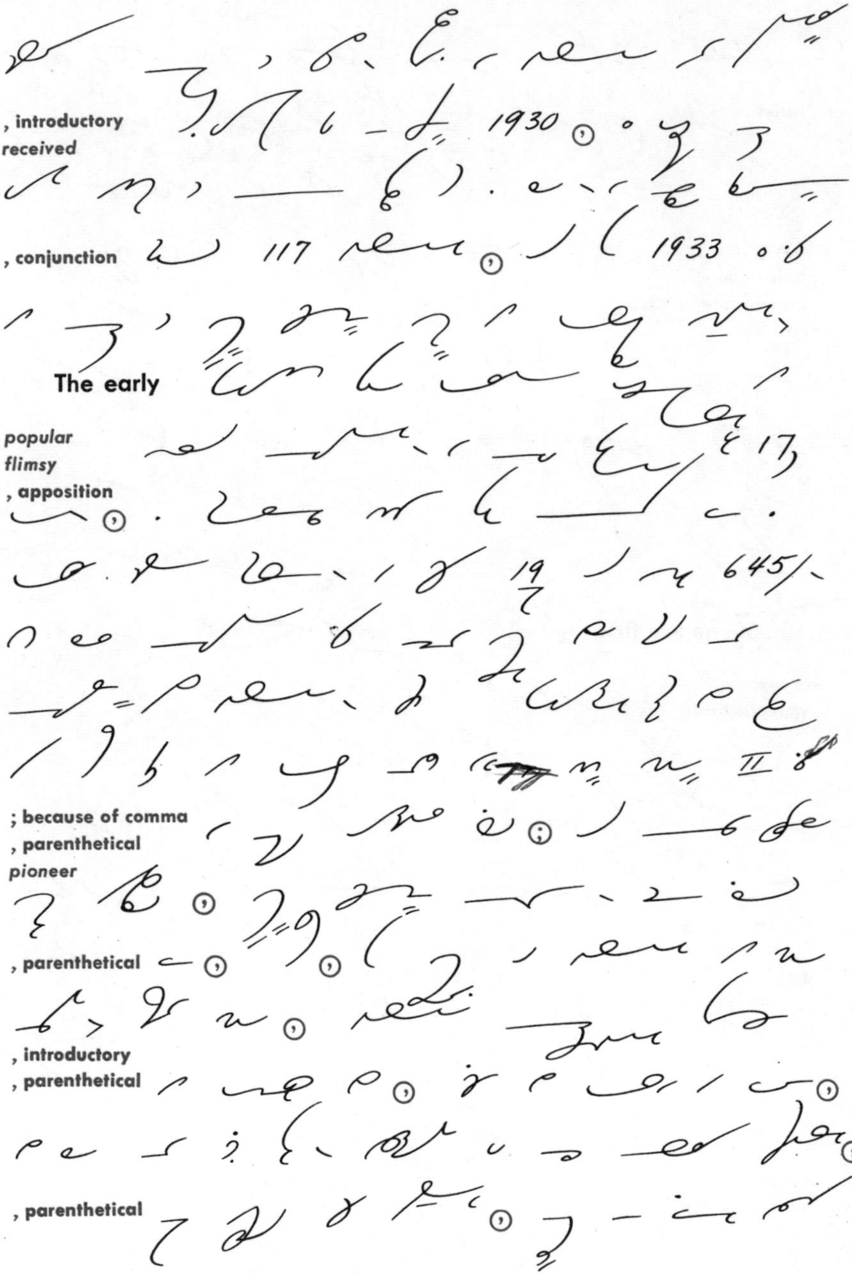

, introductory
received
, conjunction
The early
popular
flimsy
, apposition
; because of comma
, parenthetical
pioneer
, parenthetical
, introductory
, parenthetical
, parenthetical

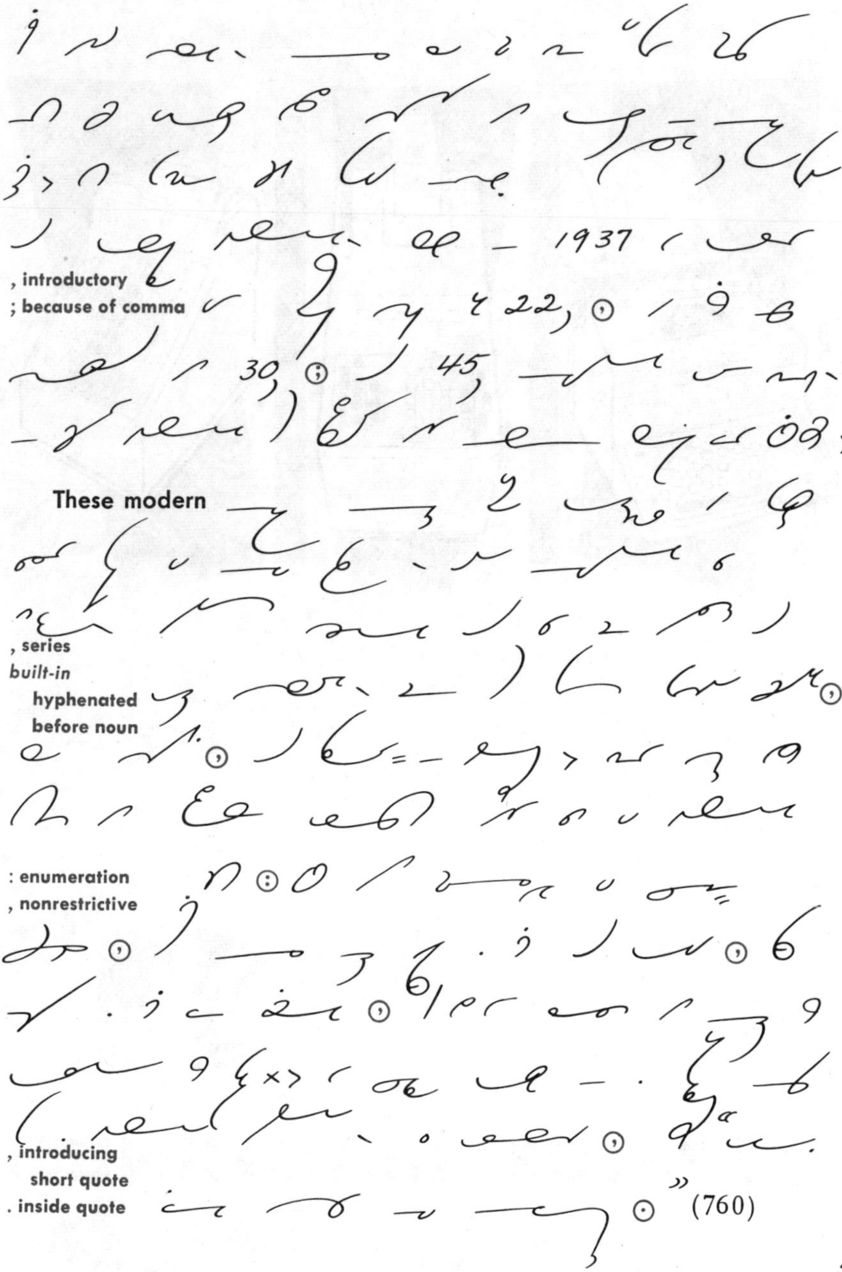

, introductory
; because of comma

These modern

, series
built-in
hyphenated
before noun

: enumeration
, nonrestrictive

, introducing
short quote
. inside quote

(760)

11

OFFICE MACHINES

LESSON 51

351. Brief Forms and Derivatives

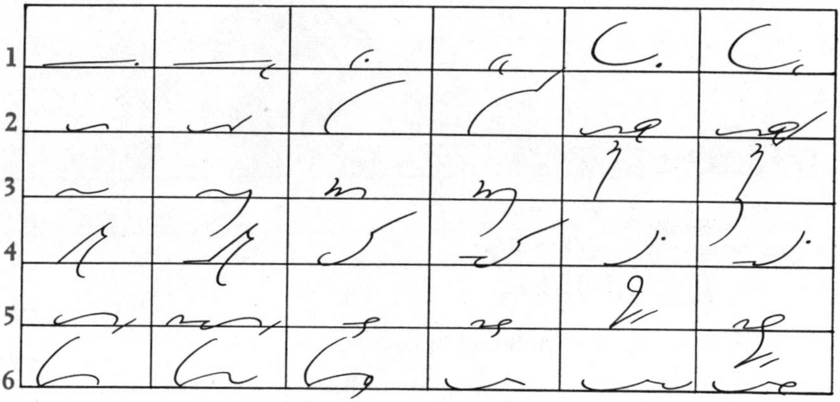

1. Morning, mornings; thing, things; billing, billings.
2. Work, worked; time, timed; recognize, recognized.
3. Correct, corrective; success, successive; suggest, suggestive.
4. Desirable, undesirable; wanted, unwanted; ending, unending.
5. Organized, unorganized; necessary, unnecessary; advertised, unadvertised.
6. Big, bigger, biggest; long, longer, longest.

352. Brief Form and Phrase Letter

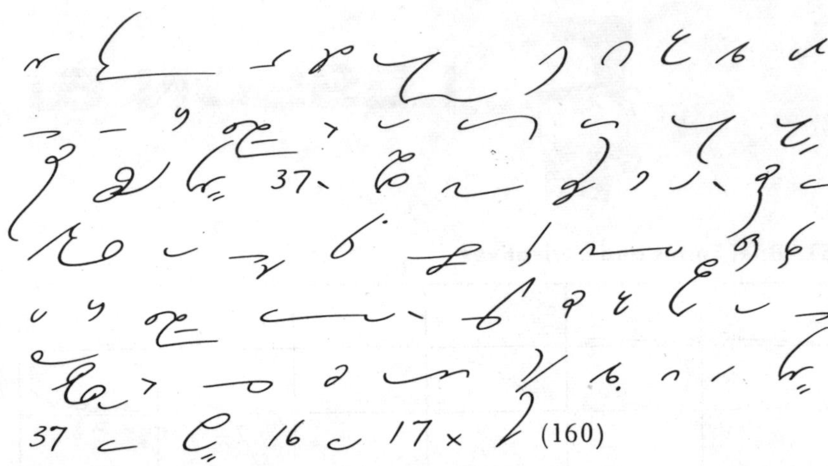

(160)

Reading and Writing Practice

353. Transcription Word Study

audio-visual Pertaining to hearing and seeing.

enlightening Shedding light on; informative.

computations Acts or processes of calculating.

354

, parenthetical

, *and* omitted

accurate

, parenthetical

, series
inventory

, apposition
: introducing long quote

. inside quote
. courteous request

(178)

355.

educational
; illustrative ,
, series

, *when* clause
undoubtedly

; because of comma
realize

, parenthetical

, introducing short quote

. inside quote
, parenthetical

(255)

356.

, *and* omitted
color

, conjunction

enlightening

(85)

Transcription Quiz. For you to supply: 7 commas—2 commas *if* clause, 3 commas series, 2 commas parenthetical; 1 semicolon no conjunction; 2 missing words.

357.

(187)

LESSON 52

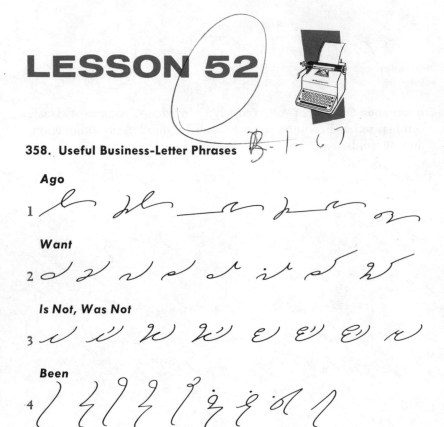

358. Useful Business-Letter Phrases

Ago

1 

Want

2 

Is Not, Was Not

3 

Been

4 

1. Days ago, few days ago, months ago, few months ago, weeks ago.
2. I want, we want, you want, they want, he wants, who wants, they wanted, if you wanted.
3. There is not, there isn't, if it is not, if it isn't, he was not, he wasn't, I wasn't, it was not.
4. Have been, have not been, I have been, I have not been, we have been, has not been, there has been, had been, would have been.

359. Frequent Names

1
2

1. Miller, Mitchell, Moore, Morgan.
2. Hortense, Ida, Irene, Jean, Jeannette, Josephine, Judith, Julia.

Reading and Writing Practice

360. Transcription Word Study

resiliency Bounce.

platen The roller of a typewriter.

prospectus An outline of an enterprise or product giving information designed to create interest and gain acceptance.

acoustical Serving to aid hearing.

361.

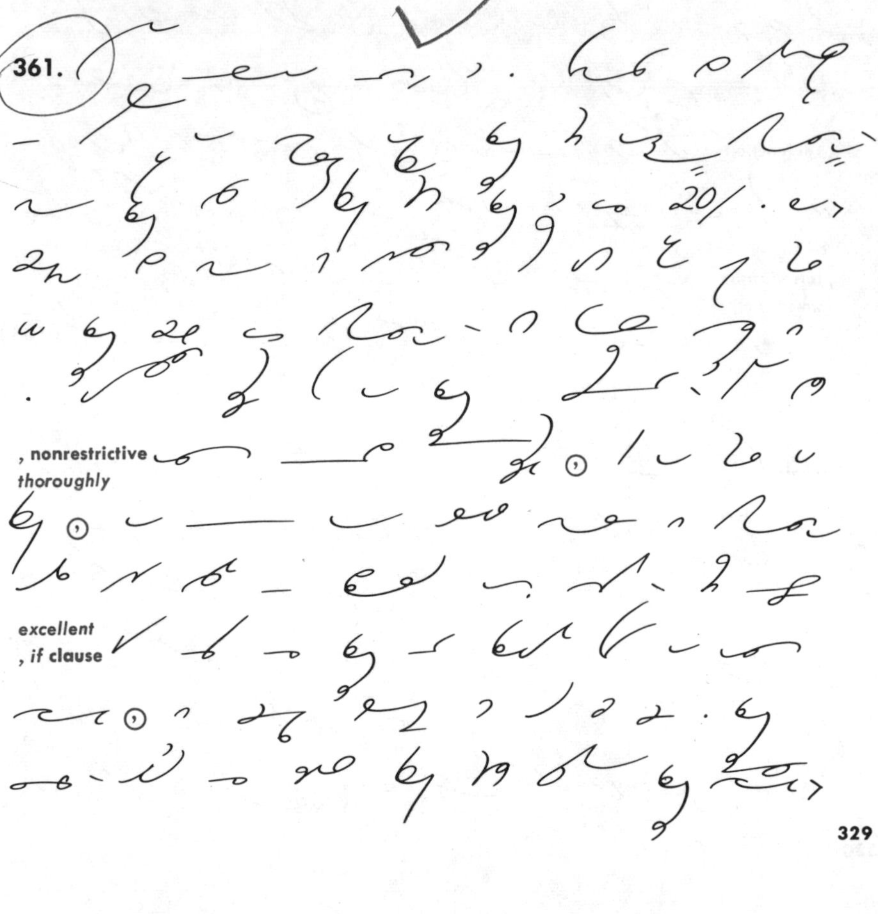

, introducing short quote

. inside quote

(173)

362.

, conjunction

, introductory

32/

, conjunction

, introductory

immediately

(104)

363.

, *and* omitted

performance

, *if* clause

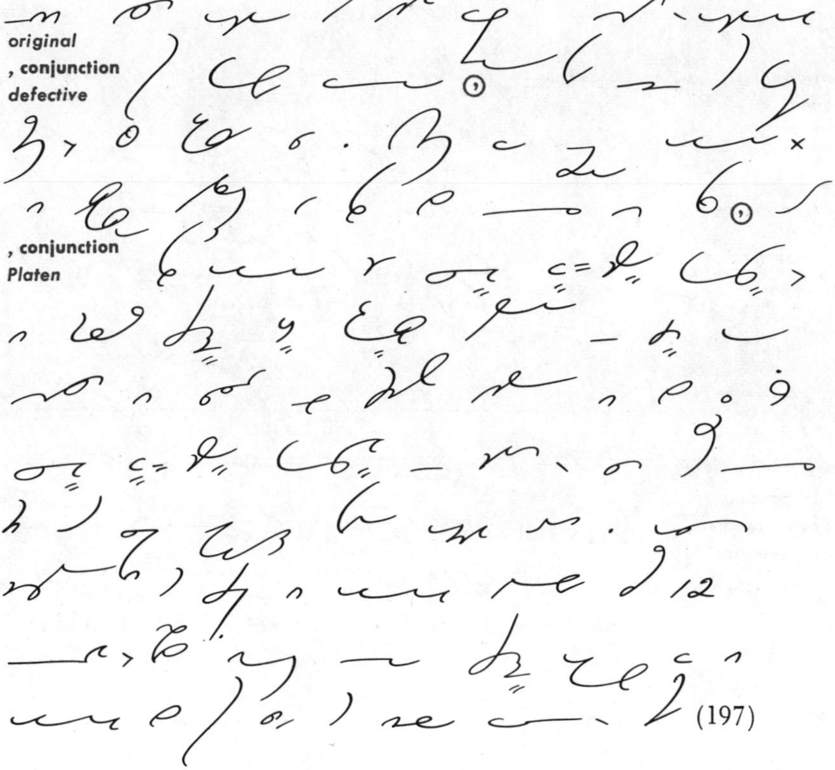

original
, conjunction
defective
, conjunction
Platen

(197)

364.

, introducing short quote
. inside quote
, introductory
, series
, apposition

associating
mind

prospectus
, series

, introductory
; no conjunction
, introductory

(214)

365.

footsteps
, series

productivity
, when clause

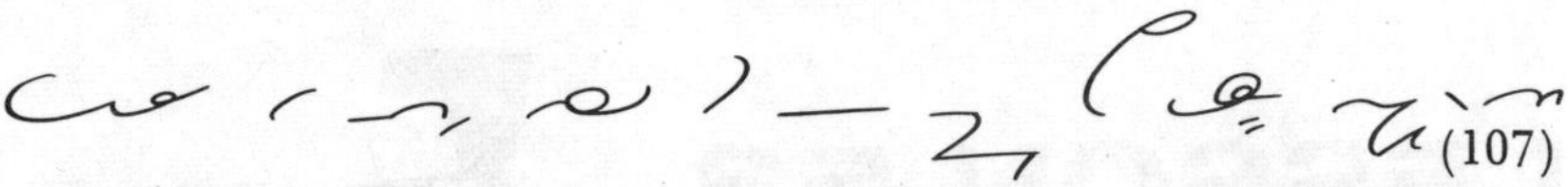
(107)

Transcription Quiz. For you to supply: 7 commas—2 commas parenthetical, 2 commas apposition, 1 comma *when* clause, 2 commas series; 2 missing words.

366.

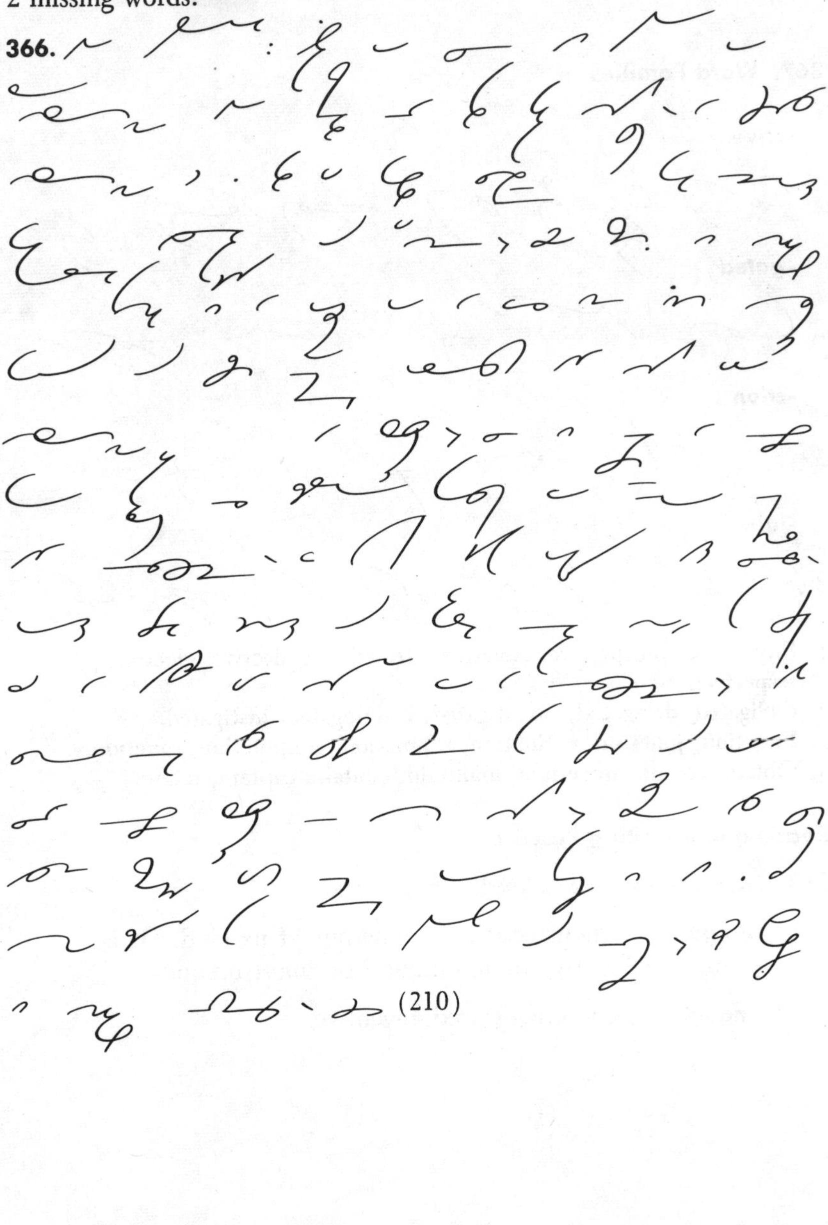
(210)

LESSON 53

367. Word Families

-ctive

1 

-gated

2 

-ction

3 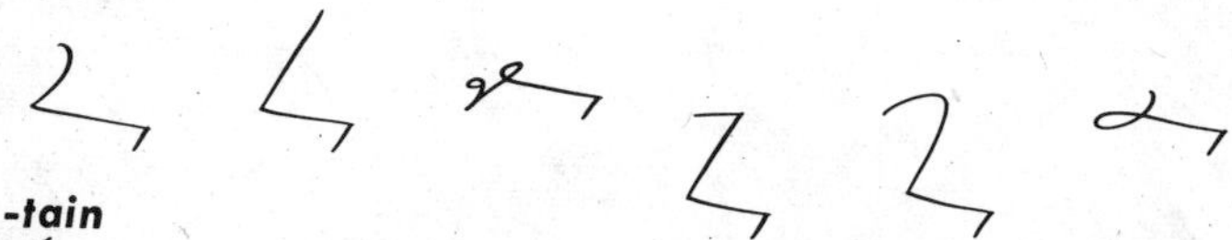

-tain

4 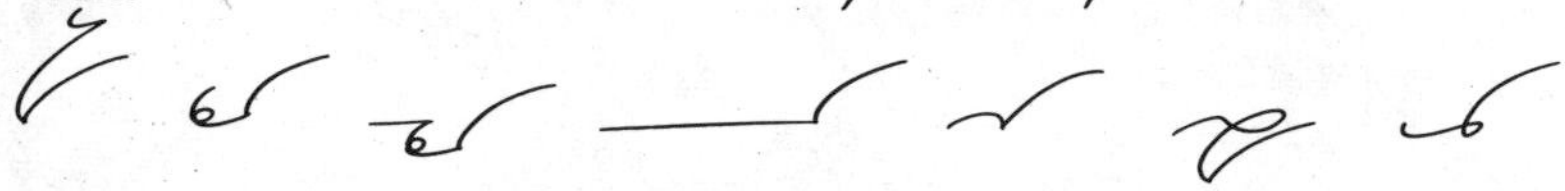

1. Productive, prospective, effective, attractive, collective, elective, respective.
2. Obligated, delegated, investigated, interrogated, instigated.
3. Function, junction, extinction, injunction, conjunction, sanction.
4. Obtain, certain, uncertain, maintain, contain, captain, retain.

Reading and Writing Practice

368. Transcription Word Study

unique Without equal; the only one of its kind. (It is incorrect to say "more unique," or "most unique.")

ingenious Cleverly devised, inventive.

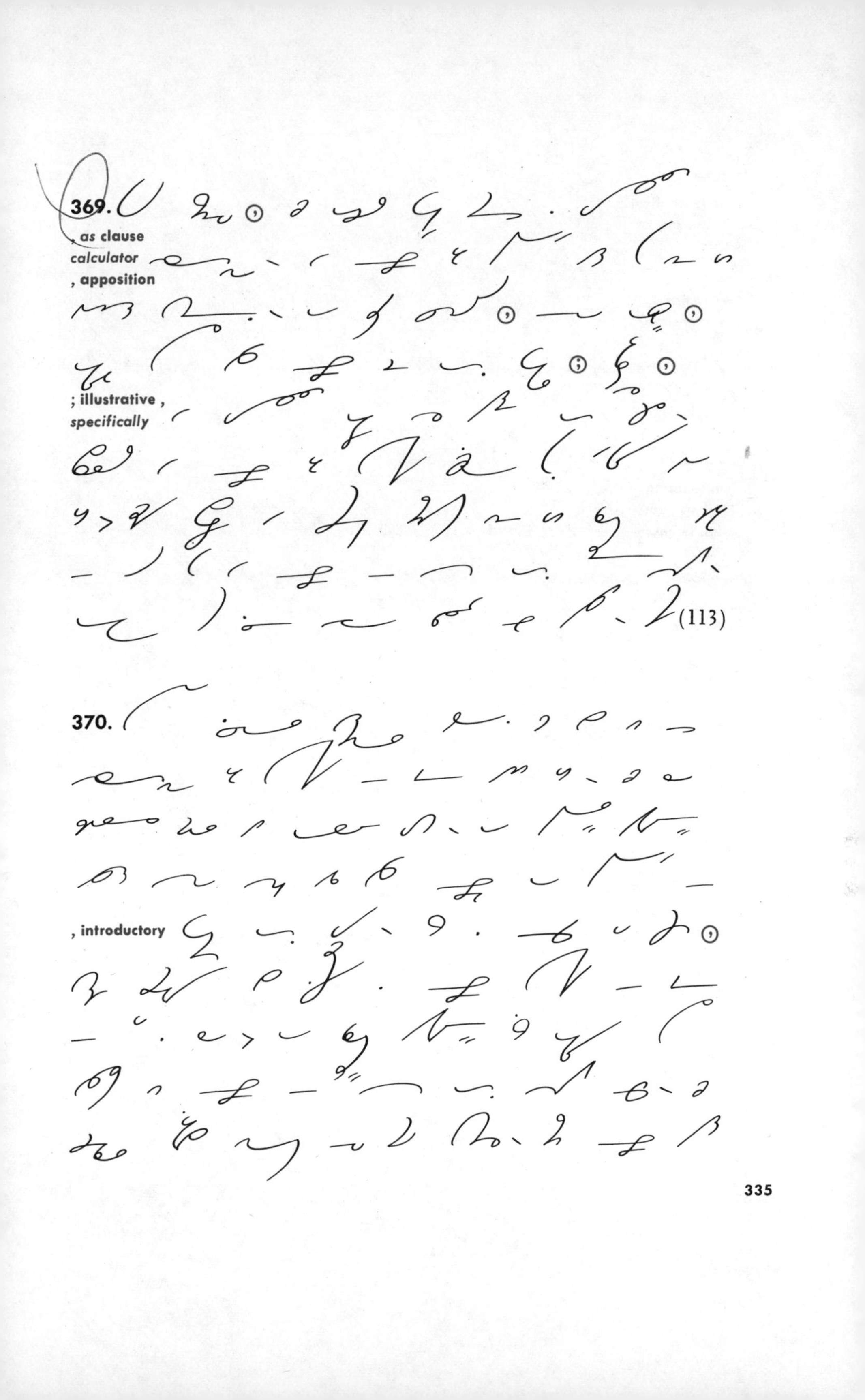

369.

, *as clause*

calculator

, *apposition*

; *illustrative* ,

specifically

(113)

370.

, *introductory*

, parenthetical
immediate
guaranteed
, conjunction

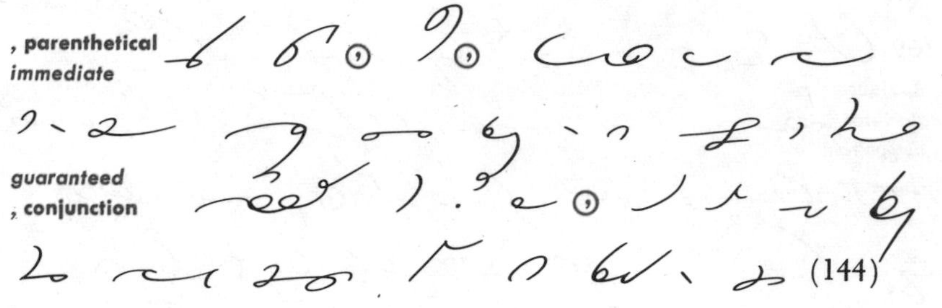

(144)

371.

, introducing short quote
. inside quote
, conjunction
, conjunction
widely used no hyphen after *ly*
unique
, introductory

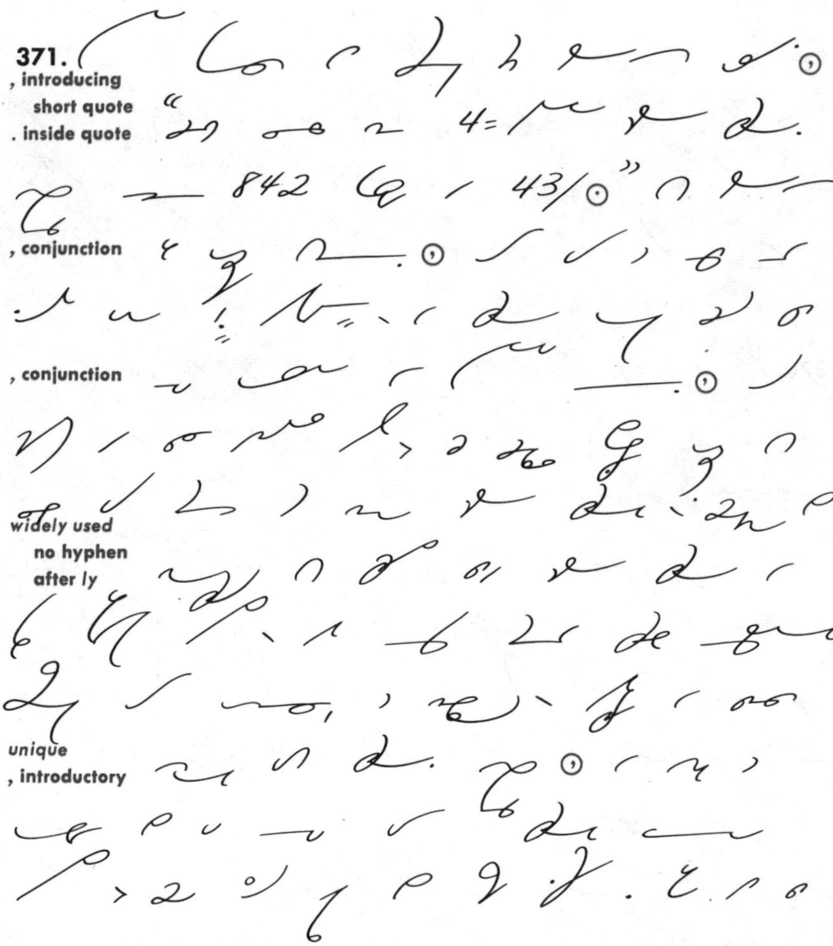

842

one-year hyphenated before noun

year's assistance

, if clause

well trained no noun, no hyphen

(259)

372. Transcribe:

November 28

28

842

, parenthetical

specialists

encountering

, as clause

, if clause

, when clause

: enumeration

, series

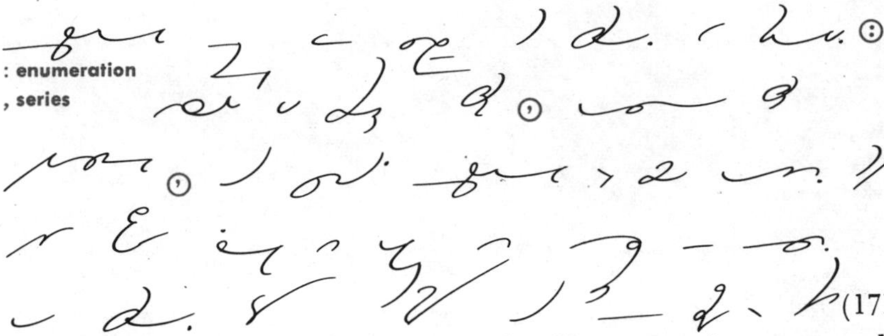

(171)

Transcription Quiz. For you to supply: 8 commas–1 comma *and* omitted, 2 commas nonrestrictive, 2 commas apposition, 2 commas series, 1 comma introductory; 1 semicolon no conjunction; 2 missing words.

373.

(148)

LESSON 54

8-2-67

374. Word Beginnings and Endings

Sub-

1 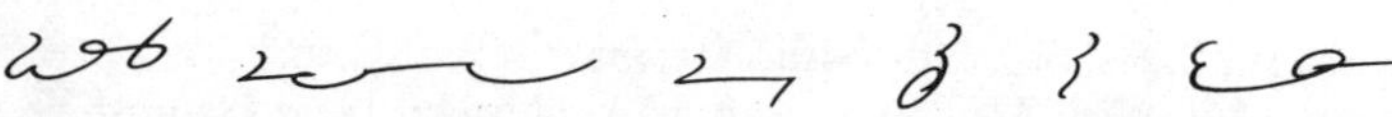

Self-

2 

-ingly

3 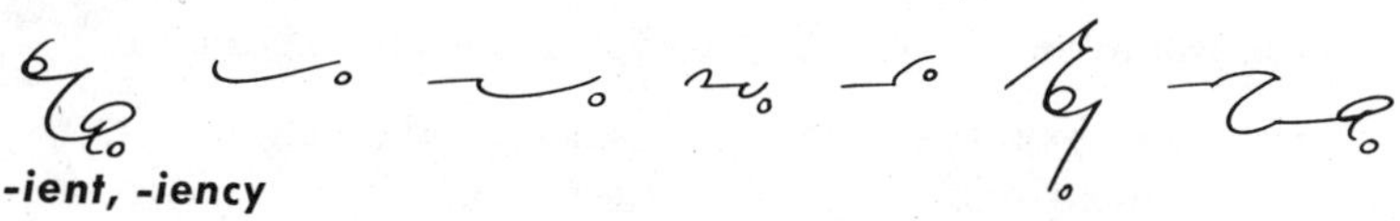

-ient, -iency

4 

-ual

5 

-hood

6 

1. Subordinate, subnormal, submission, subside, subsist, sublime.
2. Self-addressed, self-sufficient, self-esteem, self-denial, self-sacrifice, self-reliance.
3. Surprisingly, willingly, unwillingly, unknowingly, unthinkingly, disparagingly, uncompromisingly.

4. Efficient, proficient, deficient, inefficient, patient, proficiency, deficiency.
5. Manual, schedule, actual, perpetual, factual.
6. Neighborhood, falsehood, likelihood, livelihood, statehood, manhood.

375. Geographical Expressions

1
2
3

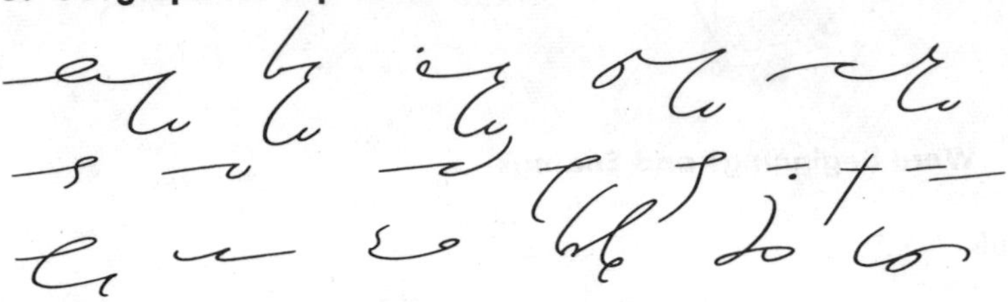

1. Marlborough, Jonesboro, Hillsboro, Attleboro, Goldsboro.
2. Mississippi, Missouri, Montana, Nebraska, Nevada, New Hampshire, New Jersey, New Mexico.
3. Naples, Rome, Sicily, Budapest, Vienna, Prague.

Reading and Writing Practice

376. Transcription Word Study

subordinates Those who are lesser in rank or importance.

overhead expenses Indirect, general costs such as rent, telephone, etc.

377.

, apposition

, nonrestrictive

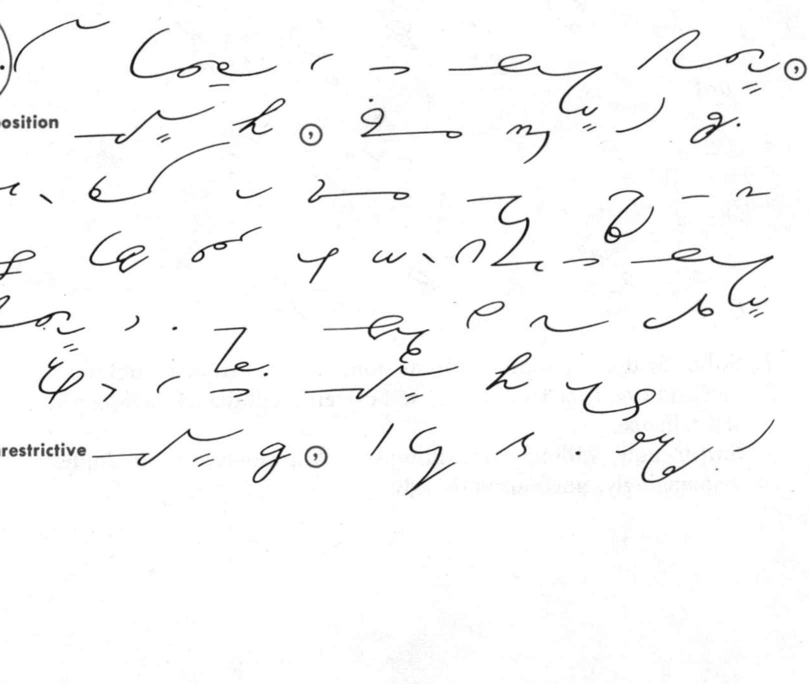

low-priced
hyhenated before noun

brilliant
, *and* omitted

convenience
, *when* clause

, introducing short quote
. inside quote
, *and* omitted

(174)

378.

, *as* clause
; no conjunction

, introductory
worn
; because of comma

, *if* clause

, introductory

(138)

379.

, series
, introductory
similar
: enumeration
men's
ingenuity
, nonrestrictive
, conjunction
, *as* clause
, parenthetical

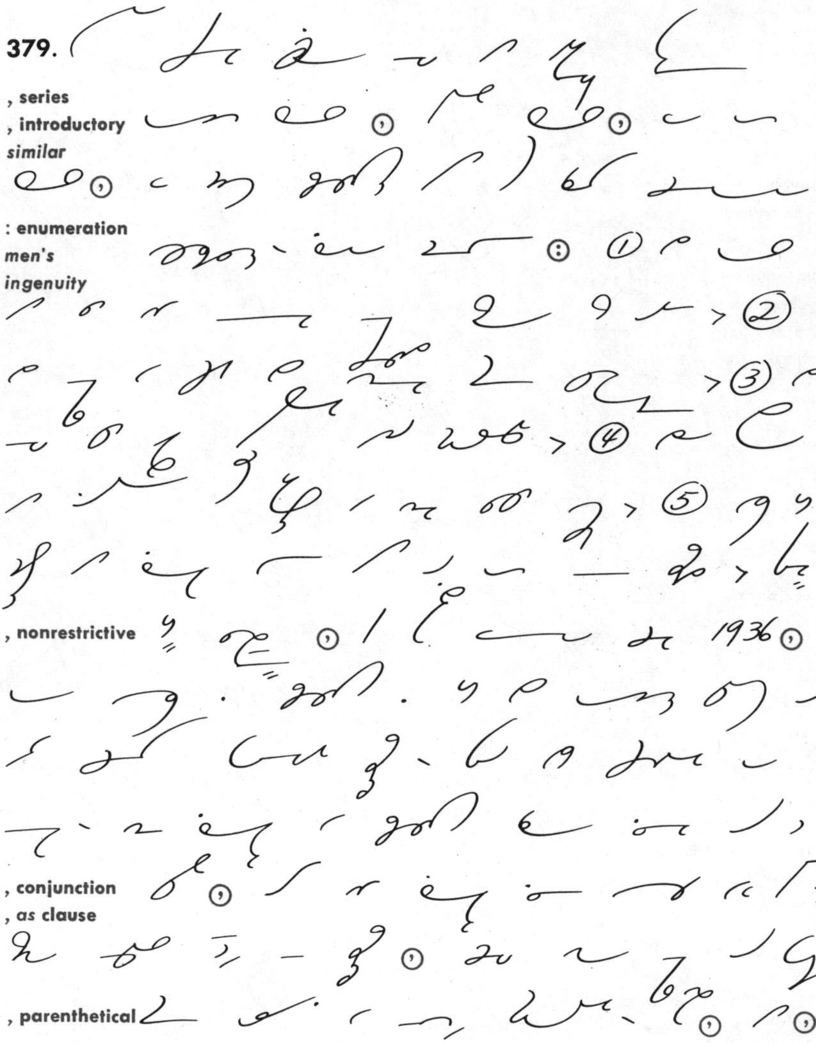

(207)

380.

; no conjunction
competent

; illustrative ,
, series
receivable

reluctance
, and omitted
, if clause

, *when* clause

, apposition

. courteous request

(229)

Transcription Quiz. For you to supply: 5 commas—2 commas series, 2 commas parenthetical, 1 comma *and* omitted; 1 semicolon because of comma; 2 missing words.

381.

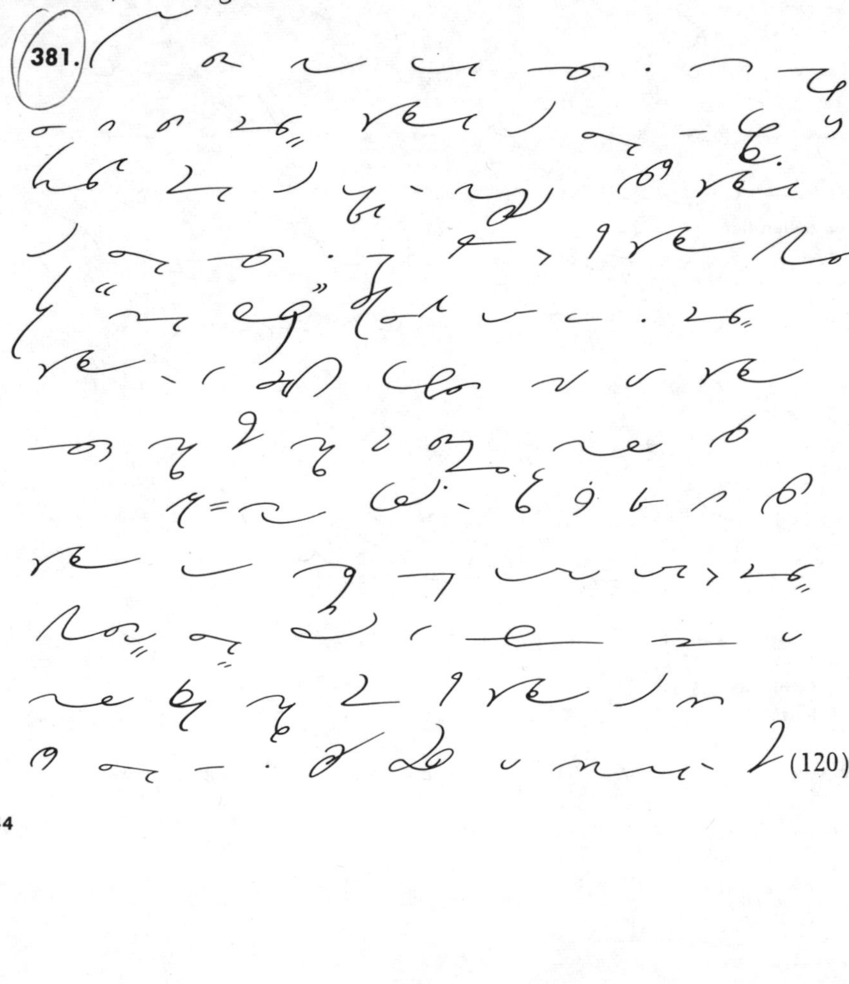

(120)

LESSON 55

382. Word-Building Practice—Blends

-rd

1 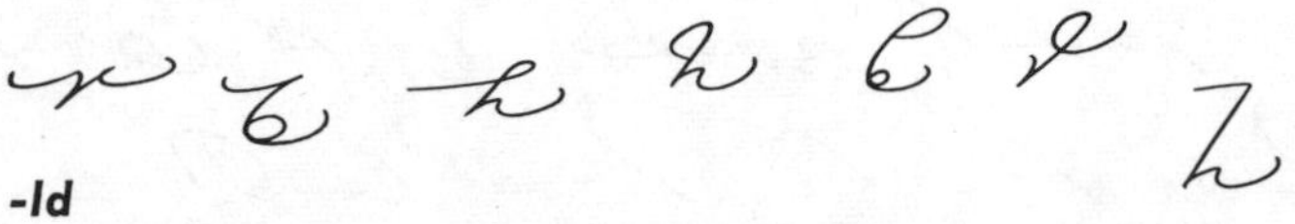

-ld

2 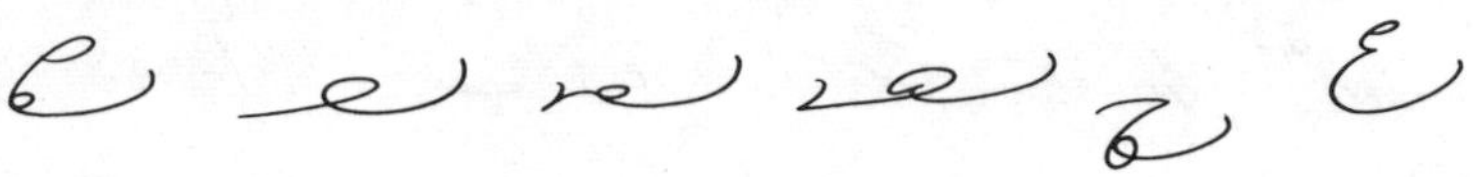

-ted, -ded

3 

Min

4 

-ses

5 

-xes

6 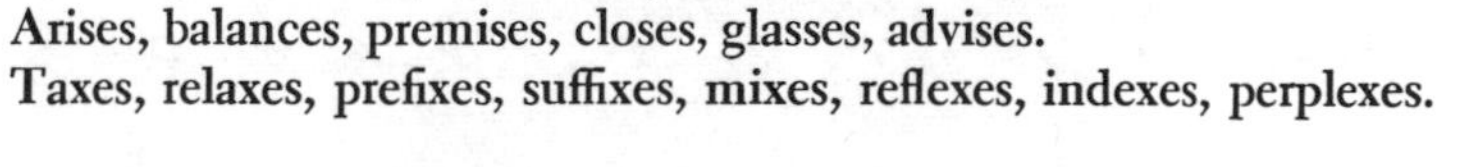

1. Restored, repaired, measured, assured, appeared, stared, injured.
2. Appealed, mailed, skilled, smiled, compiled, expelled.
3. Greeted, heated, eliminated, traded, deeded, excluded.
4. Minute, minimum, miniature, terminate, minister.
5. Arises, balances, premises, closes, glasses, advises.
6. Taxes, relaxes, prefixes, suffixes, mixes, reflexes, indexes, perplexes.

Reading and Writing Practice

383. Transcription Word Study

modulation The use of stress or expression to convey meaning.

slovenly Lacking neatness; sloppy.

articulation Distinct enunciation.

384. The Gift of Voice

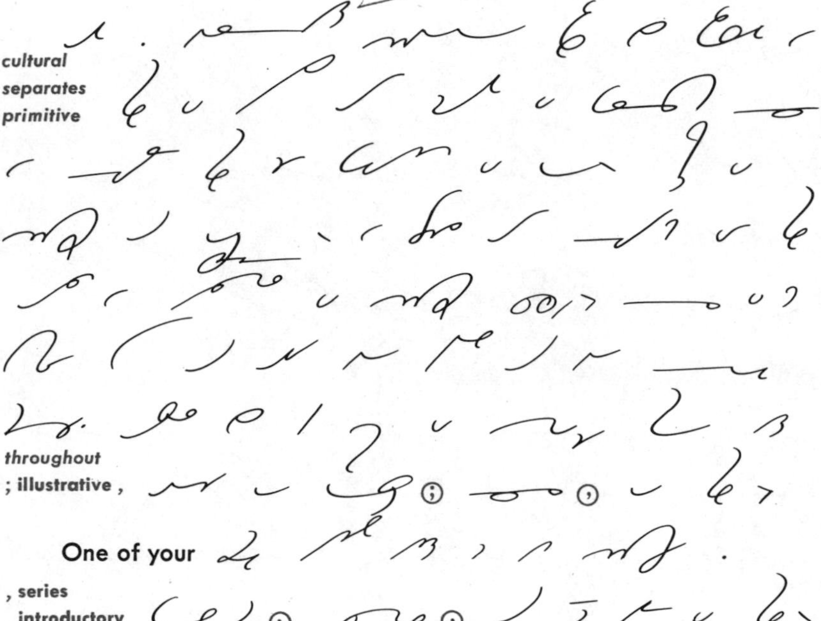

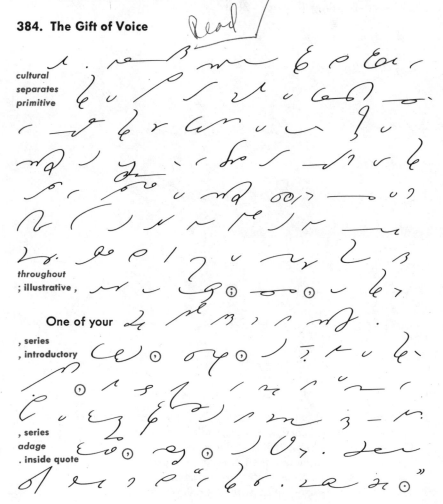

cultural
separates
primitive

throughout
; illustrative ,

One of your

, series
, introductory

, series
adage
. inside quote

, *and* omitted
; no conjunction
, *if* clause
, parenthetical
, *and* omitted
well-modulated
hyphenated
before noun
, introductory
pronunciation
, *and* omitted

We cannot all

, conjunction
articulation

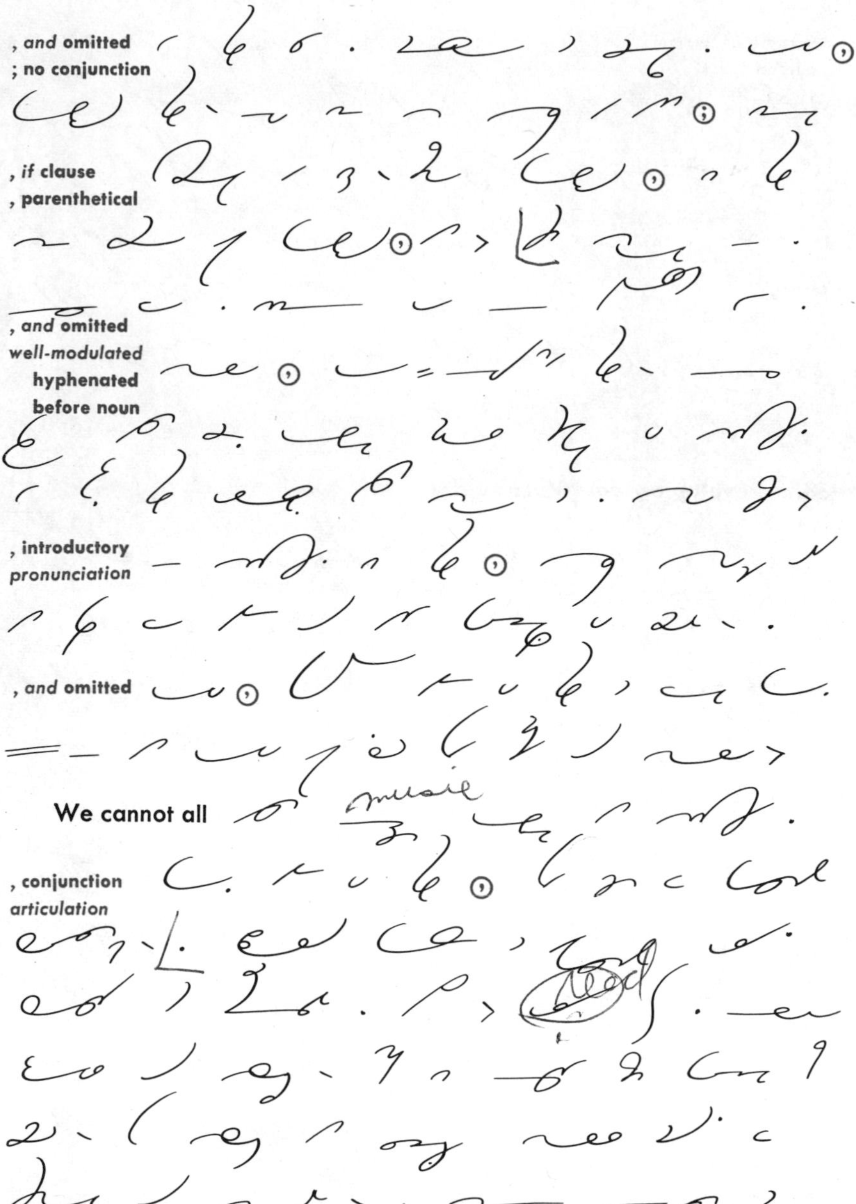

; because of comma
, parenthetical
theater
, parenthetical

(390)

385. Developing Your Vocabulary

, introductory
language
, apposition
, introducing short quote
; illustrative ,
. inside quote
, introductory
: enumeration
dictionary
, *and* omitted
intelligent

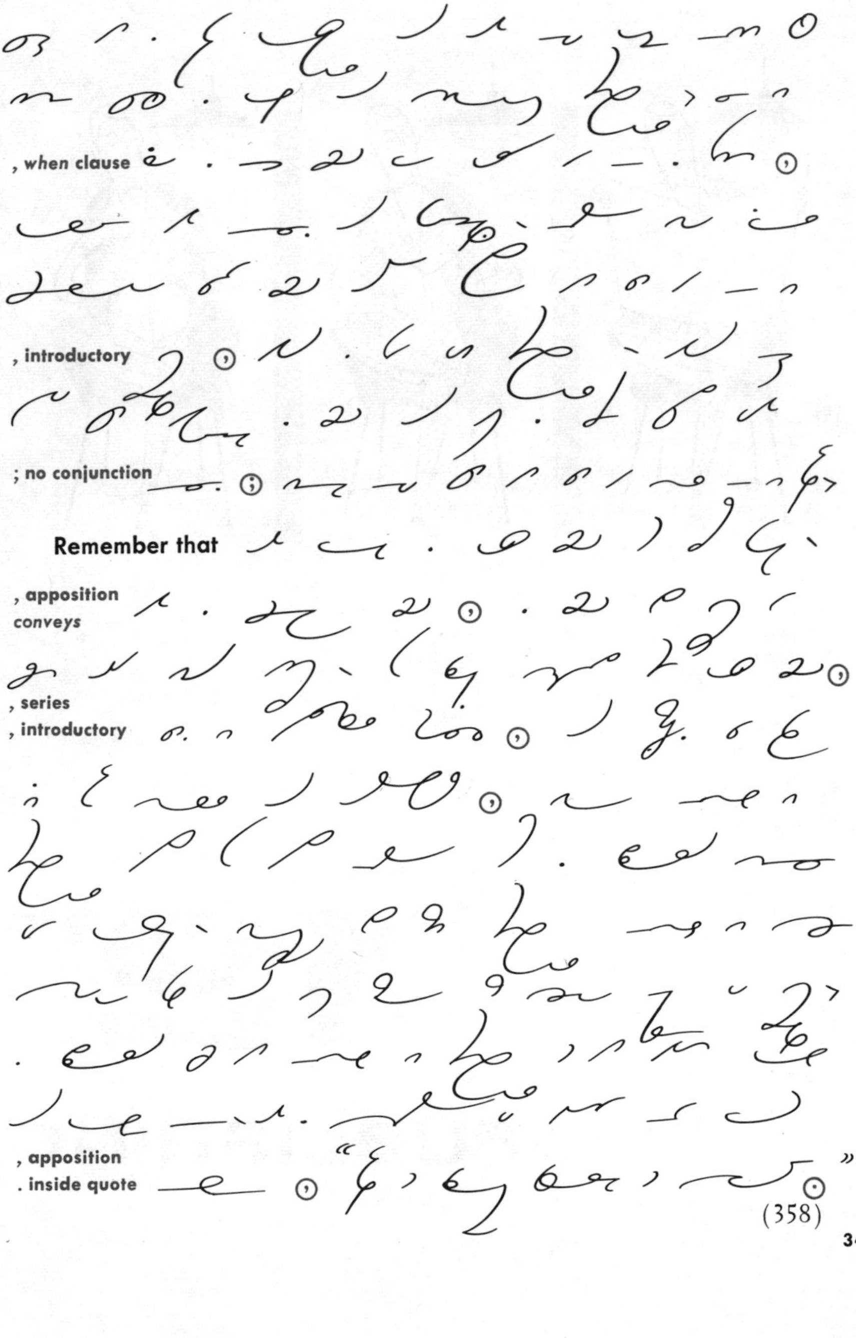

, when clause

, introductory

; no conjunction

Remember that

, apposition
conveys

, series
, introductory

, apposition
. inside quote

(358)

12

PUBLISHING

LESSON 56

386. Brief Forms and Derivatives

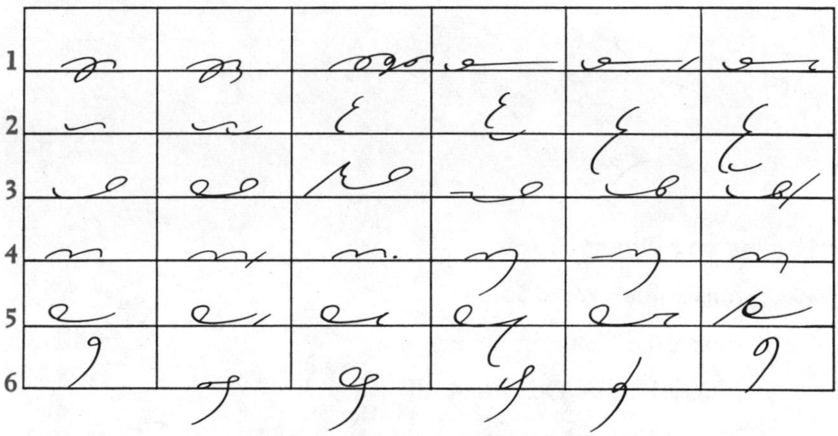

1. Character, characters, characteristic; remember, remembered, remembers.
2. Work, worker; speak, speaker; public-publish, publisher.
3. Like, alike, dislike, unlike, likely, likelihood.
4. Conclude, concluded, concluding, conclusive, inconclusive, conclusion.
5. Allow, allowed, allows, allowable, allowance, disallow.
6. Ever, whenever, wherever, whatever, whichever, however.

387. Brief Form and Phrase Letter

(137)

Reading and Writing Practice

388. Transcription Word Study

absorbing Engrossing, engaging.

procrastinate Delay, put off.

vital Essential, important.

389.
, introductory

; illustrative ,
, series

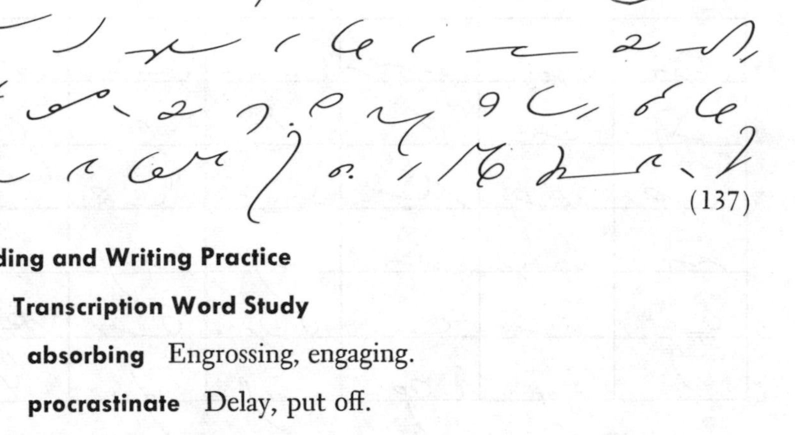

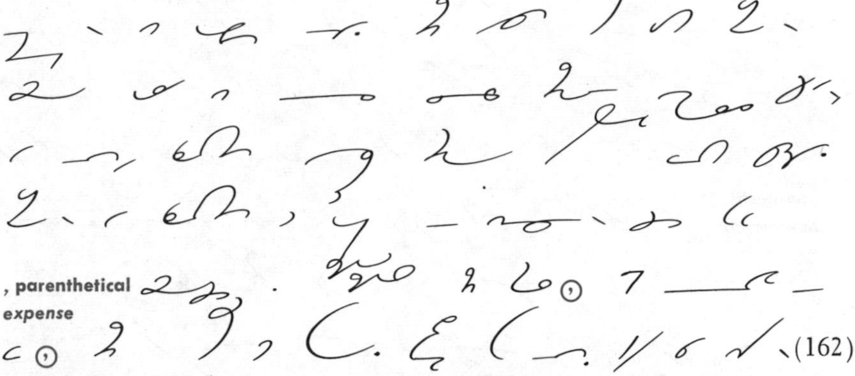

, parenthetical
expense

(162)

390.

, as clause
, introducing short quote
. inside quote
: enumeration
; because of comma
, apposition
, when clause
. courteous request

(141)

391.

, nonrestrictive

newsstands

, introductory

(158)

392.

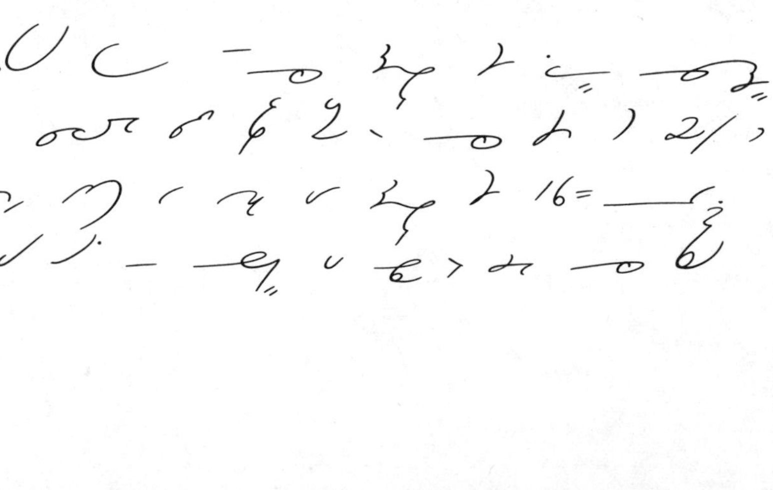

spring

, introductory

, conjunction

appreciate

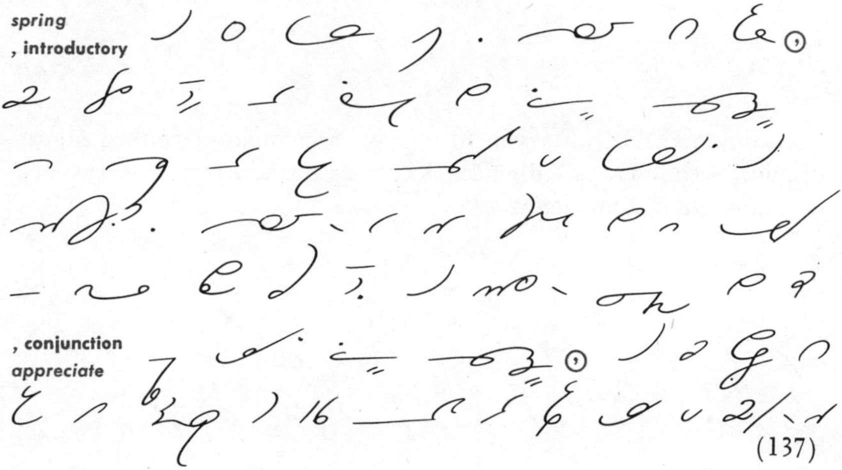

(137)

393.

, *if* clause

suggestions

humanly

, introductory

highly rated

no hyphen

after *ly*

, *and* omitted

, conjunction

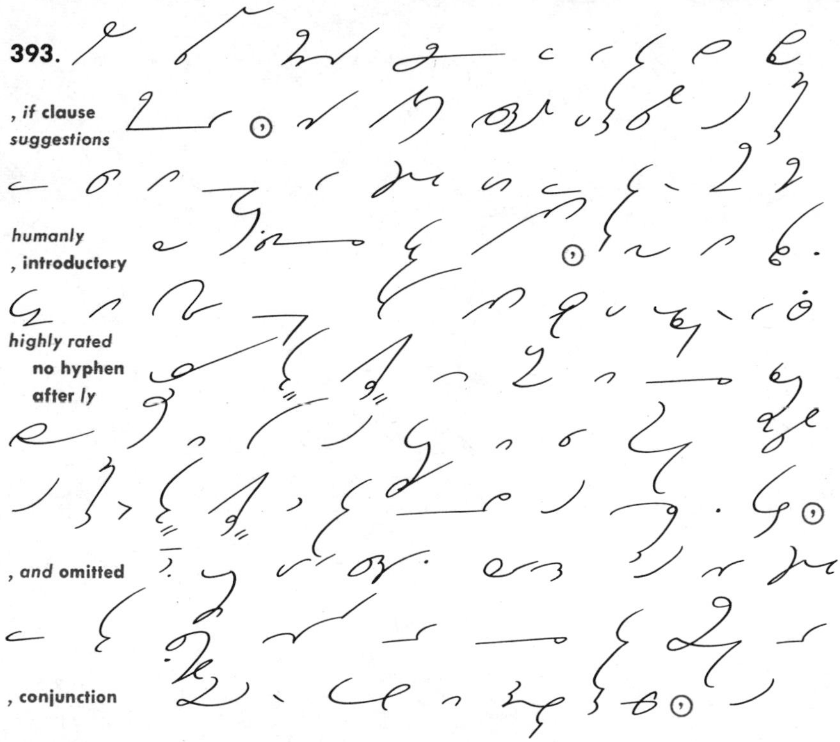

(147)

Transcription Quiz. For you to supply: 6 commas—1 comma nonrestrictive, 4 commas parenthetical, 1 comma introductory; 3 semicolons no conjunction; 2 missing words.

394.

(177)

LESSON 57

395. Useful Business-Letter Phrases

Of Course

1 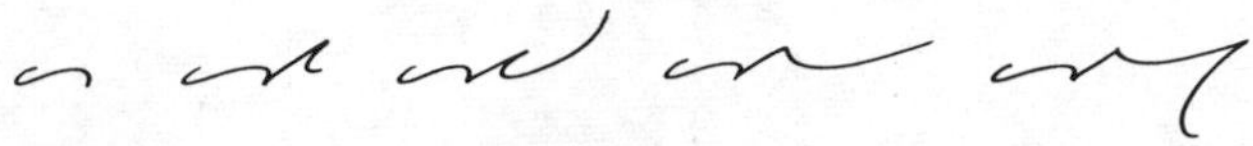

Let Us

2 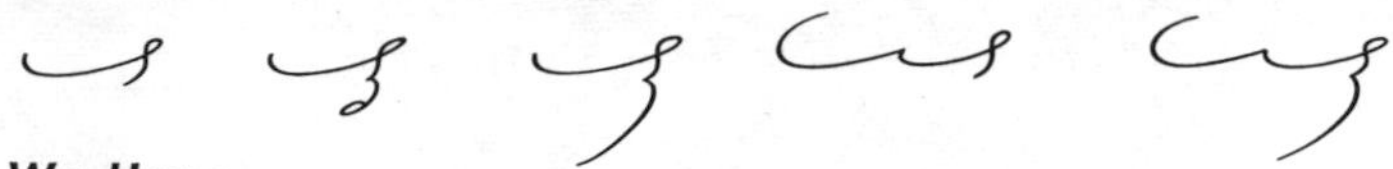

We Hope

3 

I Hope

4 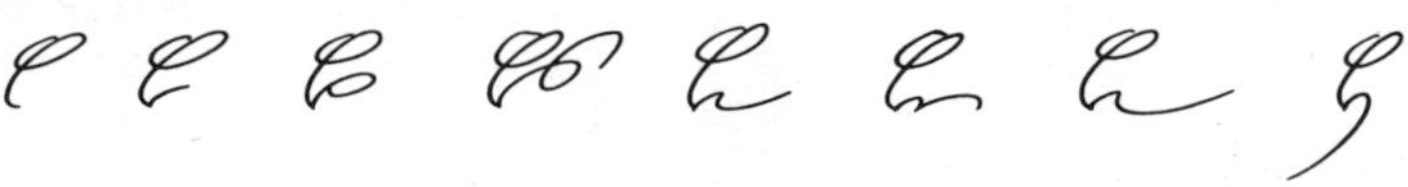

1. Of course, of course it is, of course it is not, of course it will, of course it will be.
2. Let us, let us see, let us have, please let us, please let us have.
3. We hope, we hope that, we hope that the, we hope that this, we hope you can, we hope you will, we hope you are.
4. I hope, I hope the, I hope that, I hope that this, I hope you are, I hope you can, I hope you will, I hope you have.

396. Frequent Names

1 

2 

1. Morris, Morrison, Morse, Monroe, Murray.
2. John, Joseph, Lawrence, Leonard, Louis, Michael, Nathan.

Reading and Writing Practice

397. Transcription Word Study

complimentary Free. (Do not confuse with *complementary*, which means "filling out or completing.")

house organ A magazine or periodical issued by an organization for its own employees.

398.

, conjunction
, parenthetical
Christmas

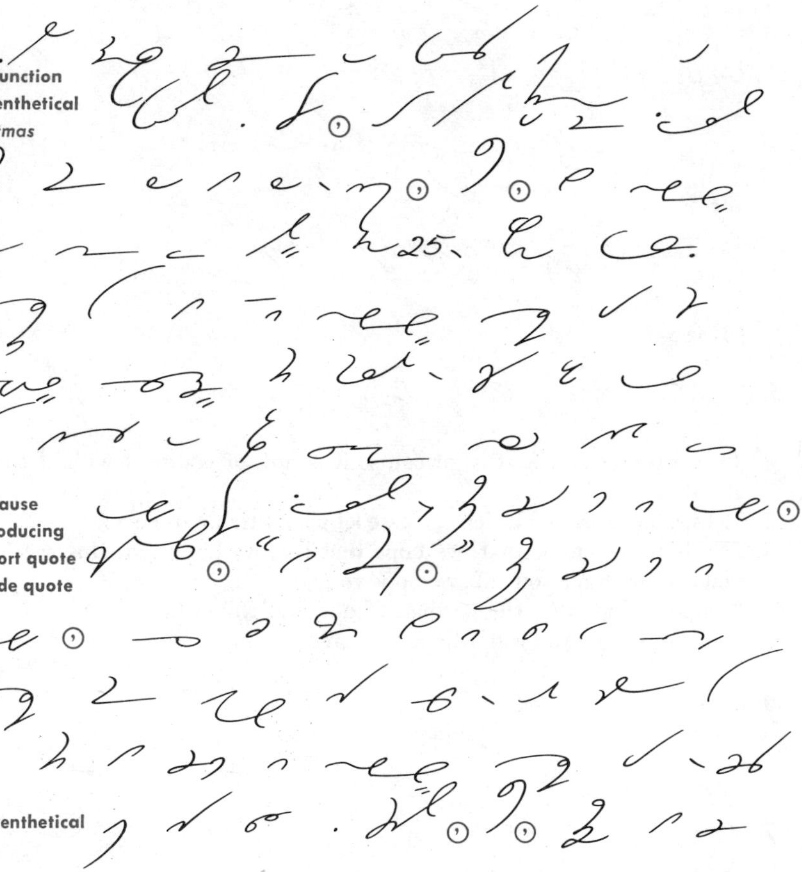

, *if* clause
, introducing short quote
. inside quote

, parenthetical

; no conjunction

(167)

399.

edition

. inside quote

, parenthetical

, when clause

ideally

, as clause

exercises

, introductory

reactions

, nonrestrictive

, *if* clause
; no conjunction

(198)

400.
personnel
, introductory
; illustrative ,
Employee
, introductory
, nonrestrictive
inside quote
, series
, *if* clause
outstanding

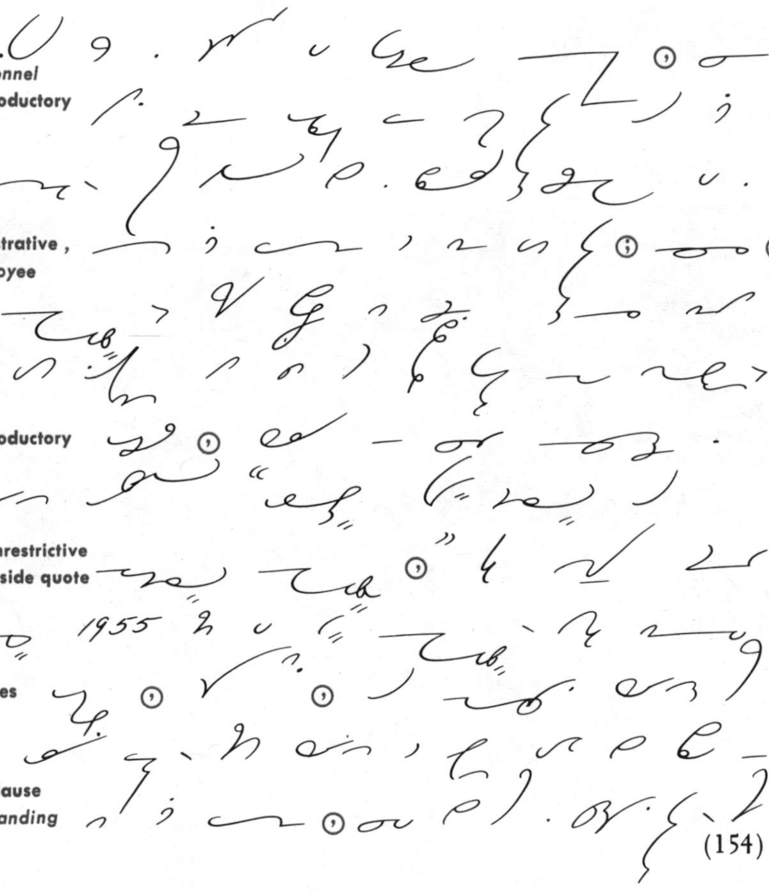

(154)

401.
, introductory

, appposition
grateful

, nonrestrictive
inside quote
, conjunction

1955

(90)

402.

; no conjunction
, introductory

. inside quote
, introductory

, introductory

, introductory

: enumeration

best-written
hyphenated before noun
, introductory

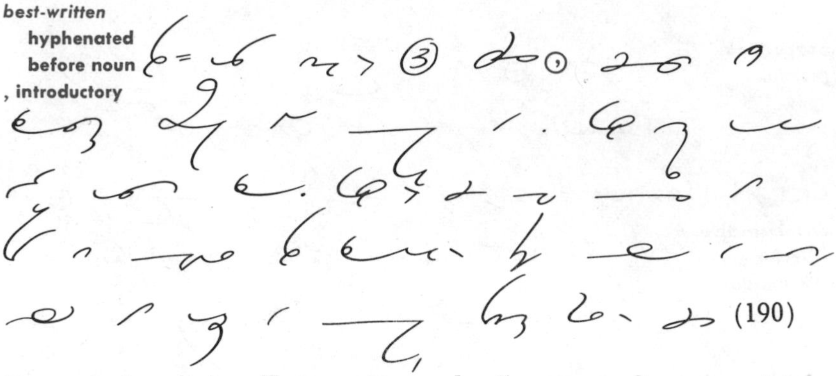

(190)

Transcription Quiz. For you to supply: 5 commas—2 commas introductory, 1 comma *and* omitted, 2 commas parenthetical; 2 missing words.

403.

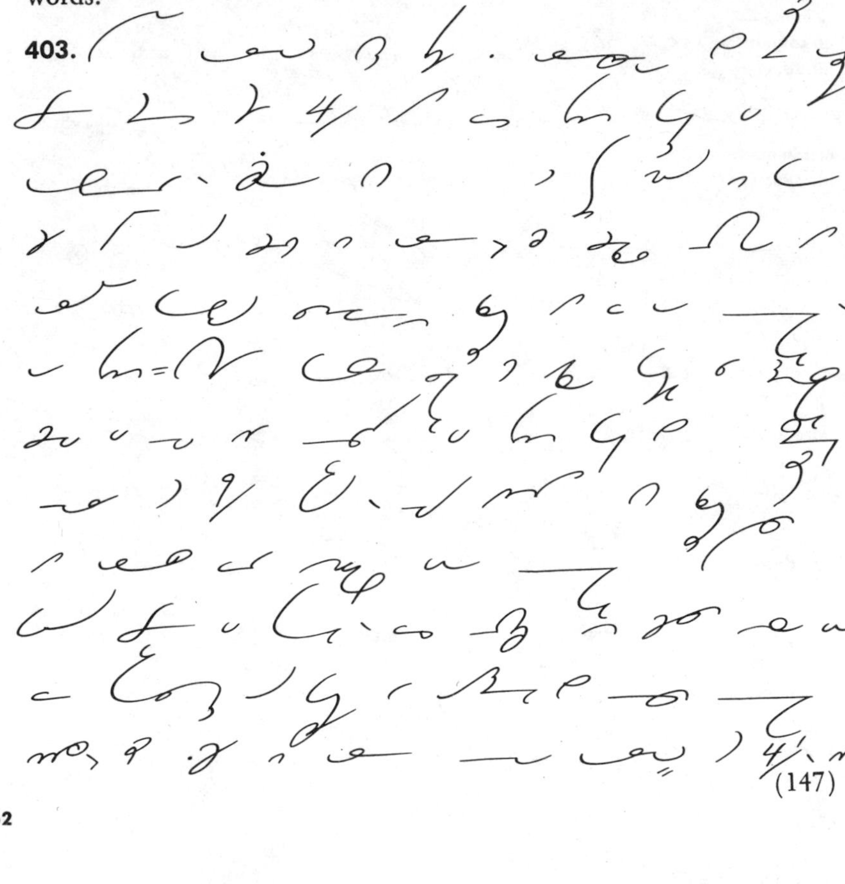

(147)

LESSON 58

404. Word Families

-tive

1 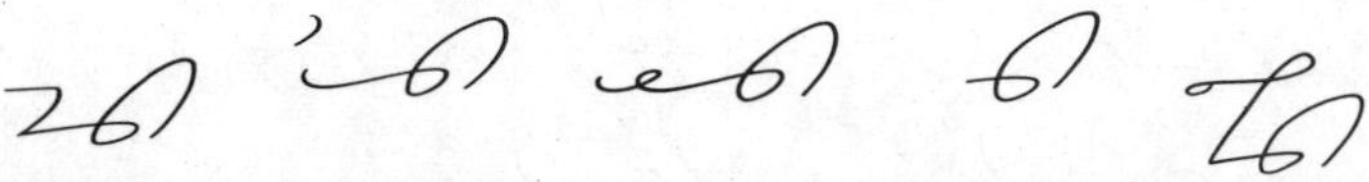

-iety

2 

-men

3 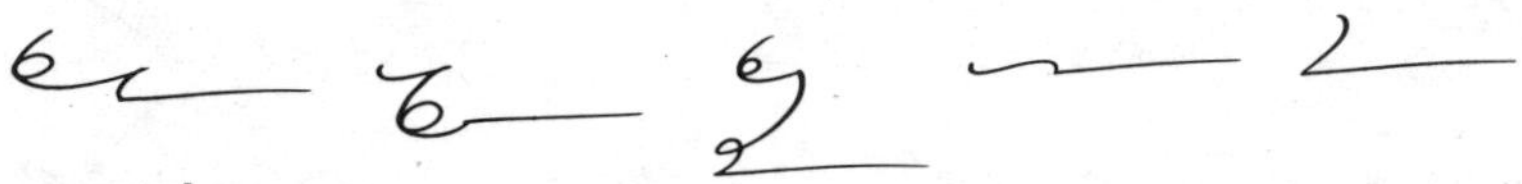

-mental

4 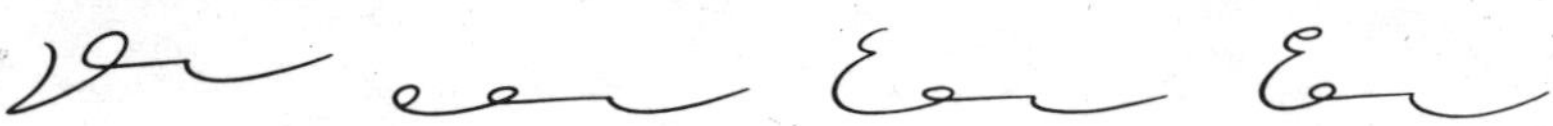

-mon

5 

-pel

6 

1. Informative, superlative, relative, native, imaginative.
2. Variety, society, propriety, sobriety, anxiety, notoriety, dubiety.
3. Salesmen, repairmen, servicemen, workmen, foremen.
4. Fundamental, elemental, supplemental, experimental.
5. Common, summon, sermon, salmon, lemon.
6. Spell, dispel, compel, propel, repel.

Reading and Writing Practice

405. Transcription Word Study

electrifying Thrilling.

fundamental Basic, essential.

salutation The introductory words of a letter; Dear Sir, for example.

406.

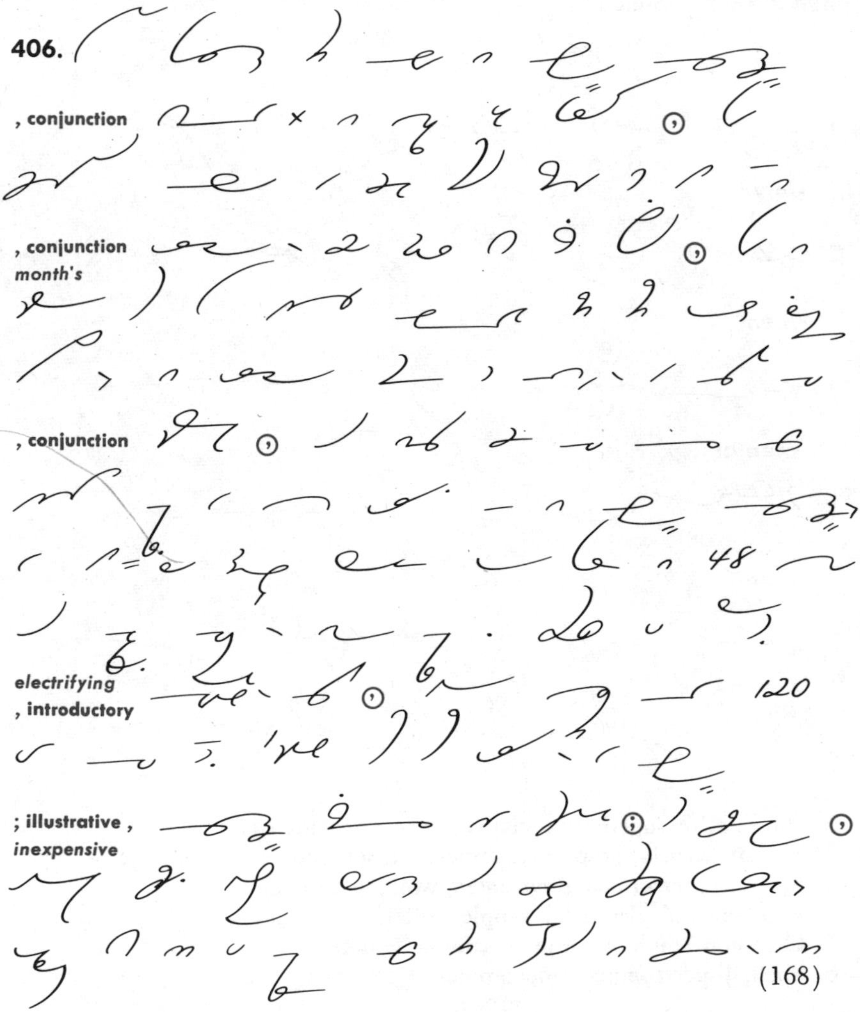

(168)

407.

, nonrestrictive

1957

, conjunction

contribute

typical

, if clause

(103)

408.

, introductory

, as clause

, conjunction

, when clause

(155)

409.

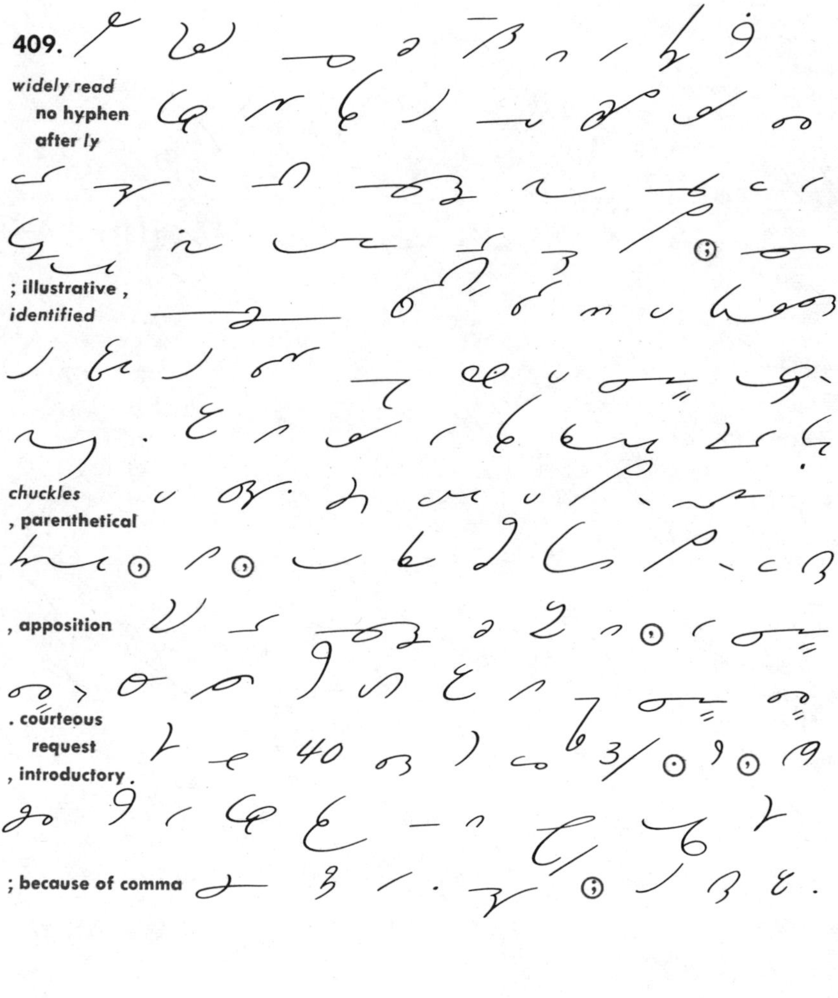

widely read
no hyphen
after *ly*

; illustrative ,
identified

chuckles
, parenthetical

, apposition

. courteous
request
, introductory

; because of comma

Personal-Use Self-Check

Do you substitute shorthand for longhand wherever possible when you

1. Take down your daily assignments?
2. Correspond with friends who know shorthand?
3. Draft compositions and reports?
4. Make entries in your diary?
5. Make notes to yourself on things to do, people to see, appointments to keep, etc.?

(209)

410.

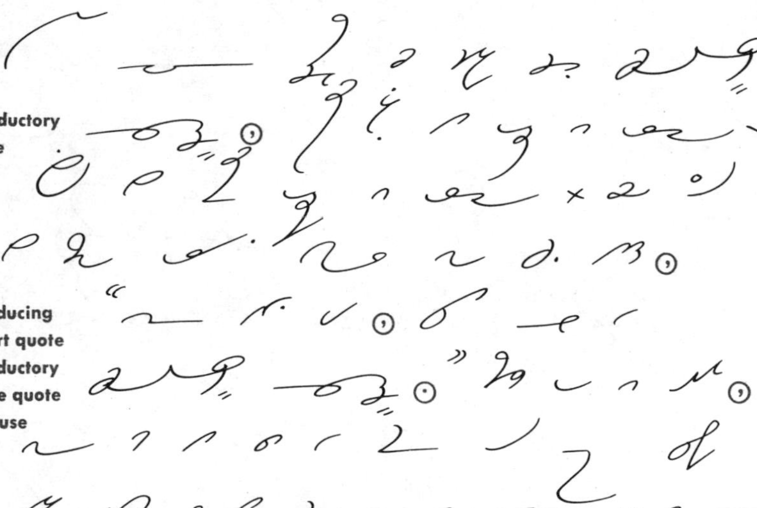

, introductory
receive
, introducing short quote
, introductory
. inside quote
, *if* clause

already
, conjunction

(105)

Transcription Quiz. For you to supply: 4 commas—2 commas parenthetical, 2 commas series; 1 colon enumeration; 1 semicolon no conjunction; 2 missing words.

411.

(176)

LESSON 59

412. Word Beginnings and Endings

De-

1 

Under-

2 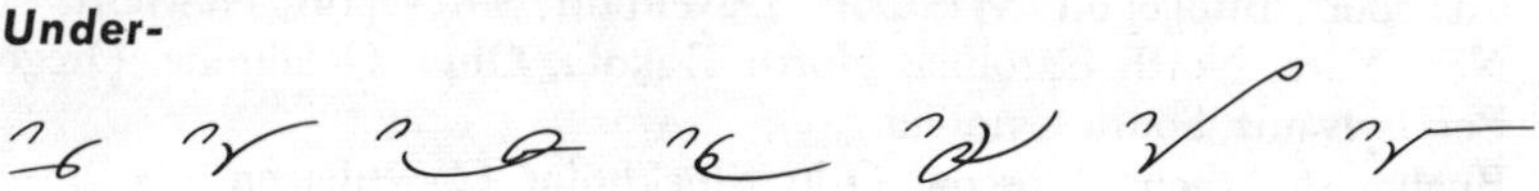

Over-

3 

Short-

4 

Pro-

5 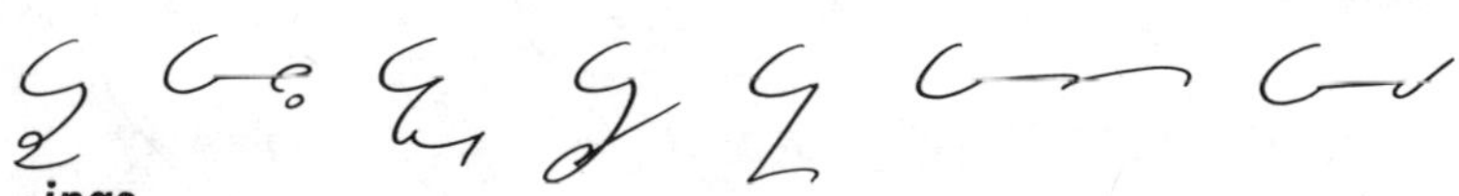

-ings

6 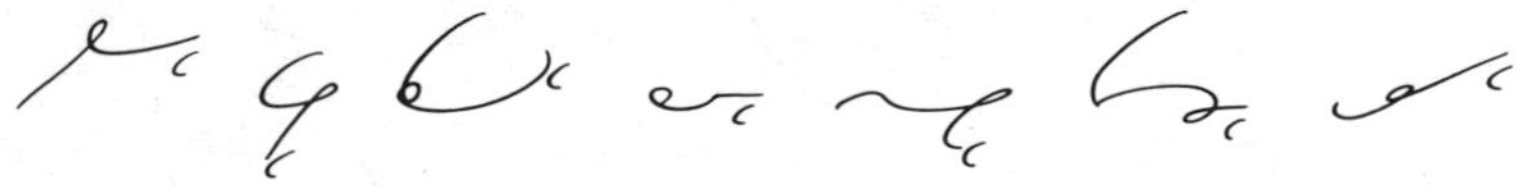

1. Design, deceive, deceit, deceitful, descend, decipher, decentralize.
2. Underneath, understand, underline, undersell, undersigned, understudy, understatement.
3. Overturn, overcome, overcoat, oversupply, overestimate, overhead.

4. Short, shortest, shortly, shorter, shortened, shortsighted, shortcomings, shortage, shortstop.
5. Professor, promisingly, proportion, provide, project, promulgate, promote.
6. Dealings, preachings, buildings, earnings, clippings, beginnings, readings.

413. Geographical Expressions

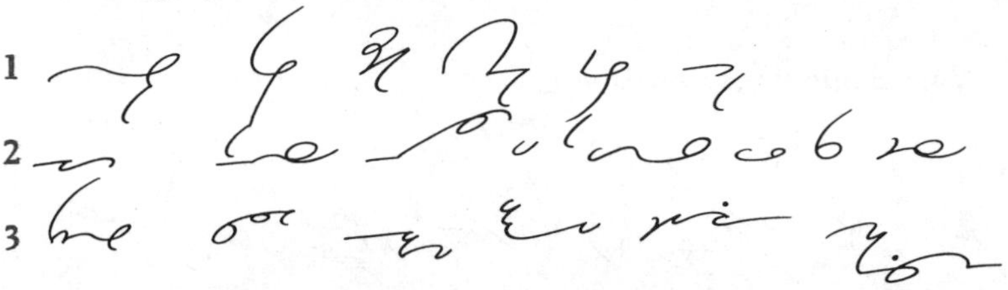

1. Glassport, Bridgeport, Westport, Davenport, Shreveport, Newport.
2. New York, North Carolina, North Dakota, Ohio, Oklahoma, Oregon, Pennsylvania, South Carolina.
3. Bucharest, Athens, Moscow, Oslo, Stockholm, Copenhagen.

Reading and Writing Practice

414. Transcription Word Study

evaluation A determination of the value of.

concise Condensed, brief.

415.

; no conjunction

, parenthetical

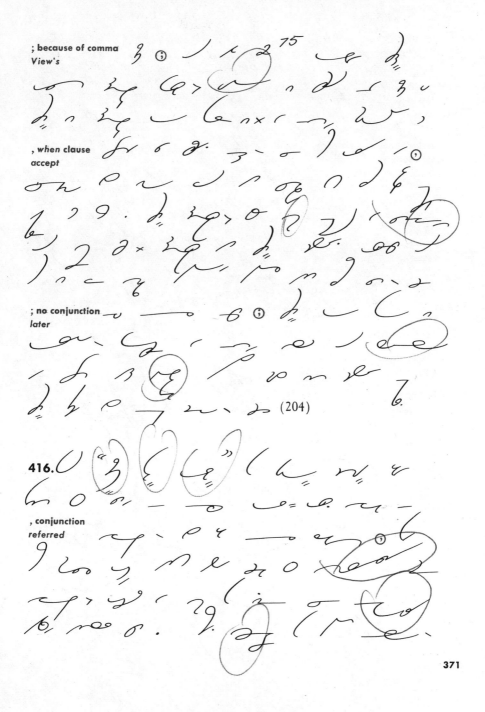

; because of comma
View's

, when clause
accept

; no conjunction
later

(204)

416.

, conjunction
referred

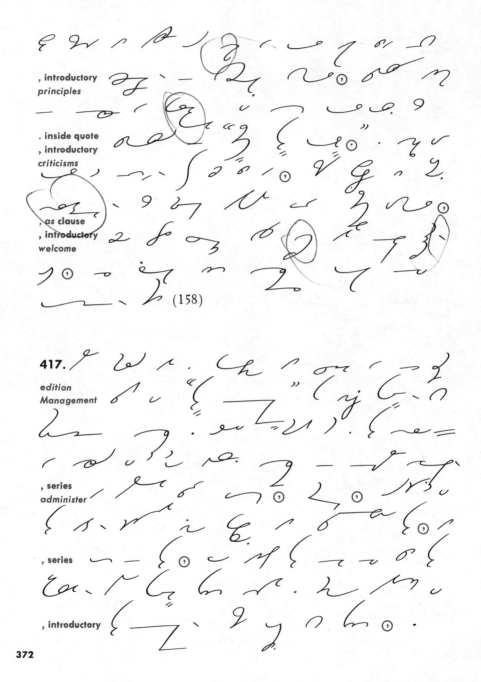

, introductory
principles

. inside quote
, introductory
criticisms

, as clause
, introductory
welcome

(158)

417.

edition
Management

, series
administer

, series

, introductory

, introducing short quote
. inside quote

: enumeration
, *and* omitted

, parenthetical

. inside quote
, conjunction

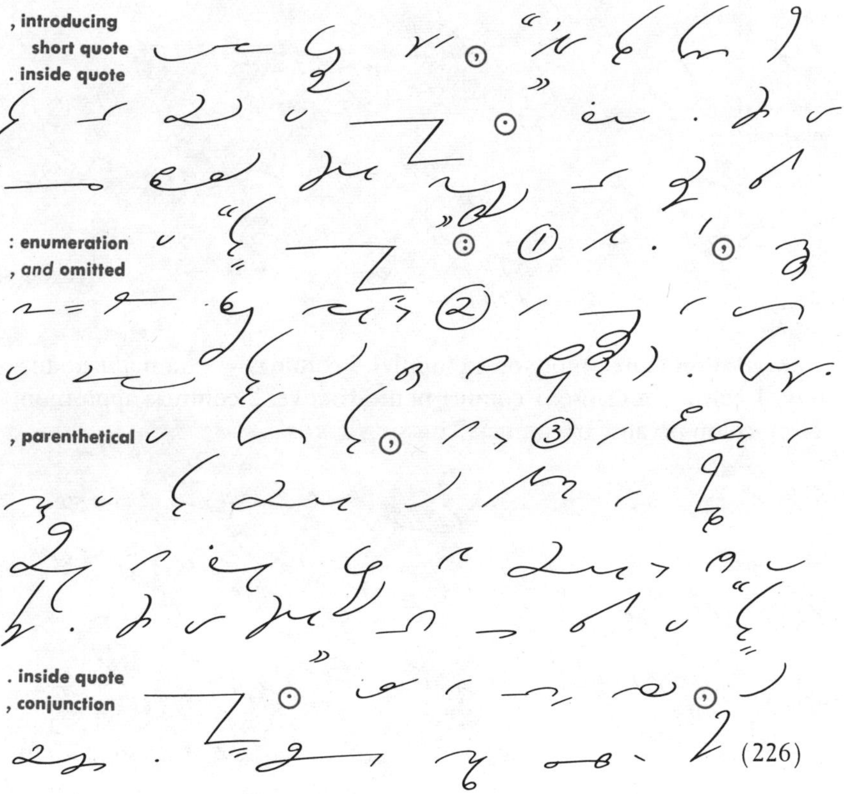

(226)

418.

; illustrative ,
, nonrestrictive

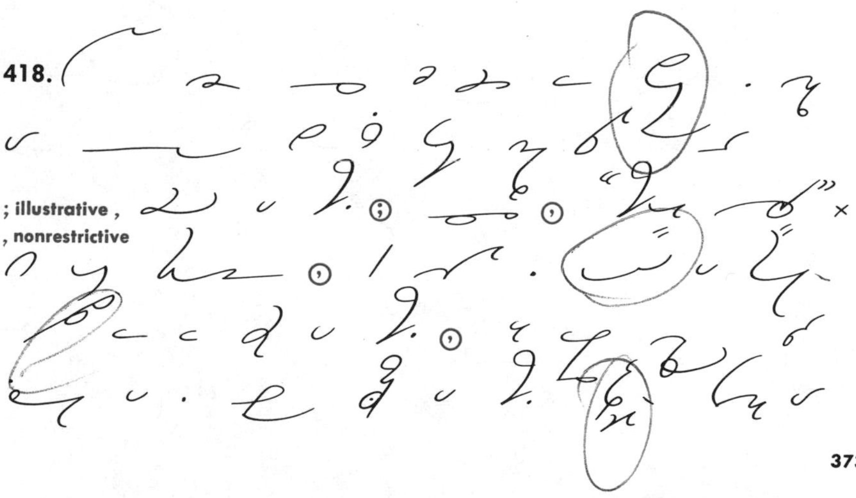

, introductory
received

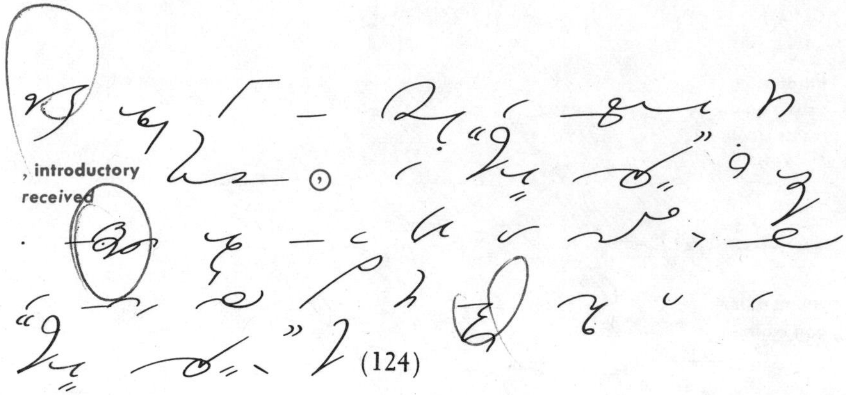

(124)

Transcription Quiz. For you to supply: 5 commas—1 comma introductory, 1 comma *if* clause, 1 comma nonrestrictive, 2 commas apposition; 1 semicolon because of comma; 2 missing words.

419.

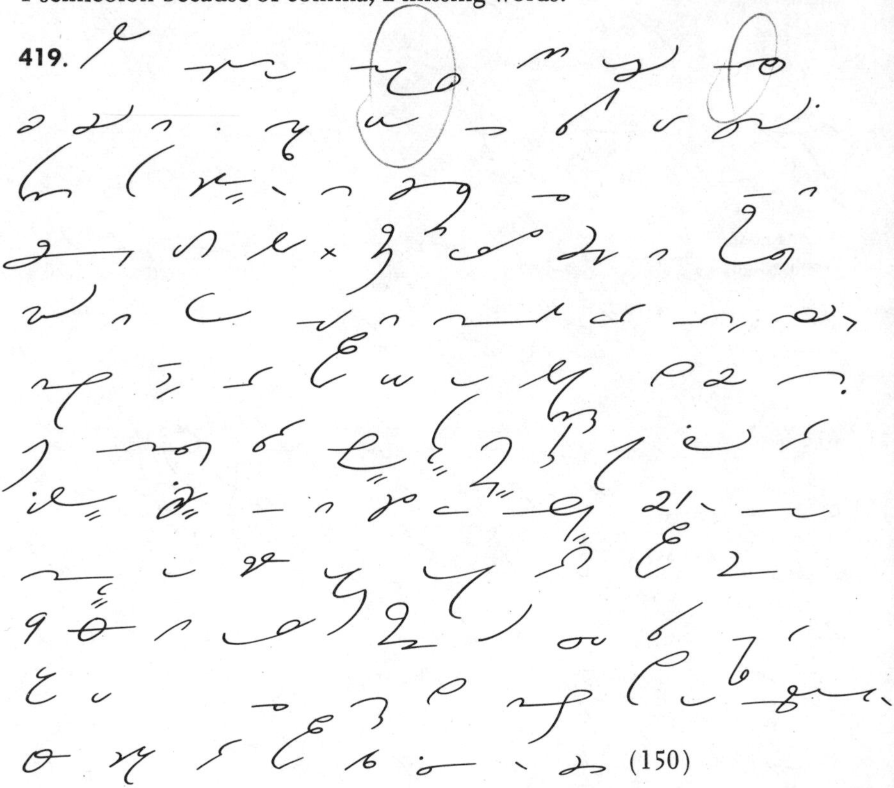

(150)

LESSON 60

420. Word-Building Practice—Omission of Vowels

Omission of Short U

1 

Omission of Ow

2 

Omission of E in Diphthong U

3 

Omission of Minor Vowel

4 

1. Touch, lunch, smudge, much, fund, refund, clutch, judge.
2. Town, down, around, surround, brown, county, crown, gown.
3. Avenue, continue, induce, inducement, introduce, produce, suit, revenue.
4. Millions, radius, miscellaneous, courteous, graduate.

421. Accuracy Practice—Curves

1 

2 

1. Present, please; brain, blame; free, value.
2. Pay, bay; see, fee, very; about, as, half, advantage; he is, if, ever.

Reading and Writing Practice

422. Transcription Word Study

denunciation Announcement or warning of impending evil.

preamble A preface, introductory statement.

sever To cut.

enshrined Cherished as sacred.

423. The Declaration of Independence

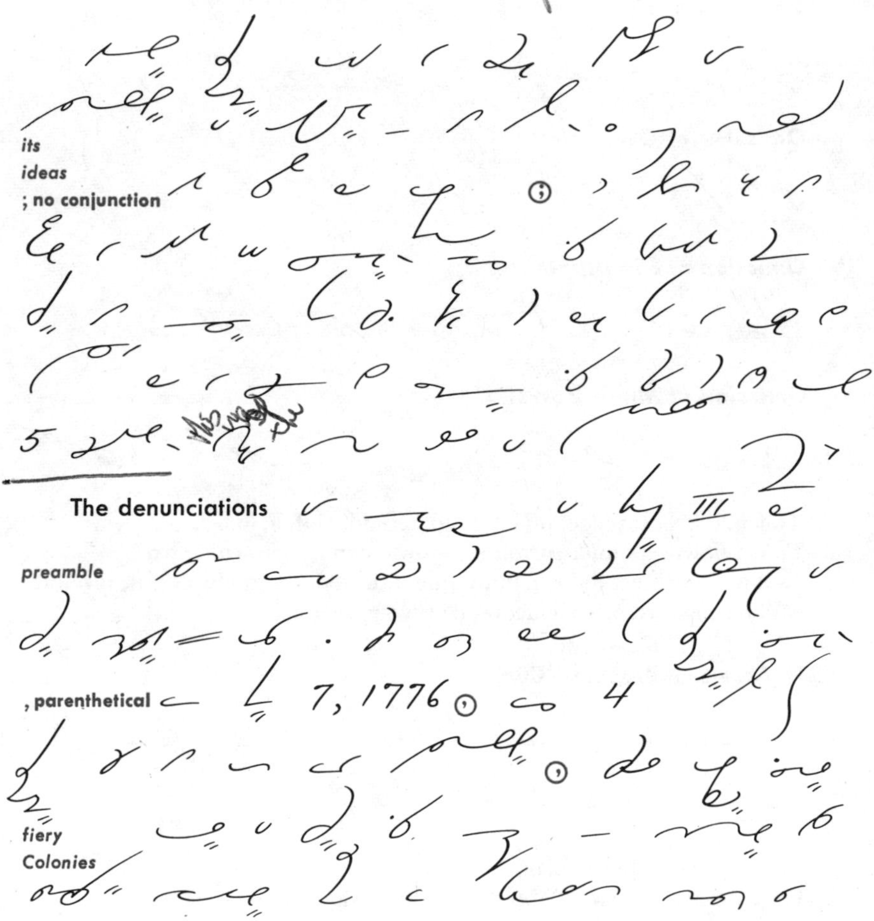

its

ideas

; no conjunction

The denunciations

preamble

, parenthetical

fiery

Colonies

Great Britain
passed
, if clause

, when clause
, apposition

28, 1776

, parenthetical

, apposition

As the debate

, as clause

, when clause

hearts
fateful

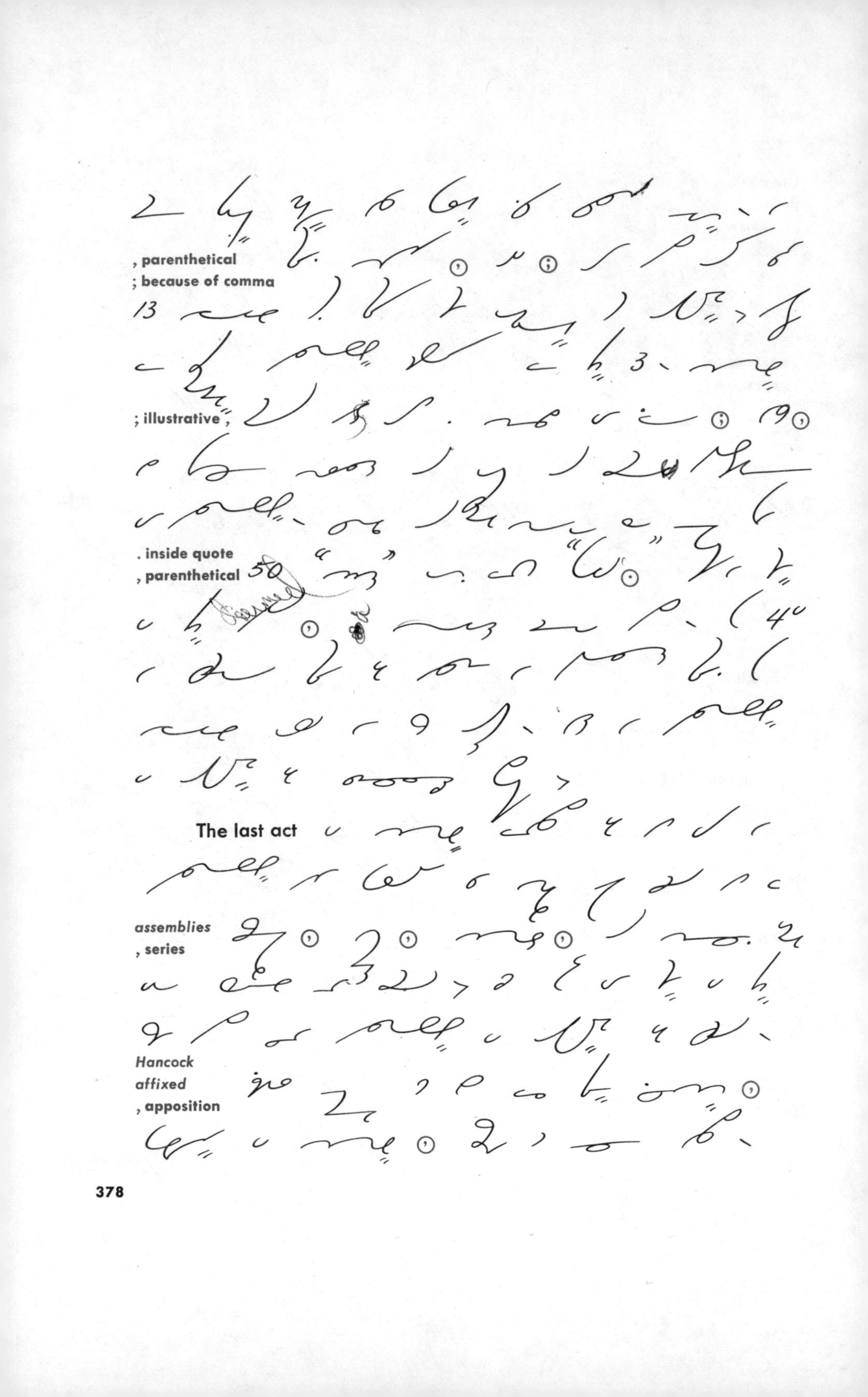

, parenthetical

; because of comma

; illustrative

. inside quote

, parenthetical

The last act

assemblies

, series

Hancock

affixed

, apposition

, conjunction
degrees

; no conjunction
losing

All that night

; because of comma
, parenthetical

, parenthetical
galloped

, introductory

; because of comma
, parenthetical

Matlack
, conjunction

To sign

, series
. inside quote

, *when* clause

(930)

PART FOUR

manufacturing
education
paper
personnel

DICTATION IN THE OFFICE

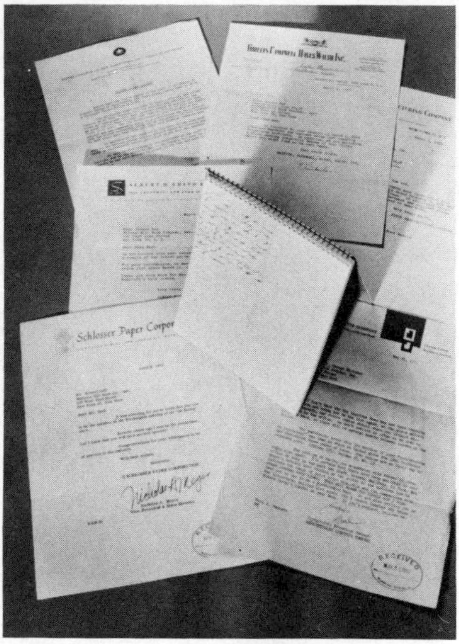

At this stage of your shorthand course, you have already read and copied and taken from dictation thousands upon thousands of words not only in practiced material but in material you have never seen before. As a result, you possess considerable skill, perhaps more than you realize. In fact, if you had to, you could take dictation from a businessman, provided his dictation were not too difficult or too fast.

You would find, however, that taking dictation in the business office is somewhat different from taking dictation in class.

Your teacher realizes that during the learning stages your skill will develop most rapidly under ideal working conditions. Consequently, his dictation is smooth and even and distinct. Most of it is carefully timed because that is the only way your skill development can be accurately measured.

The businessman, however, is not concerned with the development of your skill; he assumes that you are already skilled. His dictation will not always be smooth and even. Depending upon the flow of his thoughts, it may be slow at times, fast at others. He may change his mind about a word, a phrase, or even a sentence and substitute another. He may delete and he may insert. His dictation will never be timed!

Furthermore, your task will not be simply to take dictation and transcribe it exactly as he dictates it. A businessman is human, and all human beings occasionally err—even the most brilliant. When your employer dictates, he will unknowingly make errors – not because he does not know better but because he may become so engrossed in the thought or idea he is trying to express that he will not realize that he is using an incorrect verb, dangling a participle, or even misstating a fact.

An important part of your job as a stenographer or secretary will be to watch for these errors and to correct them. The obvious errors you can correct without calling them to your employer's attention; the use of a singular verb with a plural subject, for example. The more serious ones – particularly errors involving dates, amounts, or names – you must call to his attention – tactfully, of course!

After you have worked for a businessman for a time, you will get to know his dictation habits and will learn to take them in your stride. The most important factor in taking any businessman's dictation, however, is shorthand speed. The greater your shorthand speed, the easier you will find office dictation. There is no substitute for shorthand speed! Therefore, strive to build your shorthand speed to the highest point possible; you will never regret doing it.

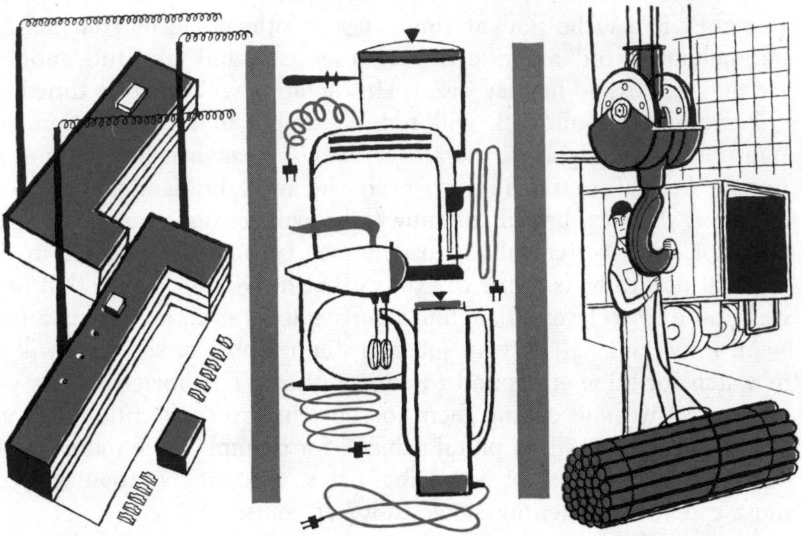

13

MANUFACTURING

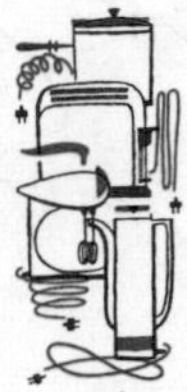

LESSON 61

424. Brief Forms and Derivatives

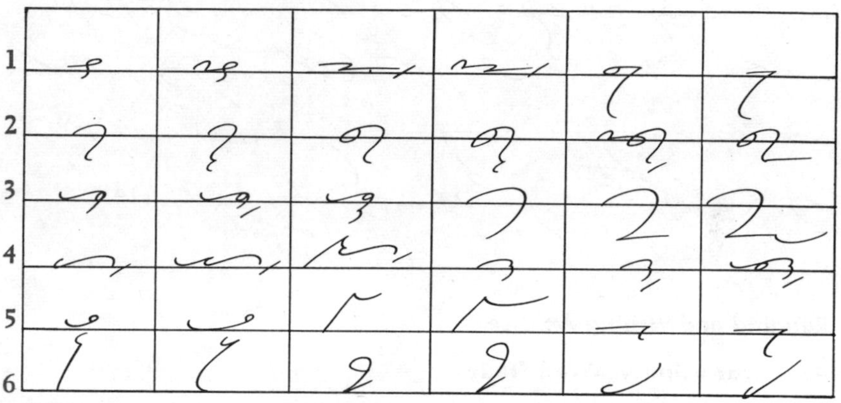

1. Necessary, unnecessary; numbered, unnumbered; enable, unable.
2. Keep-company, keeps-companies; accompany, accompanies, unaccompanied, accompaniment.
3. Request, requested, requests; govern, government, governmental.
4. Organized, reorganized, disorganized; consider-consideration, considered, reconsidered.
5. Regard, let-letter; doctor-during, deliver; must, important-importance.
6. Subject, object; after, advertise; want, order.

425. Brief Form and Phrase Letter

(141)

Reading and Writing Practice

426. Transcription Word Study

decades Periods of ten years.

depict To portray in words; describe.

fatigue Weariness.

427.

, as clause
confidential

, introductory

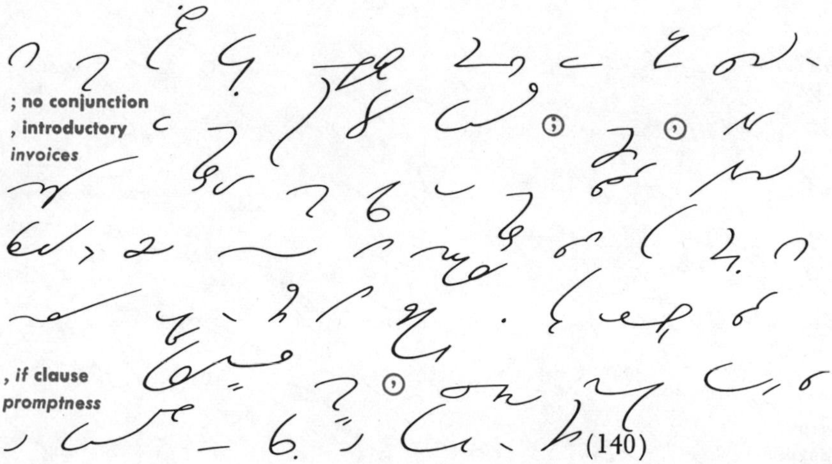

; no conjunction

, introductory

invoices

, if clause

promptness

(140)

428.

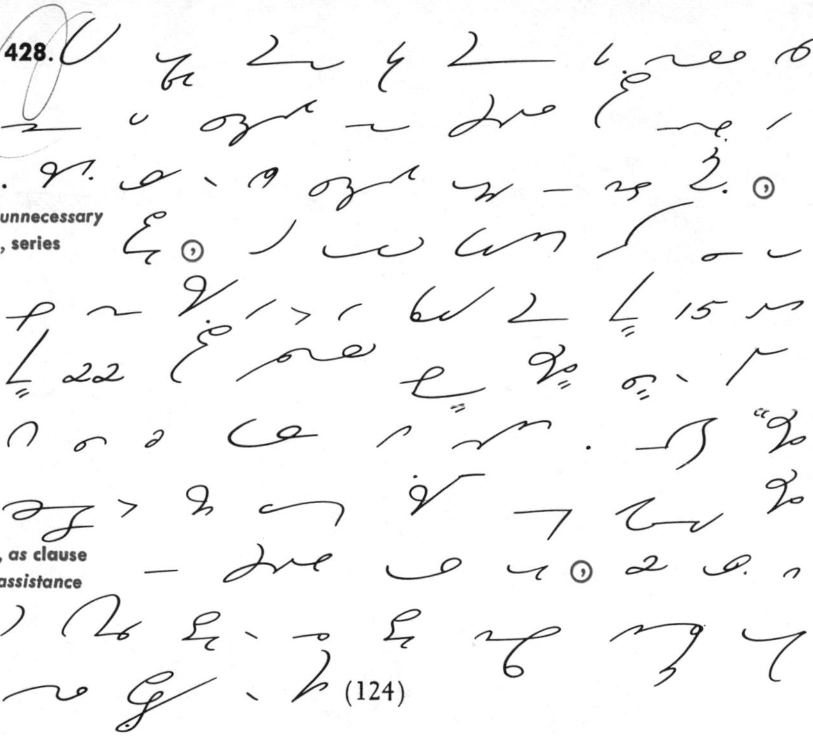

unnecessary

, series

, as clause

assistance

(124)

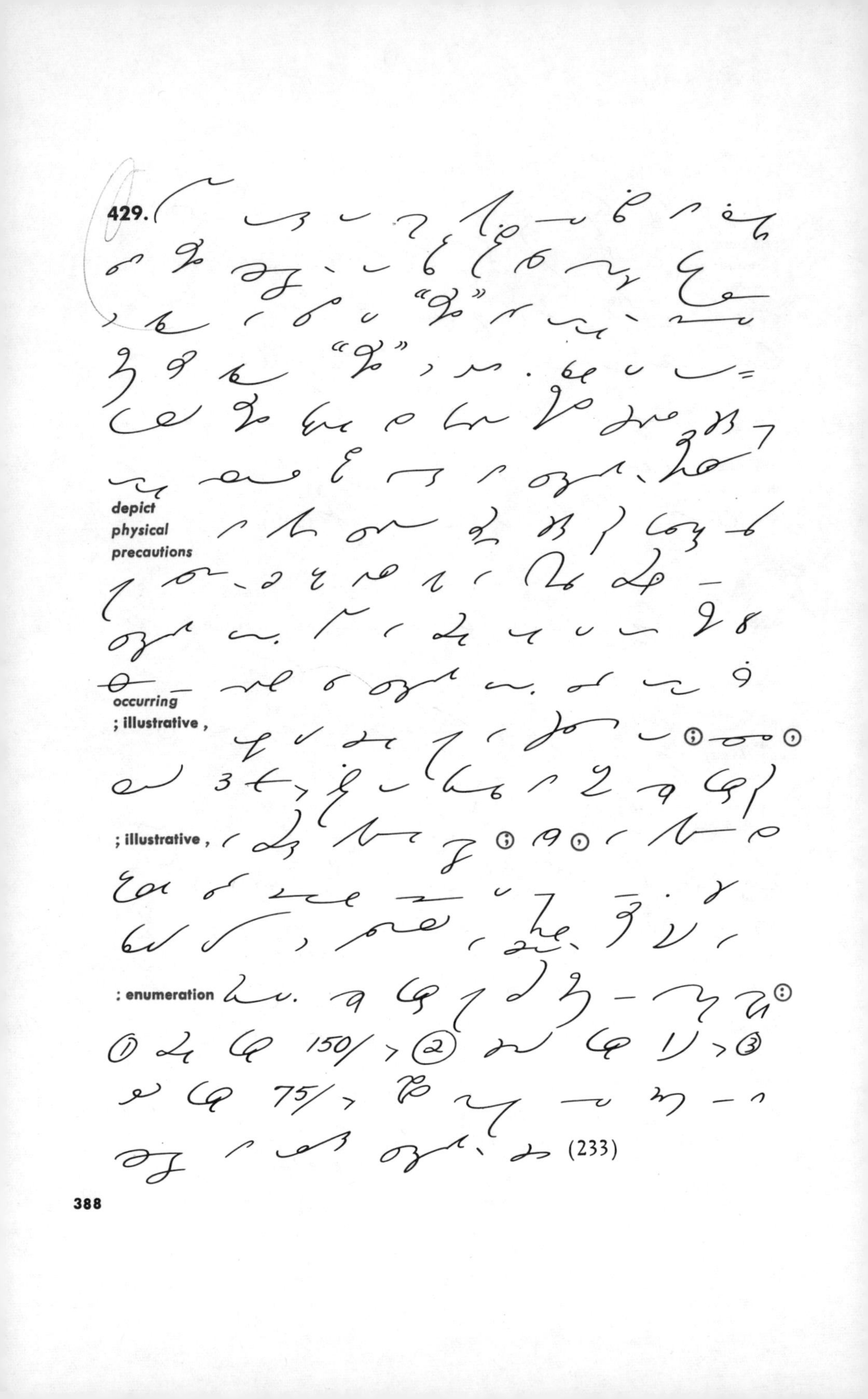

429.

depict
physical
precautions

occurring
; illustrative ,

; illustrative ,

; enumeration

150/ 1/ 75/

(233)

Transcription Quiz. For you to supply: 7 commas—2 commas conjunction, 2 commas parenthetical, 1 comma *and* omitted, 1 comma nonrestrictive, 1 comma introductory; 1 semicolon because of comma, 1 semicolon no conjunction; 2 missing words.

430.

(216)

LESSON 62

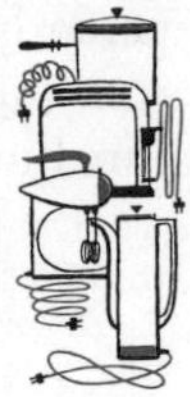

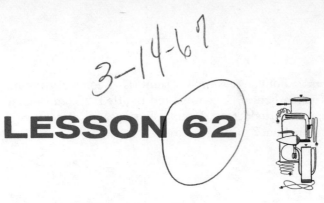

431. Useful Business-Letter Phrases

A Omitted

1 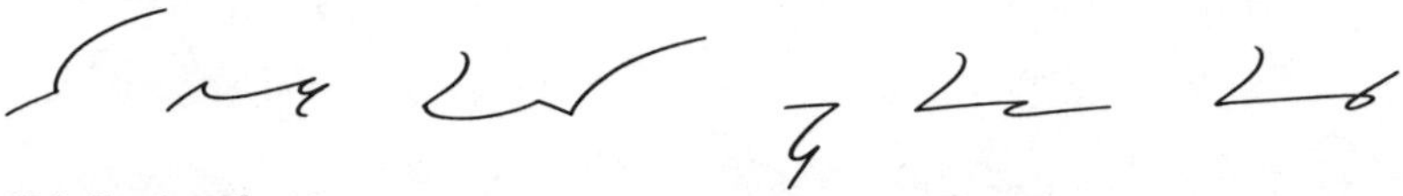

Of Omitted

2 

To Omitted

3 

And Omitted

4 

1. At a time, at a loss, for a long time, in a position, for a moment, for a minute.
2. Many of the, many of those, many of them, how many of them, number of the.
3. Glad to see, glad to say, I should like to see, I should like to say, I should like to have.
4. Men and women, more and more, less and less, here and there, up and down.

432. Frequent Names

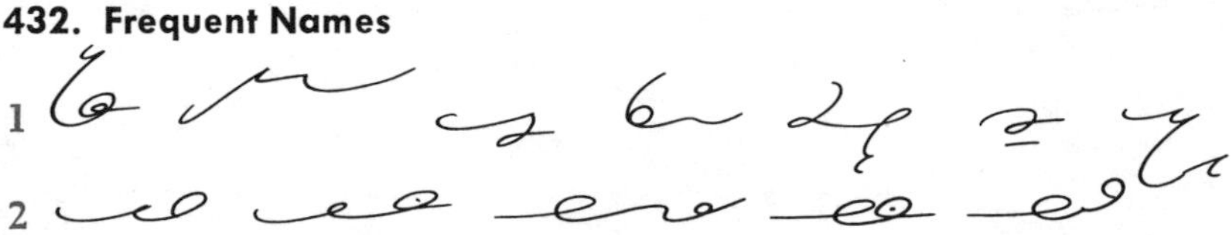

1. O'Brien, O'Donnell, Olsen, Parker, Philips, Quinn, Roberts.
2. Laura, Lillian, Margaret, Marian, Martha.

Reading and Writing Practice

433. Transcription Word Study

demolished Ruined, destroyed.

curtailing Shortening or lessening.

spacious Roomy.

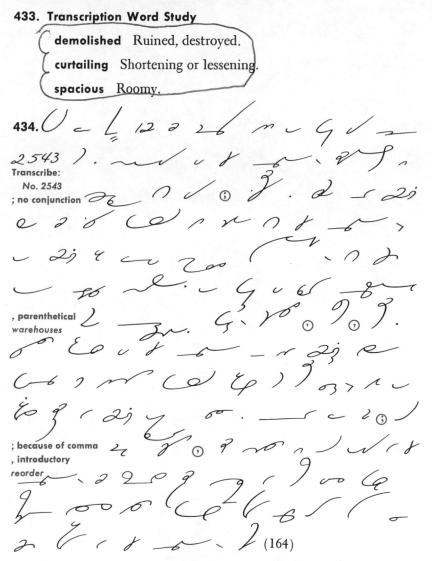

434.

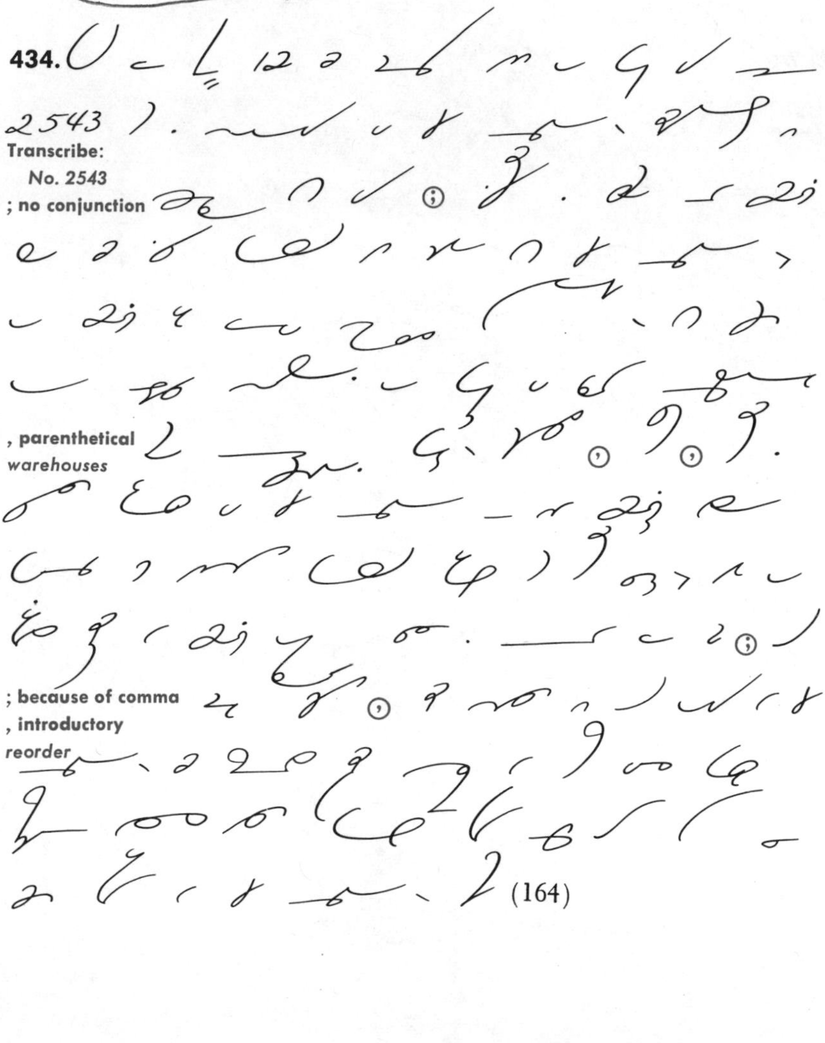

435. Transcribe:

June 15

, parenthetical

cancel

, parenthetical

temporary

, apposition

, *if* clause

. courteous request

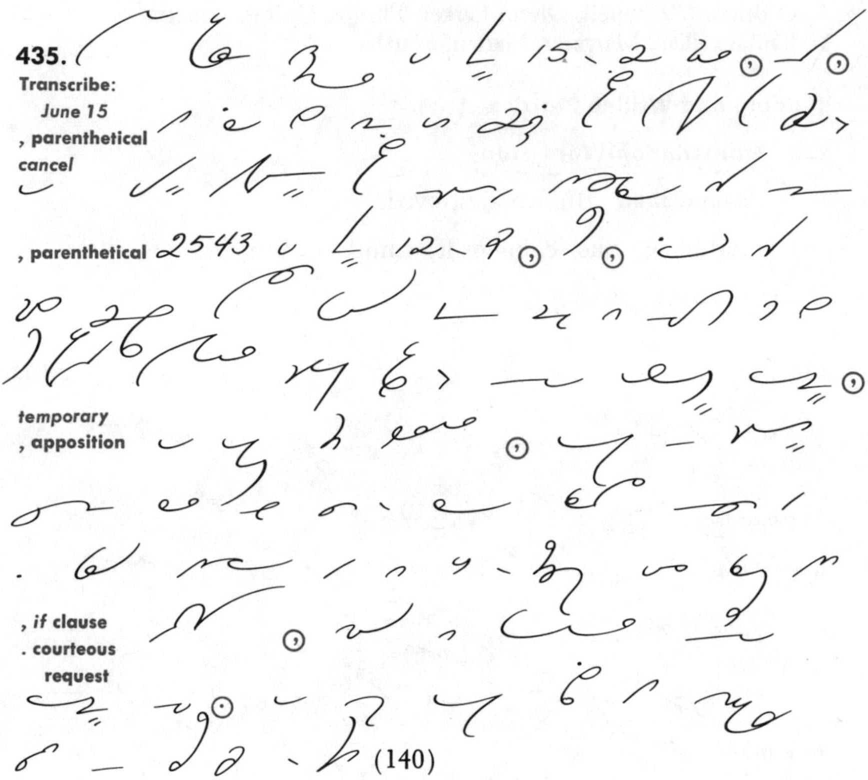

(140)

436.

, apposition

European

likely

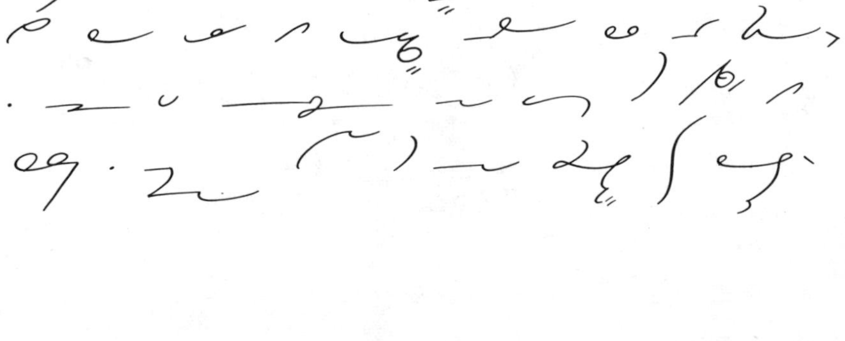

, introductory
, apposition

Philips'
, conjunction

, introductory

(177)

437.

, *and* omitted
, introductory

two-day
hyphenated
before noun

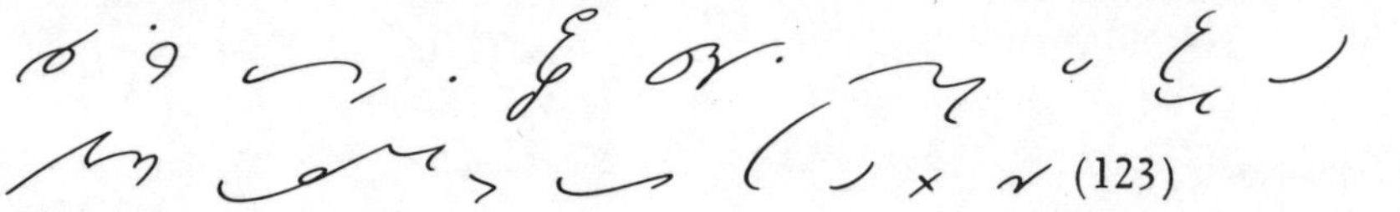

(123)

438.

Tennessee appliances

, series

. courteous request

, as clause

appreciate

, nonrestrictive

, introductory

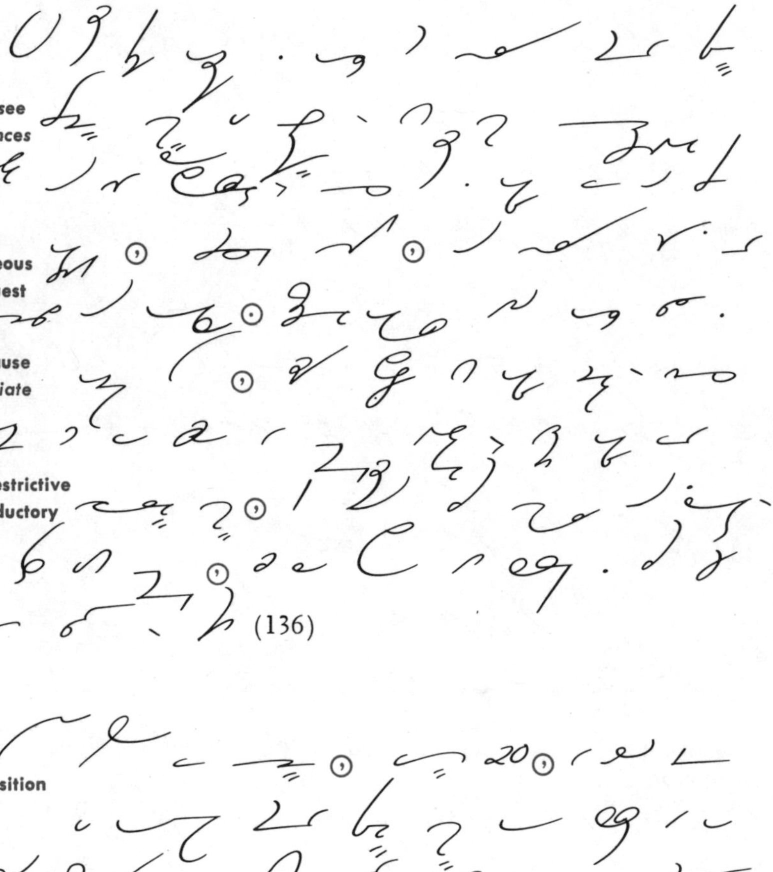

(136)

439.

, apposition

, as clause

specifications

(67)

Transcription Quiz. For you to supply: 5 commas—2 commas introductory, 1 comma *if* clause, 1 comma *when* clause; 1 comma conjunction; 1 semicolon no conjunction; 2 missing words.

440.

(226)

LESSON 63

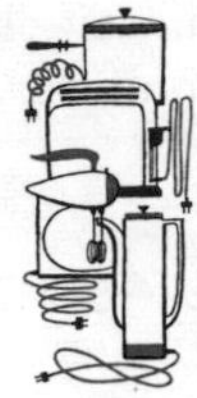

441. Word Families

-ial

1 

-ish

2 

-age

3 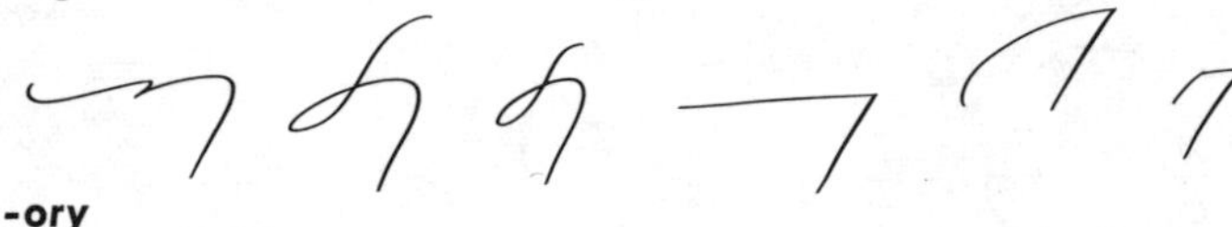

-ory

4 

-phone

5 

Comm

6 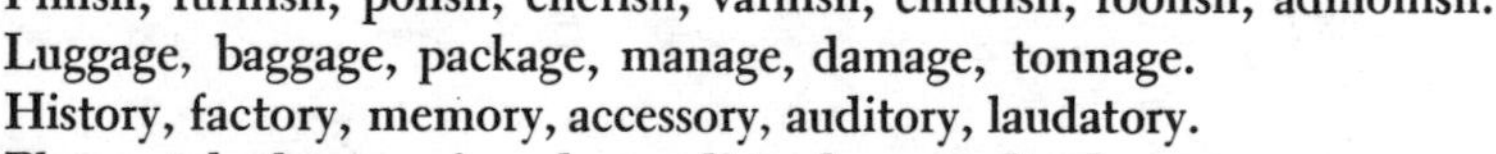

1. **Industrial, editorial, ceremonial, aerial, serial.**
2. **Finish, furnish, polish, cherish, varnish, childish, foolish, admonish.**
3. **Luggage, baggage, package, manage, damage, tonnage.**
4. **History, factory, memory, accessory, auditory, laudatory.**
5. **Phone, telephone, microphone, dictaphone, radiophone.**
6. **Committee, commit, commerce, commence, commodity.**

Reading and Writing Practice

442. Transcription Word Study

pertinent Related to the matter at hand.

rural Relating to the country as distinguished from the city.

congested Crowded.

443.

, nonrestrictive
somewhere

ideally located
no hyphen
after *ly*

industrial
, parenthetical
; because of comma

, introductory
pertinent
, when clause

(173)

444.

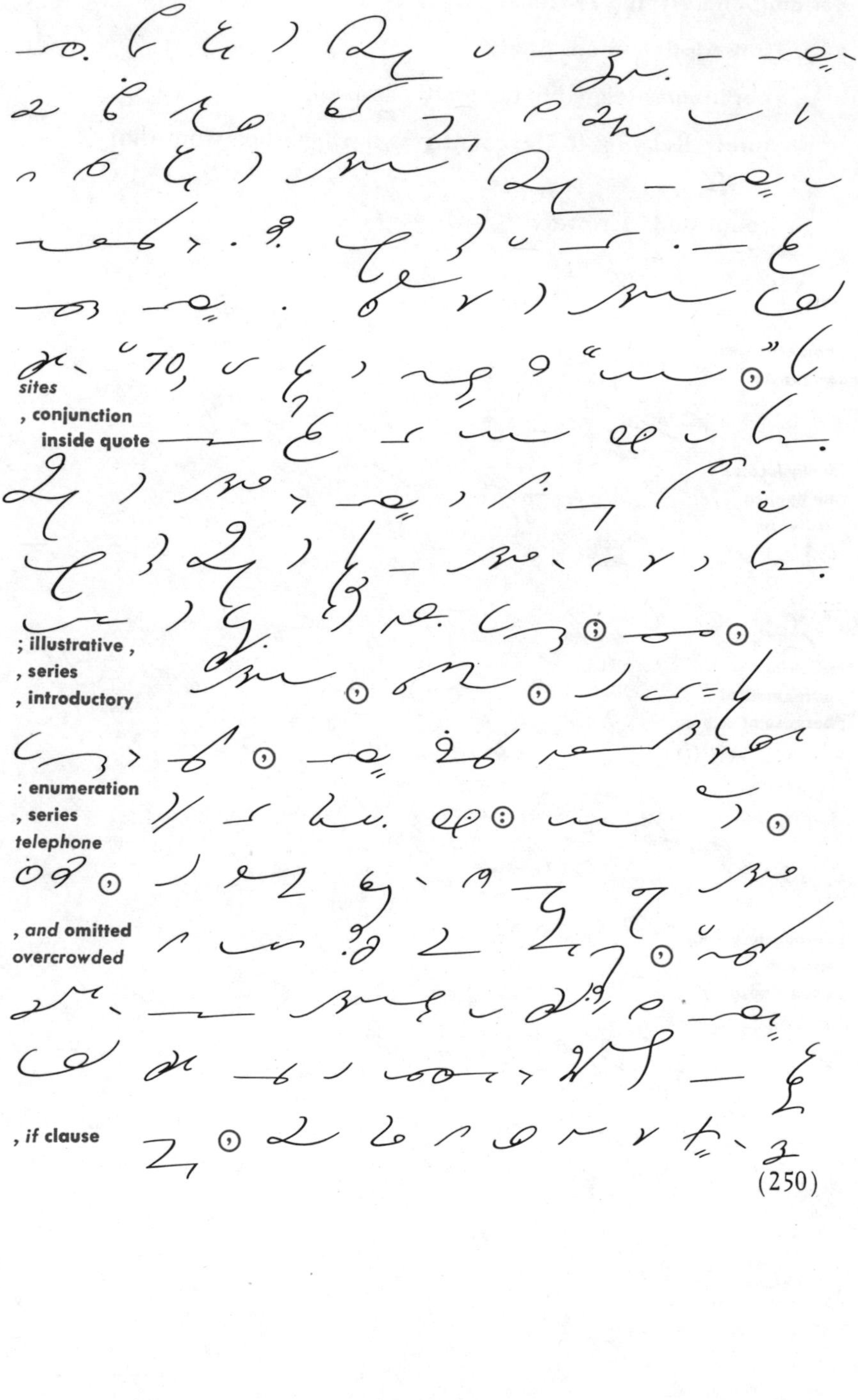
sites
, conjunction
inside quote
; illustrative ,
, series
, introductory
: enumeration
, series
telephone
, and omitted
overcrowded
, if clause
(250)

445.

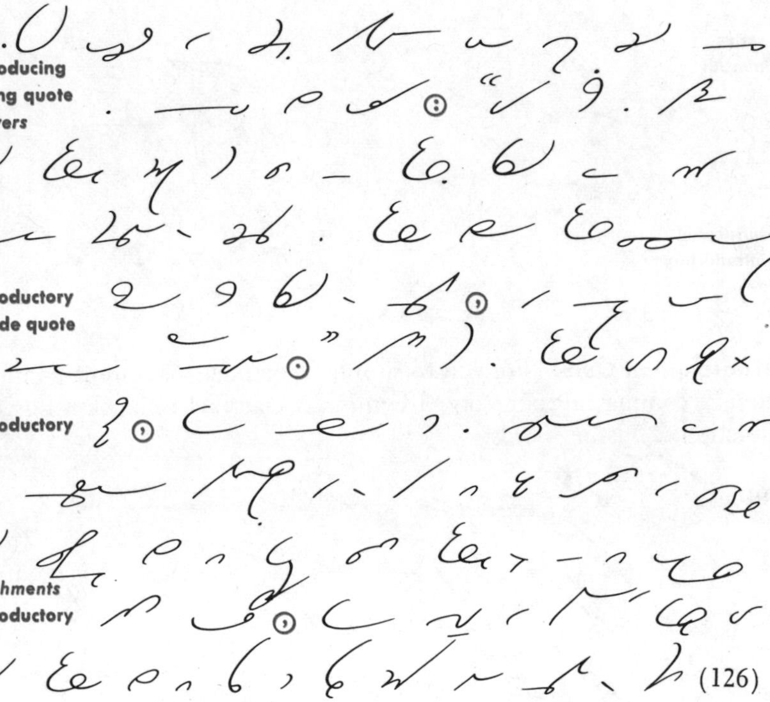

: introducing long quote

sprayers

, introductory

. inside quote

, introductory

attachments

, introductory

(126)

446.

, nonrestrictive

luggage

, series
financial

confidential
, introductory

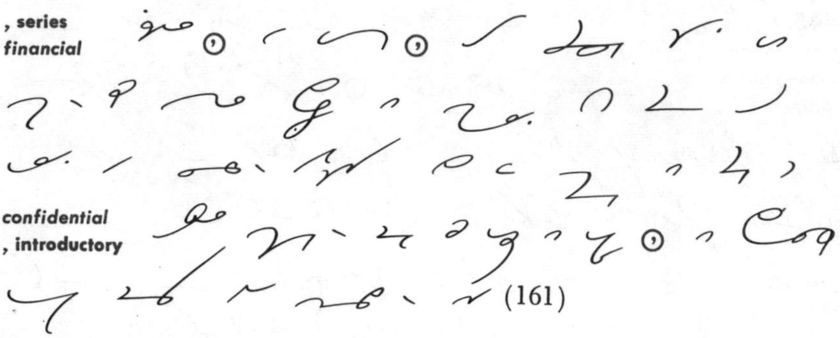

(161)

Transcription Quiz. For you to supply: 4 commas—1 comma conjunction, 2 commas introductory, 1 comma *if* clause; 1 semicolon no conjunction; 2 missing words.

447.

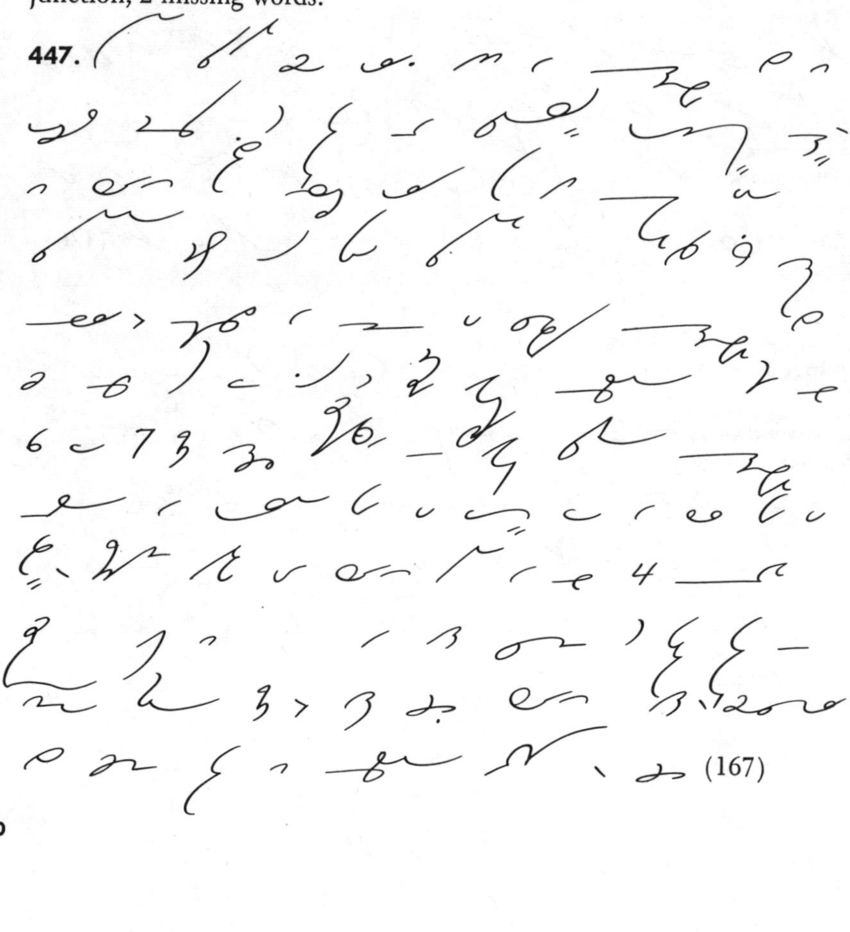

(167)

3-14-67

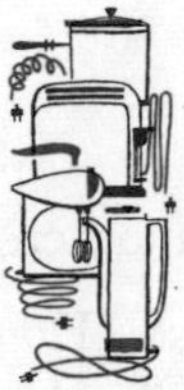

LESSON 64

448. Word Beginnings and Endings

-ure

1 

-pose

2 

Rea-

3 

Trans-

4 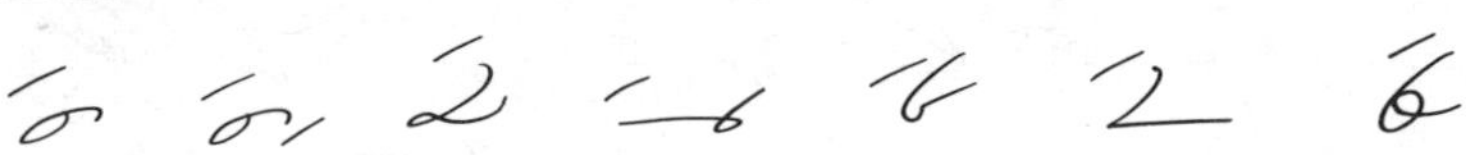

Enter-, Entr-

5 

1. Procedure, miniature, stature, conjecture, rapture, furniture.
2. Propose, proposed, proposes, proposal; dispose, disposed, disposes, disposal.
3. Readmit, readjust, reassure, reassert, reaffirm, realign.
4. Transact, transacted, transferred, transmit, transport, transform, transpire.
5. Entertain, entertainment, enterprise, enterprisingly, entrance, entrances, entered, entering.

Reading and Writing Practice

449. Transcription Word Study

exorbitant Excessive.

impartial Not favoring one more than another.

principal A capital sum placed at interest. (Do not confuse with *principle,* which means "a rule of action.")

450.

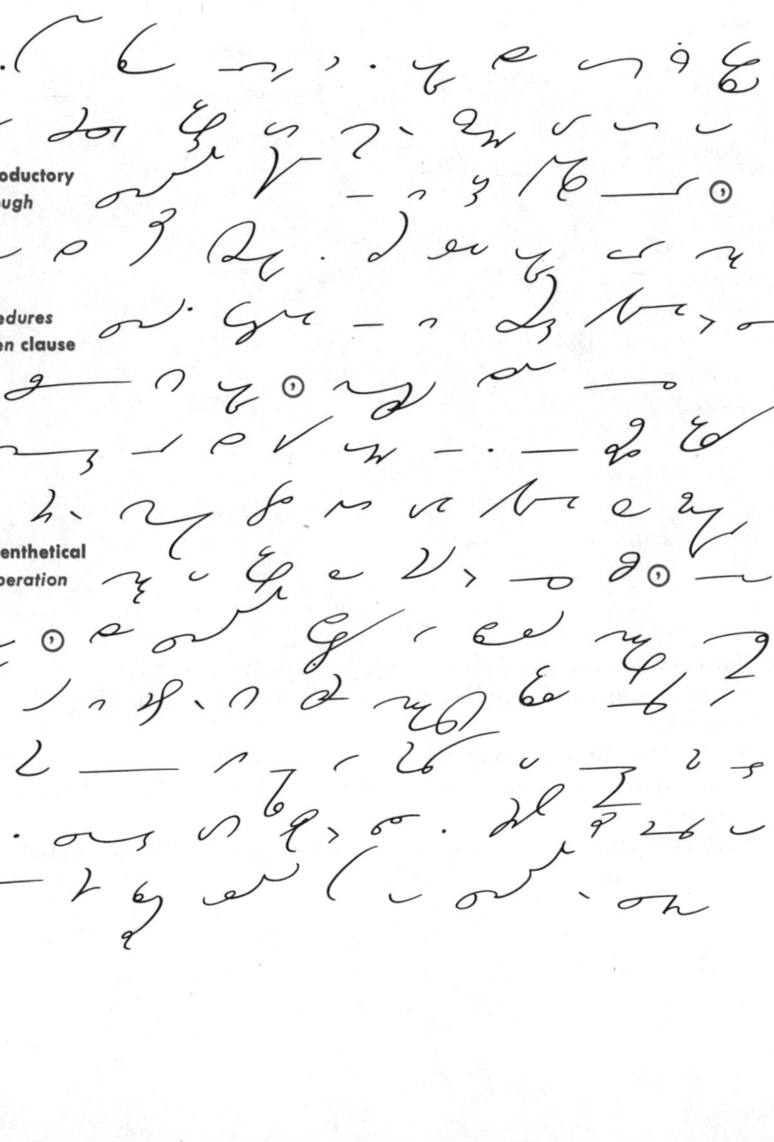

, introductory
thorough

procedures
, when clause

, parenthetical
co-operation

(215)

451.

, introductory
extensive
recommendations

proposed
, when clause

competent
, and omitted

one's
, introductory

(217)

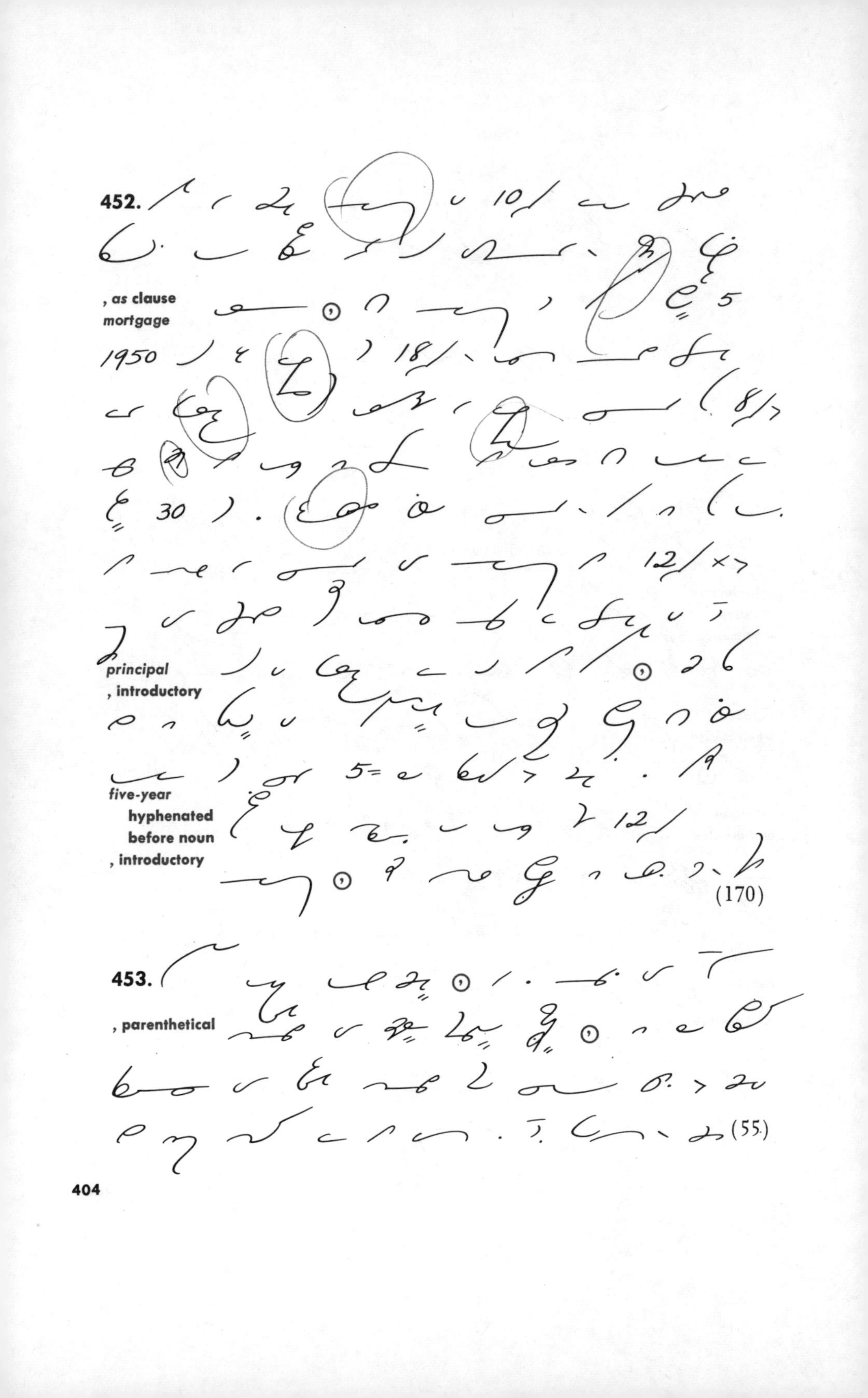

452.

, as clause
mortgage

principal
, introductory

five-year
hyphenated before noun
, introductory

(170)

453.

, parenthetical

(55)

Transcription Quiz. For you to supply. 7 commas–2 commas introductory, 2 commas series, 1 comma *when* clause, 1 comma *and* omitted, 1 comma *if* clause; 2 missing words.

454.

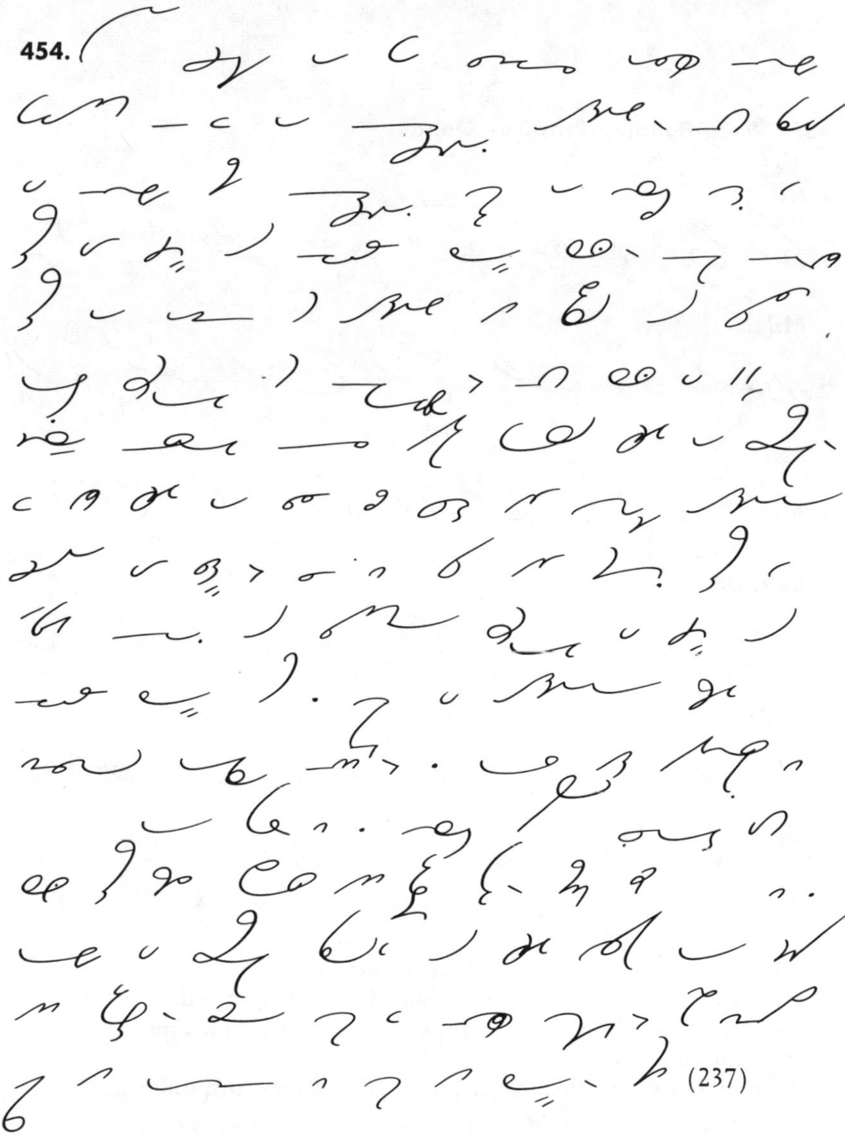

(237)

3-14-67

LESSON 65

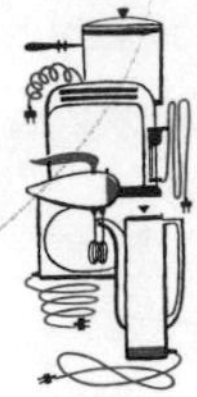

455. Word-Building Practice—Blends

Nd

1 

Md

2 

Pend

3 

Dev, Dif

4 

Den

5 

Dem

6 

1. Bind, brand, planned, second, trend, wind, land.
2. Framed, seemed, famed, named, blamed, trimmed, fumed.
3. Pending, depend, happened, opened, suspend, expend, expended, expenditure.
4. Devote, devise, develop, development, differ, different, difference.

5. Deny, student, wooden, identical, evident, accident, abandon.
6. Damage, damaged, domestic, demonstrate, seldom, medium.

Reading and Writing Practice

456. Transcription Word Study

destiny Fate.

motifs Themes or main features.

jostled Elbowed, crowded.

457. History of the Capitol Building

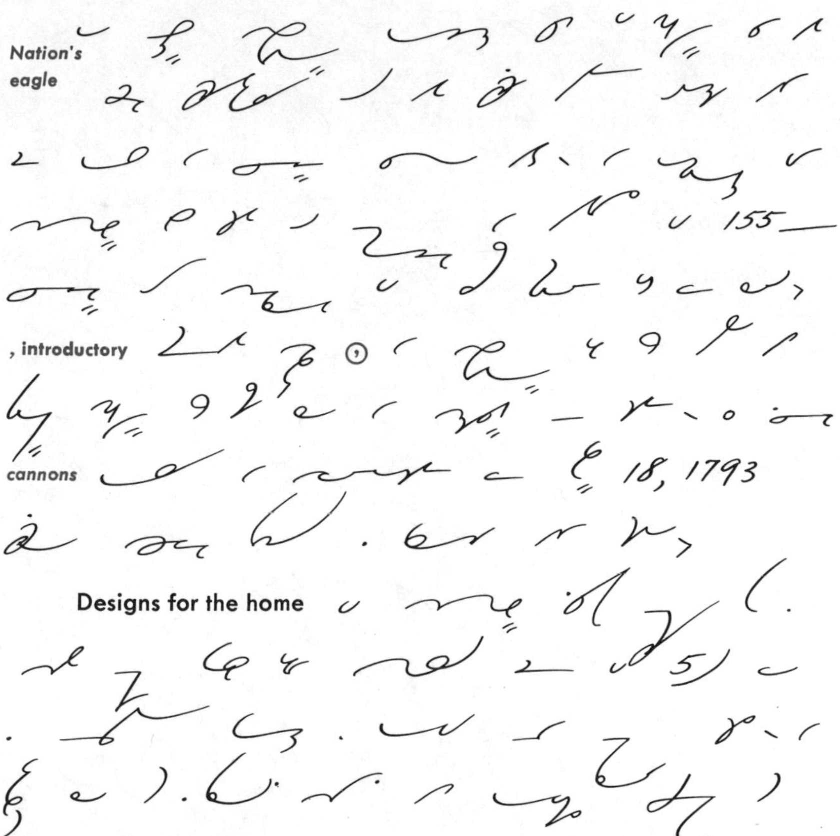

architect
Hallet
, apposition
Thornton

dismissed
substituting

The Capitol

, parenthetical
unforeseen

crumbled
chandelier

, parenthetical
befitted
era

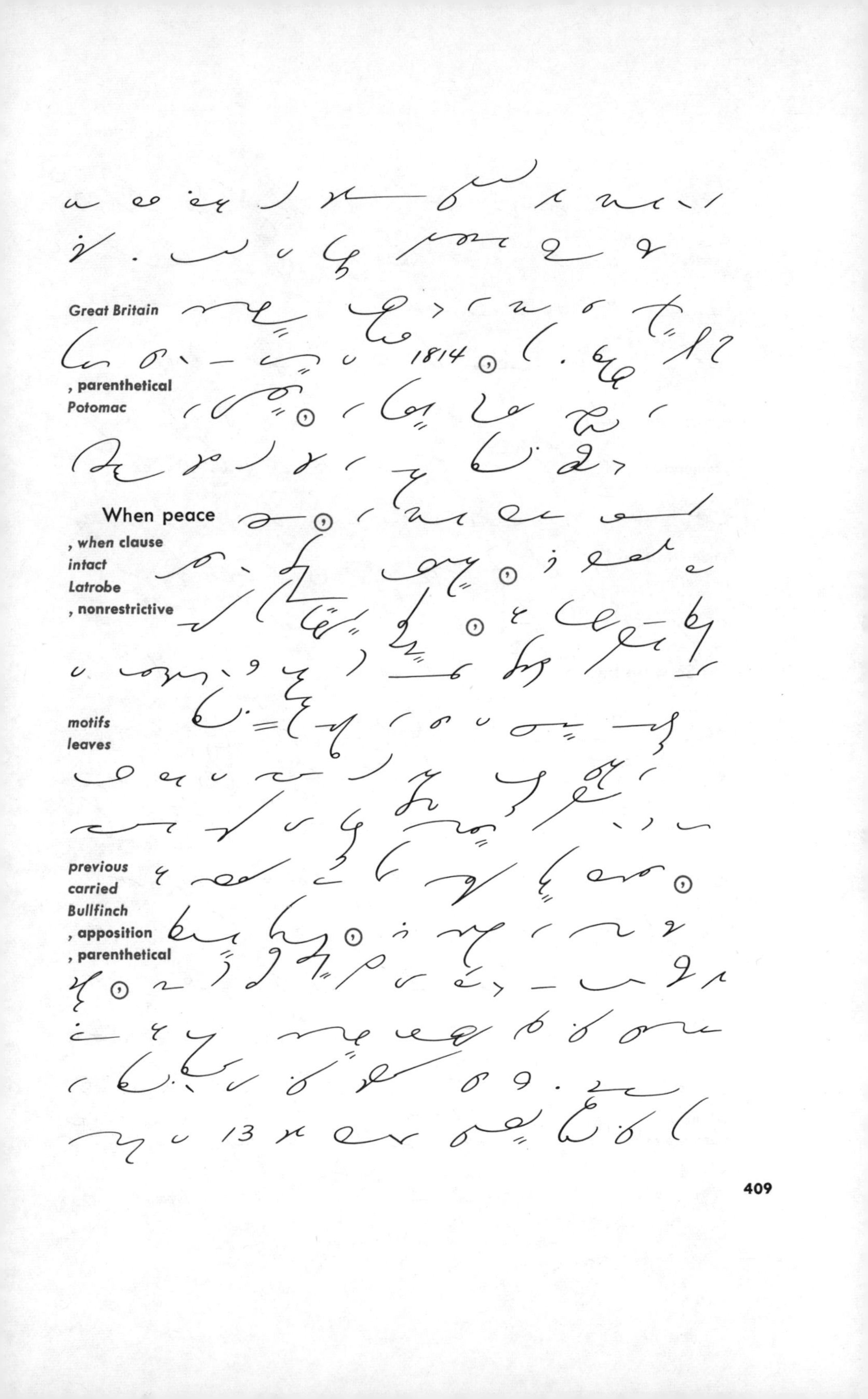

Great Britain

, parenthetical

Potomac

When peace

, *when* clause

intact

Latrobe

, nonrestrictive

motifs

leaves

previous

carried

Bullfinch

, apposition

, parenthetical

, series

, conjunction

, nonrestrictive

So were begun

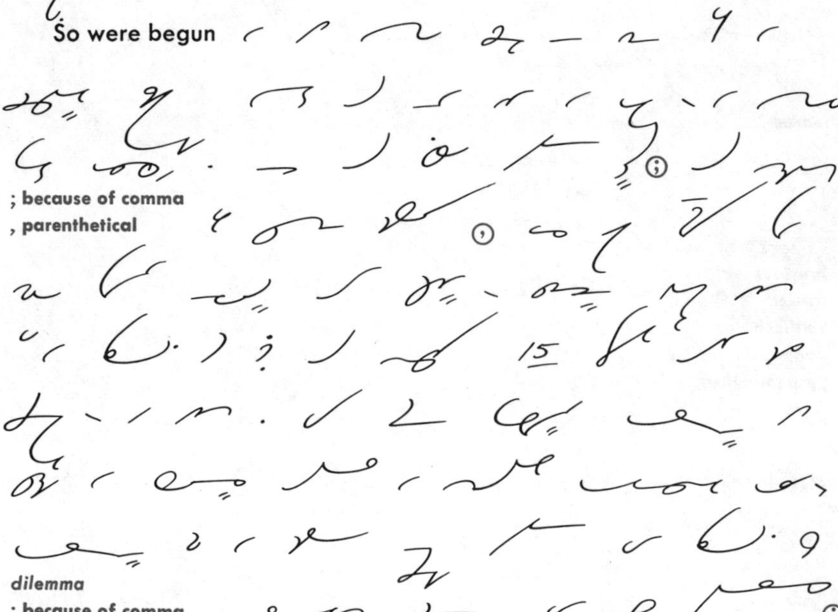

; because of comma

, parenthetical

dilemma

; because of comma

, introductory
tier
, parenthetical
plaza
miracle
285
Old style
, introductory
superbly
today's
, conjunction
, series
corridors
, introductory
galleries
(908)

14

EDUCATION

LESSON 66

458. Brief Forms and Derivatives

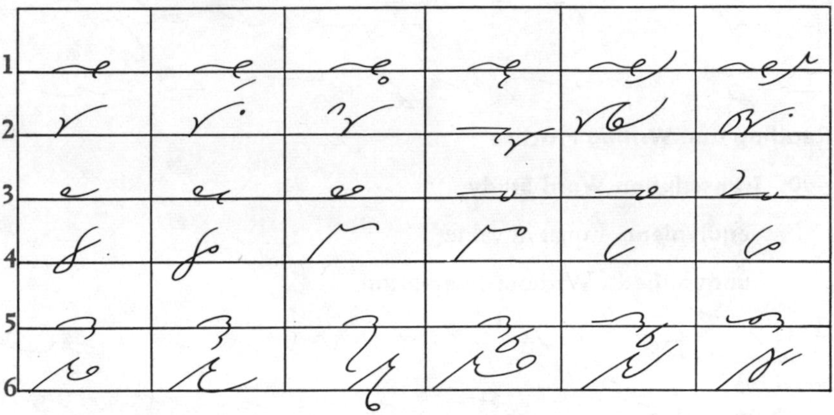

1. Correspond-correspondence, corresponded, correspondingly, corresponds, correspondent, correspondents.
2. Stand, standing, understand, misunderstand, standpoint, outstanding.
3. Were-year, years, yearly; most, mostly, foremost.
4. Particular, particularly; direct, directly; part, partly.
5. Consider-consideration, considers-considerations, considerable, considerate, inconsiderate, reconsider.
6. Disregard, displease, disbelieve, dislike, disorder, dissatisfied.

459. Brief Form and Phrase Letter

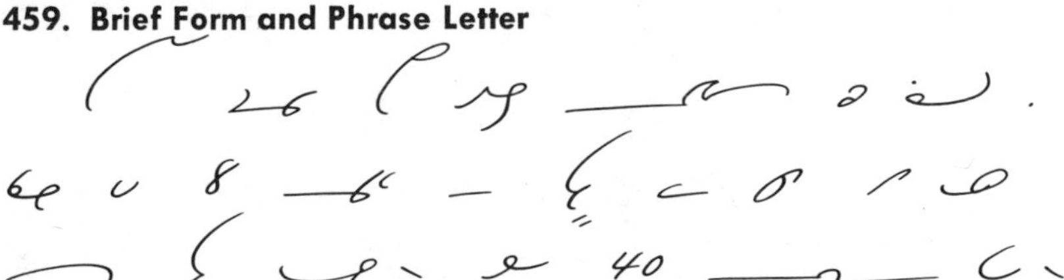

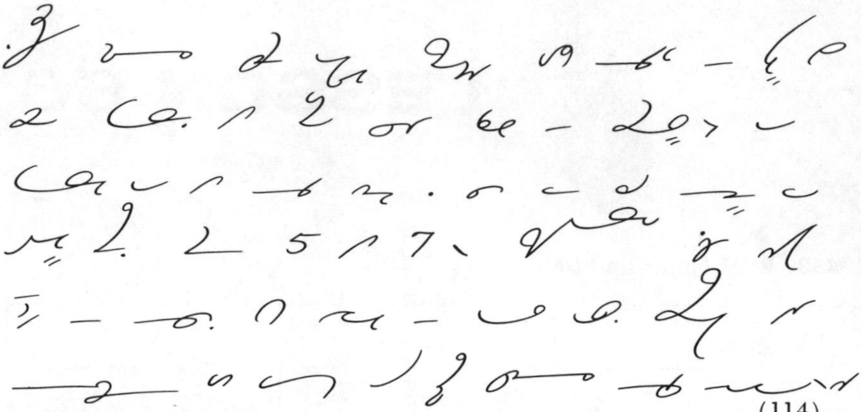

(114)

Reading and Writing Practice

460. Transcription Word Study

equivalent Equal in value.

unqualified Without reservation.

461.

, introductory
scholarships
recognized

Transcribe:
$1,000
, apposition

top-ranking
hyphenated
before noun

, introductory
; because of comma

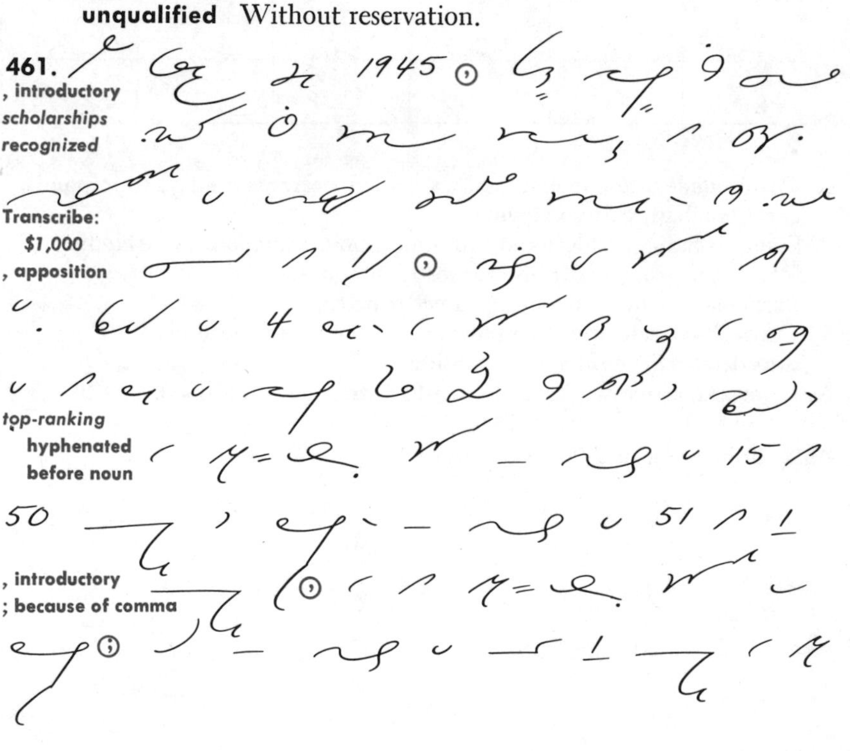

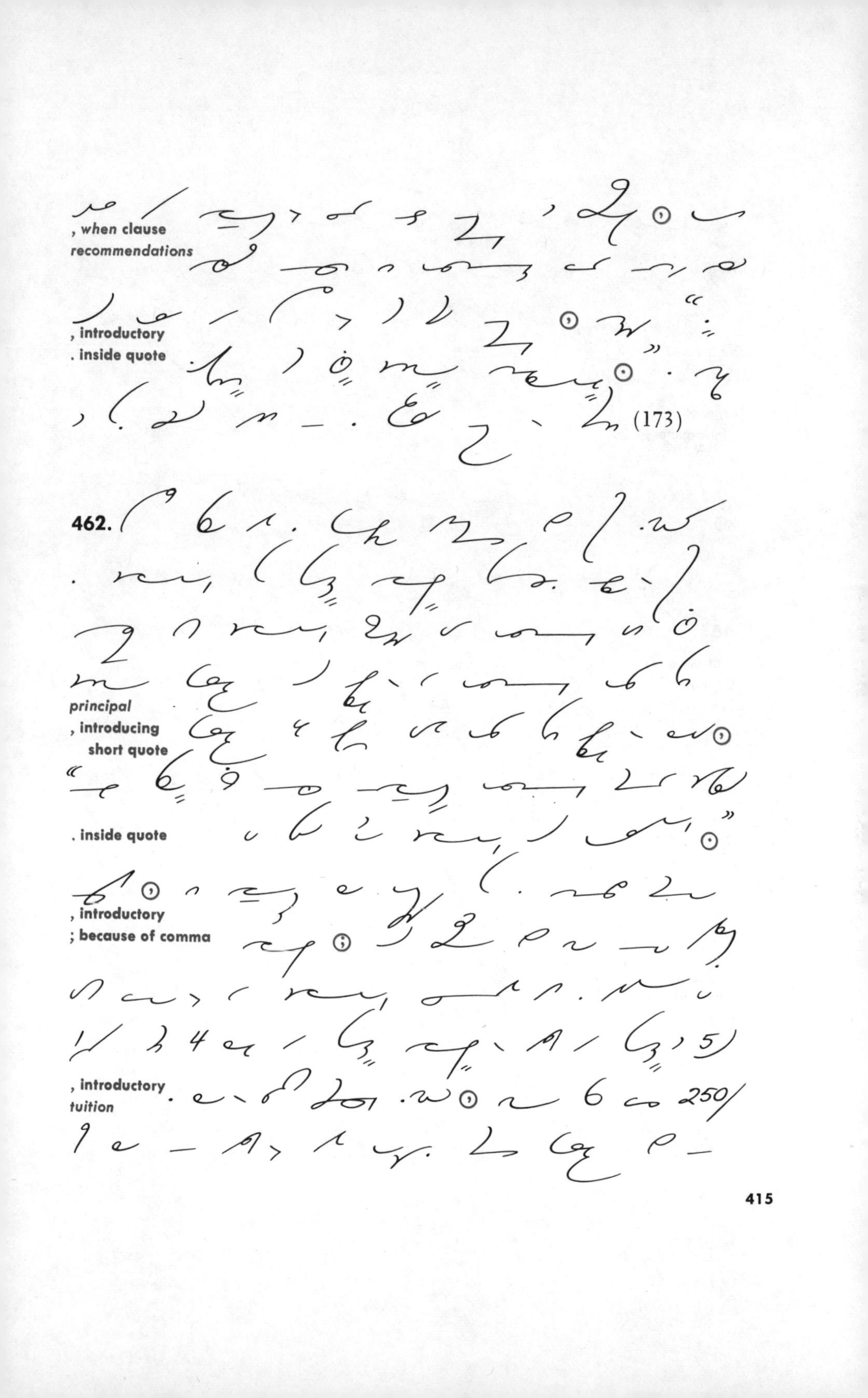

, when clause

recommendations

, introductory

. inside quote

(173)

462.

principal

, introducing short quote

. inside quote

, introductory

; because of comma

, introductory

tuition

separate
, introductory

(254)

463.

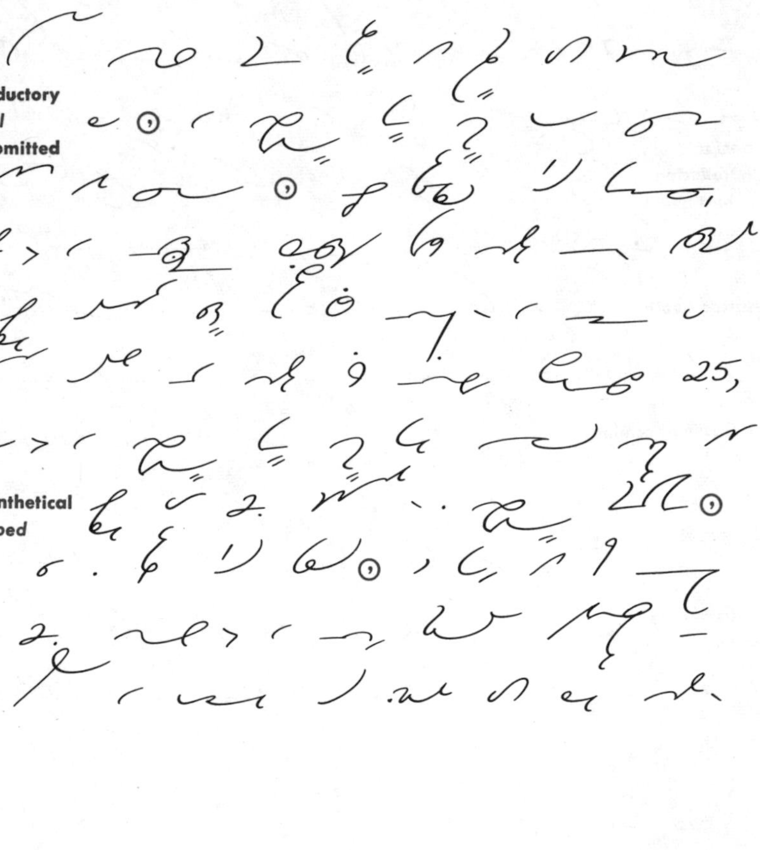

, introductory
Capital
, and omitted

, parenthetical
equipped

year's

(142)

464.

, *and* omitted

, introductory

; illustrative ,

pupils

, introductory

differentiation

practical

, introductory

(224)

Transcription Quiz. For you to supply: 8 commas—2 commas parenthetical, 2 commas apposition, 2 commas series, 1 comma conjunction, 1 comma *if* clause; 1 semicolon no conjunction; 1 colon enumeration; 2 missing words.

465.

(138)

LESSON 67

466. Useful Business-Letter Phrases

Or Omitted

1 

Of Omitted

2 

The Omitted

3 

You Omitted

4 

1. Day or two, one or two, two or three, three or four, more or less.
2. One of the, one of our, one of those, one of them, one of these, out of the, out of town.
3. By the way, in the future, in the world, about the matter, in the matter, in the market.
4. Will you please, will you please write, will you please send, will you please see.

467. Frequent Names

1
2
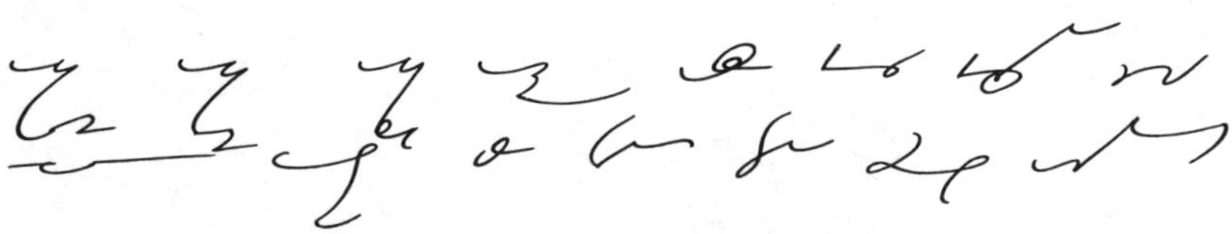

1. Robertson, Robinson, Rogers, Russell, Ryan, Schmidt, Schneider, Scott.
2. Norman, Oliver, Owen, Patrick, Peter, Philip, Rudolph.

Reading and Writing Practice

468. Transcription Word Study

recruiting Supplying with new people.

survey A study designed to provide specific information.

469.

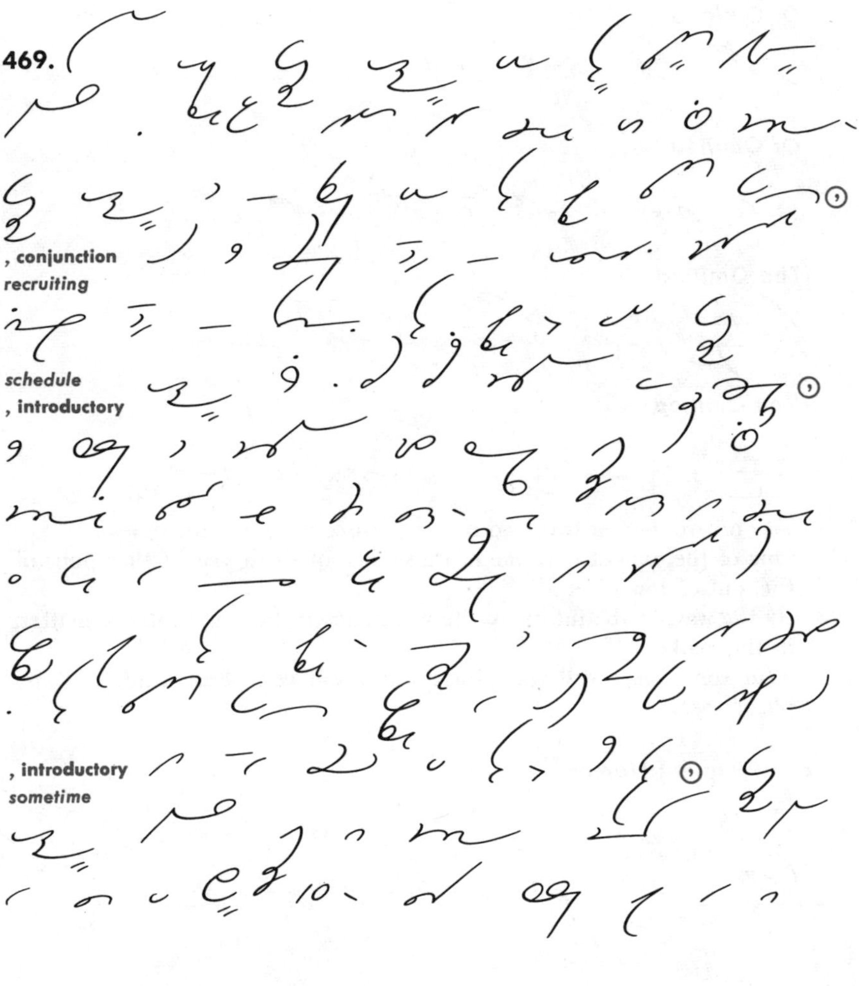

agreeable
, if clause
. courteous request
, parenthetical

(238)

470.

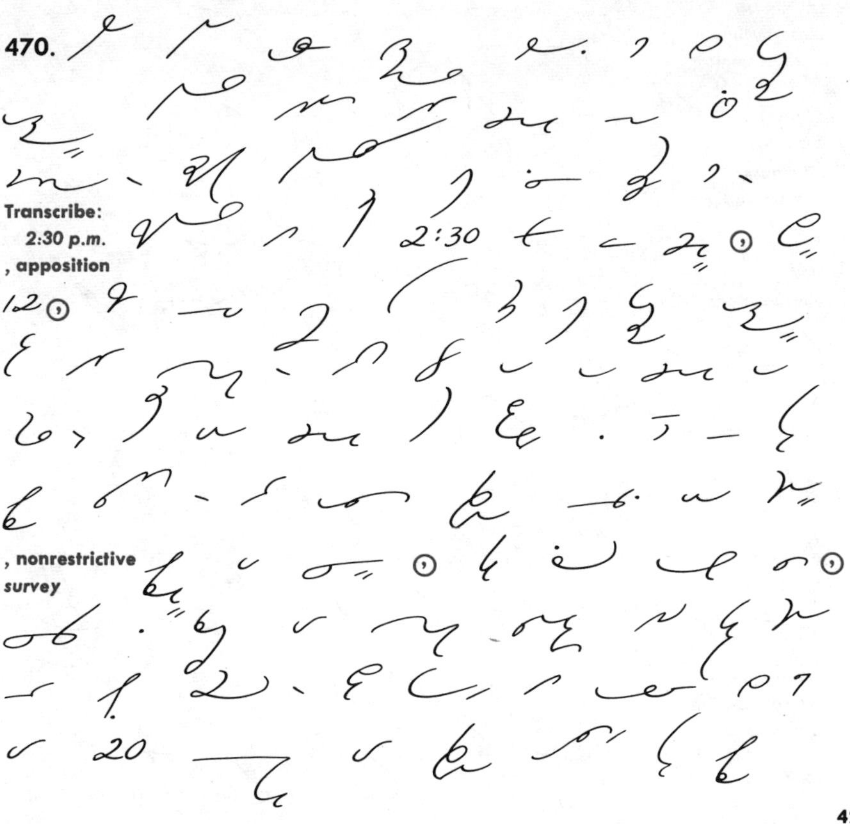

Transcribe:
2:30 p.m.
, apposition
, nonrestrictive
survey

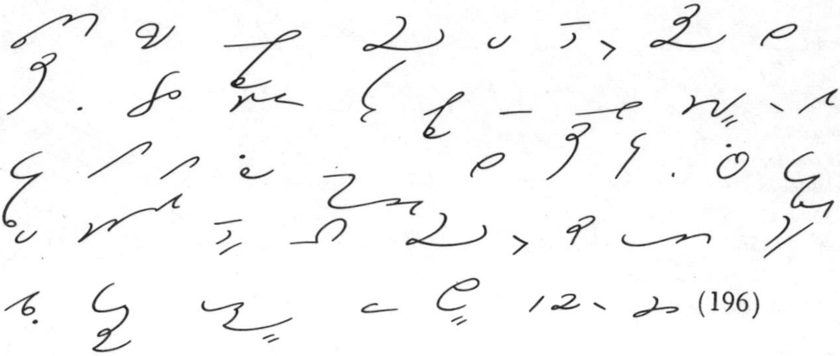 (196)

471.

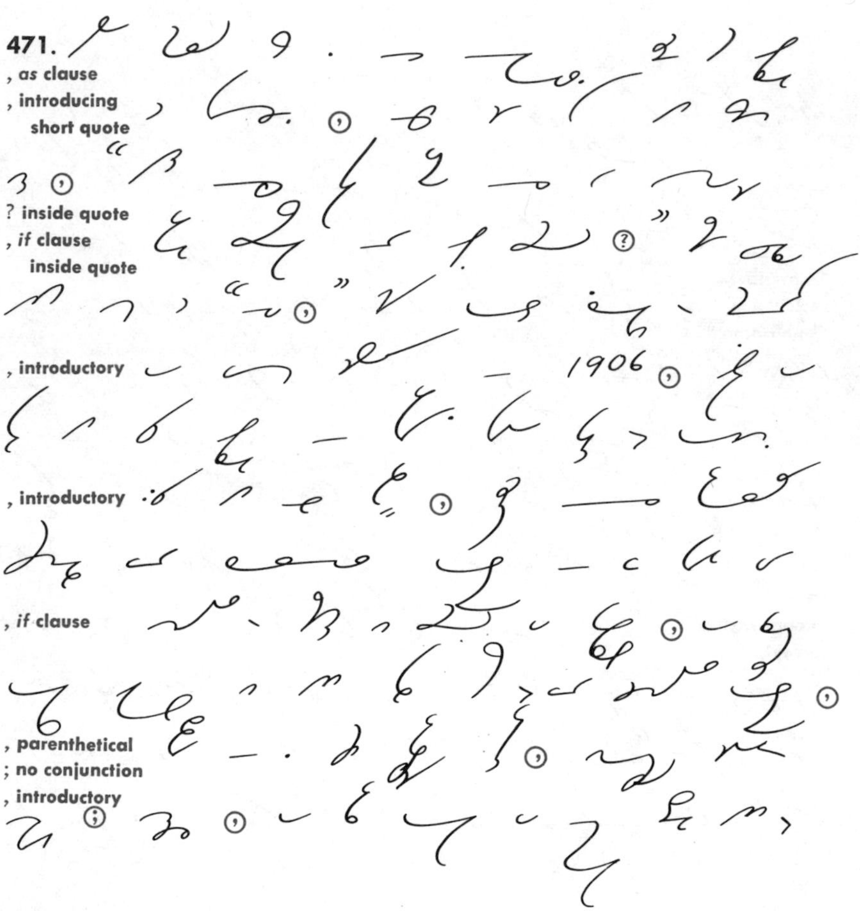

, *as* clause
, introducing short quote
? inside quote
, *if* clause inside quote
, introductory
, introductory
, *if* clause
, parenthetical
; no conjunction
, introductory

, *if clause*

(260)

472.

, **nonrestrictive inside quote**

accessible

: enumeration

, series

; illustrative , approval

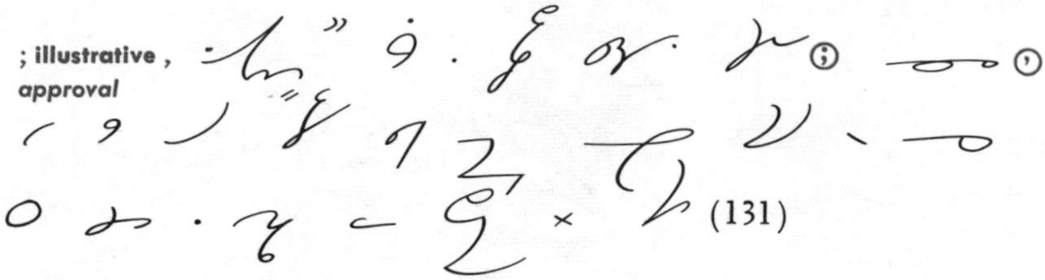

(131)

Transcription Quiz. For you to supply: 4 commas—3 commas introductory, 1 comma *and* omitted; 2 missing words.

473.

(147)

LESSON 68

474. Word Families

-sure

1 

-tance

2 

-tional

3 

-tribute

4 

1. Pleasure, treasure, measure, assure, leisure, pressure, composure.
2. Acceptance, substance, distance, admittance, circumstance, circumstances.
3. Sectional, conditional, national, rational, professional, provisional.
4. Tribute, attribute, contribute, distribute, contribution, retribution.

Reading and Writing Practice

475. Transcription Word Study

panel discussion A discussion of issues in which a selected group of persons participates.

predecessors Those who came before.

476.

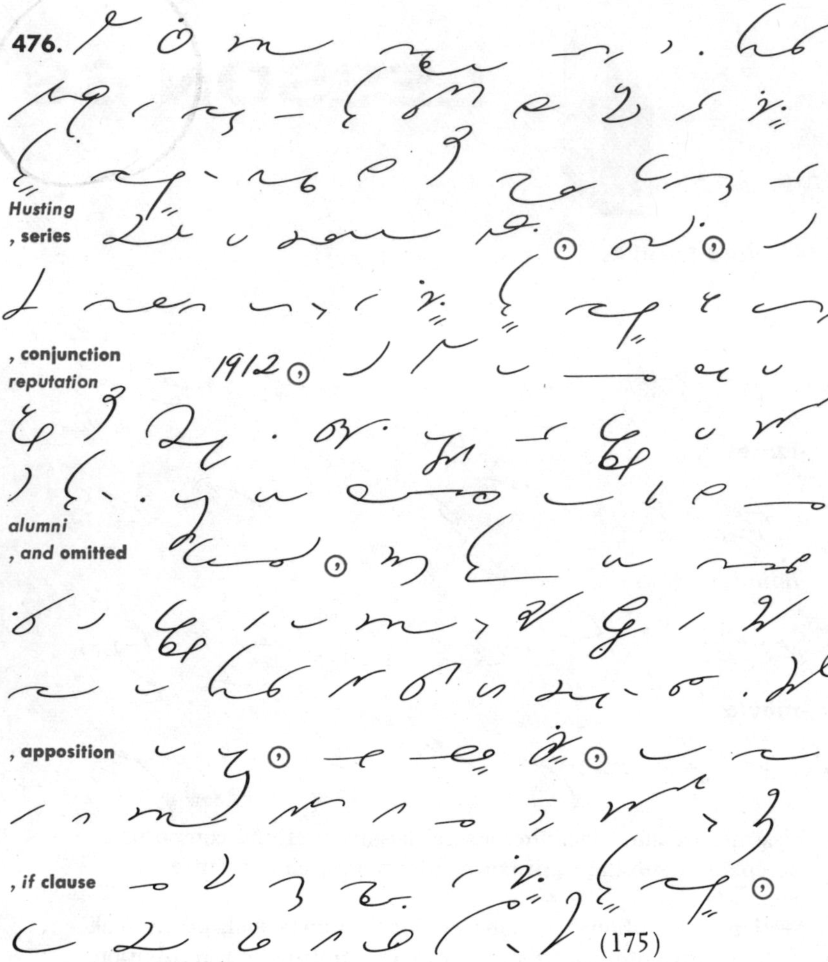

Husting

, series

, conjunction

reputation

alumni

, and omitted

, apposition

, if clause

(175)

477.

, introductory

responsibility

, apposition
; because of comma
, introducing short quote
ideal
, conjunction
. inside quote
, introductory
, apposition
, apposition
, parenthetical
. courteous request

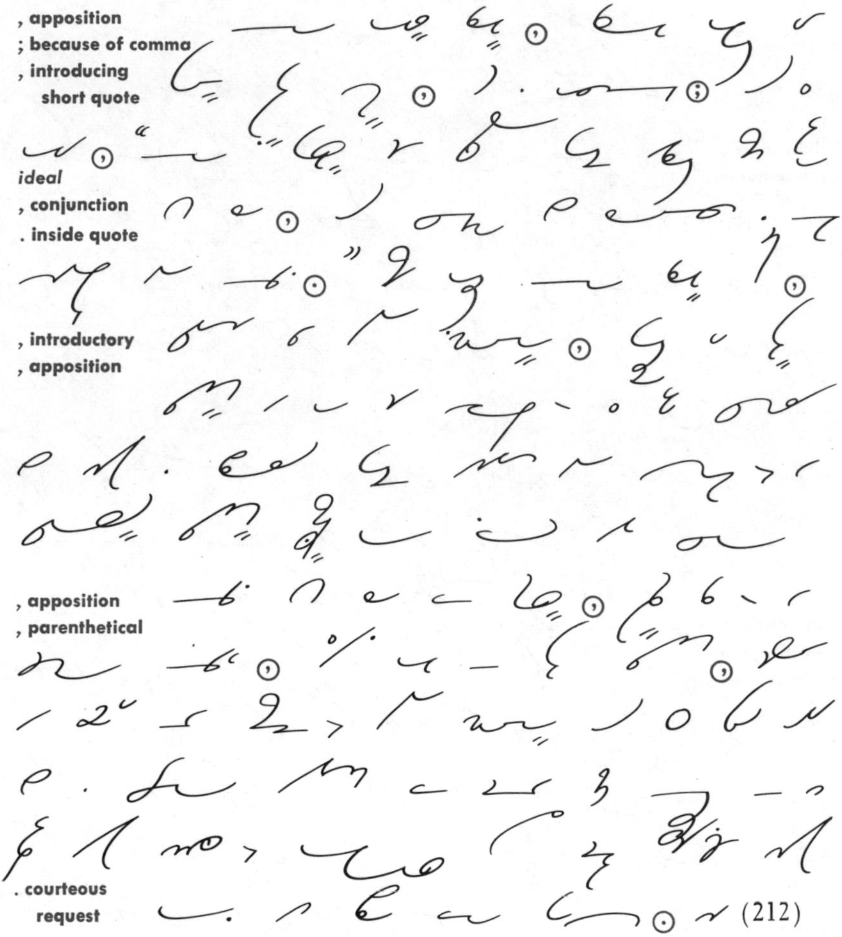

(212)

478.

, conjunction
calendar

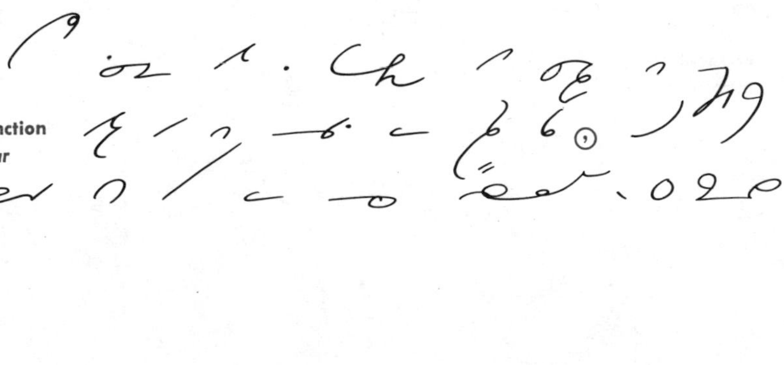

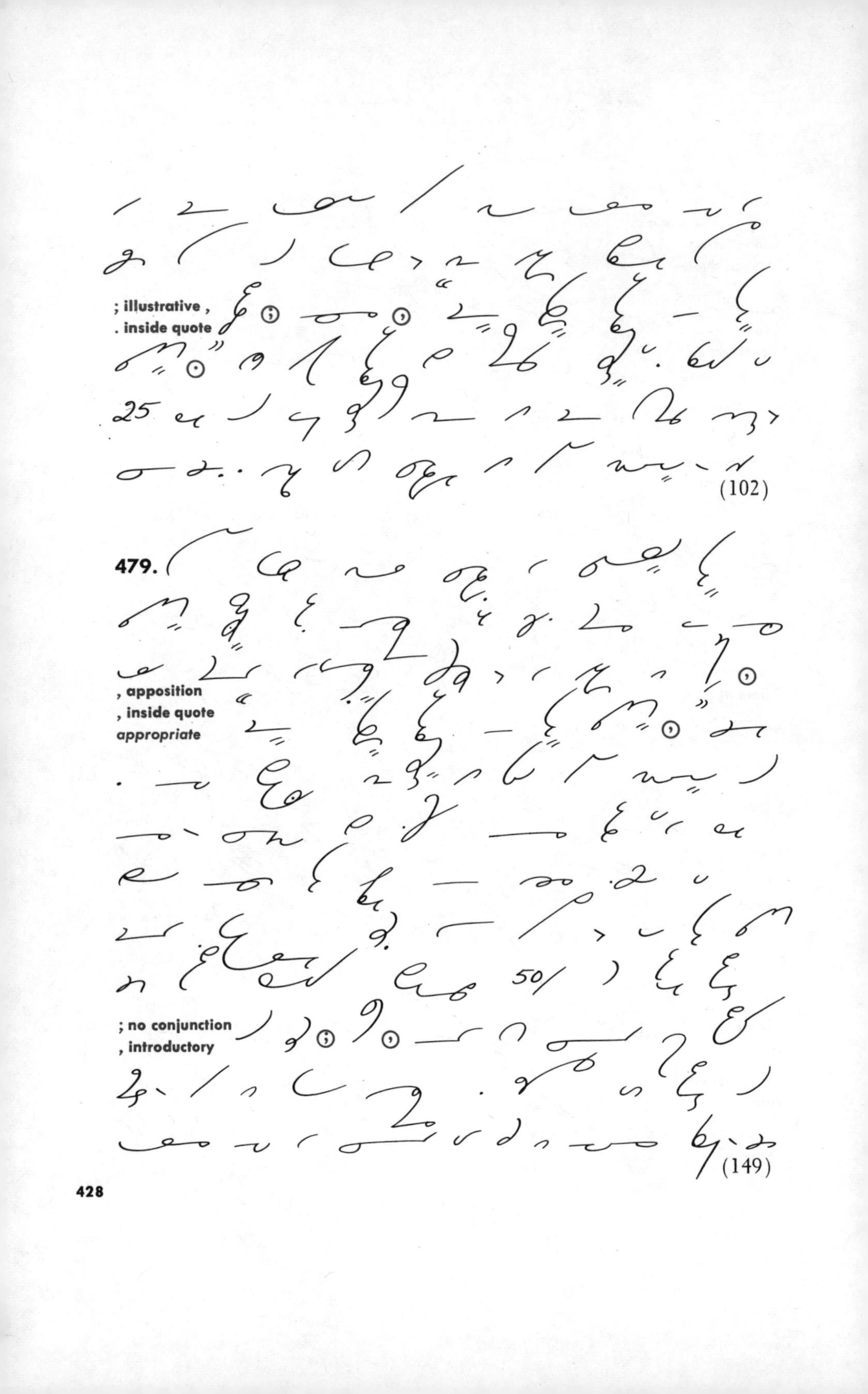

; illustrative ,
. inside quote

25

(102)

479.

, apposition
, inside quote
appropriate

50

; no conjunction
, introductory

(149)

Transcription Quiz. For you to supply: 5 commas—2 commas *when* clause, 2 commas introductory, 1 comma *if* clause; 1 semicolon because of comma; 2 missing words.

480.

(183)

LESSON 69

481. Word Beginnings and Endings

-ful

1 

-position

2 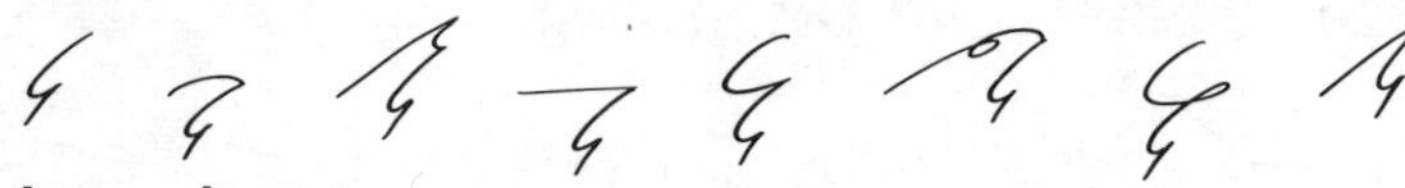

Incon-, Incom-

3 

Self-

4 

-ment

5 

Un-

6 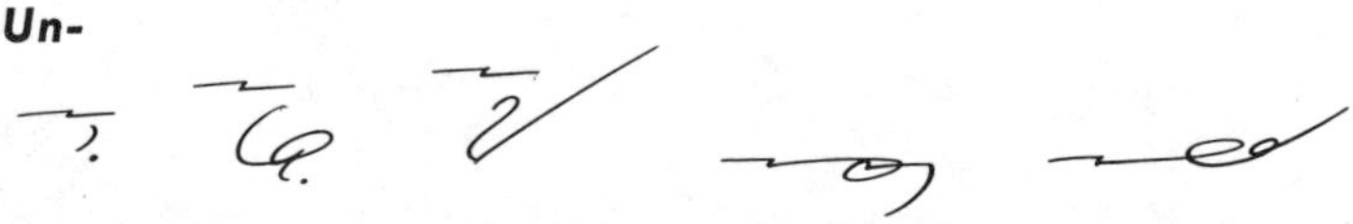

1. Meaningful, careful, thoughtful, mindful, roomful, harmful.
2. Position, composition, disposition, imposition, proposition, decomposition, preposition, deposition.
3. Inconsistent, inconvenient-inconvenience, incontestable, inconspicuous, incompetent, incomplete.

4. Self-evident, self-sufficient, self-complacent, self-indulgent, self-possessed, self-satisfaction, selfish.
5. Agreement, compliment, department, contentment, entertainment.
6. Uninteresting, unenterprising, uninterrupted, unmindful, unmarried.

482. Geographical Expressions

1
2
3

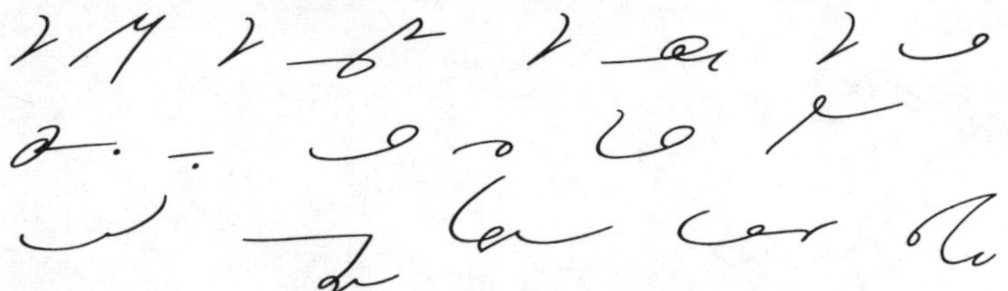

1. Fort Dodge, Fort Madison, Fort Myers, Fort Lee.
2. Wyoming, New Hampshire, Louisiana, Kentucky, Florida, Delaware.
3. London, Manchester, Bristol, Plymouth, Edinburgh.

Reading and Writing Practice

483. Transcription Word Study

reactions Responses.

intricate Involved, complicated.

484.

: enumeration
pamphlet

, introductory
, *when clause*

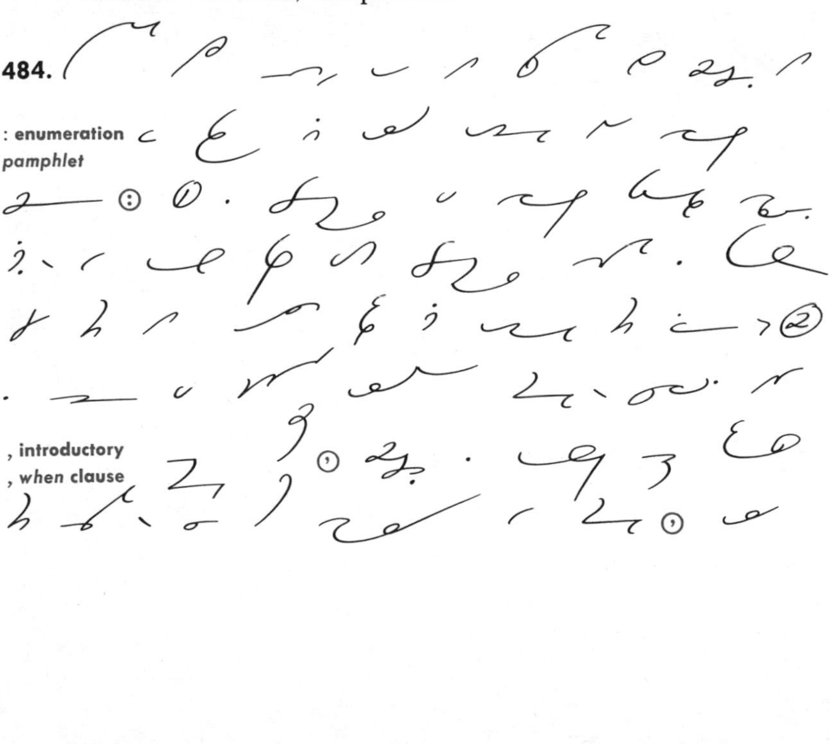

; no conjunction

, if clause
immediately

(175)

485.

warehouses
, parenthetical

8:30

, as clause

, conjunction

, parenthetical

, parenthetical
, nonrestrictive

, series
, *if* clause
accept

4-4711

(228)

486.

; illustrative ,
, series

well-equipped
hyphenated
before noun

, introductory

, introductory
, apposition

(152)

487.

. inside quote
typical

competent
intricate

, *and* omitted
co-operative

behalf
, apposition

(139)

Transcription Quiz. For you to supply: 7 commas—1 comma introductory, 2 commas *if* clause, 2 commas series, 2 commas apposition; 2 missing words.

488.

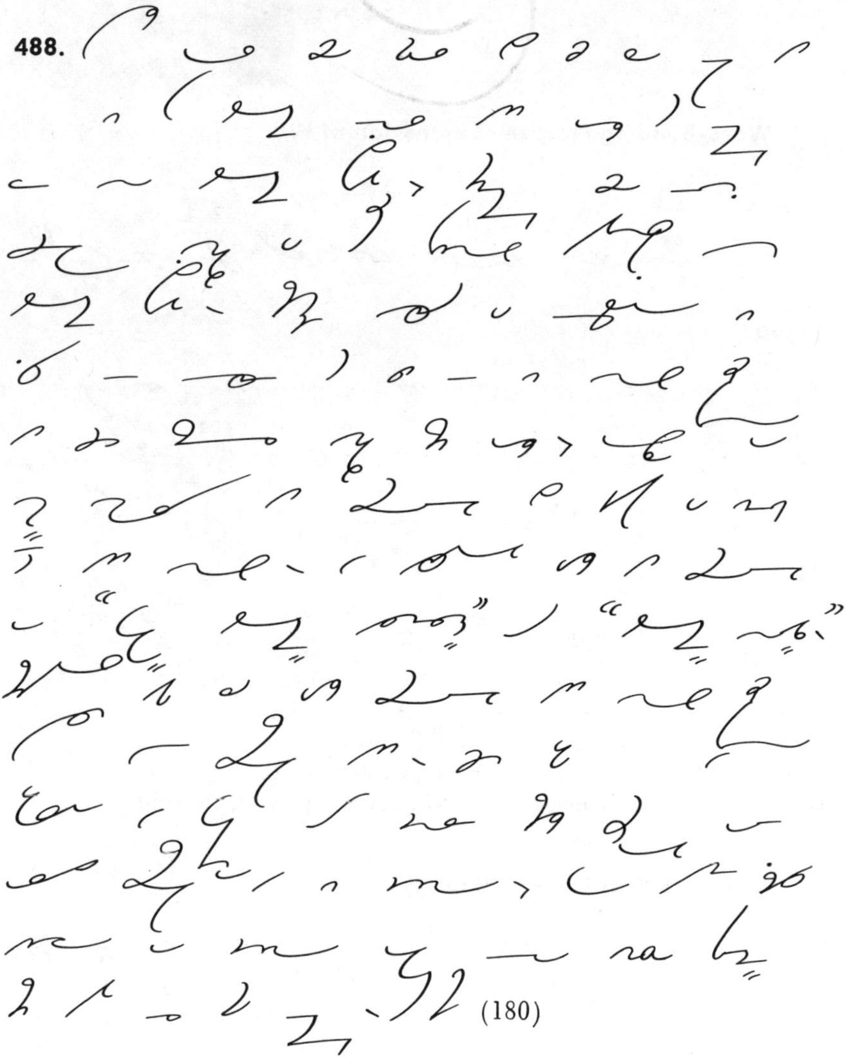

(180)

LESSON 70

489. Word-Building Practice—Expression of W

Wī

1 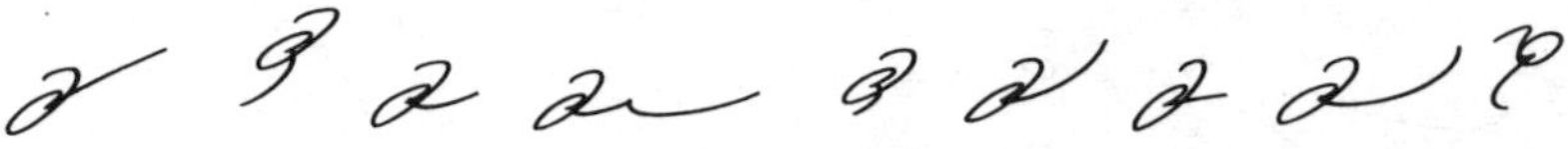

Woo

2 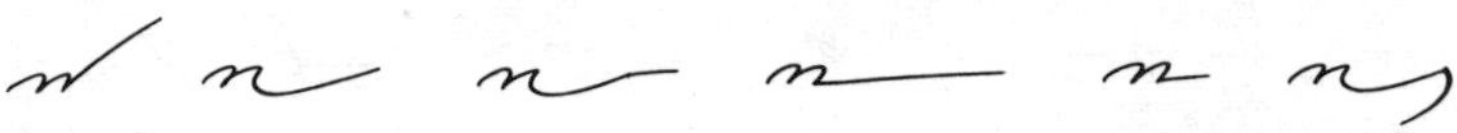

Wh

3 

Sw

4 

1. Wide, wife, wire, wireless, wise, wind, wine, wild, wipe.
2. Wood, wool, woolen, woman, wonder, wolf.
3. While, whim, whale, whistle, white, whiten, whip.
4. Sweet, swelling, swing, switch, swim, swollen, swift, sweepings.

490. Accuracy Practice—Diphthongs

1 

2 

3 

1. Use, few, human, fuel; out, ounce, now, power.
2. Point, toil, oil, royal, boil, soil, annoy.
3. Tie, pile, fine, nice, dine, wire, guide, height.

Reading and Writing Practice

491. Transcription Word Study

primarily In the first place, originally.

competent Capable.

resourcefulness Ability to make the best of available means.

492. Secretarial Work

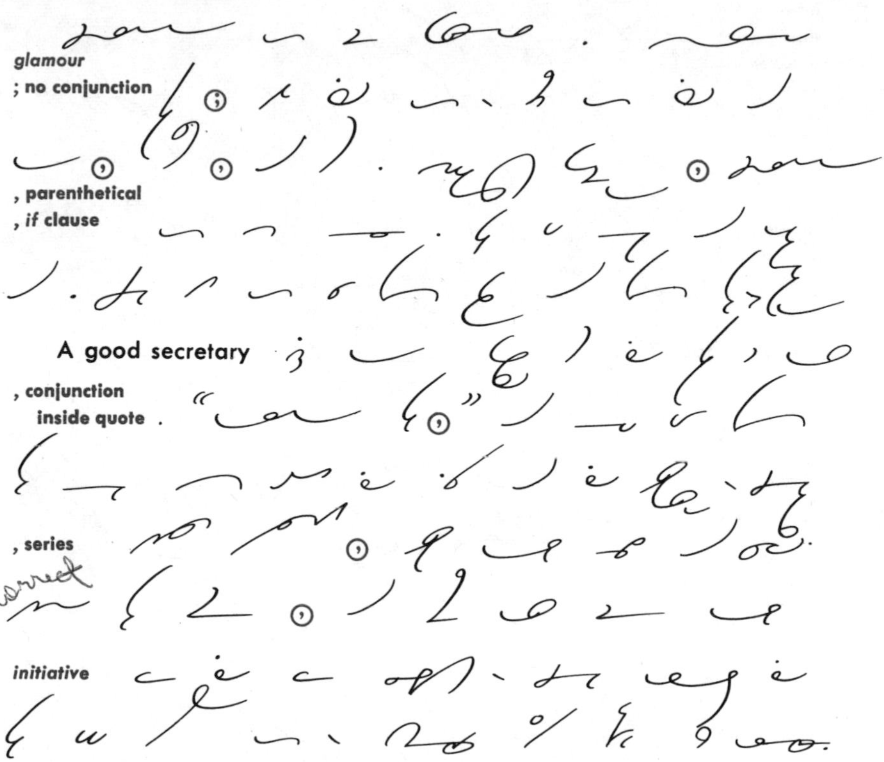

, series
occasionally

company's

, introductory
. inside quote
education

, introductory

Adaptability.

, series
criticism

, conjunction

Personal Conduct.

, series
, *and* omitted

, parenthetical

Good Health.

, conjunction

Personal Appearance.

well-modulated
hyphenated
before noun
, introductory

Sense of Responsibility.

, introductory

Wherever there are

, introductory
: enumeration

, series
brokerage

, parenthetical

municipal
, series

Mayors
, series

, series

noncommercial
, series

, series

, nonrestrictive
receptionists

wholesale
, conjunction
advancement

, series

aviation
, series

, *as* clause
, introductory

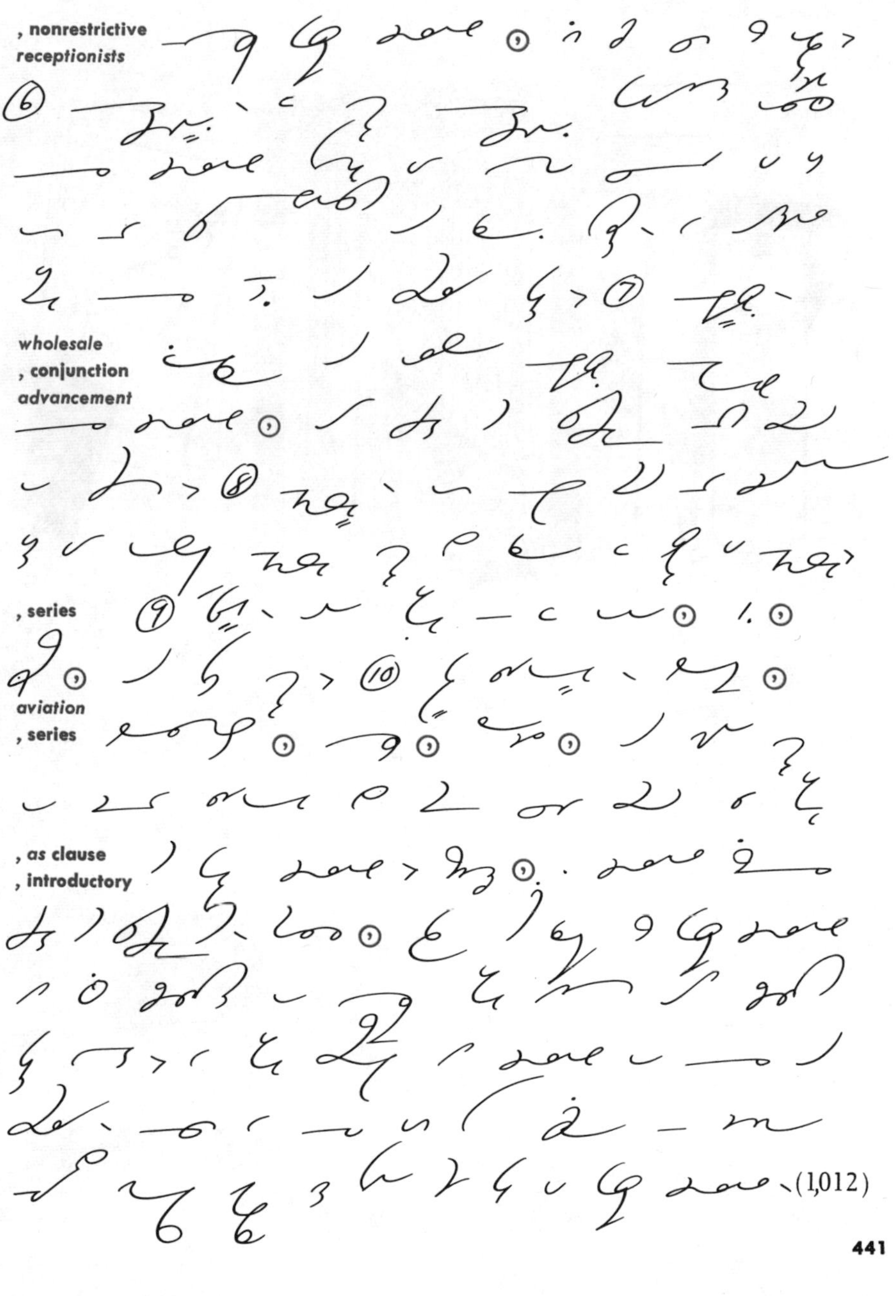

(1,012)

15

PAPER

LESSON 71

493. Brief Forms and Derivatives

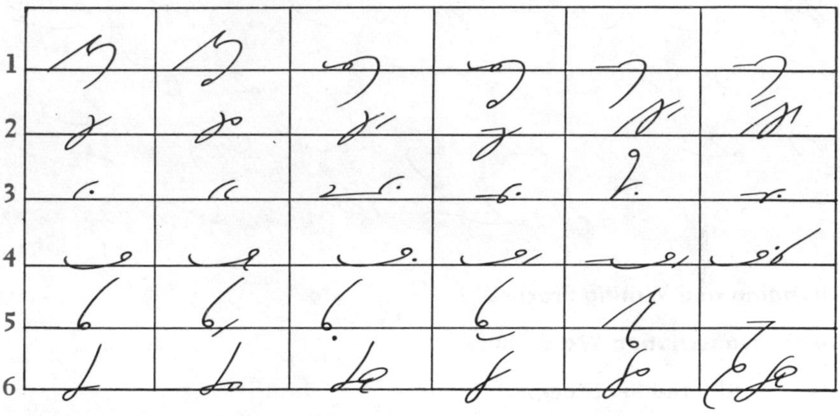

1. Discover, discovery, recover, recovery, uncover, uncovered.
2. Satisfy-satisfactory, satisfactorily, satisfied, unsatisfactory, dissatisfied, dissatisfaction.
3. Thing-think, things-thinks, something, anything, everything, nothing.
4. Let-letter, letters, lettering, lettered, unlettered, letterhead.
5. Belief-believe, believed, believing, believer, disbelief-disbelieve, unbelievable.
6. General, generally, generalize; particular, particularly, particularize.

494. Brief Form and Phrase Letter

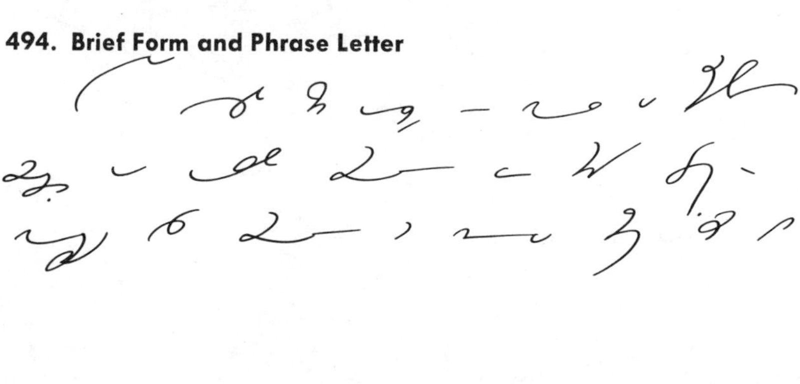

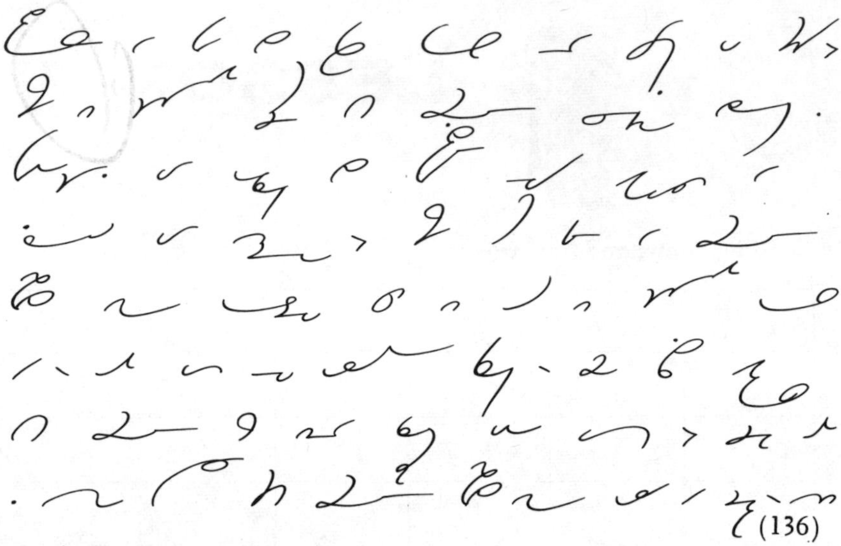

(136)

Reading and Writing Practice

495. Transcription Word Study

adhered to Stuck to.

category Class.

stationery Paper, clips, pens, etc. (Do not confuse with *stationary*, which means "in one spot.")

496.

, *when* clause

disappointed

, *as* clause

; because of comma

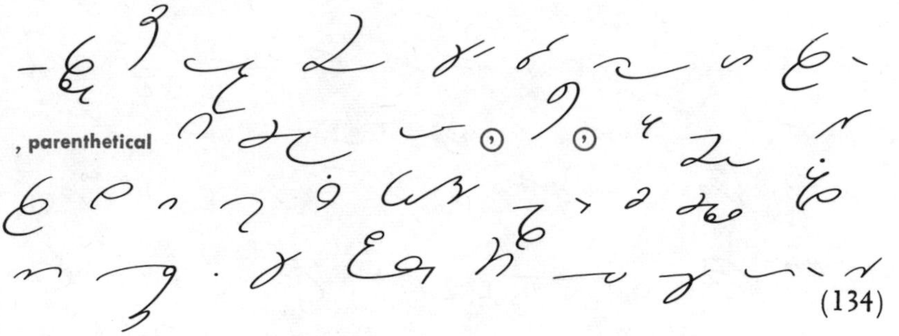

, parenthetical

(134)

497.

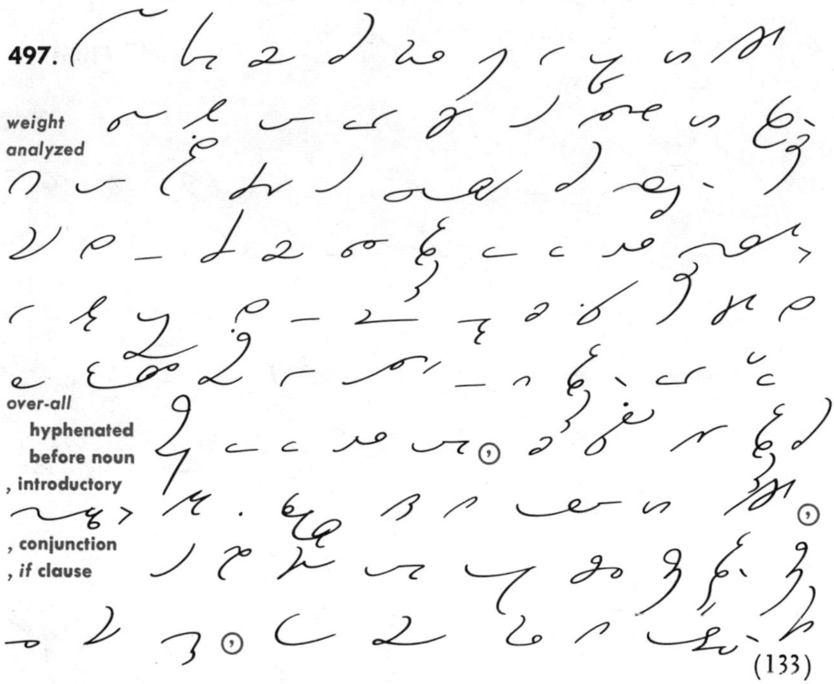

weight
analyzed

over-all
hyphenated
before noun

, introductory

, conjunction

, *if* clause

(133)

498.

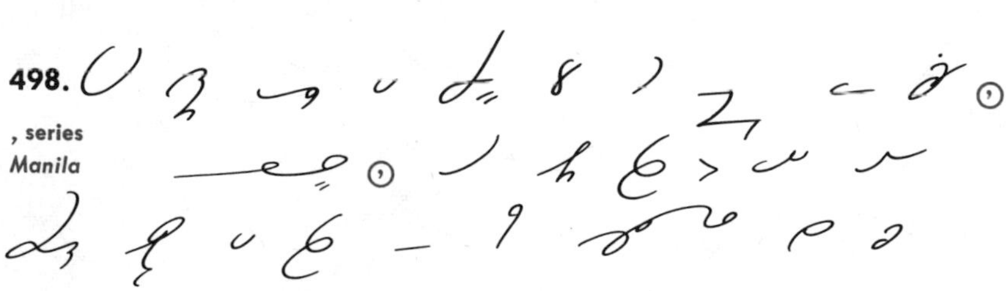

, series

Manila

, introductory

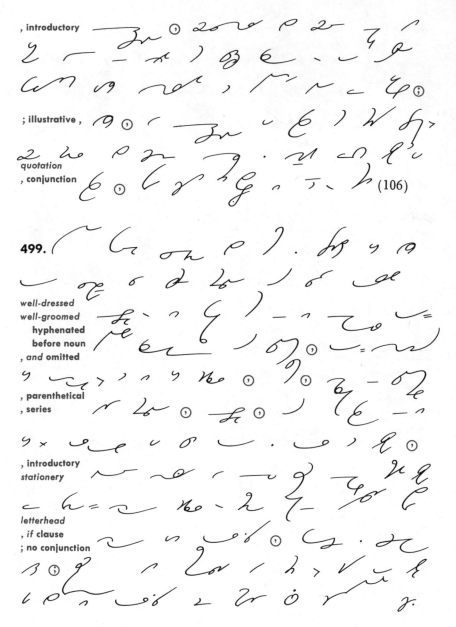

; illustrative ,

quotation

, conjunction

(106)

499.

well-dressed

well-groomed

hyphenated

before noun

, *and* omitted

, parenthetical

, series

, introductory

stationery

letterhead

, *if* clause

; no conjunction

Homework Self-Check

When you do each day's homework, do you get the most out of the time you spend on it by

1. Reading the Transcription Word Studies before you begin on the Reading and Writing Practice?

2. Reading all shorthand aloud before making a copy of it?

, introductory

, if clause

(199)

500.

, *as* clause

: enumeration

, series

Transcription Quiz. For you to supply: 4 commas—1 comma introductory, 1 comma conjunction, 1 comma *as* clause, 1 comma *if* clause; 1 semicolon because of comma; 2 missing words.

501.

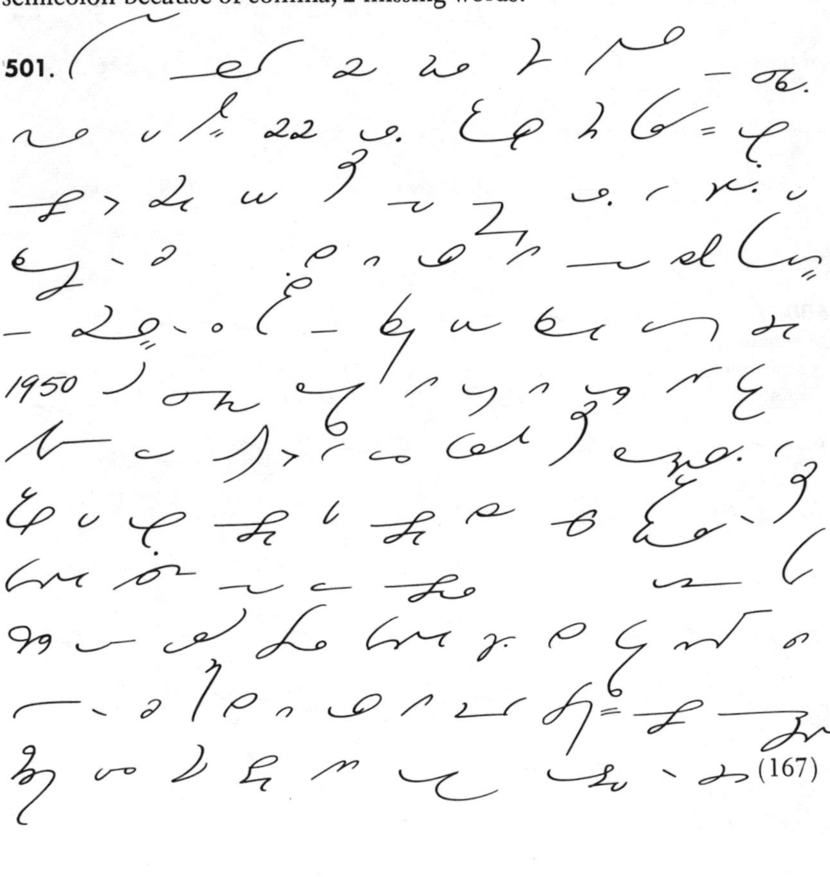

LESSON 72

502. Useful Business-Letter Phrases

Of Omitted

1 

To Omitted

2 

The Omitted

3 

In Omitted

4 

1. Some of the, some of them, some of those, some of our, some of these, some of this.
2. In addition to the, in addition to that, in addition to these, in addition to them, up to date, up to the minute, we should like to have.
3. On the part, on the question, on the subject, upon the subject, on the whole.
4. Mother-in-law, father-in-law, brother-in-law, sister-in-law, son-in-law.

503. Frequent Names

1 

2 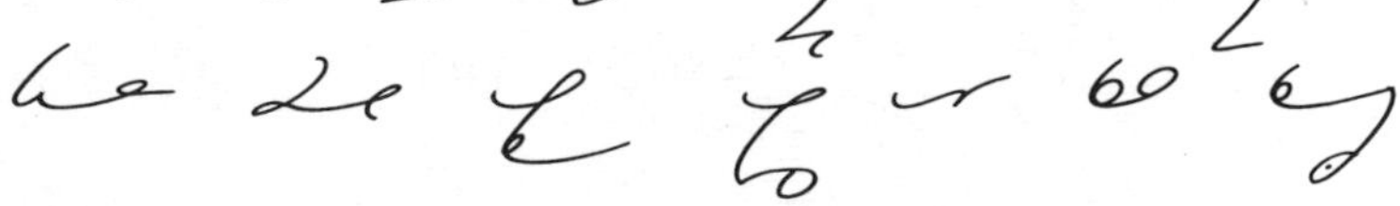

1. Shaw, Shea, Simpson, Snyder, Stevens, Stewart, Sullivan, Taylor.
2. Pauline, Phyllis, Rachel, Rebecca, Ruth, Sarah, Sylvia.

Reading and Writing Practice

504. Transcription Word Study

stimulating Exciting.

allotment The share assigned to each.

durability Power to last, not wear out.

absorption Process of soaking up, as a sponge.

505.

, introductory
attempting
develop

, introductory
occurred

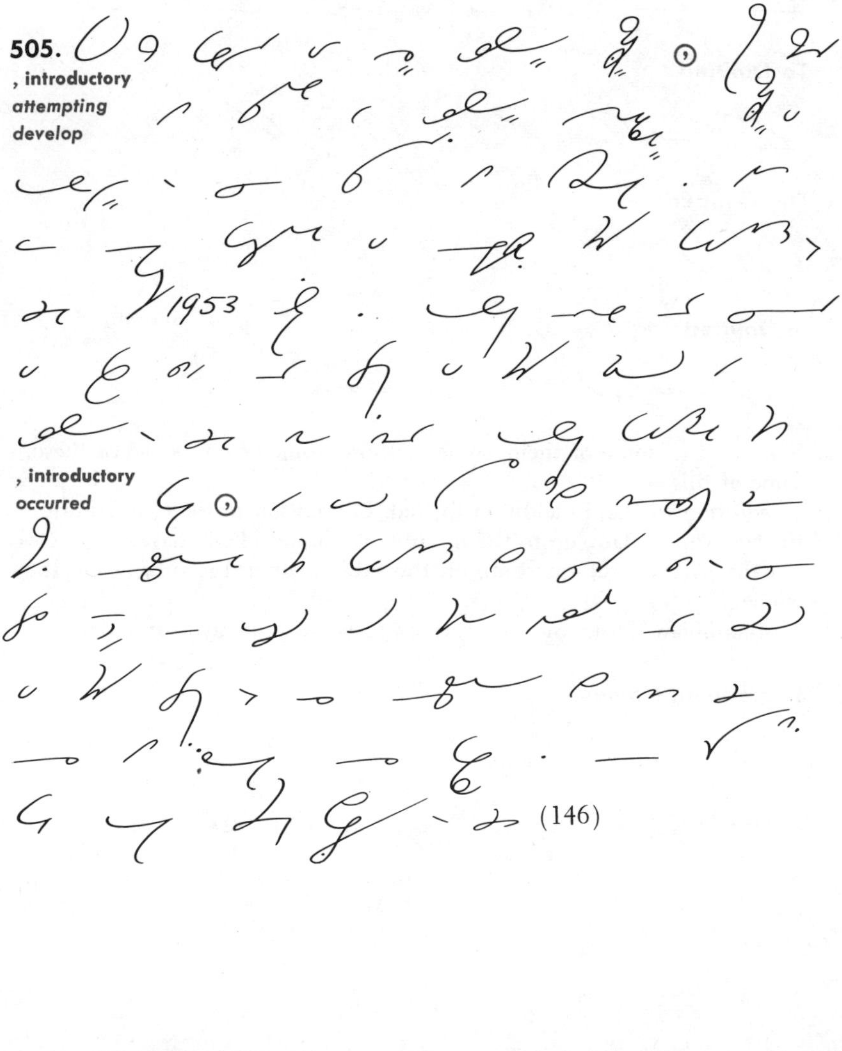

(146)

506.

, introductory
: enumeration
, series
assistance
, introductory
. courteous request

507.

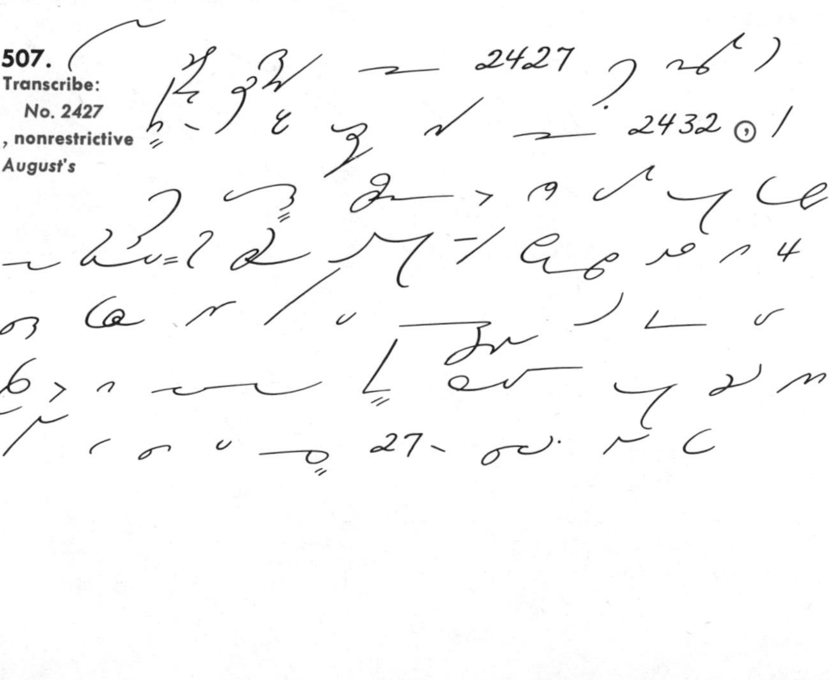

Transcribe: No. 2427
, nonrestrictive
August's

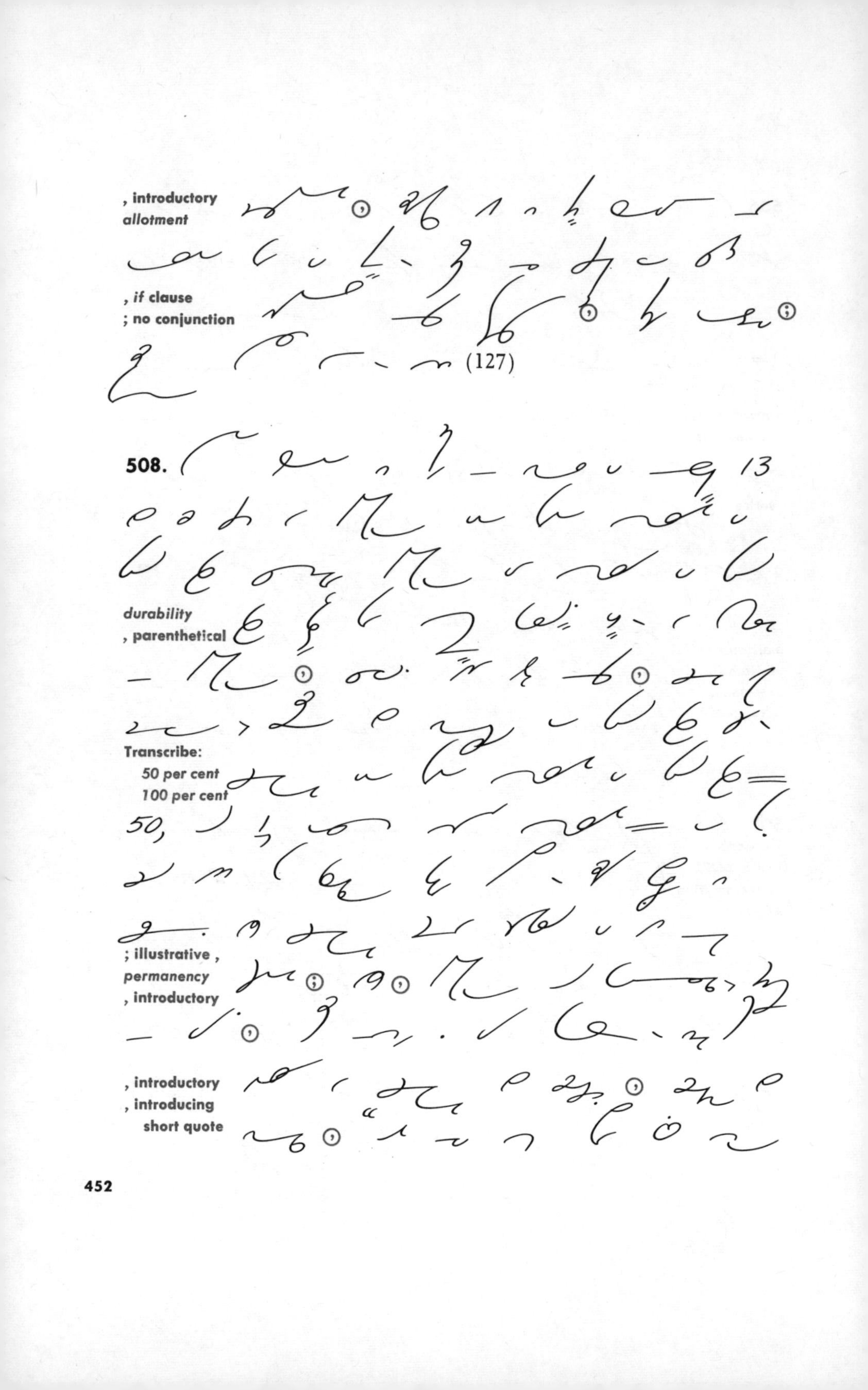

, introductory
allotment

, *if* clause
; no conjunction

(127)

508.

13

durability
, parenthetical

Transcribe:
50 per cent
100 per cent

50,

; illustrative ,
permanency
, introductory

, introductory
, introducing short quote

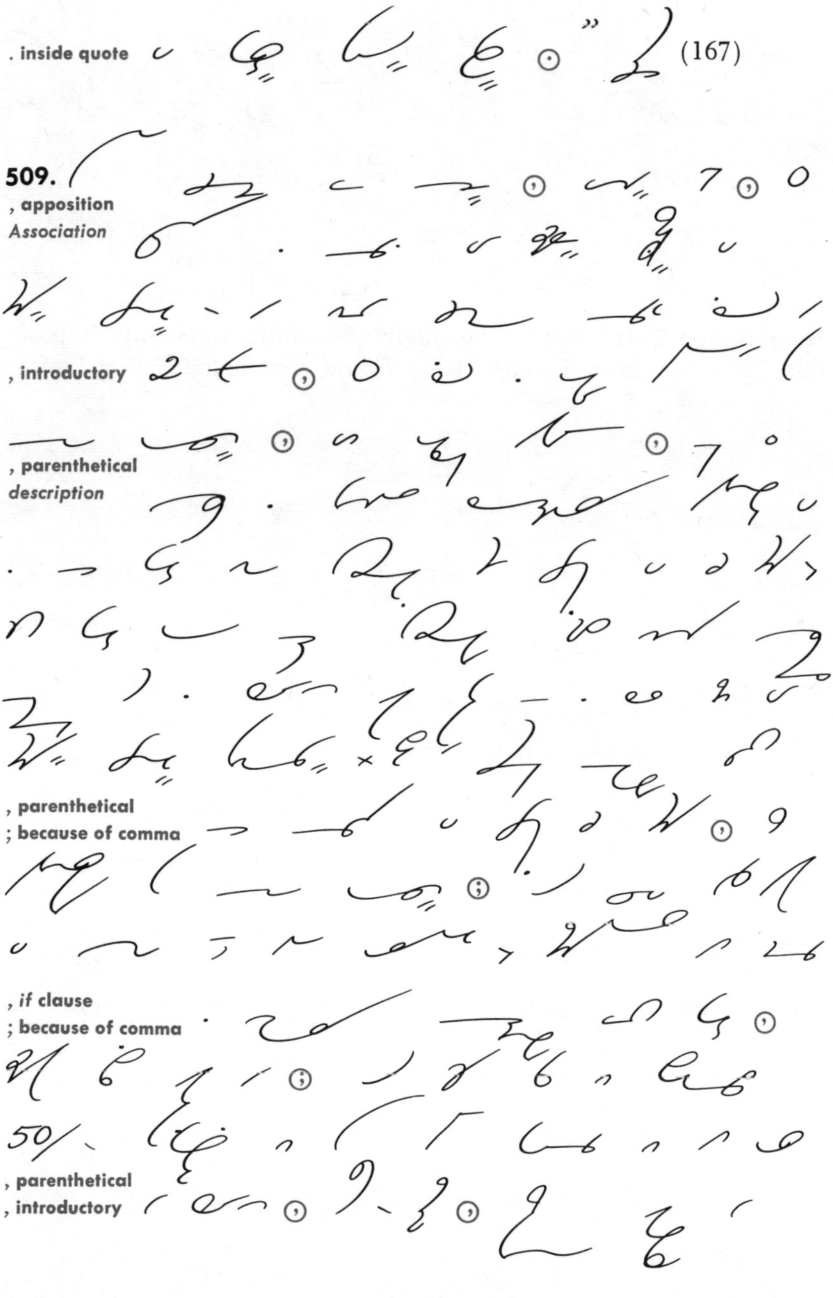
. inside quote
(167)
509.
, apposition
Association
, introductory
, parenthetical
description
, parenthetical
; because of comma
, if clause
; because of comma
50/
, parenthetical
, introductory

, introductory
forward

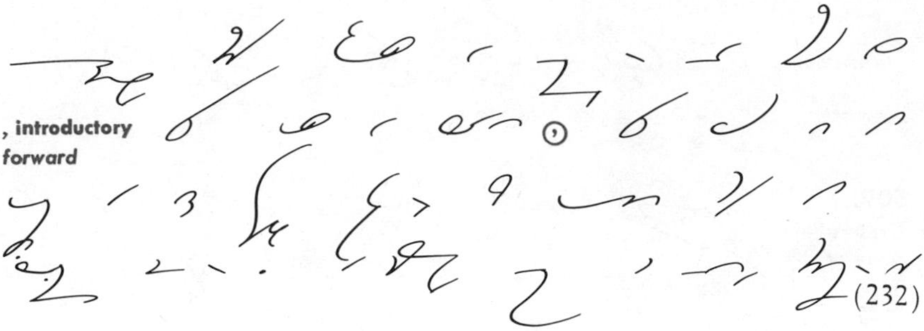

(232)

Transcription Quiz. For you to supply: 6 commas—2 commas apposition, 2 commas series, 1 comma *when* clause, 1 comma *if* clause; 2 missing words.

510.

(117)

LESSON 73

511. Word Families

-duction

1 

-lution

2 

-ment

3 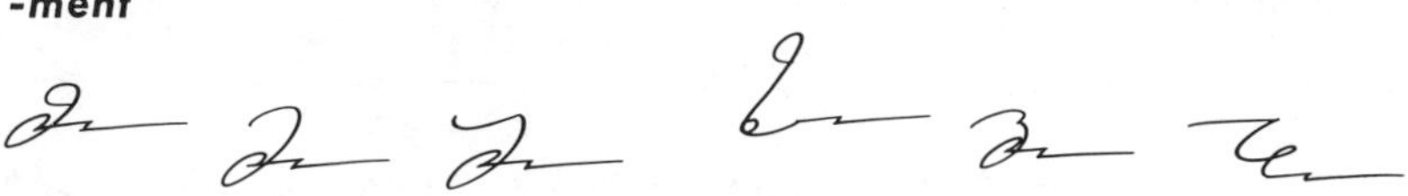

-cious

4 

-sive

5 

1. Production, deduction, reduction, introduction, reproduction, induction.
2. Solution, resolution, revolution, dissolution, evolution, allusion.
3. Assignment, confinement, refinement, adjournment, consignment, imprisonment.
4. Precious, gracious, malicious, fallacious, delicious, atrocious.
5. Extensive, expensive, impressive, defensive, comprehensive, offensive, impulsive.

Reading and Writing Practice

512. Transcription Word Study

ream A quantity of paper, usually 480 sheets, sometimes 500 sheets.

gratifying Giving pleasure or satisfaction.

participants Those who take part or share.

513.

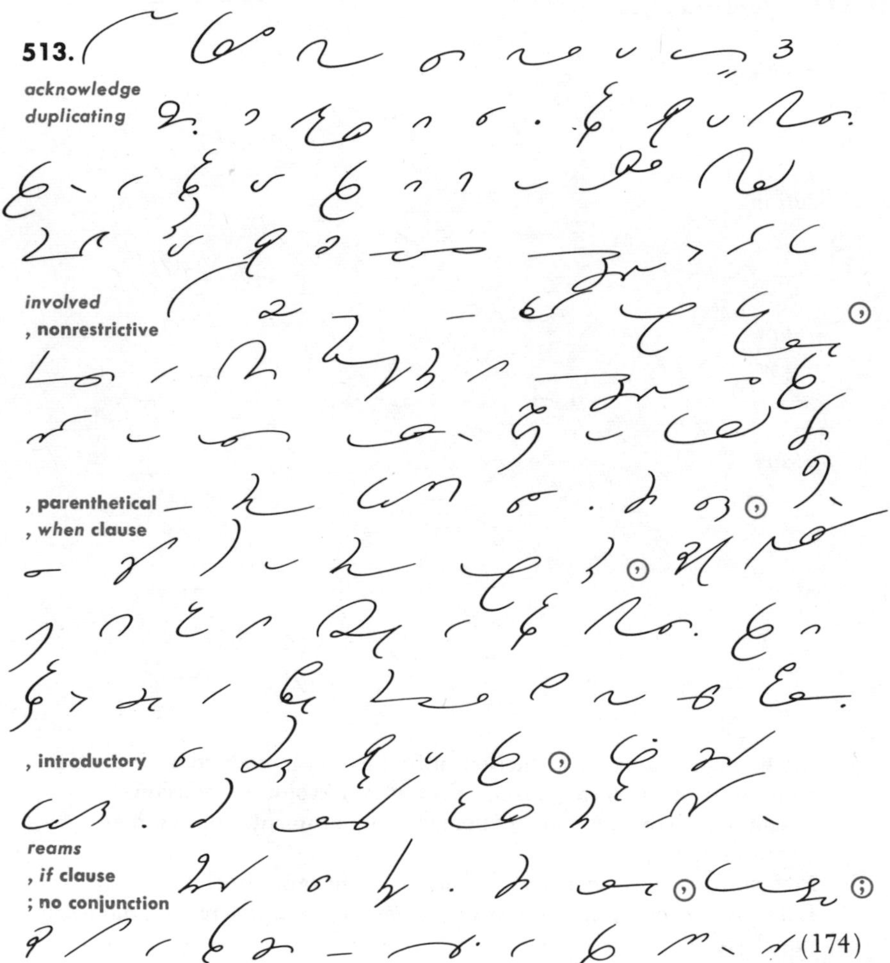

514.

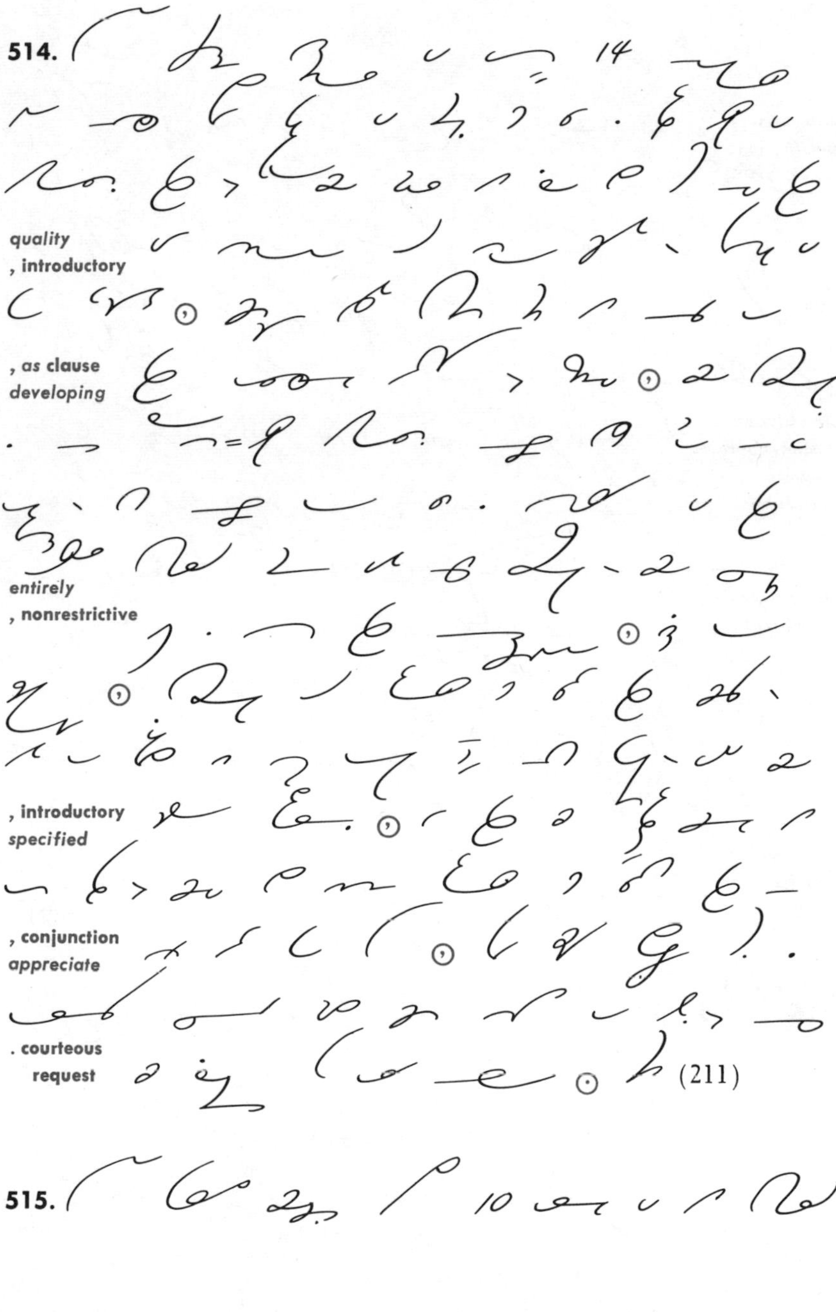

quality
, introductory
, as clause
developing
entirely
, nonrestrictive
, introductory
specified
, conjunction
appreciate
. courteous
request

(211)

515.

, introductory
specifications

, introducing short quote
capacity
. inside quote

, apposition
neighborhood

, introductory
whether

(189)

516.

co-operative
, introductory

1956

, parenthetical

, introductory

: enumeration

, series

(140)

Transcription Quiz. For you to supply: 3 commas–2 commas introductory, 1 comma *if* clause; 1 semicolon no conjunction, 1 semicolon because of comma; 2 missing words.

517.

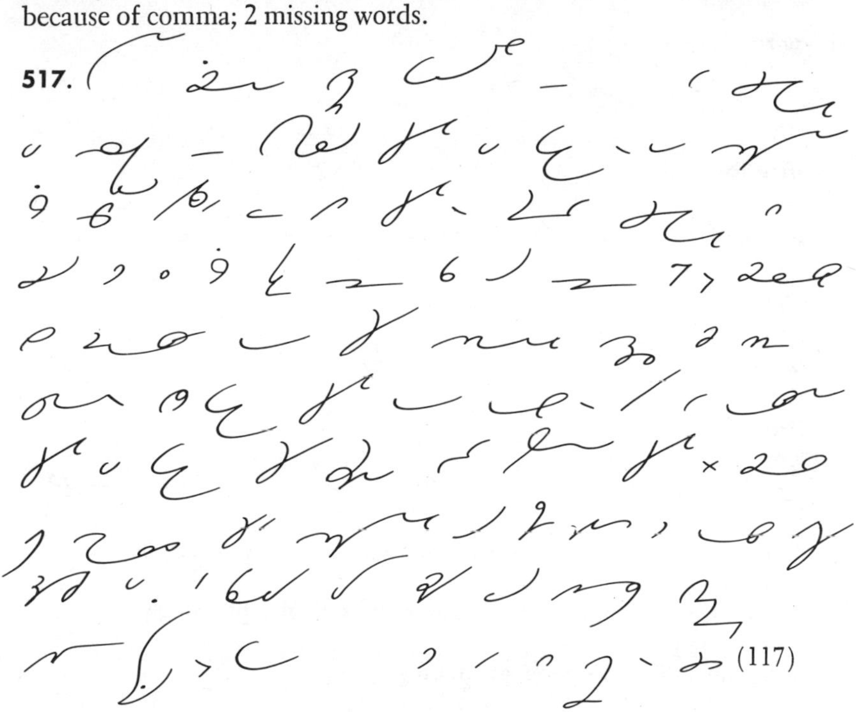

(117)

LESSON 74

518. Word Beginnings and Endings

-selves, -self

1 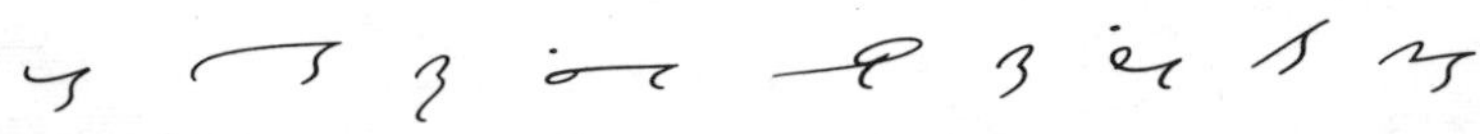

-ingly

2 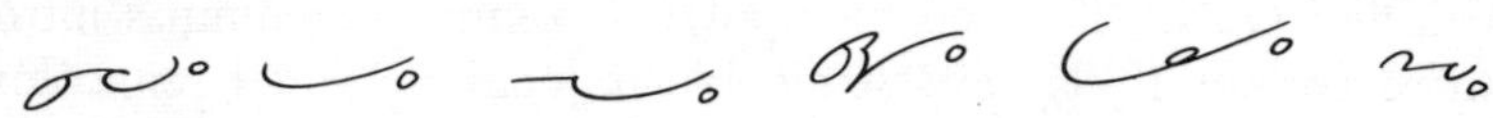

-gram

3 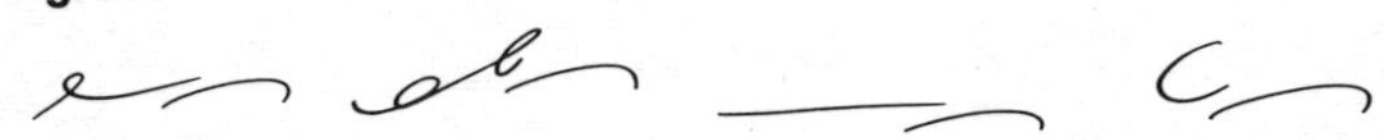

-ification

4 

-lty

5 

Circum-

6 

1. Ourselves, themselves, yourselves; himself, myself, yourself, herself, itself, oneself.
2. Accordingly, willingly, unwillingly, outstandingly, pleadingly, unknowingly.
3. Telegram, radiogram, monogram, program.

4. Gratification, notification, specifications, classification, simplification, modification.
5. Specialty, casualty, penalty, faculty, novelty, cruelty.
6. Circumstance, circumstances, circumstancial, circumvent, circumference, circumnavigate, circumscribe.

519. Geographical Expressions

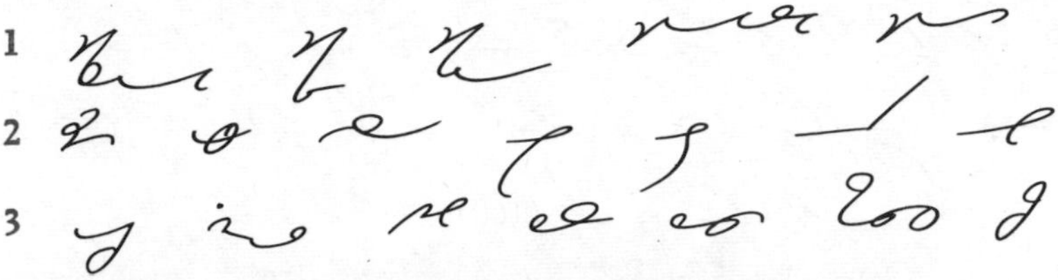

1. St. Charles, St. John, St. Paul, St. Lawrence, St. Louis.
2. Wisconsin, Rhode Island, California, Nebraska, Nevada, Maryland, Massachusetts.
3. Russia, Hungary, Tunis, Iran, Iraq, Africa, Asia.

Reading and Writing Practice

520. Transcription Word Study

prevailing Current.

hundredweight 100 pounds.

521.

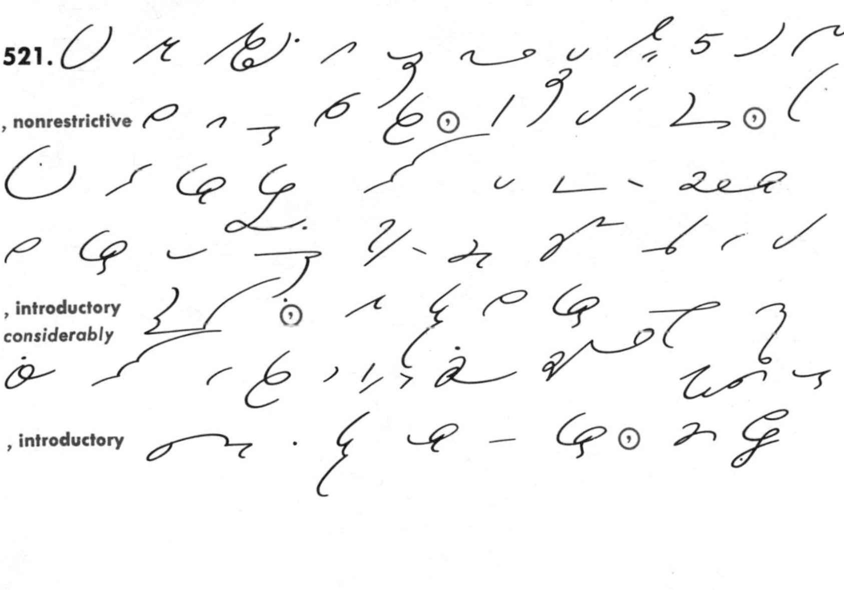

circumstances
, introductory
, parenthetical
: enumeration

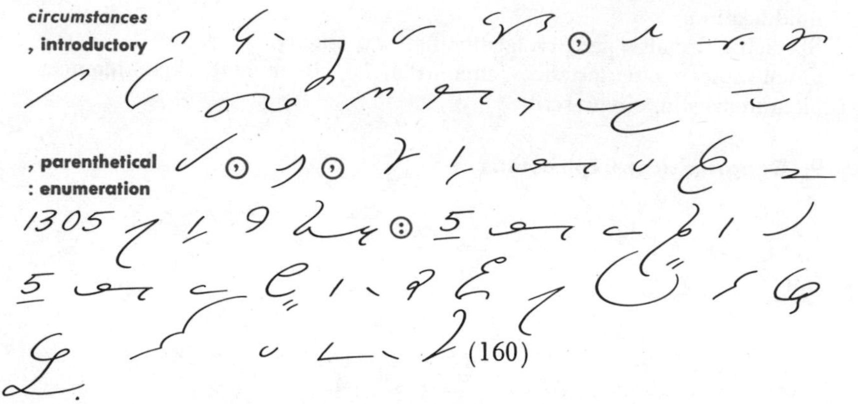

(160)

522.
accept
; illustrative ,
, introducing short quote
; no conjunction
. inside quote
accordingly
, introductory

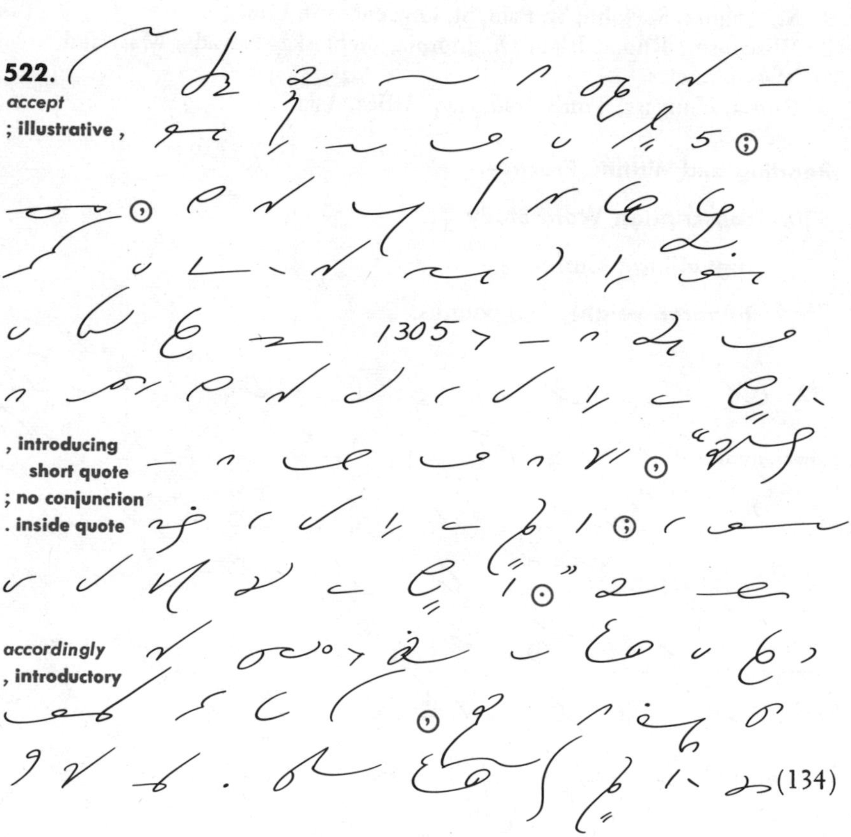

(134)

523. **Transcribe:**
50 per cent
blueprint
, conjunction
well *satisfied*
no noun,
no hyphen
, *if* clause
receive
; illustrative ,

(120)

524. **Transcribe:**
10,000
, conjunction
catalogue
separately
, apposition

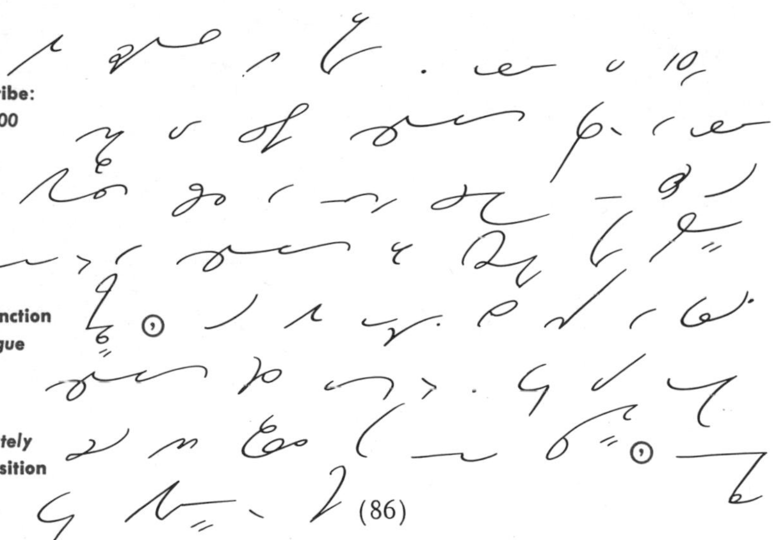

(86)

525.

Transcribe:
February 8
, as clause
, series
chemical
, as clause
, if clause
assist

(114)

526.

especially developed
no hyphen
after *ly*
, parenthetical
, introductory
wrapped

well-established hyphenated before noun

approval

, if clause

specialty

developing

, conjunction

(147)

Transcription Quiz. For you to supply: 7 commas—1 comma apposition, 1 comma *and* omitted, 1 comma introductory, 4 commas parenthetical; 1 semicolon because of comma; 2 missing words.

527.

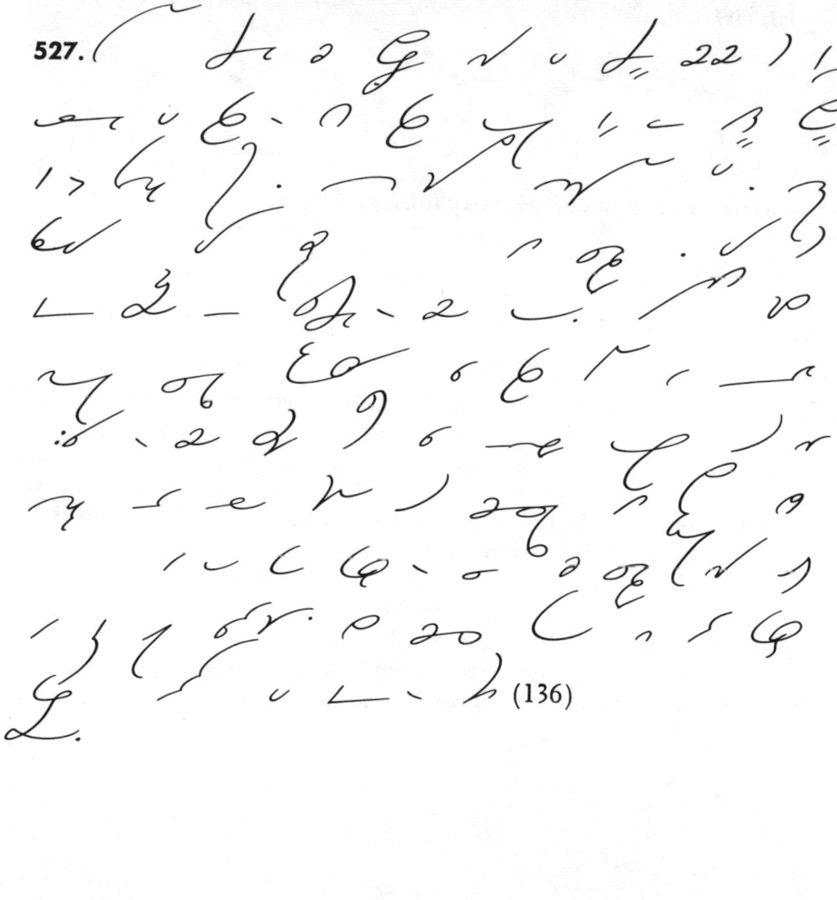

(136)

LESSON 75

528. Word-Building—Omission of T and D

-ct

1 

-est, -ist

2 

Omission of T in Seven Monosyllables

3 

Omission of D

4 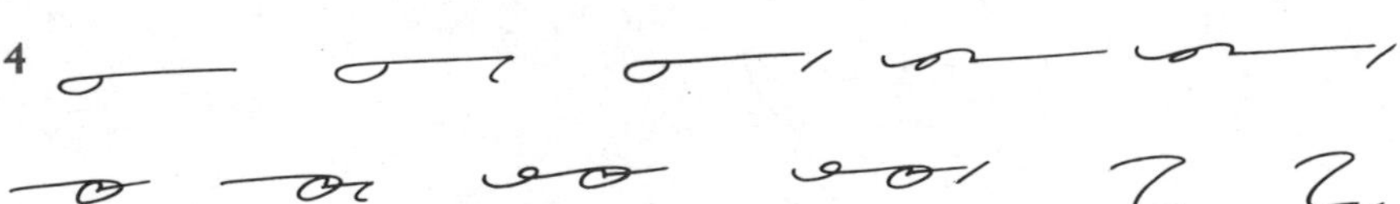

1. Affect, deduct, product, expect, elect, protect, reject, active, protected, elective, exactly, neglects, prospects.
2. Darkest, cleanest, modest, honest, deepest, coldest, sharpest, typist, vocalist, industrialist, analyst, journalist.
3. Test, rest, best, first, past, last, tested, lasting.
4. Amend, amends, amended, recommend, recommended, mind, minds, remind, reminded, compound, compounded.

Reading and Writing Practice

529. Transcription Word Study

adapted Made suitable. (Do not confuse with *adopted*, which means "taken as one's own.")

conventional Sanctioned by usage.

solicitous Full of concern.

530. The Business Letter and Collections

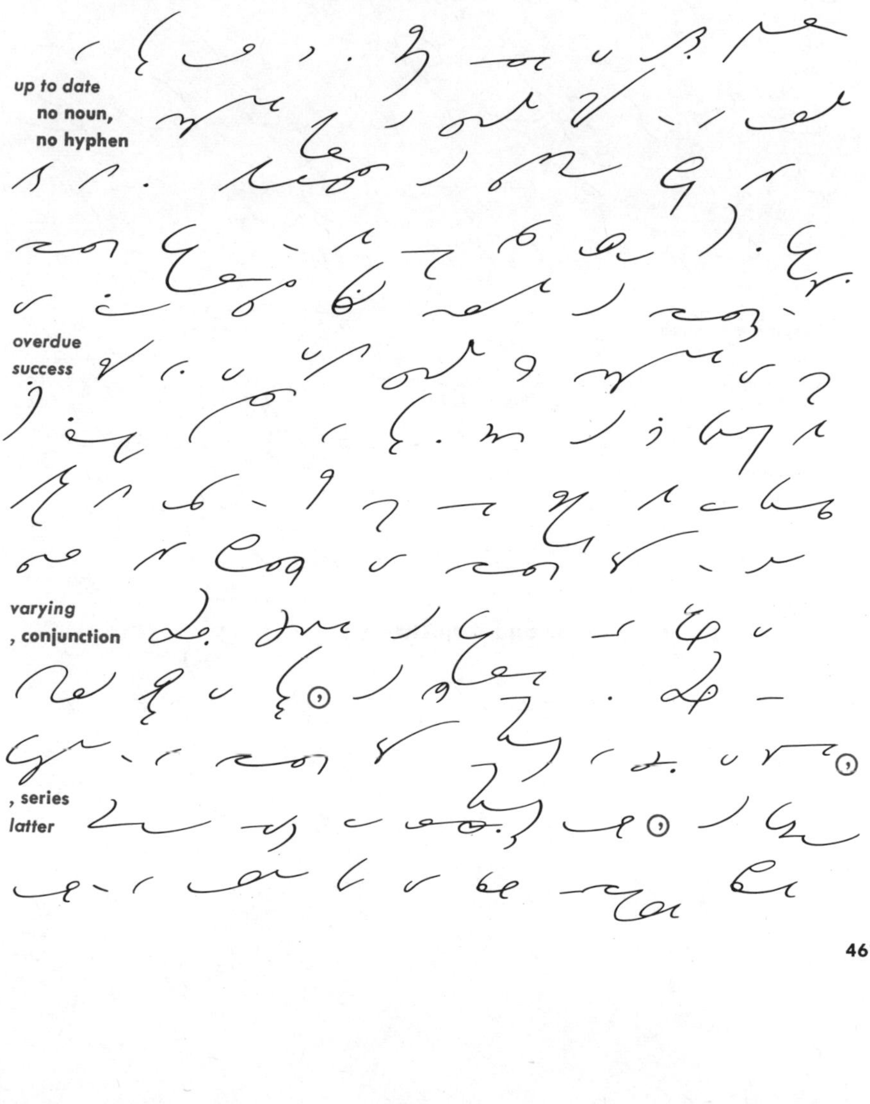

, series

, parenthetical
response

, when clause
conventional

; because of comma
capture
, when clause

, parenthetical
creditor
embarrass

(333)

531. The Business Letter and Adjustments

discourteous
, series

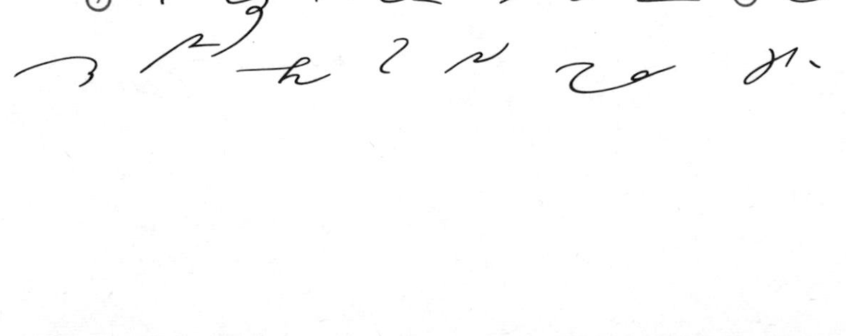

grievances

, parenthetical

adjustment

; because of comma

, parenthetical

, parenthetical

, when clause

perspective

, if clause

angered

customer's

(242)

532. The Sales Letter

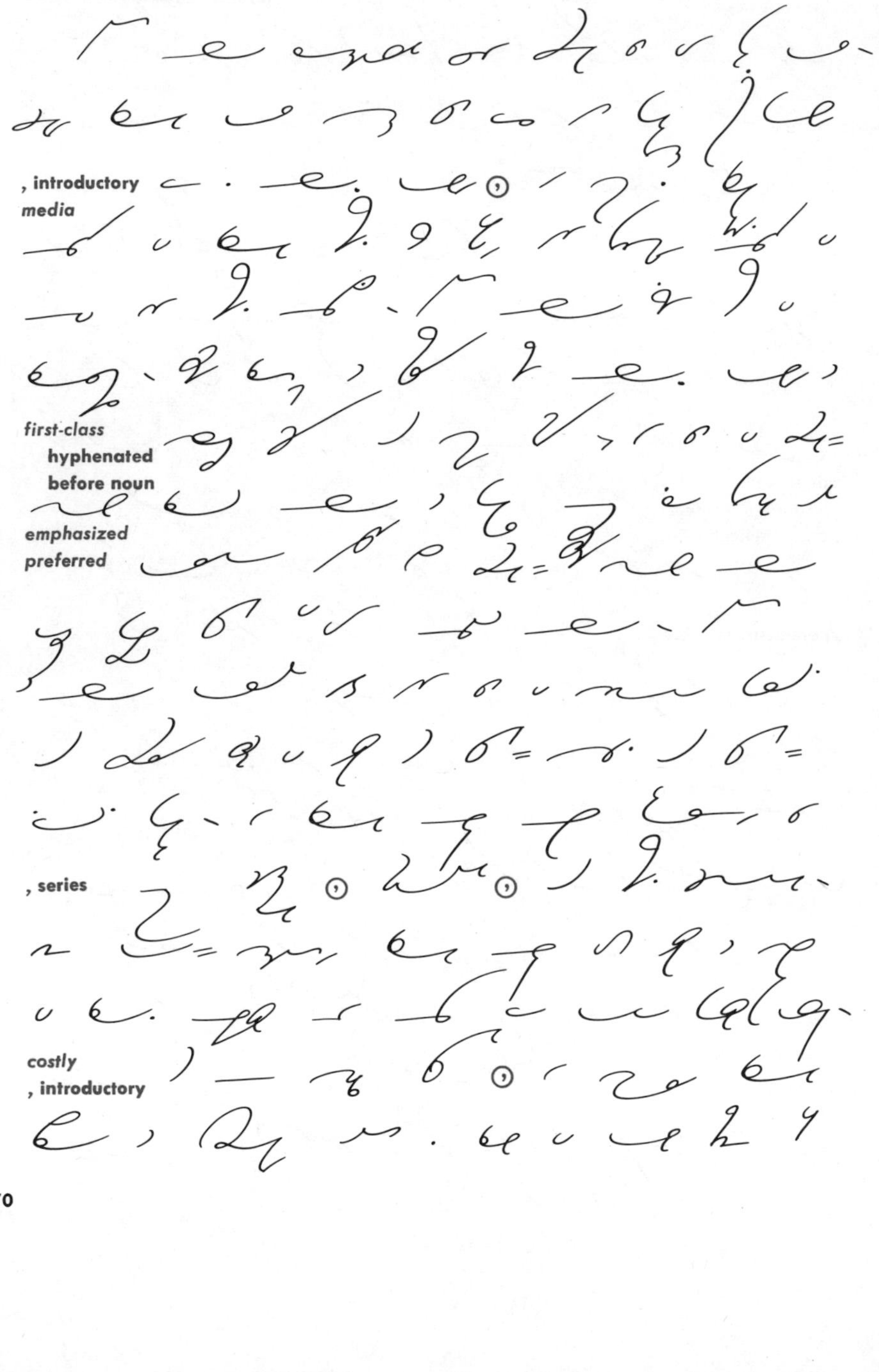

, introductory
media

first-class
hyphenated
before noun

emphasized
preferred

, series

costly
, introductory

conviction
. inside quote

An important consideration

degree
showmanship

Certainly
; no conjunction

, introductory
dramatic

arouse
novel

, parenthetical
man's

, *if* clause
, parenthetical
objective

(399)

16

PERSONNEL

LESSON 76

533. Brief Forms and Derivatives

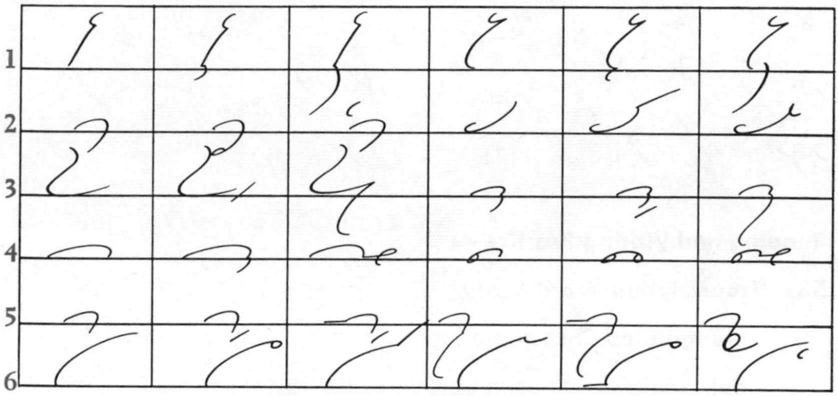

1. Subject, subjects, subjective; object, objects, objective.
2. Confident-confidence, confidently, self-confident-self-confidence; want, wanted, wants.
3. Value, valued, valuable; consider-consideration, considered, considerable.
4. Go-good, goes-goods, goodness; week-weak, weekly-weakly, weakness.
5. Question, questioned, unquestioned, questionable, unquestionable, questionnaire.
6. Time, timely, timed, timer, untimely, timings.

534. Brief Form and Phrase Letter

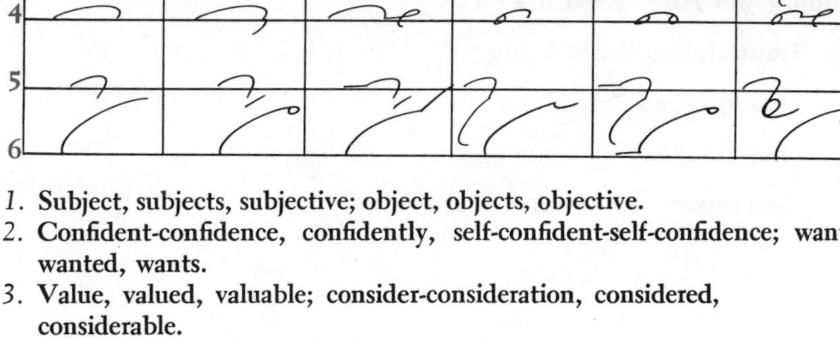

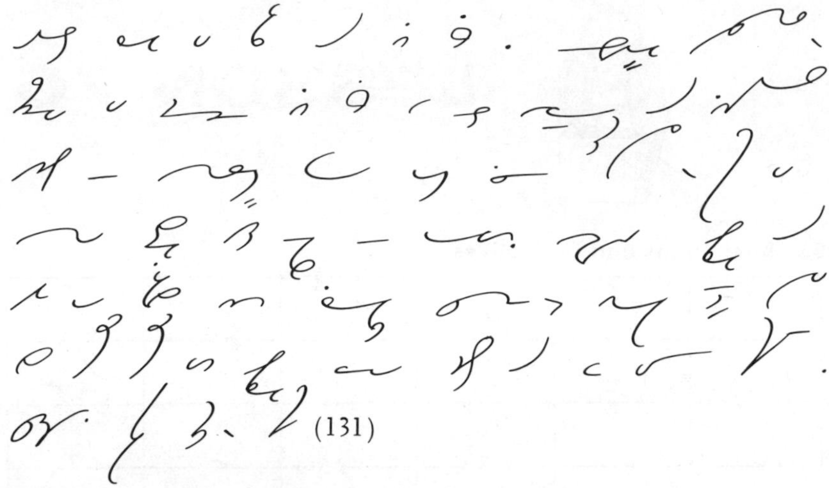

(131)

Reading and Writing Practice

535. Transcription Word Study

inaugurated Set in motion.

potentialities Possibilities.

increment An increase, a raise.

536.

, introductory
inaugurated

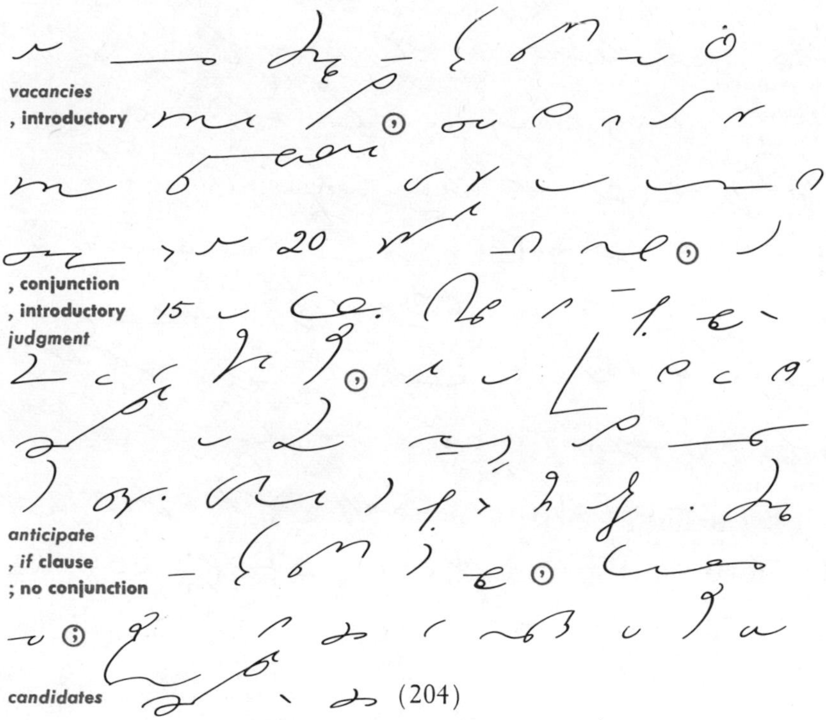
vacancies
, introductory
, conjunction
, introductory
judgment
anticipate
, if clause
; no conjunction
candidates
(204)

537.

, conjunction
, introductory

, parenthetical
: enumeration
beginning

credentials
. courteous
request

(226)

538.

, apposition
encouraging

curriculum
, and omitted

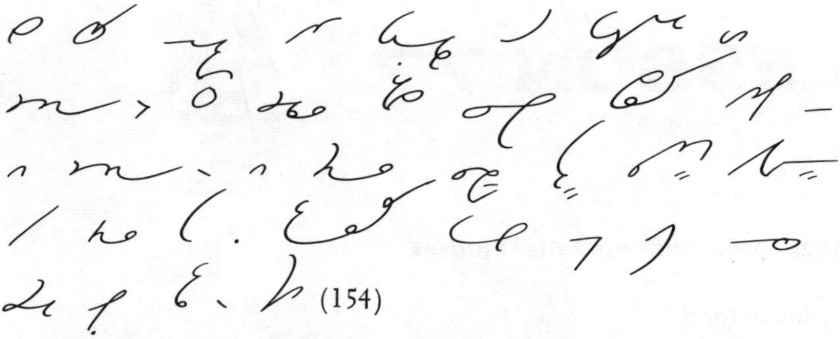

(154)

Transcription Quiz. For you to supply: 5 commas—1 comma apposition, 2 commas introductory, 1 comma nonrestrictive, 1 comma parenthetical; 1 semicolon because of comma; 2 missing words.

539.

(128)

LESSON 77

540. Useful Business-Letter Phrases

Understand

1 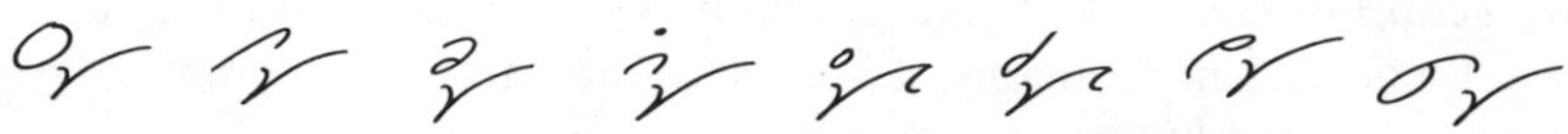

Understood

2 

Intersection

3 

Geographical Phrases

4 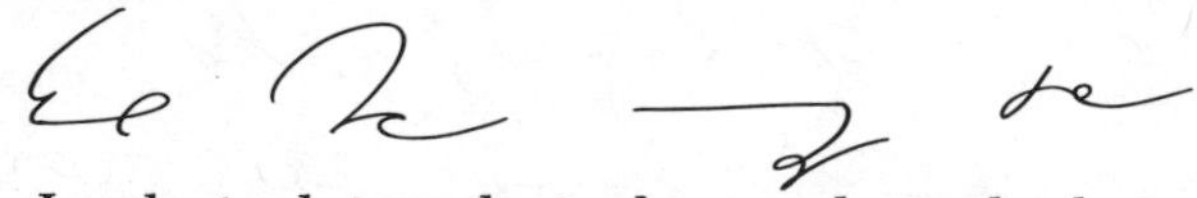

1. I understand, to understand, we understand, who understand, he understands, she understands, they understand, I can understand.
2. I understood, he understood, we understood, who understood, it is understood.
3. Associated Press, a.m., p.m., Chamber of Commerce, vice versa.
4. Boston, Massachusetts; Denver, Colorado; Memphis, Tennessee; Chicago, Illinois.

541. Frequent Names

1
2

1. Thomas, Thompson, Thomson, Turner, Walker, Walsh.
2. Samuel, Stephen, Vincent, Walter, William.

Reading and Writing Practice

542. Transcription Word Study

diversified Varied.

practical Useful.

543.

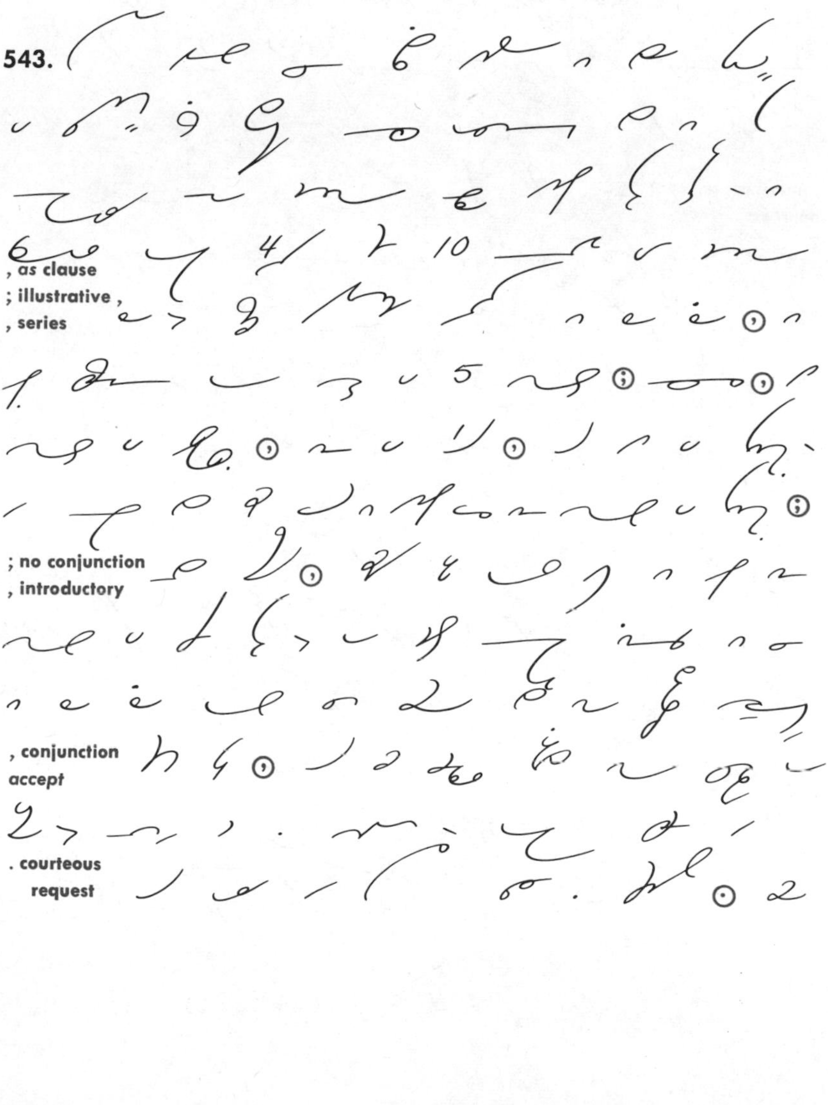

, as clause
; illustrative ,
, series
; no conjunction
, introductory
, conjunction
accept
. courteous
request

 (166)

544.

adequate

, parenthetical

, introductory

nearness

(121)

545.

, and omitted
diversified

phase
, if clause

(155)

546.

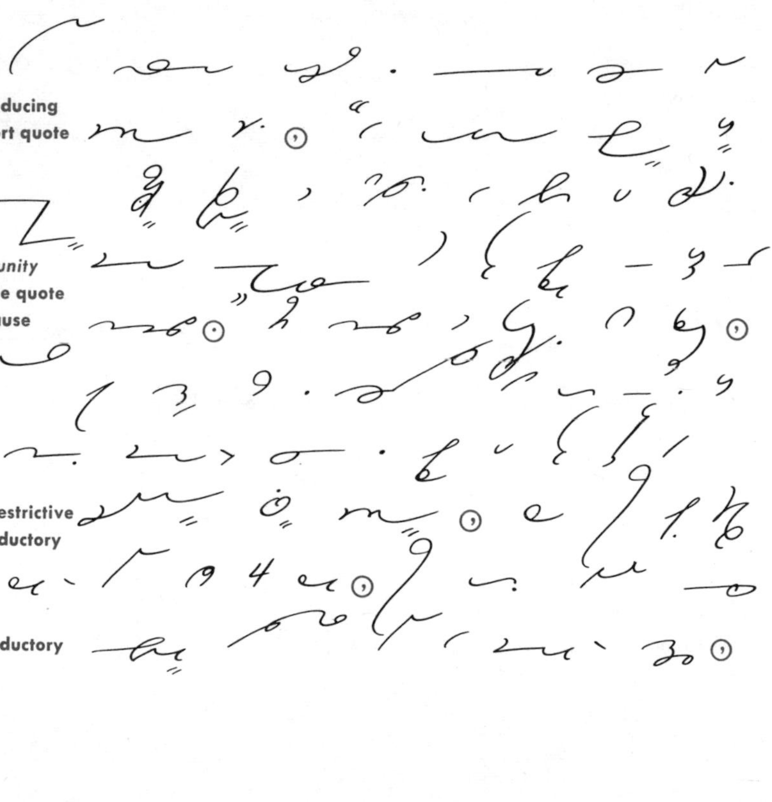

, introducing short quote
local

community
. inside quote
, if clause

, nonrestrictive
, introductory

, introductory

undergraduate
, when clause
, introductory
first-hand
hyphenated
before noun
up to date
no noun,
no hyphen
, apposition
secretarial
, introductory

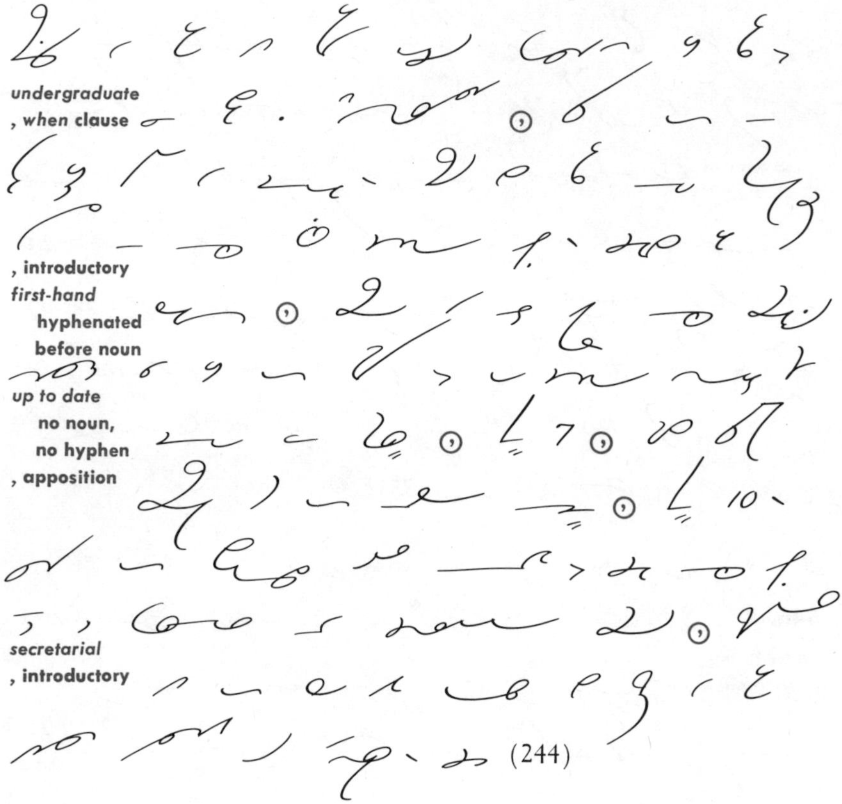

(244)

547.

stenographic
, apposition

: enumeration

application

personal

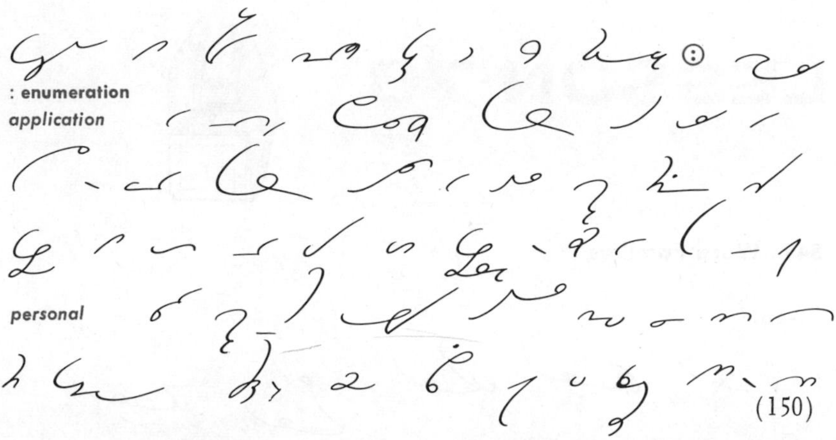

(150)

Transcription Quiz. For you to supply: 8 commas—5 commas apposition, 2 commas parenthetical, 1 comma introductory; 2 missing words.

548.

(142)

LESSON 78

549. Word Families

-ent

1 

-firm

2 

-dom

3 

-ier

4 

1. Excellent, silent, violent, prevalent, repellent.
2. Firm, confirm, infirm, affirm, reaffirm.
3. Random, kingdom, freedom, seldom, wisdom.
4. Earlier, busier, nastier, happier, heavier, prettier, fancier.

Reading and Writing Practice

550. Transcription Word Study

aggressive Enterprising, energetic.

integrity Honesty.

trainee A person who is being trained.

551.

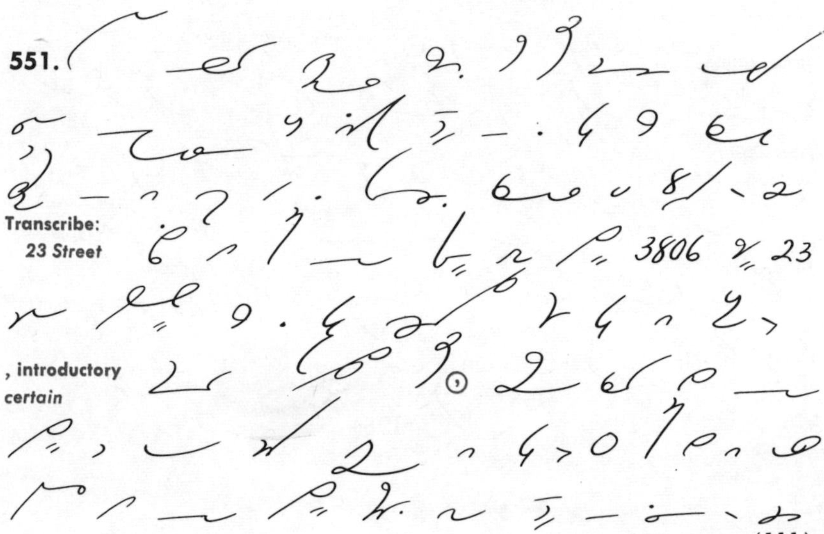

Transcribe: 23 Street

, introductory
certain

(111)

552.

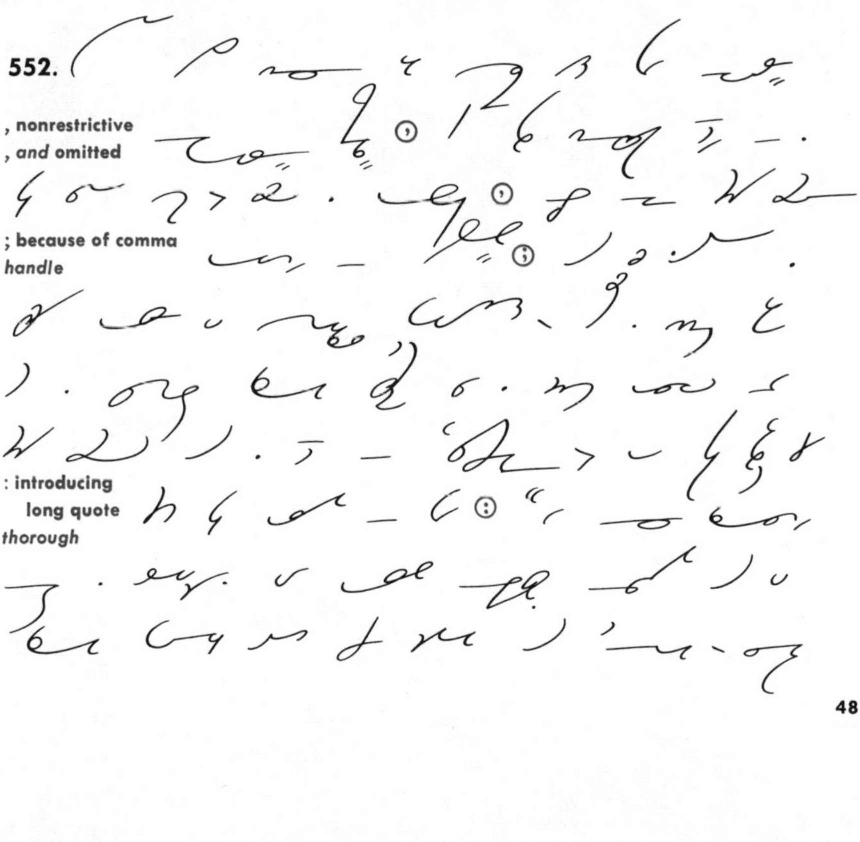

, nonrestrictive
, *and* omitted

; because of comma
handle

: introducing long quote
thorough

, series
. inside quote
responsibility
, if clause
; illustrative ,
, series

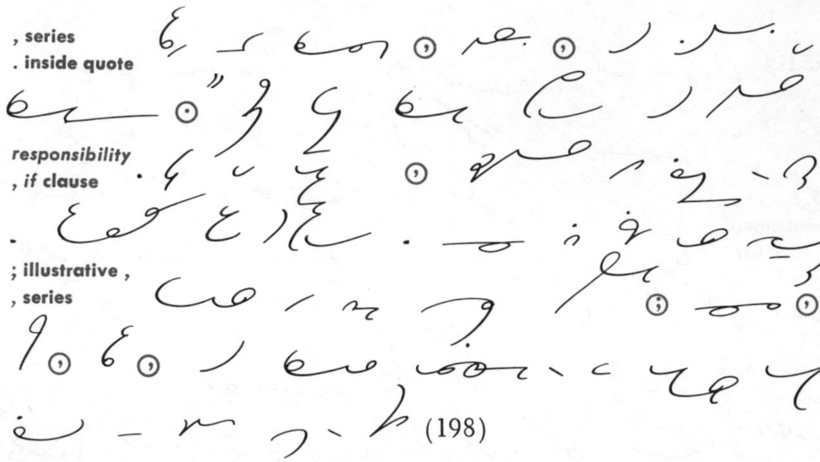

(198)

553.

vacancy
appeals
, conjunction
experience
, series
, if clause

(110)

554.

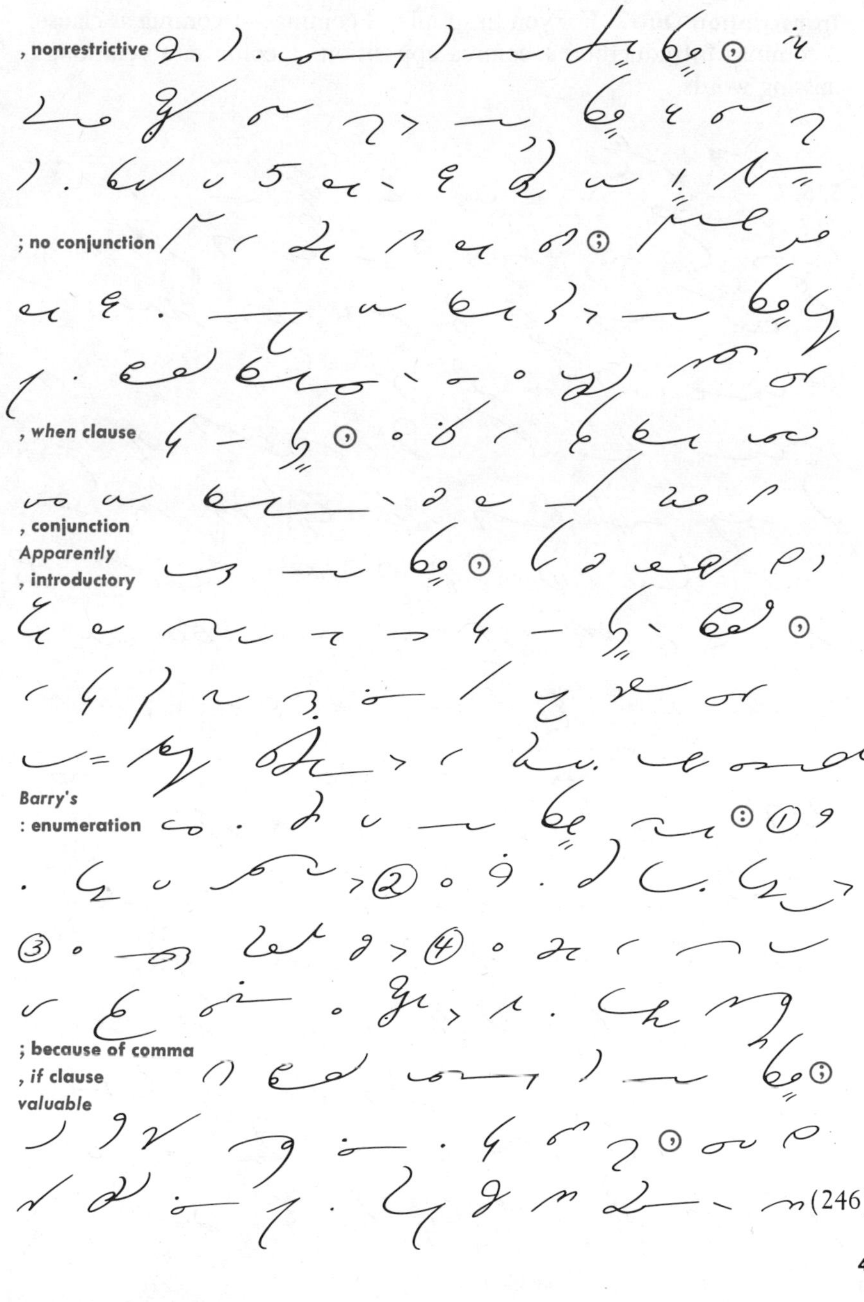
, nonrestrictive
; no conjunction
, when clause
, conjunction
Apparently
, introductory
Barry's
: enumeration
; because of comma
, if clause
valuable
(246)

Transcription Quiz. For you to supply: 4 commas—1 comma as clause, 2 commas introductory, 1 comma apposition; 1 colon enumeration; 2 missing words.

555.

(214)

LESSON 79

556. Word Beginnings and Endings

Ship-

1 

Mis-

2 

-ulator

3 

-ward

4 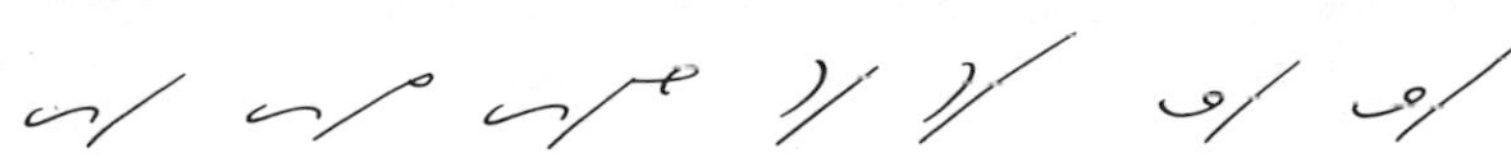

Enter-

5 

-rity

6 

1. Shipmate, shipwreck, shipyard, shipshape, shipowner, shipbuilder.
2. Misinterpret, misinterpreted, misconception, mistranslate, misfortune.
3. Regulator, speculator, insulator, tabulator, calculator, circulator.
4. Awkward, awkwardly, awkwardness, forward, forwarded, reward, rewarded.

5. Enter, entered, entering, entertain, entertainment, enterprise, enterprisingly.
6. Alacrity, popularity, similarity, mediocrity, severity.

557. Geographical Expressions

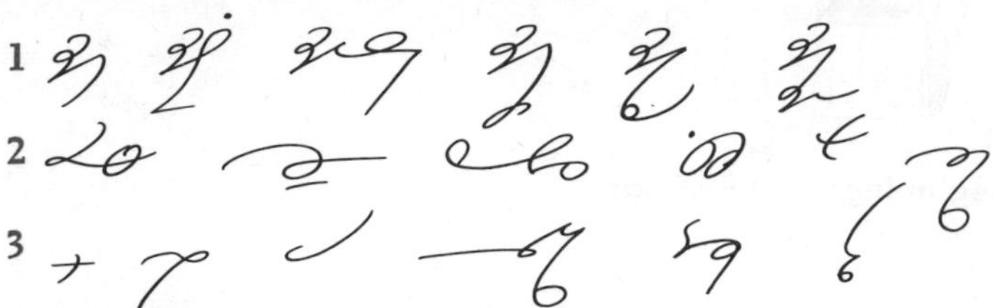

1. Westfield, West Haven, West Orange, Westview, West Bend, Westchester.
2. Philippine Islands, Guam, Alaska, Hawaii, Puerto Rico, Cuba.
3. Nova Scotia, Quebec, Ontario, Manitoba, Saskatchewan, British Columbia.

Reading and Writing Practice

558. Transcription Word Study

ingratiating Able to win one's way into the favor of another.

clients Those who use the services of a professional man, as a lawyer.

559.

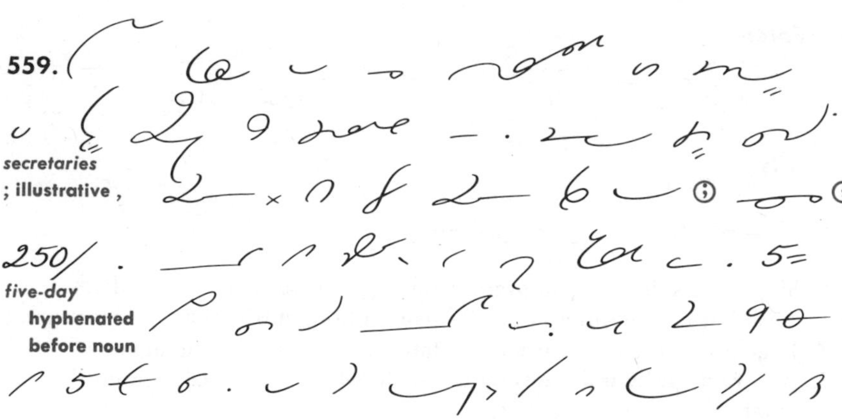

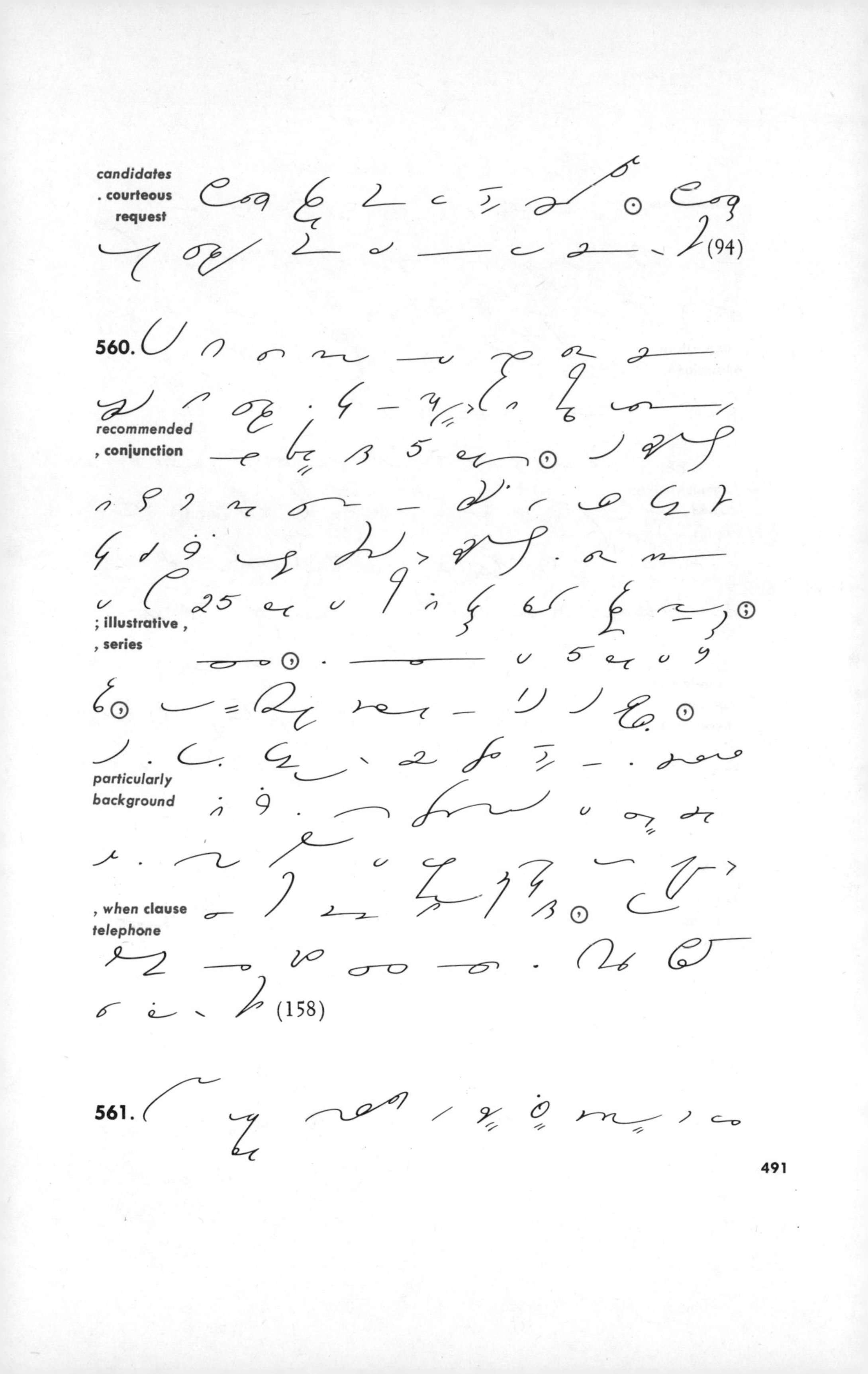

candidates
. courteous
request

(94)

560.

recommended
, conjunction

; illustrative ,
, series

particularly
background

, when clause
telephone

(158)

561.

, introductory

, apposition
exceptional

, nonrestrictive
studied
, series

, introductory
ingratiating
; because of comma

whether
. courteous
request

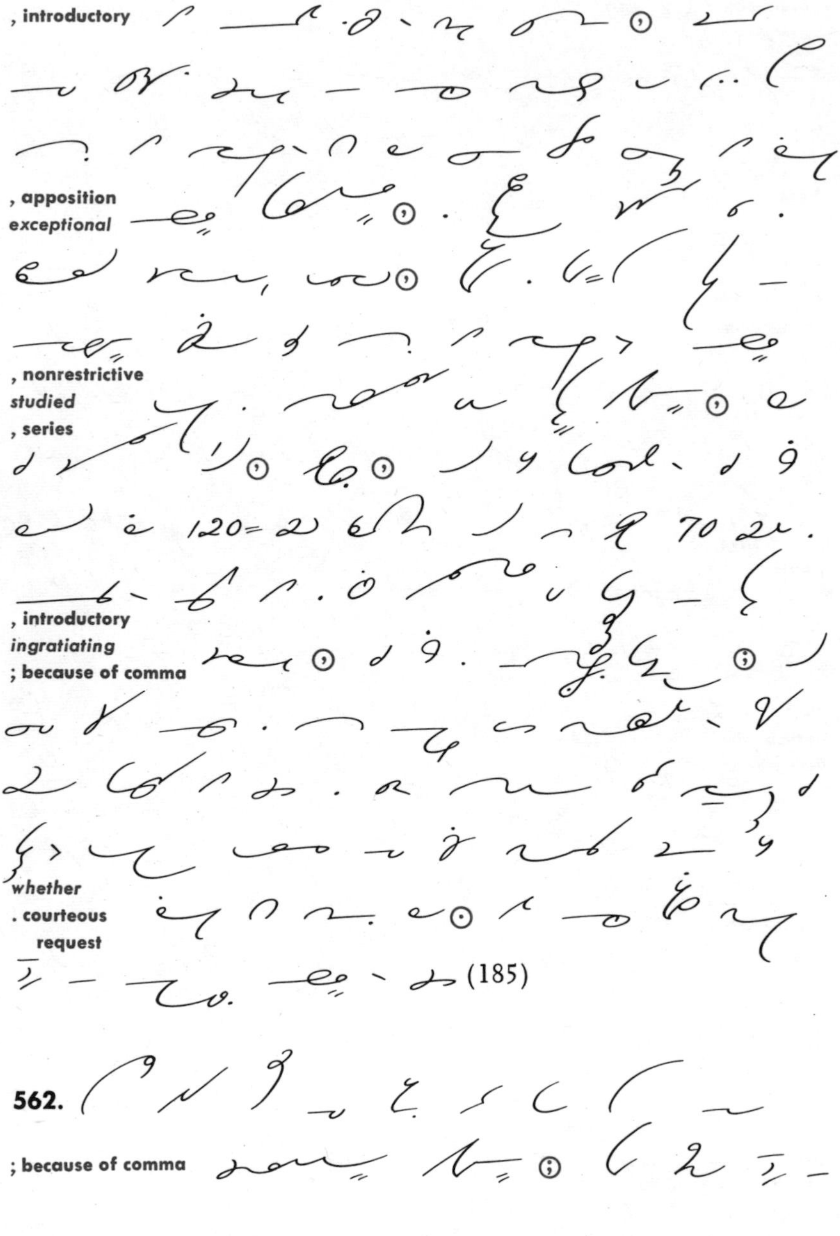

(185)

562.

; because of comma

, *if* clause

; no conjunction

, introductory

, *if* clause

: enumeration

(199)

563.

, introducing short quote

, *if* clause

extremely

. inside quote

, *as* clause

. courteous request

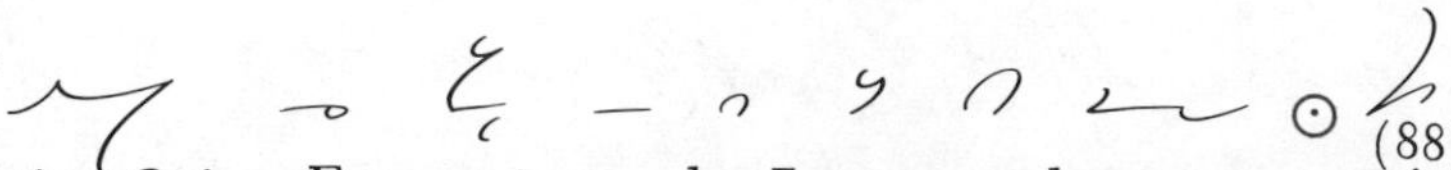

(88)

Transcription Quiz. For you to supply: 7 commas—1 comma apposition, 1 comma conjunction, 1 comma introductory, 3 commas parenthetical, 1 comma *when* clause; 1 semicolon no conjunction; 2 missing words.

564.

(212)

LESSON 80

565. Word-Building Practice—Omission of Vowels

-tation, Etc.

1 

Omission of Minor Vowel

2 

-est Following a Vowel

3 

1. Transportation, quotation, foundation, examination, discrimination, destination, repetition, reputation, transmission, additional, permission, combination, admission.
2. New, newer, newly, numerous, reduce, produce, induce, issue, suit, suits, suited, suitable, volume, manufacture.
3. Handiest, neediest, greediest, narrowest, slowest, costliest.

566. Accuracy Practice—Similar Outlines

1 

2 

1. You, this, way, say, we, see, you will, it will, you are, to our.
2. They, to me, that, with, when, yet, I think, I can, he can.

Reading and Writing Practice

567. Transcription Word Study

endurance Power to continue under hardship.

inevitably Bound to happen; unavoidable.

appraise To judge, to estimate the value of.

568. Selling Yourself

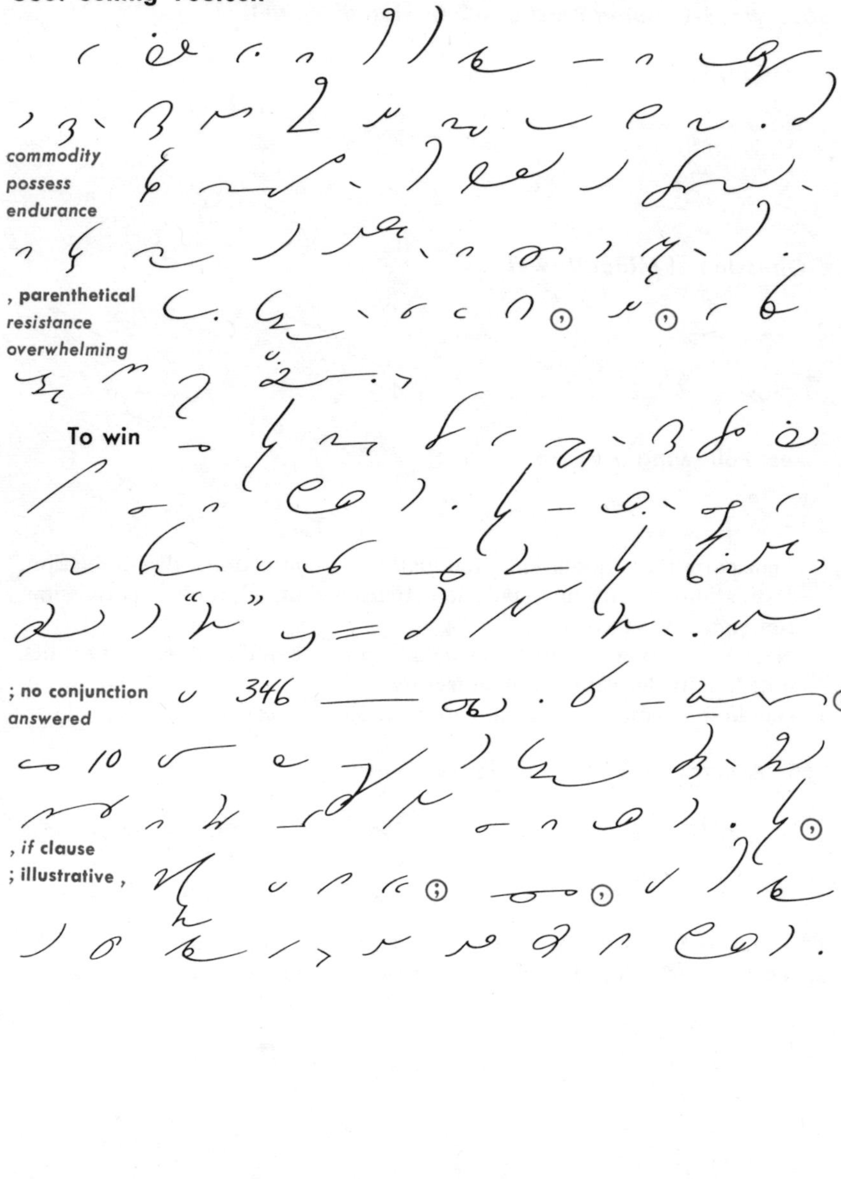

: enumeration
, series

, series

The formal application.

, when clause
, series
completeness

, if clause

: enumeration
, series

employer's
, parenthetical
survey

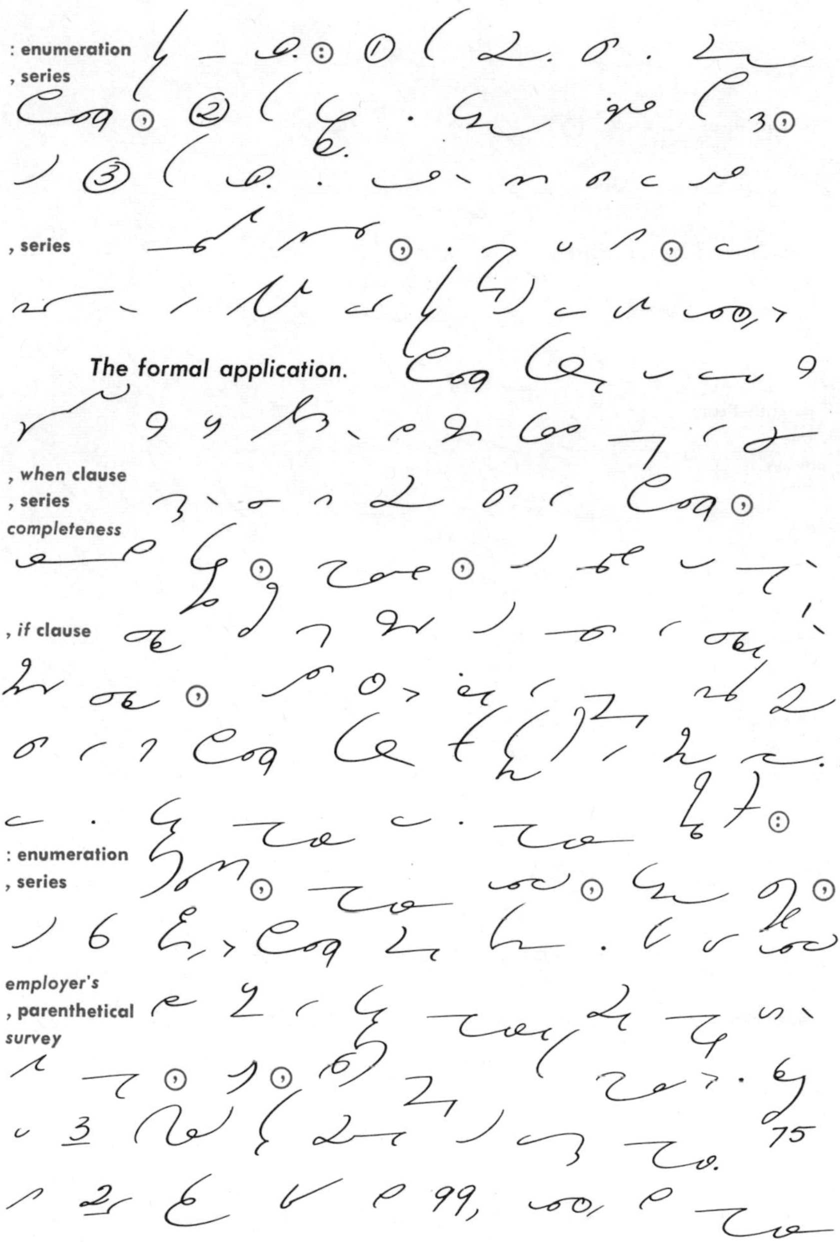

, parenthetical

The personal history.

, parenthetical
clinic
advises

: enumeration

summarize
, series
attainments

, when clause
screen

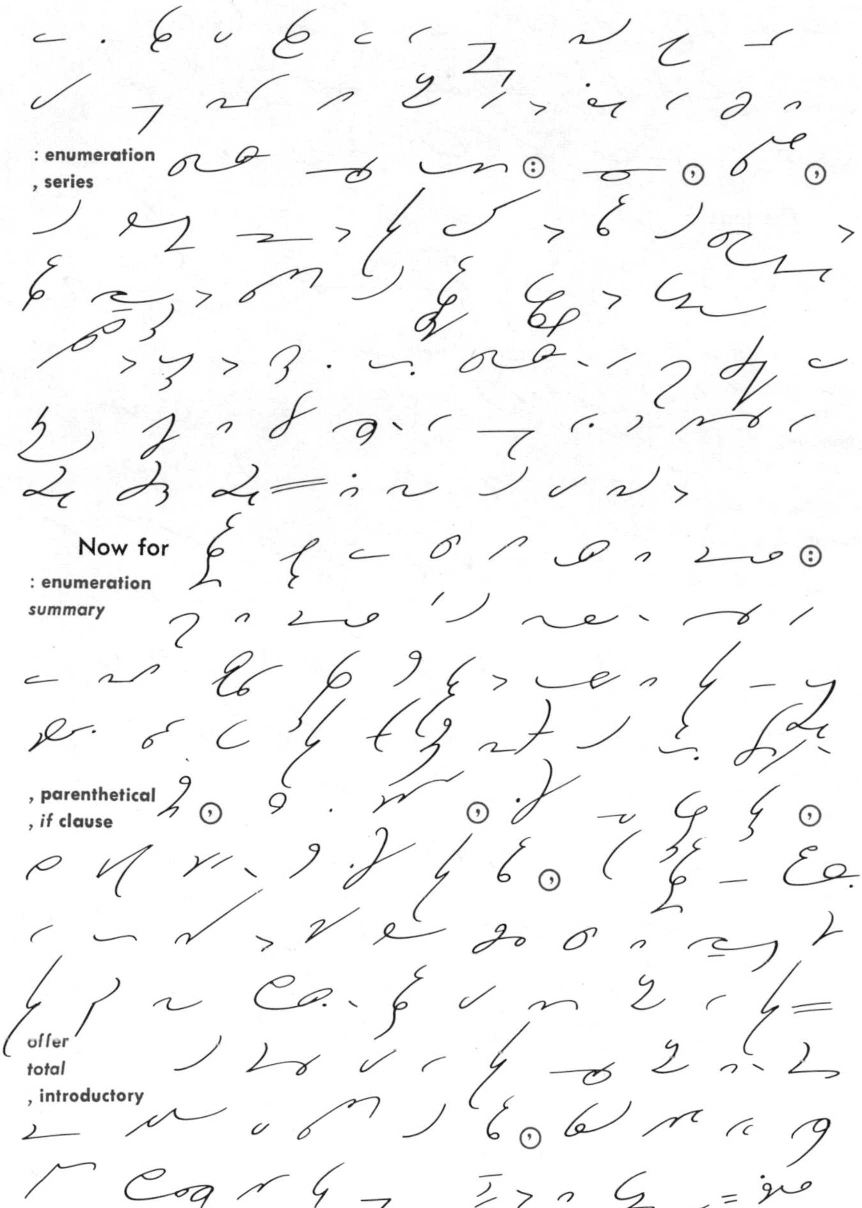

: enumeration
, series

Now for
: enumeration
summary

, parenthetical
, *if* clause

offer
total
, introductory

contact

, *if* clause

The letter.

, parenthetical

single

qualifies

busiest

, introductory

initiative

, introductory

(1,000)

APPENDIX

RECALL DRILLS

List of Joined Word Endings

1. -ment

2. -less

3. -tion

4. -tial

5. -ly

6. -ily, -ally

7. -pose, -position

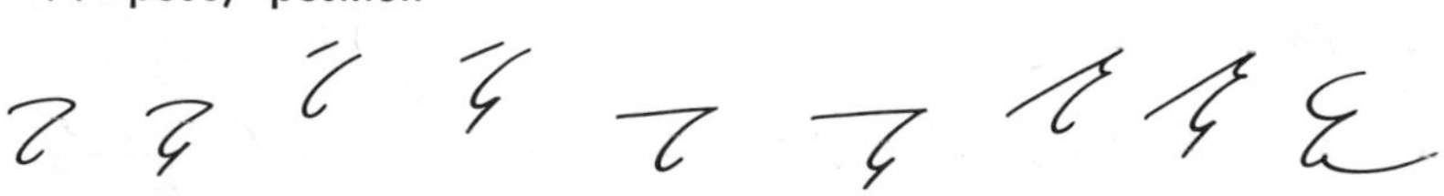

8. -ify

9. -ful

10. -sume, -sumption

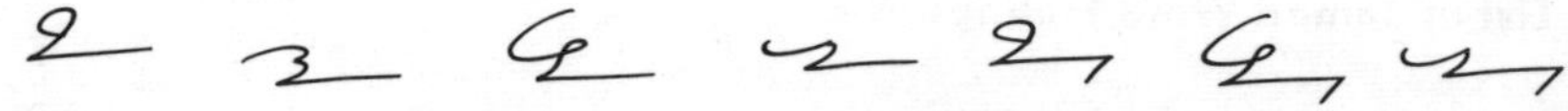

11. -ble

12. -ther

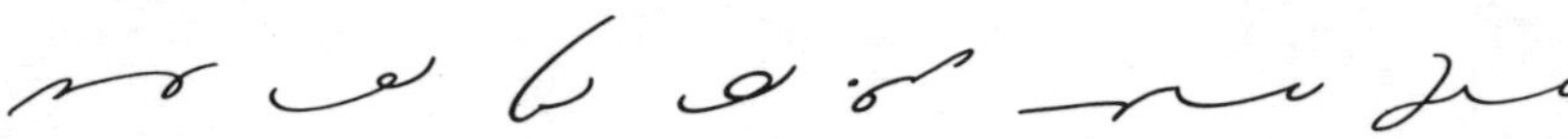

13. -ual, -tual

14. -ure,-ture

15. -self, -selves

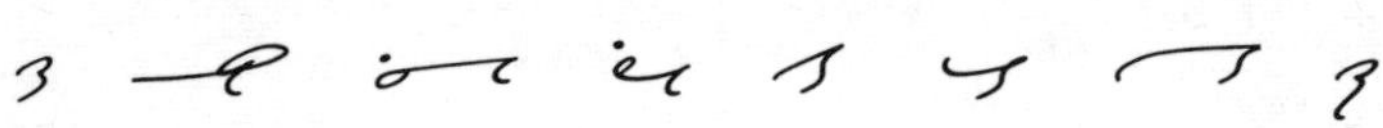

16. -ort

17. -tain

18. -cient, -ciency

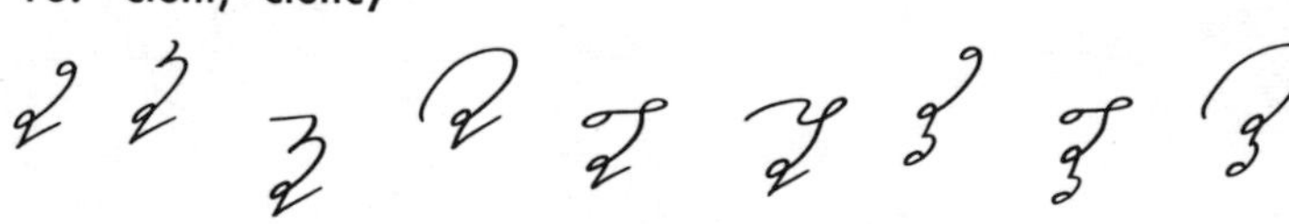

List of Disjoined Word Endings

19. -hood

20. -ward

21. -ship

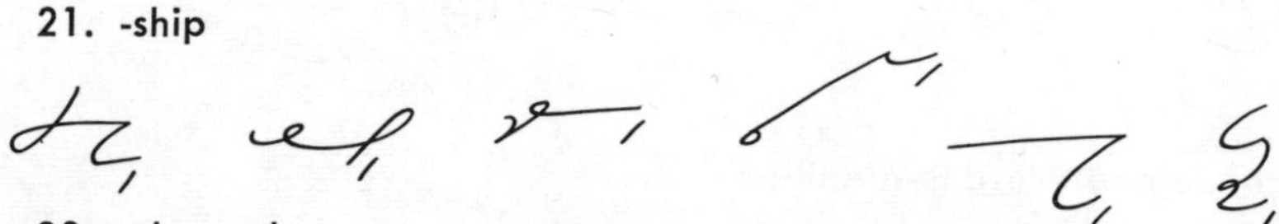

22. -cle, -cal

23. -ulate

24. -ingly

25. -ings

26. -gram

27. -ification

28. -lity

29. -lty

30. -rity

List of Joined Word Beginnings

31. Per-, Pur-

32. Pro-

33. Em-

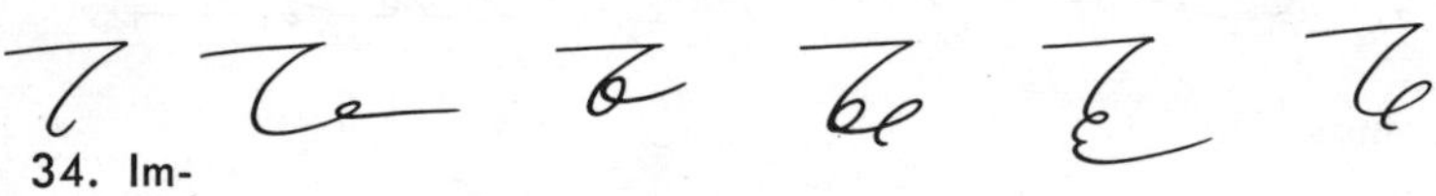

34. Im-

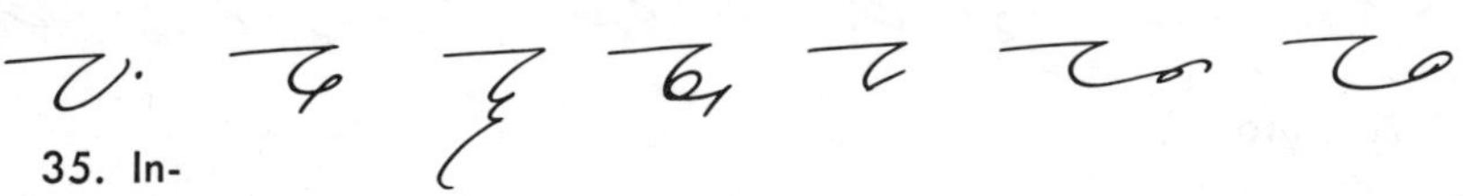

35. In-

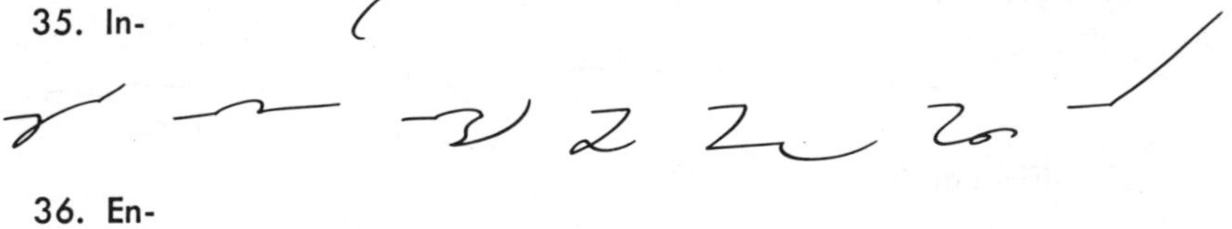

36. En-

37. Un-

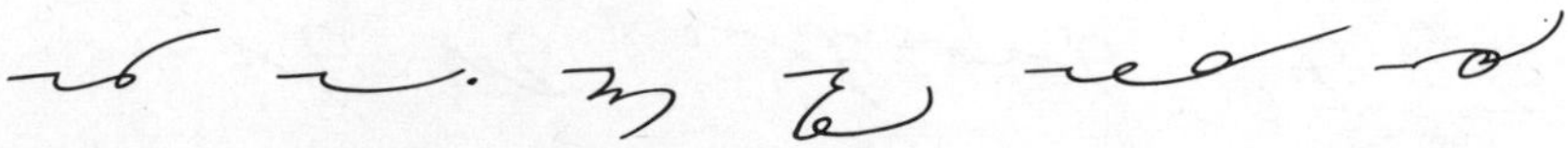

38. Re-

39. Be-

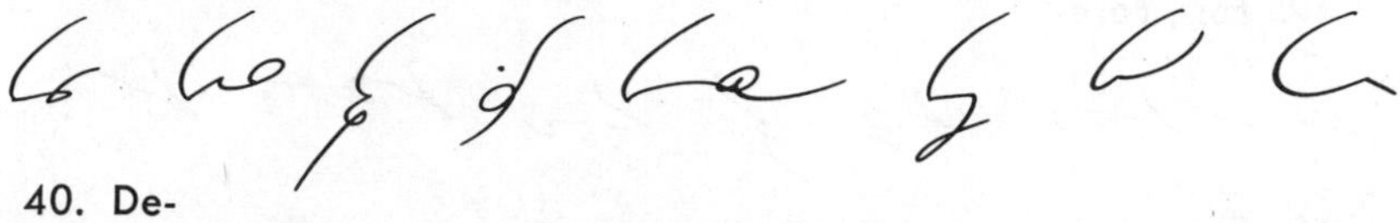

40. De-

41. Dis-

42. Mis-

43. Ex-

44. Com-

45. Con-

46. Sub-

47. After-

48. Al-

49. For-, Fore-

50. Fur-

51. Tern-, etc.

52. Ul

List of Disjoined Word Beginnings

53. Short-

54. Inter-, Intr-, Enter-

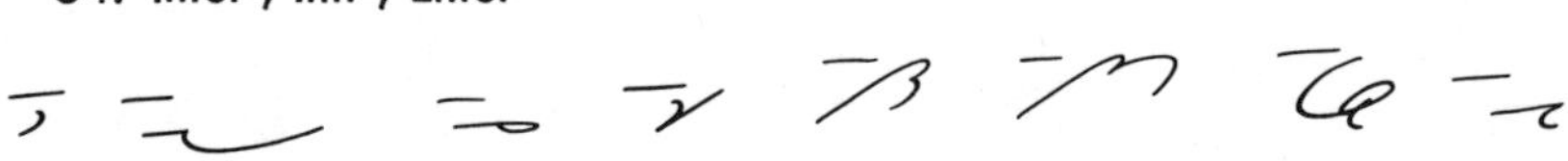

55. Electr-, Electric

56. Post-

57. Super-, Supr-

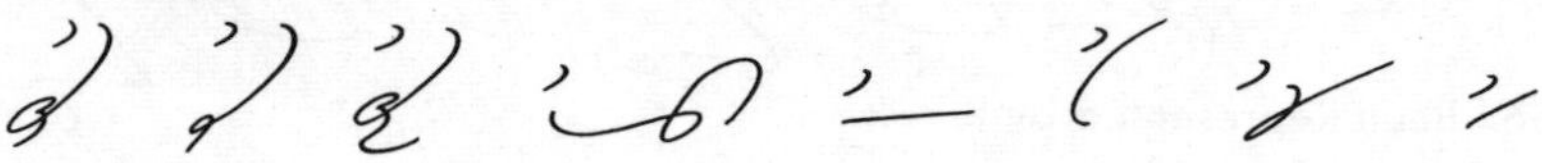

58. Circum-

59. Self-

60. Trans-

61. Incl-

62. Ship-

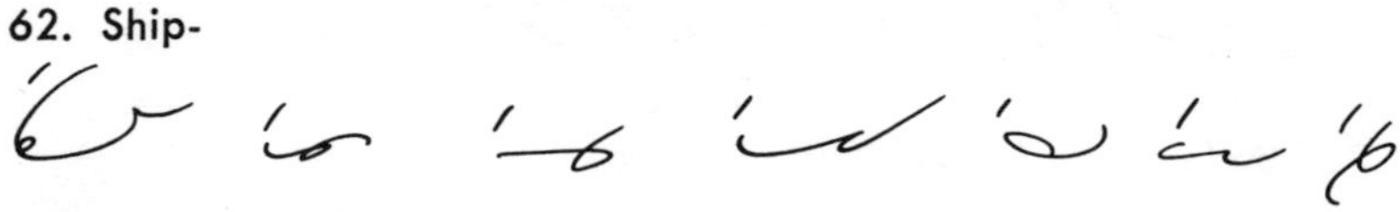

63. Under-

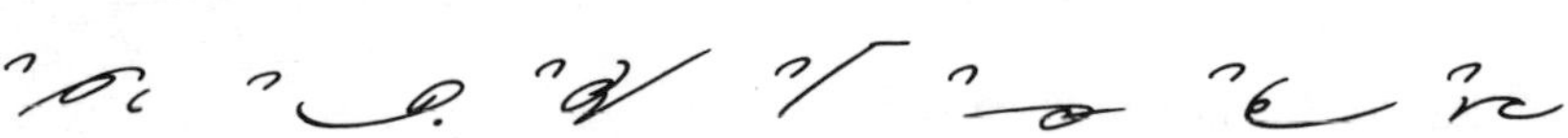

64. Over-

List of Special Phrases

65. T For To in Phrases

66. Been Represented by B

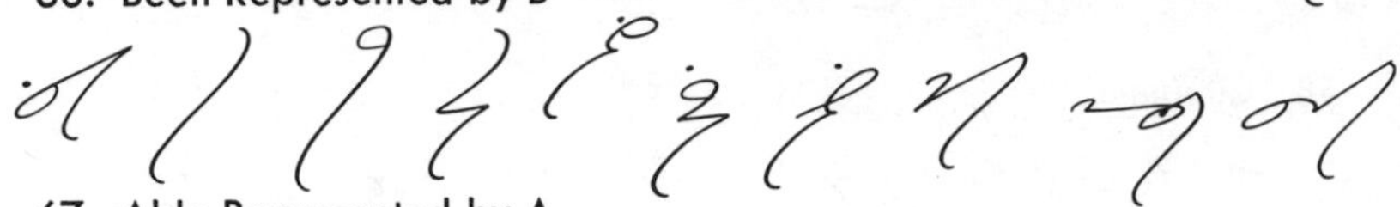

67. Able Represented by A

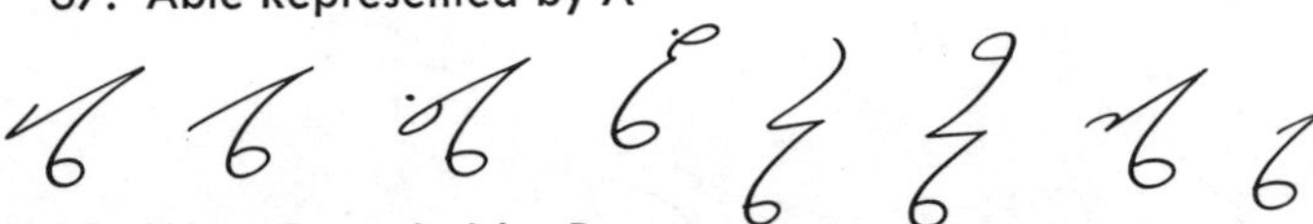

68. Want Preceded by Pronoun

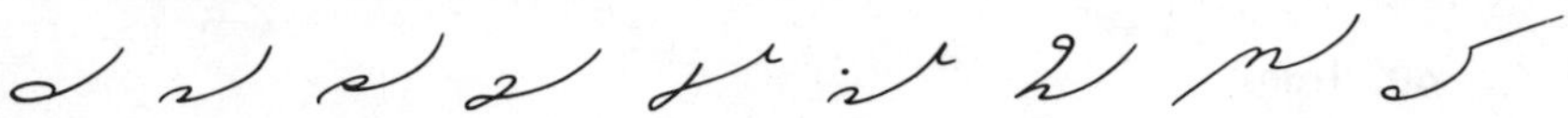

69. Ago Represented by G

70. Was Not, Is Not

71. Understand, Understood

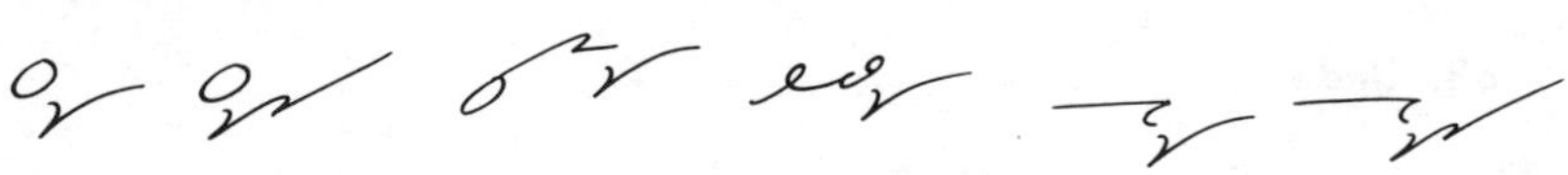

72. To Omitted in Phrases

73. The Omitted in Phrases

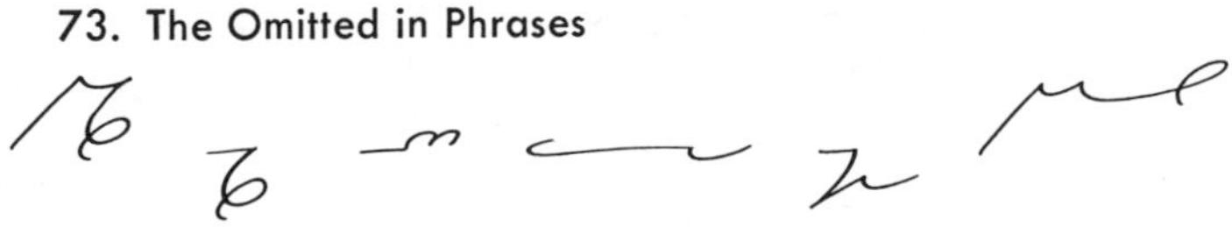

74. Of Omitted in Phrases

75. And Omitted in Phrases

76. A Omitted in Phrases

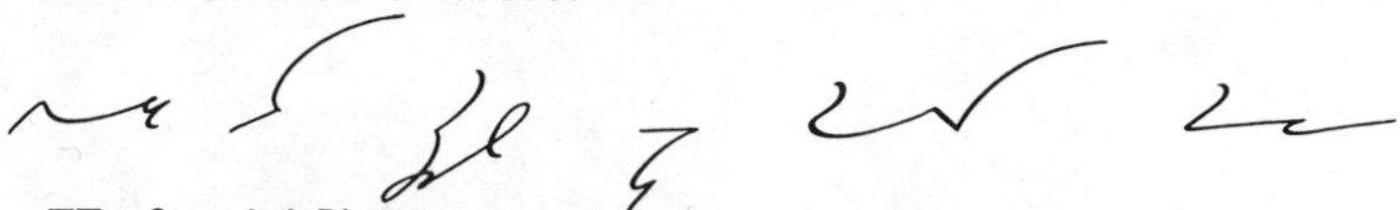

77. Special Phrases

78. Intersected Phrases

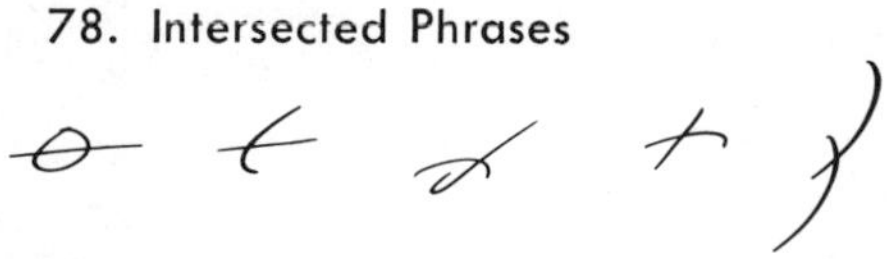

BRIEF FORMS OF GREGG SHORTHAND

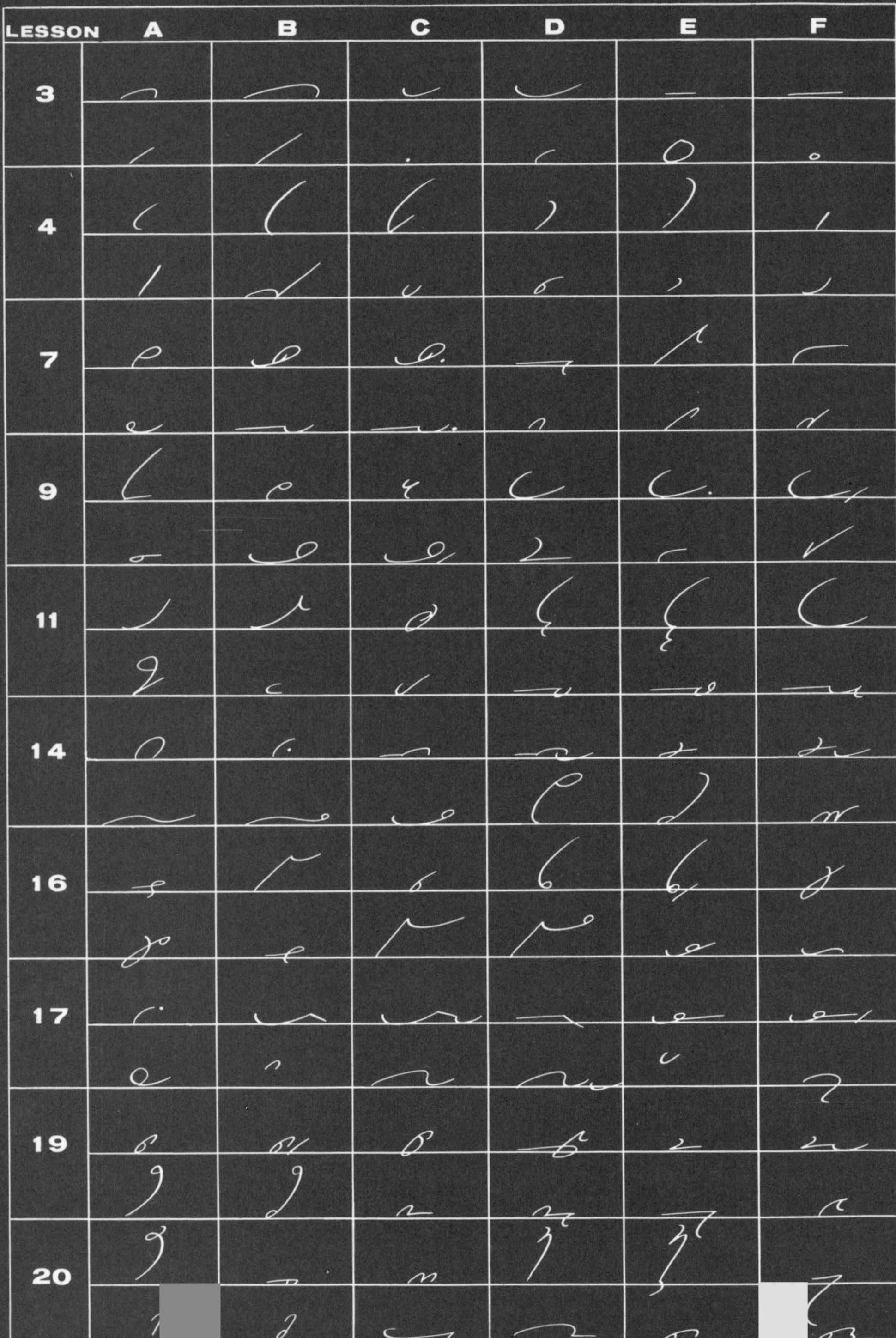